# THE LEARNED ONES

# The Learned Ones

## *Nahua Intellectuals in Postconquest Mexico*

Kelly S. McDonough

FIRST PEOPLES
*New Directions in Indigenous Studies*

The University of Arizona Press
Tucson

The University of Arizona Press
www.uapress.arizona.edu


First paperback edition 2016

Printed in the United States of America
21 20 19 18 17 16 7 6 5 4 3 2

ISBN-13: 978-0-8165-1136-5 (cloth)
ISBN-13: 978-0-8165-3421-0 (paper)

Cover design by Leigh McDonald
Cover art adapted from *Ama Tlalnamaquilistli, Quen Tiyolque (Books/ Pages of Knowledge, Origins of Man)* by Ildefonso Maya Hernández, *ixtlamatini, tlahcuilo.*

Publication of this book was made possible, in part, with a grant from the Andrew W. Mellon Foundation, and by the proceeds of a permanent endowment created with the assistance of a Challenge Grant from the National Endowment for the Humanities, a federal agency.

Library of Congress Cataloguing-in-Publication Data
McDonough, Kelly S., 1970– author.
The learned ones : Nahua intellectuals in postconquest Mexico / Kelly S. McDonough.
pages cm. — (First peoples: new directions in indigenous studies)
Includes bibliographical references and index.
ISBN 978-0-8165-1136-5 (hardback)
1. Nahuatl literature—History and criticism. 2. Nahuas—Intellectual life. 3. Nahuas—Mexico—History. 4. Nahua philosophy. I. Title.
PM4068.M37 2014
897'.45—dc23
2014007748

♾ This paper meets the requirements of ANSI/NISO Z39.48-1992 (Permanence of Paper).

*For my great-grandmother,*
*Marie (Myrtle Mae) Evans Flanagan*

# Contents

# *Illustrations*

# *Acknowledgments*

I am deeply grateful for the many people who have supported this project and shaped it in innumerable ways. Many thanks to Kristen Buckles at the University of Arizona Press for nudging me toward writing with my own voice, Natasha Varner for kind and encouraging words, and the anonymous reviewers who challenged me to rethink and clarify many of my ideas. Special thanks to Amy Den Ouden, as well as the other mentors and authors who participated in the 2012 First Peoples Manuscript Development Workshop.

My first advisor at the University of Minnesota, René Jara, set me on the path toward this book when he said, "Hija, véte a México con tus preguntas." When René passed away unexpectedly, Nicholas Spadaccini stepped in without hesitation and deftly shepherded me through the remainder of my time at Minnesota. Nick's spot-on guidance, astounding editorial skills, and unfaltering belief in the value of this project have been indispensable. I am humbled by his continued support and encouragement. Also at Minnesota, Jeani O'Brien introduced me to a wide range of scholarship on and by indigenous intellectuals in the United States and Canada and wholeheartedly supported my plan to seek their counterparts in Latin America. I could not ask for a better model to follow than Jeani—a top-notch scholar and engaged community member who adds cheer to every occasion. Heartfelt thanks also go to Ana Forcinito and Raúl Marrero-Fente for their commitment to ethical scholarship and for teaching me to become increasingly more comfortable with ambiguity.

In Mexico, thanks to John Sullivan and Delfina de la Cruz Cruz, co-founders of the Instituto de Docencia e Investigación Etnológicas de Zacatecas (Zacatecas Institute of Teaching and Research in Ethnology, IDIEZ). My first teacher of Nahuatl at IDIEZ, Victoriano de la Cruz Cruz, has been a constant interlocutor throughout the development, research, and writing of this book, and I am honored by his friendship and intellectual companionship. He is a Nahua intellectual to be watched. Sabina Cruz de la Cruz, Catalina Cruz de la Cruz, Abelardo de la Cruz de la Cruz, and Ofelia Cruz Morales have been exceptional teachers and friends, and they have pushed me to think about the implications of this project in both academic and Nahua communities today. María Pascuala Cruz and Fortino de la Cruz in Tepoxteco, don Porfirio (Juan Tomás de la Cruz Dolores) and Bina inana (María Juana de la Cruz Toribia) in Tepecxitla, and Ildefonso Maya Hernández and Felipa Olivares Cortés de Maya in Huejutla de Reyes all opened their homes to me on several occasions. *Hueyi ixtlamatiquetl* Natalio Hernández Hernández, who shared his inspiring vision of hope for a future that is expansive and inclusive enough for all peoples. *Nouhquia nitzin* Gustavo Zapoteco Sideño, thank you for always-stimulating conversations. I am especially appreciative of Jesús Villanueva Hernández, who took the time to accompany me to Milpa Alta and to share stories about his grandmother, doña Luz Jiménez. *Tlazcamati miac nochimeh*.

Thanks to Donald Frischmann for offering steady encouragement and for introducing me to both Ildefonso Maya Hernández and Natalio Hernández Hernández. Thanks to Frances Karttunen for reading more drafts of chapter 4 than she probably would have liked and for generously facilitating contact with doña Luz's family in Mexico, as well as John Charlot, son of doña Luz's compadre Jean Charlot. Thanks to Camilla Townsend for feedback on the earliest draft of chapter 2 and for the extraordinary example of how to weave together and breathe life into colonial documents. Thanks to Erika Pani and Andrés Lira at El Colegio de México, who patiently listened to half-baked ideas and promptly sent me in the right direction as I tried to piece together Chimalpopoca's life story. Thanks to Molly Bassett, who carefully read versions of chapters 1 and 3 and always asked insightful questions. Special thanks go to Stephanie Wood for her astute read of the introduction. Juanita Garciagodoy, Joanna Johnson, Dixie Lee Sullivan, and S. Kirk Walsh all helped me get closer to the story I was trying to tell. At different stages, Juan José Daneri, Marcela Garcés, Adriana Gordillo, Alexis Howe, Joseph Towle, and Naomi Wood provided important feedback, support, and camaraderie.

I finished this book at my new academic home in the Department of Spanish and Portuguese at the University of Texas at Austin. For the warm welcome to their vibrant intellectual community, many thanks to Arturo Arias, Jossianna Arroyo-Martínez, Luis Cárcamo-Huechante, Jim Cox, Héctor Domínguez-Ruvalcaba, Stephen Marshall, Lisa Moore, Jill Robbins, and Shannon Speed.

Support for this project was provided by the University of Minnesota Department of Spanish and Portuguese Studies Dissertation Research Grant; the University of Minnesota Graduate School Thesis Research Grant; the University of Minnesota Doctoral Dissertation Fellowship; the University of Wisconsin–La Crosse Faculty Research Grant; the University of Wisconsin–La Crosse International Development Fund Grant; and the Teresa Lozano Long Institute of Latin American Studies at the University of Texas at Austin from funds granted to the institute by the Andrew W. Mellon Foundation.

My grandmother Dorothy McDonough told me that she thought this book was taking much too long, and for that I am grateful. Nan and Jonathan Yurkanis sent support and energy from Seattle to wherever I was working. Joel Homme and Lupe, my sweet touchstones, kept the home fires burning while I traveled to Mexico and listened intently when I came home. Thank you both for your love, and for urging me to live and work with a calm demeanor.

# THE LEARNED ONES

INTRODUCTION

# *Ixtlamatinih*

## Nahua Intellectuals Writing Mexican Modernity

*So all this time they've been lying to us, the schoolteachers.*
*They said we were stupid* burrohmeh, *nothing but donkeys.*
*I guess they were wrong.*

—ABELARDO DE LA CRUZ, NAHUA READING CIRCLES PARTICIPANT

The *tlamatinimeh* and *tlahcuilohqueh*, the scholars and writers of pre-Hispanic Nahuatl-speaking cultures, are remembered in painted codices and early colonial-period alphabetic manuscripts of Mesoamerica as the producers, transmitters, interpreters, and guardians of knowledge. The activities of these figures often seem bound to an ephemeral and unrecoverable past, for rarely in Mexico today does one hear the words "indigenous" and "intellectual" linked together.[1] At the same time, while it is widely accepted that indigenous peoples in Mexico have always possessed a rich oral tradition, it is often thought that they have not had a longstanding relationship with the written word. This is not the case, at least for Nahuas, native speakers of Nahuatl, one of the most widely spoken and best-documented indigenous languages in the Americas. In fact, as I will argue throughout this book, Nahuas have maintained a deep engagement with the written word as one of the vehicles for their intellectual work since the introduction—some might say imposition—of the Roman alphabet in the early sixteenth century. However, similar to other minoritized cultures in the context of conquest and colonization, the existence and persistence of indigenous knowledge production, particularly alphabetic writing, has until recently been ignored, underestimated, or obscured. In joining a steadily increasing body of scholarship on indigenous knowledges in the Americas, this book takes as its task sustained attention to the complex nature of Nahua intellectualism and writing from the colonial period through the present day.[2] This broad temporal perspective shows not only the heterogeneity of Nahua writing in terms of genre, discourse, forum, and language but also that of indigenous experience in Mexico over the past five centuries.

The indigenous intellectuals whose writings and life experiences are the focus of this book offer examples of how Nahuas took up the pen with skill—dare I say delight—as agents of their own discourses and agendas. They include Antonio del Rincón, one of the few indigenous men to be ordained as a Jesuit priest during the early colonial period and the first indigenous person in the Americas to write a grammar of his native language; don Juan Buenaventura Zapata y Mendoza, a seventeenth-century elite Nahua statesman who wrote the history of his *altepetl* (city/state), Tlaxcala; Faustino Galicia Chimalpopoca, the Nahua polymath, who left his mark on the nineteenth century as a staunch defender of indigenous land rights and as a scholar of Nahua texts; doña Luz Jiménez, the only published female Nahua prose writer to date, whose short stories and *testimonio* provide a window into assimilative education for Indian children at the turn of the twentieth century; Ildefonso Maya Hernández, the prolific playwright and cultural promoter whose open-air theater and painted books light the way toward indigenous language and cultural recovery and revitalization; and Sabina Cruz de la Cruz, Victoriano de la Cruz Cruz, and Refugio Nava Nava, all present-day Nahua intellectuals who have contributed statements or think-pieces specifically for this book. The texts gathered together here alert us to fact that, contrary to popular belief, Nahuas have continued to think, produce, transmit, and interpret knowledges even after European contact and conquest. Furthermore, they demonstrate that along with oral, embodied, musical, and painted modes of expression and communication, Nahuas appropriated and adapted alphabetic writing in order to assess and influence the world around them.

A driving force of this project has been to make visible to the academic community and the general public examples of a continuous yet changeful trajectory of Nahua intellectual work and writing in modernity. Equally, it has been a priority to do the same in Nahua communities who are, more often than not, unaware of—and without access to—their own cultural heritage sources. As an exploration of collaborative research methods, I discuss the experience of reading these texts with native speakers today, some encountering Nahua intellectuals and their writing for the very first time. My hope is that this is a useful contribution to how we understand indigenous intellectual work and writing in the Americas and to Nahua people as they look to their past, present, and future, as creative knowledge producers, as intellectuals, and as writers.

* * *

At the time of the Spanish conquest in 1519, Nahuas were the largest cultural-linguistic group in Mesoamerica.[3] The Nahuatl language, often recognized as the language of the Aztecs (Mexica), was spoken in the vast territory encompassing today's central Mexico, and as far south as El Salvador, Honduras, and Nicaragua.[4] Throughout the three centuries of Spanish colonial rule, the use of Nahuatl language spread—though by no means in a standardized fashion—throughout Mesoamerica as the lingua franca, or "intermediary language" between Spaniards and other indigenous peoples.[5] Today, Nahuatl continues to be one of the most widely spoken of approximately sixty-eight indigenous languages in Mexico, with at least 1.5 million native speakers.[6] With such a seemingly robust population, along with a massive corpus of alphabetic texts—some estimate 20,000 Nahuatl-language documents from the colonial period alone—and a cadre of contemporary Nahuatl-language poets and writers, one would think that a discussion of the intellectual legacy of Nahuas, or their long-term relationship to writing, would not seem all that unusual.

But native voices and native writings, for the most part, have little presence in cultural and literary histories of Mexico, and the general public's awareness of Nahua knowledge production or writing over the past five centuries is minimal at best. I have raised more than a few eyebrows when mentioning to friends or acquaintances from Mexico and beyond—native and non-native alike—that I was researching Nahua intellectuals and their writing after European conquest and colonization. For example, recent informal surveys with parents of children attending a middle-class Mexico City elementary school consistently yielded that pre-Hispanic codices are, as one respondent stated, "a source of great pride for all Mexican people." However, when asked if they could name a codex or if they had ever seen one, all responded in the negative. When asked about writing by indigenous people, specifically Nahuas, not one had heard of such a thing. "They don't write," one gentleman informed me, in a tone that suggested I really should have known better. Another woman insisted that Nahuatl was a "dead language," and she was sure that it had never been written. "Qué lástima" (such a pity), she said. When I asked about indigenous intellectuals, most everyone seemed confused by the question. As far as they were concerned, it was possible that pre-Hispanic indigenous people may have done some worthwhile thinking and that they were talented artists. But Indians today? In the present-day imaginary, they are almost never considered to be rational, creative, thinking beings, and they certainly aren't perceived as writers. Thinking and writing: today those are non-Indian categories.

In his book *Indians in Unexpected Places*, Dakota scholar Philip J. Deloria provocatively questions how and why certain categories—or expectations—for indigenous peoples are created and outlines how the maintenance of these categories are "both the products and the tools of domination."[7] He calls into question the ideologies and discourses created by dominant culture that locate indigenous peoples in specific times and places, and associate them with certain ways of thinking and acting. These expectations of Indians—such as "they belong here, and they think and act like this; they do *not* belong here, and they do *not* think and act like this"—naturalize, and thus perpetuate, social, political, and economic relationships of inequality. Following Deloria, one of the aims of this book is to demonstrate that indigenous intellectualism and writing is not odd or even anomalous; instead, using Deloria's frame, they are activities that fall outside of the dominant culture's expectations of Indians. If Nahuas have long enjoyed a rich intellectual life that has been expressed in writing, why do most people think differently? And what might be gained by seeing, reading, and writing Nahuas in(to) the "unexpected places" of intellectualism and the world of letters?

## Intellectual, Knowledge, *(ix)tlamatini*, *(ix)tlamatiliztli*

My use of the terms "intellectual" and "knowledge producer" requires some elaboration. Both stand for individuals who are producers and interpreters of wisdom (broadly defined as cultural, historical, and political knowledges), acquired by experience and/or study and shared in and/or beyond his/her own community. This may not be precisely what is understood by a Western definition of the term, for several reasons, namely the nature and the source of knowledge. If one follows the *Oxford English Dictionary*'s definition, a Western intellectual is an individual "possessing a highly developed intellect," with intellect defined as "the faculty of reasoning and understanding objectively, especially with regard to abstract or academic matters." In addition, Roderic Camp maintains in his study of twentieth-century Mexican intellectuals and politics that the intellectual must "have access to and advance a cultural fund of knowledge which does not derive solely from their direct personal experience."[8] These definitions have certain merits for this study, but also limitations. Even if we are discussing Nahuas who regularly interacted with (or even aligned themselves with) Western cultures, their activities and obligations do not necessarily correlate precisely with Western understandings of knowledge production or intellectualism. For example, Western (or dominant) cultures tend to place greater value on what is conceived of as scientific objective knowledges than on subjective or personal experience. For dominant culture, the intellectual's source of knowledge is often related to an institution of higher learning. However, for Nahuas with whom I consulted, having availed oneself of institutional learning was neither requisite nor sufficient, in terms of being viewed by their community as an intellectual.

In several conversations regarding terminology related to intellectuals and knowledge transmission, it became clear that for many Nahuas the Spanish-language term *intelectual* is deeply associated with dominant culture and normative institutions and is therefore avoided by those we might call members of the Nahua intelligentsia today. For example, Nahua (Guerrero/Morelos) poet and activist Gustavo Zapoteco Sideño has called himself a "tlacuilo" (writer/painter), a "xochitlacuilo" (flower-writer/poet), and a "cuicajpike" ("hacedor de cantos," or a song/chant/poem-creator). Zapoteco prefers not to use the Spanish-language moniker, intelectual. Nonetheless, his description of his vocation is one that clearly marks him as a producer of knowledge in the service of his people:

> Creo que no me considero un intelectual, sino más bien una persona que trata de reflexionar, analizar, investigar, documentarme en relación [*sic*] algún tema, trato de proponer ideas, a través de la creatividad que hasta hoy he elaborado (libros, conferencias, ponencias, ensayos, cuentos, etc.) dentro del propio ámbito en que me desenvuelvo, en relación con mi propia cultura y cosmovisión en su interrelación con el entorno político, social y económico, en que estamos inmersos (pueblo, municipio, estado y nación).[9]
>
> (I don't think that I would consider myself to be an *intelectual*. Instead, I see myself as a person who tries to reflect, analyze, research, and document certain topics. I try to propose ideas through the creative work that I have produced up until now [such as books, conferences, talks, essays, short stories, etc.] within the context in which I work, and in connection

with my own culture and cosmovision, as these relate to the political, social, and economic environments in which we are immersed at local, municipal, state, and national levels.)

Zapoteco's comments resonate with Donald L. Fixico's (Shawnee, Sac & Fox, Muscogee Creek, and Seminole) discussion of what he has called "native geniuses." According to Fixico, native geniuses are "keepers of traditional knowledges who have insightful life experiences and who possess gifts of special insights to life, and whose actions benefit the people."[10] Both Zapoteco's and Fixico's explanations guide the way in which I am using the English terms "intellectual" and "knowledge" in this book. However, since direct translations seem elusive, a closer look at the terms in the Nahuatl language is in order.

The great sixteenth-century Franciscan grammarian and lexicographer Alonso de Molina glossed the Nahuatl term *tlamatini* (sing.) as "sabio" (wise person) and *tlamatiliztli* as "sabiduria, o embuacamiento" (knowledge or trickery).[11] Both have as their root the verb *mati*, or "saber algo" (to know [something]).[12] For example, *tlamatini/meh* can be broken down in the following manner: *tla* (nonspecific nonhuman object prefix [thing/s]) + *mati* (to know [something]) + *ni/nimeh* (singular/plural present agentive suffix). Tlamatiliztli is an "action noun": roughly "the act or action of knowing."[13] Present-day Nahuatl-language terminology related to intellectuals and knowledge is similar to that of the past. *Ixtlamatini* or *ixtlamatiquetl* (-quetl, like -ni/-nimeh, is a present agentive suffix) were the terms regularly offered in informal surveys as correlating with "sabio/intelectual" (wise person or intellectual), and *ixtlamatiliztli* as correlating with "sabiduría o conocimiento" (knowledge). These terms also appear in Molina's dictionary, with *ixtlamati* recorded as "sabio que usa de razon y es experimentado" (wise person who uses reason and is experienced) and ixtlamatiliztli as "prudencia, razó natural, o gestos y visajes" (prudence, natural reason, or gestures and [facial] expressions).[14] A prevalence of the modern-day incorporation of *ixtli* (face, surface, eye) to tlamatini is perhaps a lexicalized insistence that Nahua intellectuals garner much of their knowledge from lived experiences.[15] Other terms related to knowledge suggested by native speakers today were *tlalnamiquiliztli*, which Karttunen defines as "recollection, memory/pensamiento o memoria," and *ilnamiqui*, "for memory to return, sharpen; to remember, reflect on something/se refrescará la memoria de esto, acordarse de una cosa, imaginar, pensar, reflexionar, considerar."[16] Together with Zapoteco's and Fixico's insights, these Nahuatl terms and their definitions unequivocally point to personal experience as integral to knowledge work in Nahua communities.

## Writing Is Indigenous

The temporal frame of this study is from European contact in the early sixteenth century through the present; however, it is important to note that writing (in its broadest sense) is not a European import to indigenous cultures in the Americas. If we follow art historian Elizabeth Hill Boone's definition of writing as "a graphic system that keeps and conveys knowledge," we can see that alphabetic writing joined many other types of writing practices already in use—from birch bark scrolls and wampum beads to hieroglyphs and knotted *khipus*.[17] With this understanding of writing, in Mesoamerica alone we are confronted with thousands of years of indigenous writing, including the Zapotec pictographic and hieroglyphic texts of Monte Albán, Maya glottographic carvings, and Mixtec and Aztec (Mexica) semasiographic images inscribed on hide, paper, and cloth.[18] Nahuatl-speaking Aztecs (Mexica) were known to have kept painted books that dealt with a broad range of sociopolitical, religious, and economic issues. Such texts were produced and interpreted by highly specialized intellectuals, the tlamatinimeh (sages and scholars) and tlahcuilohqueh (painters/writers).[19]

The tlamatinimeh are described in the *Códice Matritenses*, one of the earlier "ethnographic" investigations of the Nahua people, carried out in the early sixteenth century by the Franciscan friar Bernardino de Sahagún in collaboration with Nahuas from leading noble families of Tepepulco and Tlatelolco:[20]

> In tlamatini: tlavilli ocutl, tomavuac ocutl hapocyo;
> tezcatl coyavac, tezcatl necuc xapo;
> tlile, tlapale, amuxva, amoxe.
> Tlilli, tlapalli.
> Hutli, teyacanqui, tlanelo;
> tevicani, tlavicani, tlayacanqui.
>
> (The wise man: a light, a torch, a stout torch that does not smoke.
> A perforated mirror, a mirror pierced on both sides.
> His are the black and red ink, his are the illustrated manuscripts, he studies the illustrated manuscripts.

He himself is writing and wisdom.
He is the path, the true way for others.
He directs people and things; he is a guide in human affairs.)[21]

Boone has characterized the tlamatini (sing.) as "a highly literate individual and a scholar, an embodiment of wisdom contained in the painted books; he or she was also a counselor and a teacher."[22] The tlamatini was, Boone states, "the most learned of the historians, orators, and poets, as well as the priests, diviners, and physicians."[23] In his study, Daniel Graña-Behrens highlighted the tlamatinimeh's role as "keepers of collective memory" known for their "intellectual capacity or skill."[24] The leading Mexican scholar of Nahua literatures, Miguel León-Portilla, has also written extensively on the tlamatinimeh, whom he understood, somewhat controversially, to be philosophers concerned with writing, teaching, and reflecting on the past, present, and future.[25]

References to the tlamatinimeh can also be found in *Coloquios y doctrina cristiana*, another text compiled by Sahagún and his Nahua collaborators. This text includes Nahua memories of the earlier attempts of the first twelve missionaries to New Spain to convert the indigenous lords of the recently conquered Tenochtitlan. The text explains how the missionaries had gathered the indigenous lords together in order to explain the truth and righteousness of the Catholic faith. It is said that after listening patiently to the missionaries, one of the noblemen defended his people's religious belief and knowledge system by explaining that they had their own wise men, the tlamatinimeh:

> Auh inhin, totecujyoane ca oncate in oc no techiacana, in techitquj, in techamama, yn jpampa in tlaiecultilo, ca in toteoua yn jntlacaceuhcava [ . . . ] in tlatolmatinjme, auh in jntequjuh in qujmocujtlauja [ . . . ] Auh in quitzticate, in qujpouhticate, in qujtlatlazticate in amoxtlj, in tlilli, in tlapalli, in tlacujlolli quitiqujticate. Ca iehoantin techitqujticate, techiacana, techotlatoltia [ . . . ] qujmocujtlauja, iehoantin yntenjz, incocol, y mamal in teutlatollj.[26]

> (But, our lords, there are those who guide us; they govern us, they carry us on their backs and instruct us how our gods must be worshiped: [ . . . ] The experts, the knowers of speeches and orations, it is their obligation; [ . . . ] Those who observe [read] the codices, those who recite [tell what they read]. Those who noisily turn the pages of the illustrated manuscripts. Those who have possession of the black and red ink [wisdom]

> and of that which is pictured; they lead us, they guide us, they tell us the way. [ . . . ] With this they busy themselves, to them it falls to speak of the gods.)[27]

This exchange highlights the important social functions of the tlamatinimeh, including their relationship to reading, writing, and guiding the people. Conquest and colonization surely disrupted the stations and practices of "those who noisily turn the pages of the illustrated manuscripts." But as we will see in the following chapters, the work of Nahua intellectuals continued in ways uniquely suited to their time, place, and purpose.

For their part, the tlahcuilohqueh (painters/writers) are thought to have worked alongside the tlamatinimeh, or perhaps were even at times one and the same. According to the description found in the Florentine Codex, the massive twelve-volume culmination of Sahagún and his collaborators' decades of research, the tlahcuilohqueh were primarily responsible for the art of writing Nahua knowledges in the painted "books" known as *amoxtli*:

> in tlacuilo, tlilli, tlapalli, tlilatl, ialuil, toltecatl tlachichiuhqui, tlatecullaliani, tlateculaniani, tlatlilani, tlilpatlac, tlapaltecini, tlapallaliani

> (The scribe: writings, ink [are] his special skills. [He is] a craftsman, an artist, a user of charcoal, a drawer with charcoal; a painter who dissolves colors, grinds pigments, uses colors)[28]

Boone notes that Sahagún seems to have understood the roles of the tlamatinimeh and the tlahcuilohqueh as distinct—one concerned with the more esoteric or abstract tasks of producing and interpreting knowledge, and the other with the more technical, artisanal practice of recording these knowledges—however, it is actually quite difficult to affirm a true distinction between the two.[29] In his study of folio 46r of the early colonial-period *Codex Telleriano-Remensis*, for example, literary scholar José Rabasa suggests the *tlahcuiloh* as both the mastermind and painter of the brilliant representation of the multiplicities and contradictions among the religious orders he/she observed.[30] At any rate, it is not whether one or two different professional classes dedicated themselves to thinking, reading, writing, and interpreting texts that matters. The point is that for Nahuas these were long-standing cultural practices.

That Nahuas embraced alphabetic writing from its earliest arrival is evidenced by the thousands of Nahuatl-language documents produced between the early sixteenth and late eighteenth centuries. The vast array of colonial-period Nahuatl-language texts scattered in archives throughout the world includes codices, ecclesiastical texts, historical annals, and plays, in addition to the copious mundane documents such as petitions to the Spanish Crown and its agents, testaments, land titles, and municipal records. Since the early 1970s, scholars of colonial Mexico have made great strides in bringing these texts, and the Nahua voices within them, to the forefront. Ethnohistorian James Lockhart,[31] linguists Frances Karttunen and R. Joe Campbell, anthropologists Luis Reyes García (Nahua) and Louise Burkhart, historian/literary scholar Miguel León-Portilla (following the pioneering work of his mentor Ángel María Garibay), and art historian Elizabeth Hill Boone, among others, have fundamentally changed the way we understand conquest, colonization, and the colonial experience in general by bringing Nahua perspectives to bear on what has long been a European version of history. They have identified and published primary sources, modeled innovative methods, and trained generations of scholars who have in turn contributed to an increasingly coherent, albeit still emerging, narrative of Nahua knowledges, written or otherwise. These combined efforts have made it clear that during the colonial period Nahuas were undeniably present in what Ángel Rama called "The Lettered City," which, in Rappaport and Cummins's terms, was "a social constellation built on an ideology of the primacy of the written word."[32] Emanating from the urban centers of the Spanish colonies, the vast web of legal and ecclesiastical writings produced by the *letrados* (the lettered elite) strategically inscribed and regulated power relations in colonial Latin America. Michel de Certeau has theorized the ways in which dominated peoples negotiate imposed systems such as that created by the letrados through a series of "tactics" or creative and unintended "uses" of the "laws, practices, and representations" of dominant culture in the social interactions of everyday life.[33] For de Certeau, the "strategies" of the powerful establish the framework of engagement, but "tactics" provide the means by which the dominated create spaces of agency *from within* a system that has located them in a subordinate position. Nahuas were not always the architects of the laws and decrees that flowed from the Lettered City, but writing provided the tactical means by which they could manipulate, contest, or even subvert the hegemonic order. We can assume that young indigenous men from noble families were trained to read and write by the friars for purposes other than contesting the colonial order, but this was one of the unintended outcomes. The avalanche of petitions, testimonies, and testaments submitted to the courts and letters directed to the king and other dignitaries are evidence of the crucial tactics Nahuas deployed in their struggles within the framework of colonialism and coloniality.

The plenary nature of Nahua alphabetic writing in the colonial period is due then in no small part to the fact that indigenous people understood—whether consciously or not—that with alphabetic writing they could shape and respond to policies and practices of the new order. The massive cache of mundane documentation can also be explained in that Nahuatl was a semi-official administrative language of New Spain up until the late eighteenth-century Bourbon Reforms.[34] During the majority of the colonial period, writing in the Nahuatl language was not only permissible in legal and ecclesiastical settings but also, as the lingua franca of New Spain, expected. But the Nahua scriptural trace trickles away and seems to disappear by the late eighteenth/early nineteenth centuries,[35] until re-emerging with the so-called Nahuatl literary renaissance of the mid-1980s, led by Nahua writers including Natalio Hernández, Juan Hernández, and Librado Silva Galeano, among others.[36] But why the two-hundred-year slumber? Had Nahuas given up on alphabetic writing? Did they, as it is commonly portrayed, fall into an intellectual stupor from which they have only recently begun to awake? Similar to their military defeat, was their vibrant intellectual life vanquished as well? Why the gap? What happened?

The explanation for the decline of writing in the Nahuatl language near the end of the eighteenth century is actually quite simple. Beginning in 1763, the Spanish Crown implemented a policy of the Spanish language as the only administrative language of the colony. Not long after, when Mexico declared its independence from Spain in the early nineteenth century, Spanish was confirmed as the official language of the new nation. The Nahuatl language was no longer an effective tool of negotiation; instead, throughout the following centuries, it became the target of waves of systematic suppression and discrimination. But Nahua intellectuals never stopped thinking, and they never stopped recording their knowledges with the written word. They adapted their practices.[37]

At times Nahua voices have been hard to hear and their writing difficult to see, muted or even concealed by discourses about indigenous peoples that categorize them as unchanging, ahistorical beings. We often fail to (or are unwilling to) grasp the fact that as the needs of indigenous communities change, so do the roles and activities of their leaders—political, spiritual, intellectual, or otherwise. One of the more significant challenges in recognizing Nahua intellectualism and writing beyond the colonial period, particularly during the nineteenth century, is that indigenous identity in Mexico has long been conflated with the use of an indigenous language.[38]

"Real" Indians are expected to speak and write in their native language. Yet when the Nahuatl language was no longer a viable medium for engaging those they sought to influence, or for protecting or asserting rights, many Nahuas added the Spanish language to their repertoire. For these reasons, I have purposefully avoided the rubric of "writes or works in his/her native language," as a determining factor of whether or not a particular figure should be considered in this opening gesture toward a more comprehensive understanding of Nahua intellectualism and writing in the context of colonialism/coloniality. For while each protagonist treated in this book does indeed work in the Nahuatl language, the sources I analyze are also in Spanish, Latin, and even a hybrid Nahuatl-Spanish ("Nahuañol"). I have been told on more than one occasion that a frame for reading Nahua intellectual production and writing that includes languages other than Nahuatl is off the mark. Regardless of the fact that some of the Nahuas discussed in this book were all deeply immersed in, and committed to, their culture and native language, it has been suggested that those that have written in Spanish aren't "real" indigenous intellectuals/writers because they use the language of the colonizer. I would argue, however, that language choices should not define or preclude one's identification as a Nahua intellectual or writer, since the language chosen to communicate ideas is not always based solely on ethnic identity; language choices can shift depending on the time, place, and audience (perceived or desired). Furthermore, an insistence on the use of an indigenous language as a sign of legitimacy ignores the fact that to be indigenous in Mexico (particularly from the late eighteenth century on) is to have experienced enormous pressure from dominant culture to stop speaking one's native language.[39] If we fail to listen to indigenous people that have—by choice or by force—utilized another language, we reveal our own categorical thinking about how and where we expect indigenous people to be. Mexican anthropologist Guillermo Bonfil Batalla takes up this issue of indigenous authenticity—that is, after all, what we are talking about here—firmly stating that the appropriation and adaptation of Western cultural elements (including language) does not imply that one is no longer an "authentic" Indian:

> La discusión sobre el monto y proporción de los elementos "autenticamente indios" (es decir, no occidentales) en las culturas actuales y su uso como criterio para determinar el grado de "indianidad," tienen un contenido profundamente colonialista: tienden a negar legitimidad a los grupos étnicos y, por otra parte, responden al estereotipo ideológico según el cual los pueblos no occidentales están fuera de la historia. Sí,

> los grupos indios que han estado sujetos a la dominación colonial han hecho suyos, de buen grado o por la fuerza, muchos elementos de origen occidental; pero la aculturación no significa desindianización ni pérdida de identidad en términos étnicos.[40]
>
> (The discussion regarding the total and proportion of the "authentically Indian" [that is, non-Western] elements in today's indigenous cultures, and its use as a criteria to determine the degree of "Indian-ness," are of a profoundly colonialist nature: they tend to negate the legitimacy of ethnic groups and, at the same time, respond to ideological stereotyping that places non-Western cultures outside of the historical record. Indeed, indigenous groups that have been subjects of colonial domination have appropriated many elements of Western culture. But acculturation does not mean de-Indianization, nor does it imply loss of identity in terms of ethnicity.)

Expectations of authentic indigenous people in Mexico are strongly linked to romantic, often imagined, ideas about the pre-Columbian past, a past that cannot be recovered. The ideological displacement of "real" Indians to the deep past does not allow for any other kind of Indian in the present. Thus, ideas of authenticity are a way in which to negate and disappear indigenous presence in modernity. In her analysis of how local histories in New England have contributed to the myth of the "vanishing Indian," ethnohistorian Jean M. O'Brien (White Earth Ojibwe) has discussed how ideas of indigenous authenticity in New England were linked to notions of blood purity and the ancient past. While discourses of indigenous blood purity differ substantially in the United States and Mexico, the insistence on "the ancient" as a marker of authenticity is common to both settings.[41] O'Brien's statement that non-native New Englanders "refused to regard culture change as normative for Indian peoples" rings true south of the border as well.[42] To release indigeneity from the confines of this mythical past, however, implies a willingness to relinquish the authority to define what it means to be a "real" Indian and instead let Indians teach us what it has meant (and means) for them. In Acoma scholar Simon Ortiz's view, for example, the appropriation of the colonizer's language has been a key element of indigenous survival:

> Along with their native languages, Indian women and men have carried on their lives and their expression through the use of the newer languages, particularly Spanish, French, and English, and they have used

> these languages on their own terms. This is the crucial item that has to be understood, that it is entirely possible for a people to retain and maintain their lives through the use of any language. There is not a question of authenticity here; rather it is the way that Indian people have creatively responded to forced colonization. And this response has been one of resistance; there is no clearer word for it than resistance.[43]

Related to his work on the recovery of a Cherokee literary tradition, Cherokee scholar Daniel Heath Justice has stated that "Mothertongues remain the worldview centers of our cultures, [but] they aren't the only viable means for Indian peoples to express ourselves."[44] As I write this book, I am not confined to only one language, my native English; I also speak and write in Spanish and Nahuatl, depending on the context. Why then do we have different expectations of Nahuas? If we are interested in what Nahuas have to say (however they have chosen to say it), we can and should listen to voices in the Nahuatl language, as well as any others they may have employed.

Even when we are willing to seek out Nahua writing in other languages, it is still challenging to identify Nahua intellectuals during the nineteenth century for the fact that, by law, Indians no longer existed. During the colonial period indigenous voices are more detectable, since indigenous identity was codified, documented, and monitored by non-Indians and Indians alike for a variety of purposes, including evangelization projects, labor extraction, and tribute collection, or for asserting and defending rights. After independence from Spain, however, ethnic affiliations were officially erased—legally disappeared—in order to unify all peoples in the Mexican territory under the rubric of "citizen." But as the saying goes, "absence of evidence does not necessarily mean evidence of absence." If we look closely at archival documents, newspapers, and pamphlets (nearly all in Spanish) that center on issues important to indigenous people during the nineteenth century (and today)—for example, their modified legal status and its effects, education for indigenous people, land and water disputes—Nahuas are present.

If Nahua intellectualism continued after the conquest, and writing has long been indigenous, how can we explain that a very different kind of story has been circulated, in indigenous and non-indigenous communities alike, over the past five hundred years? Without a doubt, the kaleidoscope of ideologies and discourses about indigenous people that have worked together to separate notions of indigeneity from knowledge production and writing are manifestations of the logic of coloniality, the "transhistorical expansion of colonial domination and the perpetuation of its effects in contemporary times."[45] Walter Mignolo's understanding of the logic of coloniality is that it functions in four interrelated domains of human experience:

1. the economic: appropriation of land, exploitation of labor, and control of finances;
2. the political: control of authority;
3. the civic: control of gender and sexuality; and
4. the epistemic and personal subjectivity: control of knowledge and subjectivity.[46]

Suggesting how domination in one area takes effect in others, under the rubric of "coloniality of power," postcolonial theorist Aníbal Quijano has posited how the "codification of differences between the conquerors and the conquered" was (and is) a key process in the organization and management of labor in the modern power structure.[47] In Quijano's view, hierarchies of difference constituted by Eurocentric notions of "race" worked to identify certain "types" of people as superior and others as inferior—certain types who would control labor and others who would provide it. Such classifications ensured, Quijano states, "a racist distribution of labor and the forms of exploitation of colonial capitalism."[48] The complex ideological (and real) maneuvering necessary to compress and maintain indigenous subjects with multiple cultural/ethnic backgrounds into a monolithic "type" or category required an elaborate regime of disciplinary practices—of bodies and of minds. In his discussion of this "new universe of intersubjective relations of domination" between Europe and its "others," Quijano argues that one of the many strategies for establishing and continuing these unequal racialized hierarchies was that Europeans "repressed as much as possible the colonized forms of knowledge production, the models of the production of meaning, their symbolic universe, the model of expression and of objectification and subjectivity."[49] Maya intellectual Victor Montejo has driven this point home by saying that "from the time of the conquest, indigenous people have been conditioned to positions of servitude and mental deficiency, and the non-Maya have insisted that the *criollos* or *mestizos* are the only *personas de razón* (people of reason)."[50] "Indigenous people," Montejo continues, "have always been perceived as incapable of thinking or reasoning like real human beings."[51] As part of this process of negating indigenous knowledges, indigenous intellectuals were, in the words of Inés Hernández Ávila (Nez Perce/Tejana) and Stefano Varese, "reduced to the catacombs, to the underground of their own communities, and turned invisible to not only dominant society, but also most of their people."[52] Indigenous knowledges were not only marginalized but also in many cases methodically eliminated. Take, for example, the book-burning sprees of the zealous friars, with only a few dozen pre-Columbian Mesoamerican texts spared. Like Europeans, imperial societies such as the Aztecs (Mexica) and Maya had linked power with the written word; those who possessed writing wielded social and political power (and vice versa). Considering this, the physical disappearance of indigenous writings coupled with the denigration and even erasure of the cultural memory of such practices can be read as a strategy of establishing and maintaining a sociopolitical hierarchy with Indians in a subordinate position.

To think that these strategies of domination were accepted without struggle would be incorrect. At the same time, I am wary of fetishizing resistance (or assigning degrees of assimilation to dominant culture). The important question for me is how Nahuas—with all of their complexities and contradictions—negotiated an ever-changing context of coloniality as thinkers and as writers. William Roseberry's reading of Antonio Gramsci's theory of hegemony provides a jumping-off point for this kind of inquiry. Gramsci argued that hegemony (domination without excessive coercion) implied the development of a "shared ideology," or a set of (dominant) cultural values and worldview that could potentially unify across class/economic lines, as well as the people to the state.[53] Whereas many studies of hegemony focus on understanding how and why subordinate peoples consent to ideas not necessarily in their best interest, Roseberry's approach highlights how hegemony provides "the common material and meaningful framework for living through, talking about, and acting upon social orders characterized by domination."[54] That is, he draws our attention to how the tools and spaces of hegemony can simultaneously be utilized for struggle and negotiation. On the one hand, representations—readings and writings—of Nahuas in certain ways (as stupefied, non-existent, or silent) have contributed to their colonization and subordination. On the other, a discussion of Nahuas who read and write (or an alternative reading and writing of Nahuas) is an operation that takes place in the same forum—the written sphere—but with distinct intentions and outcomes.

## Reading Indigenous Writing

Whether in search of a more sophisticated and comprehensive understanding of the past and present, or in solidarity with social and political movements aimed at the decolonization of marginalized peoples, academic attention to the distorted representations and silenced voices of indigenous peoples has risen significantly in the past several decades. Postcolonial/decolonial critiques that focus on ways in which alphabetic writing has been part and parcel of the colonization process have made an enormous contribution toward a fuller understanding of colonial cultures.[55] Yet in our rush to critique colonialism and coloniality, we have at times tended toward overly simplistic segregations of experiences, practices, and materialities to specific ethnic realms (i.e., colonized Indians *or* European colonizers, orality *or* writing, amoxtli *or* book, glyph *or* alphabet) that do not accurately consider the broad spectrum of colonial experience, nor indigenous modes and instruments of intellectual production.[56] For example, by correcting too sharply away from the emphasis on alphabetic knowledge, or by viewing alphabetic writing only as an imposition of Western ways, we risk overlooking how indigenous peoples have actually appropriated that tool. Recent research, however, is rethinking timeworn categories that have placed indigenous peoples outside the written sphere. Consider, for example, Frank Salomon and Mercedes Niño-Murcia's recent *The Lettered Mountain: A Peruvian Village's Way with Writing* (2011), an ethnography of five hundred years of Andean literacy in the Huarochirí Province. Salomon and Niño-Murcia challenge the stereotype of Andean Americans as "always only oral" cultures by revealing how Tupicochans adapted alphabetic writing in accordance with their own needs, particularly in the areas of governance, sacred ritual, and the recording of cultural memory. In her book *The Common Pot: The Recovery of Native Space in the Northeast* (2008), Abenaki scholar Lisa Brooks demonstrates the complementary nature of orality and writing traditions in her attention to how native space in the U.S. Northeast has been "maintained, asserted, and reclaimed" though indigenous alphabetic writing, in English no less.[57] Phillip Round's study on native print and book culture in the United States, *Removable Type: Histories of the Book in Indian Country, 1663–1880* (2010), likewise offers ample evidence of how "print and manuscript books have provided essential opportunities for Native peoples."[58] Round makes clear that native engagement with written texts "never replaced cultural traditions but have merely supplemented them."[59] Similarly, Drew Lopenzina has convincingly argued in *Red Ink: Native Americans Picking Up the Pen in the Colonial Period* (2012) that for indigenous people the appropriation of alphabetic writing was not an "either/or" proposition. Writing did not imply "turning their backs on traditional lifeways."[60] Like Round, Lopenzina insists that taking on alphabetic writing was an act of "negotiating a crucial set of tools and circumstances upon which survival and cultural continuance hinges."[61] What each of these studies have in common—and the writings of the Nahua intellectuals gathered in this book join them—is that they demonstrate how alphabetic writing has provided indigenous people with a practice and a tool with which to act, to negotiate, and to contest within the framework of colonialism/coloniality. Writing is also, as several of the above-mentioned studies have suggested, a way to imagine and create a life outside of that framework. While we must keep in mind the manner in which the Roman alphabet arrived and circulated, to ignore that which indigenous intellectuals produced with this tool would make us complicit in an ahistorical fiction of indigenous aversion to writing.

Present-day Mexican indigenous intellectuals Natalio Hernández Hernández (Nahua) and Victor de la Cruz (Zapotec) have both argued that their respective communities' long-standing relationships to the written word have been misrepresented by academic research. Hernández firmly states that "no éramos un pueblo ágrafo, ni un pueblo sin historia, como todavía sostienen las ciencias sociales y muchos científicos sociales" (we were not a people without writing, nor a people without history, as the social sciences and many social scientists continue to portray us).[62] Like Hernández, de la Cruz has criticized the academy for perpetuating the erroneous idea that some languages (i.e., indigenous) were meant to be only oral languages, not written: "El transito de la oralidad indígena a la escritura plantea problemas, aunque no en el sentido que pretenden problematizarlo algunos antropólogos, para quienes en el mundo unas lenguas nacieron para ser habladas únicamente y escribirlas sería tanto como pervertirlas" (The transition from indigenous orality to the written word presents problems, but not in the way suggested by some anthropologists, for whom some languages were born to be only spoken, as if to write them would be to pervert them).[63] As a leading proponent of the recovery and articulation of Zapotec writing, de la Cruz has stated that a major problem for Zapotec peoples today is that they lack both knowledge of, and exposure to, Zapotec writing practices, which he views as necessary "tanto para imitarlos como para criticarlos" (as much to imitate as to criticize them).[64] Working with young people in his community, de la Cruz teaches his students to read and write in the Zapotec language; they study the myriad manners of Zapotec writing utilized over the course of 2,500 years, including alphabetic script:

> El objetivo de la investigación de los nombres de los géneros literarios de los *binningula'sa'* no era revivir todas estas formas en la literatura

> zapoteca actual; sino que los jóvenes, quienes empezaban a escribir en *diidxazá*, tuvieran ante sí un panorama de su pasado literario y vieran cómo sus antepasados habían elaborado obras literarias en su lengua; y que aquellos habían tenido sus propios caminos en la creación literaria, obstruidos por el proceso colonizador.[65]
>
> (The goal of research on the names of literary genres of the *binningula'sa'* [Zapotec] writers of the past wasn't to revive them in today's Zapotec literature; it was instead so that the young people who are just beginning to write in *diidxazá* [Zapotec language] would have before them the panorama of their literary past and so that they could see how their ancestors had elaborated literary works in their language; to see that they had their own way of writing, but that it had been obstructed by the colonization process.)

De la Cruz's project is not an isolated one. Throughout the Americas there is a growing movement to recover the memory of indigenous writing and to practice old forms while cultivating new ones.[66] A notable case is the Taller de Historia Oral Andina (Andean Oral History Workshop, THOA) in Bolivia. Directed by Aymara historian and activist Carlos Mamani Condori, the THOA collective conceives of the written word not as something foreign but as part of the "genealogy of ancestral knowledge of our communities."[67] In Mexico, the "Continuity of the Yucatec Mayan Collective Memory" project is actively linking oral and written knowledges in its communities. Through this project, Mayan-language oral narratives are recorded, transcribed in the native language, and translated to Spanish for bilingual publication. Mexican indigenous literatures scholar Donald Frischmann sees this project as an example of how writing reinforces Maya orality through public intergenerational readings and discussions of the collected texts.[68] With these initiatives as my guide, the view taken for this book is that Nahua orality and writing were, and are, complementary, mutually reinforcing modes of intellectual work.[69] To be clear, this focus on alphabetic writing is not intended to undermine or predicate indigenous knowledge production outside of the logic and materiality of Western culture. But if we buy into the radical incompatibility of writing and indigeneity and discount indigenous alphabetic writing as somehow "inauthentic," we risk silencing, in historian Camilla Townsend's words, "the voices of people from whom we would otherwise hear nothing at all."[70]

A project of recognizing and recovering Nahua writing from the past five centuries requires an interdisciplinary approach, since distinct disciplines tend to focus on certain kinds of sources, theories, and methods that, on their own, reveal only a partial view of Nahua knowledge production. Historians of the colonial period have uncovered and illuminated rich examples of Nahua writing found in the archives, such as codices, annals, and mundane documents. Nevertheless, as discussed earlier, this particular line of Nahua writing fades away after the late eighteenth/early nineteenth centuries. Twentieth-century anthropological and linguistic studies of Nahua culture frequently highlight oral sources from the field; consulting only these types of sources might unwittingly suggest that Indians cannot or do not employ the written word. An emphasis on texts that are often considered "literary"—poetry, short stories, and the like—is also limiting. Present-day literary anthologies, for example, tend to only mention pre-Hispanic and early-colonial *cantares*, giving the false impression, as literary scholar Antonio Cornejo Polar has reminded us, that these kinds of activities terminated abruptly with conquest.[71] A singular focus on contemporary indigenous literatures also suggests a lengthy period of inactivity up until recent times.[72] An interdisciplinary perspective substantially increases the kinds of texts to be considered and gives a more comprehensive view of the varied ways that Nahuas have shaped and responded to specific contexts with the written word. From this angle, the Nahua grammars and dictionaries, local histories, newspaper articles, political speeches, laws, short stories, personal testimonies, and dramas appear like the ancient "geoglyphs" in the Nazca coastal planes, revealing the contours of an enduring line of Nahua thought and writing.

In the same way that suturing disciplines can help us better understand the kinds of issues Nahua intellectuals have concerned themselves with over the centuries, weaving together multiple vantage points can help tease out the experiences of the individuals treated in this book. Here I am indebted to the example of K. Tsianina Lomawaima (Creek) and Teresa McCarty, who work with a three-pronged method of analysis in their book *To Remain an Indian: Lessons in Democracy from a Century of Native American Education* (2006). By juxtaposing the discourses of American Indian educational policy with both on-the-ground practices and indigenous experiences, Lomawaima and McCarty show how a framework that brings together these potentially divergent perspectives can provide the means for a deep analysis of unique historical moments and complex indigenous lives. Throughout this book, I follow their lead by articulating theories and official policies regarding the place of the Indian in Mexico, their on-the-ground deployment, and the ways that Nahuas shaped and responded to the same.

Attention to personal experience in academic research has often been viewed as lacking in scientific objectivity and rigor. At the same time, many have convincingly argued that reading/listening to narrations of personal experience, particularly those of colonized subjects, are important critical projects.[73] Osage scholar Robert Warrior's work with native non-fiction and indigenous intellectual traditions in the United States, for example, offers an example of the productive aspects of attending to indigenous experience. In *The People and the Word: Reading Native Nonfiction* (2005), Warrior reminds us of the challenges and contradictions of utilizing "experience" as a lens through which to understand historical processes and brings to the discussion Joan W. Scott's insistence that we must not view individual experiences as incontestable nor outside of their discursive contexts.[74] Warrior cautions, however, against overlooking the possibilities that an analysis of experience can offer: "To shut down a discussion of experience runs the risk of using antiessentialist rhetoric to silence the voices of those who continue to face marginalization, while never interrogating the essentialist underpinnings of the discourse we all otherwise inhabit by default."[75] Warrior has also argued that "meaning is derived from the space between [the writer and the reader], and its production occurs in a context that includes everything that goes into producing the text and also what goes into making the writer and the reader who they are."[76] Since a substantial portion of the research for this project included reading these written texts with Nahuas, what appears on these pages is a reflection of the meaning I found in between those spaces of "me" (with my own cultural baggage), my interactions with native-speaker collaborators, and the texts we read together. I acknowledge that my own personal experience intervenes; I will not make the claim of complete objectivity or scientific distance.

Indeed, my own history has inflected how I came to this project, and how I have come to view indigenous writing. Not long before I spent my first summer with Nahua colleagues in Mexico, my grandmother and I had discovered that the records for the Carlisle Indian Industrial School, an Indian boarding school in Pennsylvania, had been organized and were available for consultation. The week before I left for my trip south, we sat at my grandmother's kitchen table reading the written forms, reports, letters, and newspaper clippings that told a small piece of the earlier years of Marie (Myrtle Mae) Evans, a young Anishinaabe girl who, on May 14, 1903, entered the school whose unofficial motto was "kill the Indian . . . save the man." On June 23, 1908, Marie, my great-grandmother, made it out alive. In these scraps of paper I saw how the Western world had categorized her, how the teachers checked off neat little boxes that quantified, codified, and categorized her identity and behaviors. But from other pages in this slim folder, I also learned that writing was powerful in Marie's hands, too. With a barrage of letters she had campaigned for the unpaid wages she had earned when she was "let out" as a maid during her summers as a Carlisle student (instead of being allowed to return home to her family for the summer, lest she revert back to her previous, undesirable state of Indianness). Later she used writing to mark her presence on the White Earth Reservation in Minnesota and to catalog the accomplishments of many of the other Carlisle School graduates there with her on the reservation. She wrote about moving to Minneapolis, about the challenges of her marriage to Raymond C. Peake (a fellow Ojibwe, whom she had met at Carlisle), the joys of a newborn son (my grandmother's oldest brother Rainsford), and her great pride in both the forty-five dollars in their bank account and a bountiful vegetable garden in their back yard. With writing, Marie defended herself and made her voice heard. I didn't know it at the time, but for that first trip, along with my clothes and books, I had carried Marie's story with me: how she was taught that who she was—and the places and the people she came from—were wholly insufficient and even a detriment to society. But I also took the story of how she wrote back. So when I listened to my Nahua teachers, who later became colleagues and friends, tell of how they learned to become ashamed of their identity and heritage, I heard echoes of my own family's past. I couldn't help but imagine the ways in which together we might tell—or write—a different story.

## Collaborative Methodologies

My introduction to the Nahuatl language and Nahua culture began at the Instituto de Docencia e Investigación Etnológica de Zacatecas (Zacatecas Institute for Teaching and Research in Ethnology, IDIEZ), an innovative Mexican research institute devoted to Nahua cultural recovery and revitalization (read more about IDIEZ between chapters 1 and 2). Over the past eight years, my interactions with Nahua intellectuals associated with IDIEZ, and the community members of the small rural villages from which they hail, have profoundly influenced the direction of this project and my research in general. Through listening to my colleagues' personal experiences and witnessing firsthand the discrimination against indigenous people in Mexico, I became increasingly aware of what Bonfil Batalla has discussed in his seminal book *México Profundo* (1996): the intense preoccupation with the glorious indigenous empires of the past, the outright disdain for the flesh-and-blood indigenous people of today, and all of the ideological maneuvering this entails. Despite being surrounded by a society that would prefer that they do otherwise, the Nahuas I worked with were deeply committed to recovering and revitalizing their language and culture. This book is aligned with their efforts as they continue this arduous process. I also learned that Nahuas are generally unaware of their own cultural heritage sources, written or otherwise, and face formidable challenges of access to the same. As an outsider academic, my knowledge of Nahua intellectual work and my ability to enter and navigate the libraries and archives where much of the evidence is held far surpassed that of my Nahua colleagues. It is not surprising then that when I began this project, Nahua intellectual Natalio Hernández Hernández directed me to "go to the books, and go to the people," firm in his beliefs that Nahuas had knowledge of ideas and people not found in books and that Nahua people needed to know about the things in the books that had been denied them. They needed to be a part of the recovery process as well. Likewise, upon asking an elder in one of the rural Nahua communities in which I worked how I might make a meaningful contribution to the community, he urged me to write about discriminatory policies and practices aimed at the elimination of indigenous ways of being. But most importantly, he said, he wanted the young people in his community to have access to the information with which I worked. They deserved to know what I (and others) knew about their people, and even more so to know how I had found it. With both of these directives in mind, a portion of this project has been a collaborative effort and has centered on bridging people, sources, and knowledges (I discuss these "bridging principles" in detail in chapter 4).

In addition to the guidance provided by Natalio Hernández and the elder in the Huasteca, the methodologies of this project are intersected by ongoing critical debates related to subjectivity, power, representation, and ethics related to research on and with indigenous peoples. Historian Florencia Mallon has called our attention to the impact that struggles for political and cultural self-determination since the early 1970s have had on today's scholarly agendas. Indigenous intellectuals emerging from these movements, Mallon explains, have brought to the forefront, among other issues, the intellectual agency of indigenous people.[77] Highlighting the colonial nature of knowledge production in academia, many indigenous intellectuals have rightly criticized how their people have been objectified as raw resources from which to extract data; how their histories have been silenced or misrepresented by dominant culture; how indigenous ways of knowing, particularly orality and storytelling, have been negated; and the overwhelming lack of indigenous perspectives and voices in research.[78] At stake for indigenous communities in their processes of intellectual decolonization are not just the kinds of stories that are (or are not) circulating about indigenous people but also who is doing the telling, and to what end. In this context, Mallon states, "scholars working on and collaborating with Native societies, whether themselves Native or non-Native, have therefore been challenged to rethink the ethical, methodological, and conceptual frameworks within which we locate our work on questions of Native histories and cultures."[79] As we have come to recognize how academic research has been (and continues to be) complicit with the (re)colonization of indigenous peoples, we have also been confronted with the challenges and benefits of developing new research methodologies in solidarity with indigenous decolonization—political, cultural, and intellectual alike.

Regarding power relations inherent to academic research and marginalized subjects, in his essay "Remapping Latin American Studies: Postcolonialism, Subaltern Studies, Post-Occidentalism, and Globalization Theory," Eduardo Mendieta has brought together some of the key debates of contemporary postcolonial/subaltern/post-Occidental theorists such as Edward Said, Gayatri Spivak, and Walter Mignolo, with the following questions: "Who is the subject who thinks what object? And more accurately still, where is this subject, and how does it project and localize its object of knowledge? Who speaks for whom and who speaks over and about whom?"[80] With many of these concerns at the heart of their theoretical-political practices, the Latin American Subaltern Studies Group (LASSG) convened during the 1990s as a working group committed to developing critical theories and methods in concert with a (leftist) political agenda identified with marginalized subjects. They proposed to develop "new ways of *looking* at the subaltern, new and more powerful forms of information retrieval, but also of building new relations between ourselves and those human contemporaries whom we posit as objects of study."[81] While these "new forms of acting and thinking politically" manifested themselves in different ways among the group's members, the idea of de-centering is the common thread that ran (and continues to run) through their various projects: a de-centering of the authority of Western epistemologies, institutions, and, paradoxically, academics.[82] As I write these words from a non-Nahua space in the U.S. academy (in English no less), this project at times feels far from the decolonization processes of indigenous communities or the de-centering model of the LASSG. There is no denying that I am in fact reading and writing *about* Nahuas. However, I have also made a commitment to a practice of collaboration, of reading and writing *with* them.

## Reading Circles

One of the tactics aimed at reconnecting cultural heritage sources with Nahuas today was to simply sit down and read together. Many of the texts brought together in this book were read and discussed in Reading Circles with native-speaker students and researchers; I consider our shared experiences in chapter 4. The participants were both male and female, between eighteen and thirty-five years old, and either completing their studies or had earned university degrees in law, accounting, education, linguistics, and social sciences.[83] They, like the intellectuals and writers in the following chapters, have worked and lived in multiple languages and cultures. During 2008, 2009, and 2011, we met over the course of several weeks (three to seven participants, one to two hours per day) and read the texts out loud while sharing our thoughts on the cultural, linguistic, literary, and thematic aspects of the readings. More often than not, the working language of the group was Nahuatl; thus, the inherent power structures of outsider academic-researcher and indigenous communities were disrupted from the beginning as I, the only non-native speaker, regularly stumbled in the language and was happily forced to defer to my eloquent colleagues. The goal of the Reading Circles was not to record and later report the details of our interactions. It was instead an exploration of collaborative methods aimed at bringing people and knowledges together in support of a common goal: the recovery and revitalization of Nahuatl language and culture. Reading Circles were a space to begin a practice of *dialoguing with* and *learning from* a people that have traditionally been talked *at* and written *about*.[84]

The Reading Circles as a space for collaboration takes its cue from activist scholarship in the social sciences, with its emphasis on, as anthropologist Charles Hale has explained, "explicit political alignments," "horizontal dialogues," and "co-production of knowledges."[85] Anthropologist Joanne Rappaport's collaborative research with Nasa people in Colombia over the past several decades has shown how intercultural dialogue—a two-way street that puts Western and indigenous intellectuals and epistemologies on equal footing—can disrupt a series of unequal power structures in academic research on and/or with indigenous people. While there is certainly an ethical component to this type of research, Rappaport also insists that one of the equally important benefits of intercultural dialogue is the potential to create powerful new analytical tools useful to all parties involved, born out of "far ranging conversations between different subject positions, their epistemologies, and the ways in which knowledge is transmitted."[86]

Along with the opportunity to experiment with intercultural dialogue, the collective critical analysis of texts in the Reading Circles provided a forum in which the group members were continuously exposed to texts that refuted the explicit and implicit disconnect between indigeneity, intellectualism, and writing, the enduring yet erroneous leitmotif of the postconquest centuries. In her work on decolonizing methodologies, Maori scholar Linda Tuhiwai Smith has made reference to Maori writer Patricia Grace's conference presentation, "Books Are Dangerous," which detailed the kinds of writing to which indigenous readers are generally subjected: they do not reflect or reinforce indigenous culture; they often leave indigenous peoples out of the picture entirely; and when they are visible on the page, many times it is a negative or untrue representation.[87] For many of the participants of the Reading Circles, the texts we discussed were the first they had encountered that reinforced a positive image of their culture and language. Our collective experience of reading together has shown that access to cultural heritage sources has the potential to increase the self-esteem of Nahua community members. One particular moment stands out: after a few weeks of Reading Circles work, one of the participants, Abelardo de la Cruz, blurted out, "So all this time they've been lying to us." When asked who it was that had been lying, the young man responded, "The schoolteachers; they said we were stupid *burrohmeh*, nothing but donkeys. I guess they were wrong." His response, I must insist, was not because Nahuas had written something down in alphabetic script. It was *what* was written, the content of what he was reading that he found so striking. In light of this experience, the repatriation of Nahua texts to Nahua people can be seen as combating the effects of what Kenyan scholar Ngũgĩ wa Thiong'o has called the "cultural bomb" of imperialist projects. In Thiong'o's words, "The effect of a cultural bomb is to annihilate a people's belief in their names, in their languages, in their environment, in their heritage of struggle, in the unity, in their capacities, and ultimately themselves."[88] The texts we read gave evidence of how Nahuas have grappled with many of the same issues that figure in the agendas of Nahua intellectuals and their communities today: questions of how the Nahuatl language ought to be written and taught; ways of remembering and recording histories; questions of autonomy and citizenship, agrarian reform, sacred ritual, education, and identity formation as indigenous people and citizens of the Mexican nation. A reincorporation of these kinds of texts to Nahua cultural memory can inform discussions, potentially leading to actions on these issues today. Indeed, books can be dangerous.

Distributing copies of the texts I have worked with, providing practical instruction in locating them (navigating databases and conducting archival research, for example), and reading together are some of the basic steps I have taken toward re-connecting Nahua communities with their intellectual legacy. I have also understood the elder in the Huasteca's request for "access" to cultural heritage sources along the lines of Tuhiwai Smith's call to demystify scholarship: "The responsibility of researchers and academics," she states, "is not simply to share surface information (pamphlet knowledge) but to share the theories and methods which inform the way knowledge and information are constructed and represented."[89] Similarly, anthropologists Kay Warren and Jean E. Jackson have noted that "few foreign investigators spend substantial amounts of time working with indigenous researchers and students, enabling them to gain access to the analytical skills routinely taught at national and foreign universities."[90] In light of this, one of the mutually agreed-upon goals during our Reading Circles sessions was to maintain a certain sense of transparency with how I was going about my own approach to the texts. I did this by sharing a variety of analytical strategies and theoretical approaches as a springboard for conversations on what might resonate with my colleagues from within their own cultural practices of approximation and interpretation of signs, sounds, performances, and other texts. In this way, we each came to the table as teachers and as learners, not unlike the way that educator/philosopher Paulo Freire envisioned collaborations in his essay, "Creating Alternative Research Methods: Learning to Do It by Doing It":

> If I am interested in knowing the people's way of thinking and levels of perception, then the people have to think about their thinking and not be only the object of my thinking. This method of investigation which involves study—and criticism of the study—by the people is at the same time a learning process. Through this process of investigation, examination, criticism and reinvestigation, the level of critical thinking is raised among all those involved. Thus, in doing research, I am educating and being educated with the people.[91]

These may seem to be relatively small gestures. But they are essential in creating space for Nahuas to decide if they wish to join local and global academic conversations as they relate to their culture, conversations from which they have been traditionally excluded. These are their stories after all.

* * *

The chapters that follow are organized chronologically, but need not be read in that order. Whether the writer produced his/her work hundreds of years or only a few months ago, the issues upon which they reflected are still pertinent to the present moment. History has not marched through and past the concerns of Nahua people as related to, for example, indigenous languages, land tenure, intercultural politics, education, gendered experiences, or cultural survival. Indeed, as Rabasa has stated, "the past is not something that happened a long time ago but a presence that *faces* us in its immediacy."[92] The shorter pieces in between the chapters, entitled *Tlen naman* (that which is of today), are meant to signal this present/presence. Along with my own short description of the decolonizing methodologies and current projects at IDIEZ (where this project began), the interludes are written reflections by present-day Nahua intellectuals Refugio Nava Nava, Victoriano de la Cruz Cruz, and Sabina Cruz de la Cruz. Each in different ways has been my teacher, and I am honored by their willingness to contribute their time, energy, and words to this project.

"Describing Nahuatl Language to Others in Early Colonial Mexico" centers on the linguistic work of Antonio del Rincón (1566–1601), a grammarian and Jesuit priest descended from the Nahua royal house of Texcoco. Rincón, perhaps the only indigenous man ordained by the Jesuits during the colonial period, is also the first native-speaker person in the Americas to write a grammar and linguistic treatise of his own language, *Arte mexicana* (1595). His intellectual activities provide a platform from which to discuss religious education for indigenous peoples and native-language legislation in the early colonial period, as well as the rapidly shifting social terrain characterized by attempts to contain and manage native populations. Through an analysis of Rincón's grammar, I discuss the alphabetization and categorical description of indigenous languages, with special attention to what the native speaker can tell us that the non-native speaker could not (or did not) in regards to the Nahuatl language, in this case its phonological aspects. Once used to facilitate the conversion of indigenous people to Catholicism, today, Rincón's text is an important resource in the recovery and revitalization of the Nahuatl language.

"Writing Tlaxcalan Memories that Matter" focuses on the historical memory of a community compiled, edited, and expanded upon by seventeenth-century Tlaxcalan elite statesman don Juan Buenaventura Zapata y Mendoza (16xx–1688). Along with the year-to year account of territorial and political disputes, transfers of power, public works, and natural/climactic phenomena, his annals offer rich examples of indigenous political negotiation in a context of domination. In this chapter, I deal specifically with Zapata's records of public performances of Tlaxcalan political authority and rights, as these were being modified and restricted. This is Zapata's legacy to his descendants, a record of Tlaxcalan agency that forcefully interrupts any storyline that would suggest his people as passive victims of the colonial project.

"Defending Indigenous Citizens when 'Indians No Longer Existed'" analyzes the career and writings of Faustino Galicia Chimalpopoca (ca. 1802–1877), Nahua politician, attorney, scholar of colonial Nahuatl texts, and personal Nahuatl teacher and interpreter to Emperor Maximilian I. Through these readings, I address the rhetoric of nation building during the nineteenth century, including the denial and disappearance of indigenous people in the discourse of citizenship. Long relegated to an unpopular footnote in the historiography of Mexico for his outspoken support of the short-lived French occupation of Mexico (1864–1867), Chimalpopoca's far-reaching activism aimed at securing and assuring the rights of indigenous peoples as full citizens mark him as an important nineteenth-century indigenous intellectual. Add to this that he was one of the most active scholars of Nahuatl language and culture of his time—as determined a defender of his language and culture as he was of indigenous rights—all at a time when, by law, Indians no longer existed.

"Knowing, Speaking, Teaching, and Writing" engages the testimonial writings and short stories of doña Luz Jimenez (1897–1965), who, along with being muse and model for artists such as Diego Rivera and Jean Charlot, was a teacher of her language and a cultural intermediary for a series of well-known anthropologists and linguists. Through doña Luz's life story, we are offered a vision of how indigenous people experienced the scientific and economic policies and discourses of Social Darwinism manifested in the nation's resolve to deal with the so-called "Indian problem" of the early twentieth century. Her recollections and tales of day-to-day life during the Mexican Revolution and experience with assimilative schooling come to us as a joint project with Mexican anthropologist Fernando Horcasitas. This collaborative process of her work provides the impetus for a discussion of outsider academics and indigenous communities, including my own work in Reading Circles with Nahuas today.

"Performing the Recovery of Indigeneity" examines the work of playwright, artist, and teacher Ildefonso Maya Hernández (1936–2011). Along with a discussion of my interviews with Maya, I analyze his play

*Ixtlamatinij* (*The Learned Ones*), a biting critique of the cultural annihilation inherent to bilingual education programs for indigenous people in the twentieth century. The chapter closes with a consideration of Maya's work as a modern-day tlahcuiloh. In pre-Columbian times, the tlahcuiloh was responsible for painting and interpreting the knowledge and history of his/her people. Whereas the genre of the painted book (amoxtli) fell into disuse with the arrival of the Roman alphabet, Maya returned to this style as a move to recover and redesign indigenous discursive and material communication tools. Like his pre-Columbian predecessors, he observed, interpreted, wrote, and painted his world.

I have been asked why I chose to write about these particular individuals to initiate a project of the recovery of Nahua intellectualism and writing. My decisions were based primarily on practicality, having much to do with the fact that each was already mentioned in the literature of several disciplines. A "blip" on the radar in narratives of the early indigenous-language grammars, Antonio del Rincón stood out in his role as a "first": first Jesuit grammarian of an indigenous language, first native speaker to write a linguistic treatise in the Americas, and first to explain contrastive vowel length in the Nahuatl language in a systematic way.[93] Don Juan Buenaventura Zapata y Mendoza's manuscript, one of the more detailed of the Nahua annals genre, has been recently made widely available thanks to a critical edition by the late Luis Reyes García (Nahua) and Andrea Martínez Baracs, and pioneering studies by ethnohistorians James Lockhart and Camilla Townsend have cleared the path for further discovery. Faustino Galicia Chimalpopoca caught my eye for being repeatedly and energetically criticized by one of Nahuatl Studies's greatest scholars, Ángel María Garibay. The sheer quantity of texts that Chimalpopoca's hand had supposedly botched led me to believe that he was deeply immersed in the study of his culture and language, and perhaps deserved a second look. Thanks to Frances Karttunen's book *Between Worlds* (1994), I learned that the woman portrayed in Diego Rivera's ubiquitous flower-seller images, doña Luz Jiménez, was not silent but instead spoke—and wrote—volumes. Mexican indigenous literatures scholar Donald Frischmann introduced me to the work of Ildefonso Maya Hernández and the man himself. Maya's lengthy career as a playwright and theater director happily contradicts Diana Taylor's pessimistic pronouncement that Latin Americans lack the option of "using their native languages in a step toward cultural decolonization [and that] most playwrights have no 'native' languages to turn to; they would have to learn them and even then they could address only miniscule populations."[94] "There is no question," Taylor continues, "of returning to a native drama."[95] For Nahuas, the case is not closed: Maya's work is a fine example of the tenacity and persistence of indigenous theater in Mexico. Finally, my collaboration with the researchers at IDIEZ began with my study of the Nahuatl language at a summer intensive course and has continued throughout the research for this book. It is thanks to these present-day indigenous intellectuals that I was drawn to explore this untapped vein of intellectual work and writing in postconquest Mexico. I did not consciously choose these Nahua intellectuals in order to demonstrate such a wide diversity of experiences and perspectives. This is, however, precisely what has occurred. I only hope that my words do justice to the extraordinary, courageous, complex individuals whom I have attempted to know better in the pages that follow.

## A Note on Orthographies and Translations

The reader will note that the Nahuatl texts I reproduce in the following chapters do not follow a single unified orthography and that they employ varied spacing, spelling, and punctuation conventions. While I discuss this more fully in the chapter on doña Luz Jiménez, suffice it to say that the lack of a standardized orthography is one of the hallmarks of Nahuatl writing.[96] These orthographic variations reflect the different geographical origins and ideological orientations, as well as the producers and perceived audiences of the texts. My own use of Nahuatl terms is italicized on first appearance, utilizing a modified colonial orthography that marks glottal stops with an *h*. Quoted materials are faithful reproductions of the original texts.

In publications related to Nahuatl literatures, it has unfortunately been common practice to omit the Nahuatl original in favor of a translation (normally to Spanish) or to bury the original Nahuatl text in a footnote or appendix. I have intentionally included the Nahuatl original as well as translations within the main body of the chapters. Following Gayatri Spivak, I believe that translation should be a "practice rather than a solution."[97] That is, the original Nahuatl texts are not silenced but instead supplemented with tentative translations, thus maintaining the possibilities of native and non-native linguistic and cultural exploration. Translations to English are my own, unless otherwise noted, and were completed in collaboration with either Sabina Cruz de la Cruz or Victoriano de la Cruz Cruz, both native speakers from the Huasteca region of Veracruz, Mexico. I take full responsibility for any and all errors.

CHAPTER 1

# Describing Nahuatl Language to Others in Early Colonial Mexico

Antonio del Rincón

Descended from nobility of Texcoco, and the first indigenous person in the Americas to write a grammar of his own language, Antonio del Rincón (1555–1601) has been called "el primer lingüista nativo del Nuevo Mundo" (the first native linguist of the New World).[1] Through the figure of Rincón—perhaps the only indigenous man ordained by the Jesuits in the early colonial period—we are offered a unique perspective from which to consider how Nahua intellectuals responded to Spanish Crown and Catholic Church policies related to the colonization and evangelization of the native population of New Spain.[2] In the case of Rincón, he worked from within the ranks of the Jesuit order to promote Christian evangelization among Indians, taught the Nahuatl language to other priests, and wrote one of the earliest grammars of his native tongue to facilitate this process. To better conceptualize his writing, I focus in on the debate regarding the place of indigenous men in Church affairs during the early colonial period, as well as the role of language in the colonization and evangelization project. The chapter closes with attention to Rincón's intellectual contribution related to the categorical description of his native language, taking into consideration the two other extant sixteenth-century Nahuatl grammars, both written by non-native speakers: Andrés de Olmos and Alonso de Molina.

Rincón lived and wrote in a world marked by (proto)racialized socio-political tensions, which are manifest in the abundant administrative documents of the Spanish Crown and Catholic Church. Sixteenth-century decrees and laws indicate a (re)organizing impulse in New Spain, aimed at locating, and subsequently maintaining, colonial subjects in specific positions in the social, political, and economic hierarchy. Historian Yanna Yannakakis has observed that Iberian notions of lineage or descent as marking difference—both between groups and within them—transferred to the new context, but also combined in new ways with legal constructions of colonial social identities.[3] For example, pre-conquest central Mexican indigenous society was highly stratified, and the Crown recognized and supported such distinctions between indigenous nobles and commoners when it served its interests. Yet by the 1540s, consistent efforts were made to compress and incorporate indigenous peoples of varying ethnicities and social classes "toward a single level and condition," that of *indios,* inferior to wealthy *peninsulares* and *criollos.*[4] Subsumed into the legal category of *indio,* indigenous people were understood to be minors and wards of the Crown, distinct from the other major categories of *negro* or *español.* This special legal status, which afforded certain protections and privileges, simultaneously codified difference.[5] It also gave the illusion of an identifiable social group that could be managed and contained. As the complexities of colonial society increased—with subsequent waves of Spanish immigrants, African slaves, and regular biological and social mixing between the three major groups—so did anxieties over the unmanageability of the progressively diverse population as a potential threat to the desired social order. These preoccupations would translate to increased attempts to identify and assign the place (social, political, geographic, and even occupational) of individuals (or groups) in a hierarchy that inevitably located the small group of Spaniards and their descendants at the pinnacle of the social pyramid.[6]

But these efforts were met by colonial subjects—indigenous or otherwise—with regular subversions and transgressions of imposed boundaries. As the social and political place of Indians was progressively modified in order to limit access to power and resources, many noble-class indigenous men such as Rincón maintained or achieved varying degrees of power and prestige, often in their indispensable roles as cultural intermediaries. As Yannakakis has ascertained, in their roles as translators, cabildo members and governors, linguistic and cultural "informants," and in other positions within local churches, indigenous intermediaries proved to be extraordinarily capable of negotiating, appropriating, and deploying discourses of power.[7] Rincón's story echoes that of many other colonial-period native intermediaries in New Spain: they tended to be young men from prominent indigenous families who had been educated by the Catholic priests. This education then resulted in (whether intentional or not) an entire class of "alphabetically, bureaucratically, and legally bicultural, bilingual, and literate" individuals.[8] Responsible for communication and mediation across ethnic, political, and religious lines, these men made possible the exchange of symbolic and material power between cultures.[9]

Indigenous people who resisted the colonial project (as opposed to mediating exchanges between cultures) during the early colonial period have tended to gather much of the critical attention in recent times, while a somewhat conservative figure such as Rincón has received scant consideration. Yet Rincón and others like him are crucial to understanding the colonial experience. Literary scholar Rolena Adorno has remarked, for example, that without native voices our understanding of complex colonial cultures in contact is incomplete.[10] I would also add that we must listen to native voices regardless of their perceived degrees of resistance to or collaboration with the colonizers. A more productive frame for addressing indigenous intellectualism and writing, especially during the early colonial period, is perhaps what Philip J. Deloria has called an analysis of the "wreckage and the opportunity generated by colonial encounters."[11] It is in this space of wreckage and opportunity that we find this Nahua intellectual writing the first linguistic treatise of his own language, building a bridge between Jesuits and native speakers of Nahuatl.

Historians place Antonio del Rincón's birth around 1555 and his death in 1601. General consensus is that he hailed from the *altepetl* of Texcoco and was descended from the revered *tlahtoani* Nezahualcoyotl, although there is some speculation regarding whether both of Rincón's parents were indigenous or if he was mestizo (defined at this time as one who is of mixed European and indigenous descent). Jesuit historian Andrés Pérez de Ribas recorded the following bibliographic information for Rincón: "Nació en la ciudad de Texcoco, cuatro leguas distante de la de México, de muy nobles y cristianos padres, los cuales le criaron en temor de Dios, en honestidad, en toda virtud (He was born in the city of Texcoco, four leagues from the city of Mexico, to very noble and Christian parents, who brought him up with fear of God, honesty, and virtue).[12] Frances Karttunen posits a Spanish father and noble Texcocan mother.[13] We cannot know for sure as no concrete evidence has surfaced related to his parentage, although this scenario would not be surprising, as we know that intermarriage between Spaniards with highborn Indian women was not unheard of, and it was a common occurrence for noble Indians to be, or profess to be, Christians, particularly those of Texcoco.[14] At any rate, whether both or only one of his parents were indigenous is not important: his much-cited connection to Texcocan nobility, and his innovative scholarship on phonological aspects of Nahuatl as recorded in his grammar, clearly mark him as a native speaker of the language.[15]

Rincón's origins become intriguing, however, when we take into consideration the fact that he was ordained as a Jesuit priest during a time when Indians were theoretically prohibited from ordination according to the Church's provincial council decrees as well as by the Spanish Crown. How could an Indian—or even a mestizo for that matter—have become an ordained priest at this time? We can assume that certain concessions were made by the Church in order to bridge the massive gap between the theories and practices of ministering to the indigenous populations. Specifically, at the time of the Jesuit arrival in the late sixteenth century, epidemics were again decimating the native population (smallpox, measles, and then typhus).[16] Tending to the afflicted was a priority for the priests, yet communication with the native populations was challenging since few were fluent in the indigenous languages.[17] The Jesuits had great need not only of native speakers but also specifically of those who had a command of the Texcocan regional variation, considered by natives and non-natives alike to be the most refined and elegant manner of Nahuatl speech. Texcocan Nahuatl would appropriately reflect "the high seriousness of [the priests'] sacred purpose, [the Indians would hear] in 'lordly speech' an echo of the authority of the true Faith."[18] Louise Burkhart explains, "the friars could successfully manipulate the system only by adapting to it."[19] That is, their best recourse in convincing native speakers of the authority of Christianity would be to learn the indigenous language, in the appropriate (symbolically powerful) register. Thus, Rincón as a son of Texcoco would be an ideal recruit to the Jesuit order for his linguistic abilities. Add to this the fact that a Texcocan would also solidify already strong links between Texcocan nobility and the Church, forged in the earliest days of conquest.

The noble class of Texcoco, the pre-Hispanic intellectual center of the Aztec Triple Alliance (Tenochtitlan, Texcoco, and Tlacopan), expressed varied reactions to the arrival of the Spaniards and Christianity. For example, don Hernando Ixtlilxochitl (Ixtlilxochitl II, son of Nezahuapilli, installed as ruler by Hernán Cortés) embraced Christianity and European customs from the very beginning, and it is said that he even threatened to burn his own mother alive if she did not follow suit.[20] In return for being selected by Cortés as the new lord of Texcoco, Ixtlilxochitl ordered baptisms, Christian marriages, and the establishment of the first church in New Spain.[21] The Flemish Franciscan, Pedro de Gante, began his study of the Nahuatl language and his evangelization project as a houseguest of don Hernando Ixtlilxochitl's family.[22] Other Texcocans famously resisted the imposition of the new religion. Consider the case of don Carlos Ometochtzin Chichimecatecuhtli (half brother to Ixtlilxochitl), burned at the stake in 1539 for being a "heretical dogmatizer" who dared to suggest not only indigenous sovereignty but also the coevalness of the varied religious practices of indigenous people and Europeans.[23] The lesson of being burned at the stake might have encouraged Indian obedience to the new religion.[24] At the same time, a Christian identity was required in order to maintain or achieve any degree of power in the new social hierarchy.[25] Motivated by fear, a grasp for power or prestige, or a true calling to the ministry—as far as Rincón's rationale for becoming a Christian priest, we can only guess; he did not write on this topic.

What we do know of Rincón's lifetime, however, is that he studied ecclesiastic law at the Real y Pontificia Universidad de México, an institution founded in 1551 with the idea of offering an education such as that of Spain for "naturales e hijos de españoles, sin ninguna distinción" (Indians and sons of Spaniards, with no distinction).[26] Margarita Menegus and Rodolfo Aguirre point out that an education at the Real y Pontificia was a viable strategy utilized by the noble indigenous families to access the benefits and privileges of education as well as a way to attain the (secular) priesthood.[27] Studying at the Real y Pontificia, and thereafter joining the recently arrived Jesuits, was a logical path for an indigenous or mestizo man intent upon becoming a priest at this particular moment in time. From scant biographical traces, we know that Rincón followed the traditional Jesuit route to the priesthood.[28] Joining the Company of Jesus as a novice on August 25, 1573, he took his first vows (as a brother) in September 1575.[29] From there, he began his Scholastic period, normally a four-year educational process, with the first two years devoted to the humanities and arts (such as grammar and rhetoric) and the third and fourth years devoted to philosophy. During this time, he is known to have studied at the Colegio de San Pedro y San Pablo.[30] The next stage of Jesuit education toward the priesthood is the Regency, where the man is sent out from the monastery, generally to teach or carry out some form of ministerial work. For his Regency period, Rincón was sent to Puebla de los Ángeles around 1578–1579, where he would be instrumental in the early years of the Colegio de la Compañía de Jesús de San Jerónimo as its first rector, as well as at the Casa de la Compañía del Nombre de Jesús de

Espíritu Santo.[31] In Puebla, Rincón taught Latin and Nahuatl grammar, explained Christian doctrine to the Indians, tended to the sick, and carried his message to prisoners in the jails and the workers at the *obrajes* (sheep farms, textile mills). In the late 1580s, he suffered a stroke, leaving his left side paralyzed, but the record states that he nonetheless returned to Mexico City in 1581 to study theology with Pedro de Ortigosa before being ordained on September 30, 1583.[32] From here it appears that Rincón returned to Puebla to work as a priest and confessor of Indians.[33] His trace is minimal during what is termed the Tertianship, when the Jesuit traditionally embarks upon a period of contemplation, study, and prayer before petitioning for final vows, which Rincón took in 1592.[34] During the last decade of the sixteenth century, Rincón is mentioned in the annals of Jesuit history as visiting Tepotzotlan and Mexico City, where he more than likely taught Nahuatl to novices and priests. He would have commenced his work on the grammar, *Arte mexicana*, in 1584, since, as he explains in the grammar's dedicatory letter to the bishop of Tlaxcala, Diego Romano, dated Saint Ambrose's Day in 1594, it took him ten years to complete. The choice of Saint Ambrose's Day for the dedication is appropriate, as this patron saint of bees and beekeepers was known for his eloquence in preaching and was sometimes called the "honey-tongued" bishop. With the lessons in Rincón's *Arte mexicana*, the Jesuit priests would skillfully instruct and cultivate new adherents to the Christian religion.

## Colonization, Evangelization, and Language

Four religious orders (Franciscans, Dominicans, Augustinians, and Mercedarians) were originally authorized by the Crown to preach in the New World, yet only the first three would commence the first missionary projects of New Spain. The Franciscans arrived in 1523, followed not long after by the Dominicans in 1526 and the Augustinians in 1533. Each dominated distinct geographical areas, worked in a wide variety of indigenous languages, and held distinct views regarding the evangelization process, education for Indians, and the formation of an indigenous clergy.[35] The Franciscans initially intended to educate and train elite indigenous men for the priesthood, whereas the Dominicans and the Augustinians did not share this goal. The Jesuits, relatively late arrivals to the scene, began their work in New Spain in 1572 after receiving authorization from King Philip II. Well known for their missions in the unwelcoming northern reaches of the Spanish Empire and in Puebla, they were also quite active in Mexico City, responsible for establishing the renowned centers of learning such as El Colegio Máximo (Colegio de San Pablo y Pedro), the Colegio de San Ildefonso, the Casa Profesa, the Colegio de San Gregorio, and the Colegio de San Andrés. The Jesuits' later arrival was to their benefit, as they could see what had worked—and what had failed—in the experience of the first three orders. By and large, experience had shown that conversion efforts and ministering to Indians in New Spain was most effective in the native languages. Whereas the Crown's wish was that priests would eventually teach the Indians the Castilian language, the priests concentrated their efforts with the native populations on learning and preaching in the indigenous language or, in the case of the Franciscans and the Jesuits, in Latin, teaching and ministering in the language of the Church.[36] Their priority was to evangelize, not Hispanicize.[37] Practical experience told the priests that without a deep understanding of the indigenous languages, evangelization was nearly impossible, thus the religious orders worked closely with native speakers of indigenous languages such as Rincón. The following brief detour outlining sixteenth-century linguistic and educational policies provides a frame of reference for understanding the role of language in the evangelization process in colonial Mexico and its implications for indigenous intellectual protagonism.

Long before Hernán Cortés's arrival in Tenochtitlan, the 1512 Laws of Burgos had already established "the who and the how" of the education of Indians in the so-called New World. The Spanish Crown initially established the encomienda system, which rewarded the conquistadors for their efforts by supplying them with Indian labor and tribute. Spanish encomenderos with more than fifty Indians in their "care" were responsible for their evangelization and education. The proposed method was that one Indian would memorize Latin prayers, learn the Castilian language, and receive instruction of the new religion in his native tongue. He would then go on to teach the rest of the Indians.[38] From very early on it was apparent not only that the method was unrealistic but also that the encomenderos were much more concerned with organizing and controlling labor than teaching Castilian or evangelizing and therefore ignored this obligation. In fact, recognizing the difficulties of this situation, in 1524 Cortés wrote to King Charles V requesting that the clergy (not the encomenderos) take over the responsibilities of indigenous conversion and instruction.[39] By 1535, King Charles V officially turned this enormous task over to the Church and informed New Spain's viceroy Antonio de Mendoza that all religious representatives must learn an indigenous language and that the Indians were to learn the Castilian language. Shirley Brice Heath tells us that "encomenderos and Crown administrators were ordered to provide schools for the sons of Indian caciques, or local chieftains. In these schools, under the tutelage of friars, the young men would learn 'Christianity, good customs, civility, and the Castilian tongue.'"[40]

The Franciscans complied with the Crown's directive to instill European norms by opening schools for indigenous elites (the classic example being the Colegio de Santa Cruz de Tlatelolco), but Castilian had limited importance or presence in the curriculum. The reality of New Spain was such that the use of Castilian in dealings with indigenous people was uneven at best, and for the most part impractical. Indeed, it would not be until the Bourbon Reforms of the late eighteenth century that the idea of Castilian as the language of the Spanish Empire would be unilaterally deployed across the colonies and embraced by both Crown and Church.[41]

By 1542, the encomenderos had become perhaps too powerful, and the 1542 New Laws declared that the Indians were no longer their property but were to be transferred as "free vassals" to the Crown. In this way, Charles V effectively reduced the power of the faraway encomendero class in the colonies and compressed indigenous hierarchies into one lump identity of "subjects," diminishing that group's claims to power as well. Soon thereafter, in 1550, Charles V again declared that Castilian should be the language of the Christian educational program organized by the friars. This time his stated rationale was that the mysteries of the Catholic faith were unattainable in the indigenous languages. Interestingly, he does not insist on Latin for Christian instruction. In his opinion, Castilian would not only suffice but also be the ideal language of Christianity. He also insisted that this education should be extended to all Crown subjects, not just the native elite.[42] In this single decree the monarch clarified the pecking order, establishing Castilian (and by extension the Spanish Crown) above Latin (the Vatican) and indigenous languages (natives). However, this assertion had little effect on the ground in New Spain, where the friars continued to enjoy more immediate results by working in the indigenous languages. It seems that Charles V had begun to sense that besides the encomenderos, the Franciscans were becoming perhaps more influential than he preferred, and by extension the natives associated with them. In that same year he sent word to the Dominican and Augustinian provincials, requesting that they agree with his plan of establishing Castilian as the language of religion. It is not surprising that Charles V would attempt to ally with the Dominican and Augustinian orders in light of the fact that these groups traditionally viewed Indians as neophytes and had no designs on establishing an Indian clergy, as did the Franciscans. The monarch would need to do everything in his power to manage and control from so far away, and this included ensuring that Indians did not go beyond their defined social boundaries as vassals of the Crown. He did not even attempt to persuade the Franciscans, leaving them oblivious to his conversations with the other two orders.[43]

If Charles V faced the formidable task of wrangling a jumble of factions that all believed themselves to have prestige and rights, his son and successor Philip II was equally saddled with the conundrum of how to manage the expansive and unruly empire from afar. A nagging problem was that Indians had become increasingly adept at moving within the new social system, with many of the elite indigenous men having benefited from their education with the friars, particularly those associated with the Colegio de Santa Cruz de Tlatelolco.[44] As Barbara Fuchs has argued, whereas the goal in educating Indians was "to reinforce existing class hierarchies [ . . . ] the nobles thus taught did not learn to be willing subjects of the colonial masters, but rather their equals."[45] Especially in their roles as intermediaries, educated indigenous men had the potential to dominate important positions that the colonial structure was not prepared to concede, since the economic success of New Spain depended on maintaining Indians in a subordinate social category.[46] Not surprisingly, Philip II's reign, 1556–1598 (coincidentally, nearly mirroring Rincón's lifetime [1555–1601]), was characterized by repeated attempts to control indigenous behaviors, including language use, through law.

In what seems to have been a flash of insight as to the realities of the linguistic landscape of the New World, in 1565 Philip II declared that all missionaries should learn the language of the indigenous population with whom they were working.[47] Where it might appear that Philip recognized the linguistic plurality of his empire, with this decree he shows himself perhaps unaware of just how many languages or ethnic groups there were, let alone the fact that each religious order worked among various peoples. It is possible that he began to understand the enormous difficulties that this directive posed after all, for in 1570 he declared Nahuatl the official language for all Indians in New Spain.[48] Whereas Heath reads this as Philip II's "iron sense of Christian mission" aimed at simplifying the linguist kaleidoscope in order to better disseminate Catholic teaching in the colony, it could be argued that this was a shrewd tactic to circumvent the potential unification of Indians and criollos/mestizos against the Crown.[49] This brief universalization of Nahuatl for all of New Spain's Indian subjects deploys the idea of language as companion of empire, not only in facilitating administrative tasks but also, more importantly, in maintaining distinct social/racial categories. The categorization, separation, and visual codification had already been set in motion with reorganized physical space (*república de indios* and *república de españoles*), as well as with material identifiers classified in sumptuary laws. Now language would also "mark" and locate Indians and non-Indians in the social/racial hierarchy. Besides assigning a social place for (presumably all) Indians, this would have managed to create a clear division between Indians and other colonial subjects, thus circumventing any kind of mutual identification. Understanding themselves as "different" from each other, the criollos, but especially mestizos, would be hard-pressed to find common ground with the Indians and would therefore be less inclined to form an alliance against the Crown. This imposition of Nahuatl as the official language of all of New Spain's Indians demonstrated the Crown's attempts to control the subjects of the empire by legislating economic, political, and social differences. However, as a classic example of Michel Foucault's conceptualization of power as circulating through a "net-like organization" where people are "simultaneously undergoing and exercising this power," Philip's move to contain one group unwittingly created space for others to advance their own agendas.[50] The Jesuits, while latecomers, shrewdly established their own niche as able speakers of the Nahuatl language by adding to their ranks the gifted *nahuatlahto* (interpreter/scholar of Nahuatl), Juan de Tovar, and eight native-speaker students, one being Antonio del Rincón.[51]

Whereas the Jesuits strategically responded to Philip II's decree of Nahuatl for all Indian subjects, most others largely ignored the decree. A unifying language for the indigenous population may well have been an easy solution to a series of Crown concerns in territories that had already had contact with Nahuatl. But there were substantial populations that had never had any contact with the Aztec Empire or its dominant language, particularly in areas where the Dominicans and Augustinians worked.[52] This is yet another example of the differences between theory and practice in the New World context, and it demonstrates what historian James Lockhart has suggested as the hallmark of Spanish American administrative/legislative iteration: noncompliance. According to Lockhart, "legislation, regulations, and policies are declared intentions but cannot be presumed to have been carried out; in the Spanish American context in fact the presumption is very much in the other direction."[53]

With indigenous languages playing such a vital part of the initial colonization and evangelization of New Spain's indigenous subjects, from today's perspective it would seem that Rincón's experience as a native-speaker priest would have been the rule rather than the exception. But this was not the case; the ordination of Indians was both infrequent and controversial, but certainly not unheard of. As we have seen, and as we will see in the following discussion of indigenous men in the priesthood, often theories articulated at an administrative level had little to do with the realities and pragmatic responses to day-to-day life in the colonies.

## Indian and Mestizo Priests in the Early Colonial Period

In 1524, the first twelve Franciscans arrived in New Spain and, following the example of Pedro de Gante who had arrived one year earlier, began the process of evangelization. To do so, they quickly learned the dominant indigenous language of Central Mexico, Nahuatl, and established primary schools for noble Indians. Stafford Poole characterizes this first stage of Franciscan work with Indians (1524–1555) as one of idealism in terms of both the Church's perception of the effectiveness of their missionary efforts and their goal of establishing an Indian clergy.[54] In line with the 1539 Junta Eclesiástica that decreed that Indians could be ordained to the four minor orders in preparation for the priesthood, at this time the Church did not see Indians as "perpetual neophytes," as would be the case later in the century.[55]

The second stage, punctuated by the meetings of the Mexican provincial councils of 1555 and 1585, is characterized by the Franciscans' realization that not all Indians would accept (nor, according to the friars, understand) Christianity, tempering the initial strong support of the idea of indigenous men groomed for the priesthood. The councils' discussions show increasing caution in terms of indigenous education and access to sacred scriptures. In fact, the First Provincial Council of 1555 formally excluded Indians (as well as mulattos and mestizos) from the priesthood. The bishops of the Mexican councils were not alone in the debates regarding Indians and the priesthood; the king of Spain and the pope weighed in as well. Between 1575 and 1578, Philip II issued a series of *cédulas* (royal decrees) regarding what the (perhaps too) powerful religious orders and his Indian subjects were doing in his empire.[56] Sent to the archbishops and bishops in the colonies, the cédulas explicitly "forbade the ordination of mestizos," which Poole reads as a sign of anxiety over possible separatist movements among mestizos, arguing that "it can be surmised that the social advancement involved in ordination to the priesthood was viewed as a potential power base for mestizo separatism."[57] As a sign of papal and royal disagreement, on January 25, 1577, Pope Gregory XIII issued the *Nuper ad Nos*, which stated that "the illegitimate sons of Spaniards and Indian women, as also of Spaniards who live in the Indies, [can] receive all the orders, hear confessions, and preach the word of God, provided they master the native language and have the qualities that the Council of Trent prescribes for ordination."[58] The Vatican's ruling had assessed the colony through the lens of Christian evangelization, not the consolidation of imperial Spain's power. The reality the pope interpreted was that of an increasingly mixed population and a chronic shortage of priests who were fluent in the native languages. With explicit reference to the Council of Trent, we are also reminded that the Church was more concerned with its own internal divisions than with Spain's fears of separatism in the colonies. In this particular "war of the wills," the pope was victorious in that he succeeded in securing the revocation of Philip's cédulas in 1588.[59]

The Third Provincial Council of 1585 appeared to still have great concerns regarding the suitability of Indians in the clergy, stating that "whence also neither those of mixed blood, whether from Indians or Moors, nor mulattoes in the first degree are to be admitted to orders without great caution."[60] However, the wording of the decree was ambiguous enough to provide a loophole for Indians to enter the priesthood.[61] According to Poole, the decree was based on earlier peninsular council documents that did not treat the topic of Indians or *castas*, so the Mexican bishops added a line specifically barring Indians, mestizos, and mulattos. Rome, however, added the phrase "without great caution" to the decree, opening the door to the legal ordination of Indians and others of mixed lineage. He also identified that due to a change in the original wording of the conciliar text—this addition of "without great caution"—from 1591 and on, there was in fact "no formal legal exclusion of Indians from the ranks of the clergy, and only a qualified one for mestizos and other *castas*."[62] The provincial council's hesitance to allow Indians to enter the priesthood reflects the heightened racial prejudices in New Spain: increased social and biological mixing was resulting in an increasingly unmanageable (albeit minoritized) majority that threatened the social, political, and economic dominance of the Europeans and their offspring (the majoritized minority). In this context, the constant vigilance and limitation of minoritized groups' access to power was crucial in maintaining the colonial hierarchy. As an example, Ignacio Osorio Romero points out that if the peninsulares or criollos had accepted Indians as equals on the religious sector, they would have been obliged to do so in civil society as well, something they were simply not willing to do.[63] The fact that a native clergy was never fully developed can therefore be read as a sign of the race/class divisions in colonial Mexican society. Of course, as was the case in the differences between linguistic theory/legislation and quotidian practice, there were surely cases of Indians and mestizos entering the "clerical ranks under false designations" when social and racial prejudices were tempered by necessity.[64] "Practical accommodation," according to Poole, characterized the end of the sixteenth and beginning of the seventeenth centuries when it came to who entered the priesthood.[65] However, while it is true that Indian and mestizo ordination was for all intents and purposes legal by this time, it would be quite a stretch to say that the European-born clergy or the peninsular and criollo classes approved of the idea.

Taking into consideration the escalating social tensions of the second half of the sixteenth century in New Spain, and the racialized politics surrounding the intellectual and spiritual capacities of the Indian visible in the Mexican provincial council papers, it was indeed a rarity—but certainly not an impossibility—that an Indian or mestizo would be admitted to the Company of Jesus. Moreover, while Rincón's ordination in 1583 occurs before the ruling of the Third Provincial Council that (perhaps unintentionally) cleared the path for indigenous entrance to the clergy, we can certainly imagine the extent to which the Jesuits obeyed the pope before all other masters. That is, through Rincón's experience we are presented with an example of how in certain circumstances laws and decrees were ignored in favor of solutions that responded to daily life in New Spain. In the previous section, Rincón's unique historical context has been established by reviewing official linguistic and educational policy in relation to quotidian practice, as well as the perceived (and actual) place of Indians in the priesthood. The missionaries knew that to identify and uproot pagan customs, and to successfully replace them with the new religion, they needed to learn indigenous languages. They quickly realized that they could not do this without the active participation of the native speaker.

## Indigenous-Language Grammars

During the three hundred years of imperial Spain's rule of present-day Mexico, fifty-seven indigenous-language grammars (*artes*) and dictionaries (*vocabularios*) were written to support the task of Indian conversion to Christianity. While the bulk of colonial-period grammars and dictionaries dealt with the Nahuatl language, other larger language populations such as Otomí, Tarasca (P'urhépecha), Zapotec, Mixtec, Maya, and others received their share of attention.[66] Rincón's brief grammar and glossary, *Arte mexicana* (1595), is the sixth of New Spain's indigenous-language grammars and the third of the Nahuatl language, following Franciscan friars Andrés de Olmos's *Arte para aprender la lengua mexicana* (1547) and Alonso de Molina's *Arte de la lengua mexicana y castellana* (1555–1571).[67] *Arte mexicana* is the first grammar from the Jesuit order and, it bears repeating, the first written by a native speaker of an indigenous language in the Americas.

It is well known that the religious orders appropriated indigenous languages, wrote grammars and dictionaries, and recorded indigenous cultural practices and histories to better evangelize/colonize the so-called pagan populations of the Americas. In this way, the languages themselves became, in Walter Mignolo's words, "instruments of Christianization."[68] The alphabetic representation of the languages can indeed be seen as suppression or even an attempted destruction of one technology and the imposition of another. At the same time, Nahua appropriation of the alphabetic script, and of the Latin and Castilian languages, was just as much a "possession."[69] In fact, from the outset Indians energetically appropriated the new technology and utilized it to their own ends. Indigenous elites associated with the religious orders and their centers of learning were not just instrumental but also crucial protagonists in the accumulation of written knowledge on their culture, which led, perhaps paradoxically, to the preservation of indigenous languages and cultural knowledge. Latin, Nahuatl, and Castilian alphabetic writing were used to record indigenous versions of events and also regularly utilized to demand and defend property and hereditary rights throughout the colonial period.[70] Yet others took on the technology of the alphabet and practice of writing, not necessarily to preserve the old ways but to support their own present-day agenda. Such was the case of Rincón, who used his knowledge of the intricacies of his native language (not to mention Latin and Castilian) in order to evangelize and tend to the Indian population.

## *The First* Artes

Published in 1595 by Pedro Balli, *Arte mexicana* is divided into five sections and includes a glossary of approximately 650 words. In comparison with the other sixteenth-century Nahuatl grammars, Rincón's is the most compact, with seventy-three pages devoted to grammatical explanation and nineteen to the glossary. Fellow Jesuit and renowned twentieth-century scholar of Nahuatl Ángel María Garibay ranked Andrés de Olmos's text as "uno de los mejores artes antiguos," (one of the best older grammars) and Alonso de Molina's as "excelente" (excellent), while Rincón received a lukewarm "bueno" (good).[71] Garibay's assessment of the grammars is accurate if the criterion used is whether or not the text is appropriate for self-study and/or actual work in the field. But not all early colonial-period (or beyond, for that matter) grammars were written for this specific purpose. While unified in certain aspects, each of the grammars is stylistically distinct from the other. Each has strengths in areas where the other does not. Olmos's oeuvre is much more an ethnographic text than the others, particularly with his inclusion of the *huehuehtlahtolli*, or exhortations, of the Nahua elders.[72] Molina, more often known for his monumental dictionary *Vocabulario en lengua castellana y mexicana* (1555, 1571), demonstrates his talent for lexicography with a text that is quite user-friendly to the non-native speaker in that Nahuatl words are nearly always accompanied by their Castilian translation.[73] For his part, Rincón appeared to be much more concerned with the articulation of phonological aspects. Furthermore, it is true that Rincón's grammar is not ideal for self-guided study of the language since, in contrast to Olmos and Molina, he provides very few translations for the Nahuatl words he uses in the body of the text. Many, but not all, of the Nahuatl terms are instead found in the glossary at the end of the grammar. Nor does Rincón include Nahuatl translations of prayers, as does Molina, with his detailed translation and gloss of the *Pater Noster*. John F. Schwaller sums this up in saying, "[Rincón's] grammar of Nahuatl represents not so much practical hints on how to use the language but a scholarly treatise on the structured language."[74] The *Arte mexicana* was perhaps used more as a reference guide for a teacher in preparing class plans, as opposed to a tool for the autodidact or a classroom textbook.[75] Besides distinct approaches in style and content, the three grammars (each separated by at least two decades) also bear witness to an evolving Nahuatl-centric approach to the description of the Nahuatl language. While each grammar is clearly indebted to the work of the renowned Latin/Castilian grammarian Antonio de Nebrija, the manner in which each engages Nebrija's work over the course of the century is markedly different.[76]

It was not Nebrija's famous treatise on the Castilian language (*Gramática de la lengua castellana* [1492]), but his earlier work on Latin (*Introductiones latinae* [1481]) that would provide the model for the grammatical descriptions of indigenous languages in the New World, and this is the case for the early Nahuatl grammars.[77] Like Olmos and Molina, Rincón acknowledges Nebrija's Latin grammar as the starting point. In the license portion of *Arte mexicana*, Rincón's slim manual is described as being a grammar of "la lengua castellana y mexicana"; however, the metalanguage is a combination of Latin and Castilian languages utilized to explain Nahuatl. There is an underlying assumption that the audience will have a command of Latin's grammatical structure and descriptive vocabulary. This reminds the present-day reader that the audience for Rincón's work was a small group of priests educated in the humanist tradition, in which a command of Latin and specifically Latin grammar was a requirement. The following excerpts from each of the three earliest Nahuatl grammars offer an idea of how each writer engaged Nebrija's Latin grammar as model, as well as how he perceived Nahuatl in relation to the language of the Church:

> Olmos: En el arte de la lengua latina creo que la mejor manera y orden que se ha tenido es la que Antonio de Lebrixa sigue en la suya; pero porque en esta lengua no quadrara la orden que el lleua por faltar muchas cosas de las quales en el arte de gramatica se haze gran caudal como son declinaciones, supinos y las especies de los verbos para denotar la diuersidad dellos, y lo que en el quinto libro se trata de acentos y otras materias que en esta lengua no se tocan, por tanto no sere reprehensible si en todo no siguiere la orden del arte de Antonio.[78]
>
> (In regards to the grammar of the Latin language I believe that the best method and order is evidenced in that of Antonio de Lebrixa; but since in this language [Nahuatl] the order doesn't quite match the way he outlines Latin because it lacks many things that in grammars one normally sees much of such as declensions, nominalized verbs, and the type of verbs used to note their differences, and that which in [Nebrija's] fifth book dealing with accents and other materials that in this language are not utilized, therefore I won't deserve condemnation if I don't follow exactly the same order as in Antonio's grammar.)
>
> Molina: Es de aduertir que no ponemos aqui las significaciones de muchas dictiones de la lengua Mexicana, imitando en esto a Antonio de Lebrixa en su Arte de latin, el qual dexo a sabiendas y de industria por declarar las significaciones de muchas dictiones, para con mas facilidad se entendiesse la dicha Arte de latin: lo qual hazemos aqui nosotros, para que este Arte de la lengua Mexicana sea mas breue; saluo quando fueremos compelidos a declarar algunas dellas, las quales no se entenderian, sino se pusiesen y declarassen sus significaciones: especialmente en la conjugacion de los verbos para saber y entender la diuersidad de los tiempos y modos.[79]

(Be advised that I do not record here the meanings of many dictions of the Mexican language, imitating Antonio de Lebrixa in his Latin grammar, in which he intentionally avoided declaring the meaning of every single item, so that one could understand more easily said grammar of Latin: this is what I am doing here also, so that this grammar of the Mexican languages will be brief, except in the case where I am compelled to clarify something, such as that which would not be understood without explicit explanation of the meaning: especially in the conjugation of verbs to be able to know and to understand the different kinds of tenses and moods.)

Rincón: No se puede negar sino que el camino mas llano y breue para aprouechar en qualquiera de las lenguas, es, el que an hallado la latina, y griega, como se vee por el artificio con que se enseñan y aprenden [ . . . ]. Por lo qual hauiendo yo de escreuir Arte para deprender y enseñar la lengua mexicana no me pareció apartarme del ordinario camino por donde procede la lengua latina, que es mas sabida entre nosotros, ni tampoco me he querido obligar aseguir del todo sus reglas, porque seria lleuar muy fuera de proposito (y como dizen) de los cabellos muchas cosas que aca piden muy diferentes preceptos. [ . . . ] De manera que en aquello que me e podido aprouechar de la gramatica latina siempre me yre arrimando a ella pero en las demas cosas, en que esta lengua se diferencia de la latina por ser ellas nueuas a sido forçoso reducirlas a nueuas reglas, con el nueuo estilo que se require.[80]

(It can not be denied that the most straightforward and concise route to best learn any language is that which has already been articulated in the study of Latin and Greek, as seen in the manner in which they are taught and studied [ . . . ]. Therefore, in needing to write a grammar to learn and teach the Mexican language, it did not make sense to stray from the traditional route of the Latin language, which is the most familiar to us, nor did I wish to be obligated to follow all of [Latin grammar's] rules, because it would be contrary to my goal (and as they say) out of place, since many things here require different rules. [ . . . ] When it made sense to utilize the Latin grammar I always returned to it, but in other areas, where this language was different than Latin, since these aspects were new, it was necessary to create new rules, and a requisite new style.)

In these examples one can see that Nebrija's Latin grammar served as touchstone for these early studies and descriptions of the Nahuatl language. However, as work in the language progressed, so did the approach to grammatical explanation. Olmos, the pioneer, was a Spaniard with no other New World model. Therefore, it is logical that he interpreted Nahuatl vis-à-vis Nebrija as lacking due to his literal Eurocentrism. Molina, a Spaniard who spent nearly his entire life since childhood in New Spain, moved to an increasingly flexible imitation of Nebrija with the recognition that the language was indeed different, but not necessarily lacking. His approach seems more representative of one who had the ability to appreciate fully both cultures, perhaps due to his early exposure to Nahuas and their language.[81] Rincón, the native speaker, boldly closes the sixteenth century by stating that Nebrija's work is indeed useful but will require modification to accommodate Nahuatl. In fact, his prologue begins with a radical assertion: "No es possible guardarse en todo un mismo methodo y arte, en enseñar todas las lenguas, siendo ellas (como lo son) tan distantes y diferentes entre si" (It is not possible that one single method or grammar can be used to teach all languages, since they are all so different). Latin here is just as "different" as Nahuatl. Rincón's interpretation of the Nahuatl language could point to ethnic pride or simply reflect the Jesuit perspective that tended to respect the many languages of their flock. Regardless, if in the earlier examples of grammatical description of the Nahuatl language the rules were made to bend to Nebrija, in the hands of the native speaker, Nebrija bends to Nahuatl. Rincón's grammar is an example of the appropriation of something that is quite functional (Latin grammar) and its modification to the context (Nahuatl language in New Spain). This would be the pattern for grammatical investigations throughout the ensuing years of the colonial period, which progressively developed a Nahuatl-based grammatical tradition that became increasingly attuned to the specific needs of the indigenous language.[82] Rincón's Nahuatl-centric grammatical research is most evident in the fourth chapter of *Arte mexicana*, where he replaces Latin syntax with "Composiciones," outlining how the polysynthetic language's word-phrases are constructed. In the prologue, Rincón expands upon the issue of the limitations of the Latin grammatical model, specifically in dealing with pronunciation:

> El V y ultimo libro trata de la pronunciacion y accento, y aun en esto auiendonos aprouechado del latin en lo que el mexicano le es semejante: van juntamente puestas reglas para la pronunciacion y accentos nueuos que a esta lengua le son propios, y no se hallan en las demas.[83]

(The fifth and last book deals with pronunciation and accent, and while in this area I have taken advantage of Latin [grammatical explanation] in terms of what it has in common with the Mexican language, I also include pronunciation and accent rules which are specific to Nahuatl, and not found in other languages.)

It is in these last books of Rincón's grammar that we see his groundbreaking elucidation of key phonological aspects of the language, specifically his scholarship on contrastive vowel length and pronunciation that had previously eluded the non-native grammarians. Similar to Inca Garcilaso de la Vega, who in his *Royal Commentaries of the Incas* (1609) wrote of the Quechua language and how pronunciation can have radical semantic implications that non-native speakers either do not or cannot ascertain, Rincón, as a native speaker, was able to grasp and explain how pronunciation can change the meaning of a word.[84] Garcilaso explained: "There are three different ways of pronouncing some of the syllables. They are quite different from the pronunciation in Spanish, and the differences of pronunciation give different meanings to the same word; [ . . . ] The Spaniard who thinks he knows the language best is ignorant of nine-tenths of it, because of the many meanings of each word and the different pronunciation that a word has for various meanings."[85] Rincón, for his part, was the first to systematically describe this feature of the Nahuatl language. In book five of his *Arte mexicana*, he explains in detail contrastive vowel length (long [acute or grave accent] or short [short, moderate, or saltillo accent]). In the appendix of his *Arte mexicana*, we find as examples a list of eighty-seven words grouped in thirty-six "pairs" and five sets of "triplets" that include descriptions of their pronunciation (*largo*, *breve*, *grave*, *agudo*, or *salto*) along with their definitions.[86] A few examples from this list highlight the perils of incorrect pronunciation:

Atlacatl, salto en la primera hombre sin raçon.
Atlacatl, salto en la segunda, hombre del agua, como el marinero o pescador.

(Atlacatl, glottal stop in the first [syllable], man who does not think or use his faculties.
Atlacatl, glottal stop in the second, man of water, as in a sailor or fisherman.)

Chichi, largo en la primera. Mamar.
Chichi, breue en la primera. Es perro.
Chichi, salto en la primera surzir alguna cosa, y tambien es la saliua.

(Chichi, long vowel in the first [syllable]. To suckle.
Chichi, short [vowel] in the first [syllable]. It is a dog.
Chichi, glottal stop in the first [syllable] is to mend something, it also is saliva.)

Macehualli, largo en las dos primeras, hombre vil y plebeyo.
Maceualli, salto en la. I. el merito.

(Macehualli, long [vowels] in the first two [syllables], unworthy or common man.
Maceualli, glottal stop in the first [syllable], merit.)

Matequi, salto en la ma. laueme las manos, ninomatequi.
Matequi, largo en la ma, corteme las manos, ninomatequi.

(Matequi, glottal stop in the ma. I wash my hands, ninomatequi.
Matequi, long [vowel] in the ma, I cut my hands off, ninomatequi.)

Pati. largo en la. I. derretirse.
Pati. salto en la primera. sanar.

(Pati. long [vowel] in the first [syllable]. to melt.
Pati. glottal stop in the first. to heal.)

Tepiltzin. largo en la I. hijo de alguno.
Tepiltzin breue en la. I. verbum turpe.

(Tepiltzin. long [vowel] in the first [syllable]. the son of someone.
Tepiltzin short [vowel] in the first [syllable]. an obscene word [which Rincón does not define].)

Toloa. largo en la. I. bajar la cabeça.
Toloa, breue en la primera, tragar.

(Toloa. long [vowel] in the first [syllable]. to bow the head.
Toloa, short [vowel] in the first [syllable], to drink.)

In these examples we see the potential for riotous miscommunication with the simple misuse of a long vowel instead of a short, or emphasis on the incorrect syllable. Instead of offering to heal someone's son, the priests could just as easily be understood to be offering to melt down an [expletive!]. With incorrect pronunciation, before a meal an indigenous man might be directed to cut off his hands and drink, as opposed to washing his hands and bowing his head. A man could be called an unthinking or bad man (as opposed to his actual occupation, that of fisherman), and an indigenous woman asked to mend a piece of clothing might instead understand the priest to be requesting that she suckle something. As these entries suggest, proper pronunciation was paramount if the priests were to ensure clarity in their message and avoid offending their new converts.

This important issue of pronunciation and its potential effect on the meaning of a term had not entirely escaped the earlier grammarians. Olmos, a non-native speaker, had recognized this aspect of the language, but had not felt capable (or perhaps had not fully understood its significance) to elaborate on the issue: "No hablo en el acento por ser muy vario [ . . . ], y porque algunos vocablos parecen tener algunas vezes dos acentos; por lo qual lo dexo a quien Dios fuere seruido darle mas animo para ello, o al uso que lo descubra" (I don't discuss pronunciation because it varies [ . . . ], and because some words appear to sometimes have two pronunciations; therefore I leave this to whomever God inspires, or through more practice discovers [the rhyme or reason of] this).[87] Molina, bilingual from a young age, appears to have been aware of the subtleties of Nahuatl pronunciation. In his *Arte*, he points out how improper pronunciation can cause problems in religious ceremonies. The example he offers is the word *motlatiz*, which when pronounced one way means to light something (as a candle) and when pronounced in another way implies that something was extinguished.[88] One can imagine the calamity this might cause in a Christian Mass, with the solemn priest directing native-speaker assistants to do one thing (light a candle) and the result being the opposite of what was intended. Both Olmos and Molina were aware of this important detail of the language, but it is the native speaker, Rincón, who is able to cogently identify and articulate the issue, offer evidence of the ramifications of mispronunciation, and finally pave the way for future elaboration in this area. We know, for example, that Rincón's work would later form the basis of fellow Jesuit Horacio Carochi's diacritical system for marking vowel length, as seen in his own exceptional *Arte de la lengua mexicana* (1645).[89] Rincón's treatise, as Karttunen remarks, "representa una de esas iluminaciones que clarificó el camino seguido por Horacio Carochi y nos alumbra a nosotros al vía que debemos seguir" (represents one of those illuminations that made clear the path followed by Horacio Carochi and lights the way to where we should continue).[90] Rincón, like the *tlamatini* described in the *Códice Matritenses*, lights the way for future work on his language: "In tlamatini: tlavilli ocutl, tomavuac ocutl hapocyo; [ . . . ] teyacayani, tehutequiani" (The wise man: a light, a torch, a stout torch that does not smoke; [ . . . ] He is a teacher of guides; he shows them their path).[91]

Earlier I mentioned that we have little information regarding why Rincón chose to enter the priesthood. We do, however, have a better idea of why he wrote his grammar, thanks to the license and dedication portion of his text. As with other books written in sixteenth-century New Spain, Rincón's grammar was subject to a series of inspections before being granted license to publish. In the elaborate *Licencia* of the *Arte mexicana*, don Luis de Velasco (son of New Spain's second viceroy by the same name) affirms that Rincón "a compuesto vn Arte con que se podrá saber perfectamente la lengua Mexicana, y que para que se pudiesse comunicar a todos los que la quisieren tenia necessidad de imprimirla pidiendome le mandasse dar licencia para ello" (has compiled an Arte with which one can perfectly know/understand the Mexican language, and in order to communicate with all that might be interested, he needed to print it and so requested from me a license to do so). We are reminded of the context of the Inquisition and preoccupation with religious orthodoxy in Bachiller Pedro Ponce de Leon's review found in the first pages of the *Arte mexicana*, wherein he confirmed Rincón's grammar as being free of anything "contra nuestra fe catholica y buenas costumbres" (contrary to our Catholic faith and good manners/customs) and was therefore publishable. Esteuan (Esteban) Paez, the provincial of the Company of Jesus who approved the request to print the *Arte mexicana*, and the governor, don Ihoan (Juan) de Cervantes Arcediano, weighed in after receiving approval of the content from esteemed Nahuatl-language expert Iuan (Juan) de Tovar, who claimed that Rincón's *Arte* was "vtil y necessaria para los ministros de los sacramentos á los naturales" (useful and necessary for the ministering of the sacraments to the Indians).

A dedicatory letter that Rincón addressed to "don Diego Roman, Bishop of Tlaxcallan" then follows the license. The letter begins with the story of how in the beginning all of the trees and plants were abundant and gave fruit without need of human tending or toil. Rincón explains that because humans have sinned, their punishment is that they are forced to work for their sustenance; humans must now tend their gardens in order to ensure survival. He then goes on to compare the labors of the Church in this same manner: "las tiernas plantas" (the tender young plants) are the indigenous populations that must be cultivated. At one time, Rincón continues, the apostles might have been able to understand all languages and could preach the gospel without linguistic barriers; now that time was long gone.

Affirming the Church opinion that indigenous languages were the best vehicle for evangelization, Rincón states that the "tantas y tan preciosas plantas" (so many very precious plants) in the burgeoning garden of the Church in New Spain will bear fruit, that is, embrace the Holy Faith, by hearing the word of God. However, if the priests do not know the native language, this task will be impossible. The priests must study and work diligently to attain some level of accuracy in the language they preach in (or, he rather comically adds, expect a miracle [prologue]). Rincón offers his *Arte mexicana* so that his Jesuit brothers may more readily achieve the linguistic capabilities necessary.

Rincón states that he intends his *Arte mexicana* to assuage the linguistic difficulties that fellow Jesuits encountered "entre estas bárbaras naciones donde estamos" (among these barbarous nations where we are). The words "donde estamos" (where we are) surely implied Puebla and the surrounding missions, where Rincón is known to have been working during the writing and publication of his text. In his reference to being "among these barbarous nations," it is possible that he is revealing his own sense of difference from other Indians, even as the peninsulares and criollos were attempting to consolidate various native groups into a single, inferior entity. Regardless of the efforts to create clearly segregated groups (and subgroups) of "us" (Europeans and their descendants) and "them" (all Indians), Rincón's mention of nations (plural) suggests that ethnic and altepetl affiliations continued to hold weight. But what did he mean in reference to barbarous? Here we may refer to Bartolomé de Las Casas's mid-sixteenth-century treatise on "The Meanings of Barbarous" found in his *Apologética historia sumaria* to arrive at a more clear idea of Rincón's use of the term. The four manners in which people may be called barbarous, according to Las Casas, are as follows:

> The first way, taking the term broadly and improperly, is because of some strangeness, ferocity, disorder or unreasonableness [ . . . ] [that] somehow become or are fierce, hard-hearted and cruel [ . . . ]. These are men who seem to have stripped themselves completely of their human nature.
>
> The second kind of barbarous people is something narrower; under it come those who do not have a written speech that corresponds to their language as Latin does to ours—in brief, who lack the use and study of letters. These peoples are said to be barbarous *secundum quid*, that is, according to some part or quality, which they lack—which they would

> need in order not to be barbarous. [ . . . ] Likewise, a man is apt to be called barbarous, in comparison with another, because he is strange in his manner of speech and mispronounces the language of the other [ . . . ]. But from this point of view, there is no man or race which is not barbarous with respect to some other man or race [ . . . ]. Thus, just as we esteemed these peoples of these Indies barbarous, so they considered us, because of not understanding us.
>
> There is a third kind of barbarous people [ . . . ] They neither have nor care for law, right, nation, friendship, or the company of other men, because of which they lack towns, councils, and cities, since they do not live socially. And so they neither have nor endure lords, or laws, or political rule. [ . . . ] These are the men of whom Aristotle particularly speaks [ . . . ] saying they are slaves by nature and should always serve and be subject to others.
>
> [The fourth kind] includes all those who lack true religion and the Christian faith, that is, all pagans, however wise and prudent they may be as philosophers and statesmen.[92]

Puebla and the surrounding missions were often portrayed as presenting extraordinary challenges to the religious orders in terms of the pagan and "unruly" behaviors of the natives. Jesuit historian Alegre states that Rincón worked tirelessly in Puebla, even while surrounded by what Alegre termed "escuelas de maldad y unos pequeños ensayes del infierno" (schools of wickedness and little manifestations of hell on earth). Rincón could have been referring to the first and the third Lascasian definitions (ferocity and lack of recognizable social organization).[93] However, as a grammarian and priest, it is more likely that he was ultimately concerned with the second and the fourth, of peoples marked by unintelligible languages and lack of Christian faith. His subsequent reference to Nahuatl as the mother or root of other "barbarous" indigenous languages supports an interpretation of "barbarous as unintelligible":

> es general en todas estas prouincias de la nueua España, [ . . . ] ella misma es como madre de las demas lenguas barbaras que en estos reynos se hallan, y assi me parescia seruia á todos en abrir y llanar el camino de la lengua Mexicana pues por este se entra á las demas, fuera de que esta misma lengua a menester todas estas ayudas para hazer algun progreso en ella, por los exquisitos primores y elegancias que tiene.

(it is the general [language] in all of the provinces of New Spain, [ . . . ] it is the root of the other barbarous languages that we encounter in those regions and so it seemed to me too it would be useful to all and create easier access to the Mexican language since through this language we can understand the others, besides the fact that [to learn] this language we need all the help/assistance we can get to make any progress at all in it, due to the exquisite intricacies and elegances it contains.)

This final point regarding the complexity and elegance of his mother tongue also implicitly argues along the lines of Las Casas, who urged against conflating linguistic alterity and inferiority. Here perhaps we also hear intertextual whispers of Cicero, the great Roman philosopher who insisted on linguistic eloquence as the marker of civilization.[94] Besides being the knowing subject, Rincón also squarely places himself in the center of "civilization," establishing his own place in the colonial hierarchy, while simultaneously rejecting the notion of indigenous inferiority.

Here we have come full circle, returning to the shifting ideas of "race" and place in New Spain. Attention to the case of Antonio del Rincón in the "unexpected" realm of the priesthood has provided a distinct viewpoint from which to discuss the first century of Spanish colonization, evangelization, and imposition/appropriation of the Roman alphabet, as well as an example of indigenous intellectual activities in the midst of these changes. His story reminds us that communication between cultures, possibly the most crucial aspect of the evangelization and colonization process, was impossible without the protagonism of the native speaker, underlining the paradoxes of the imperial project. Equally, his experience in and of itself is emblematic of the next four hundred years of Nahua intellectual activities. Regardless of the fact that after conquest indigenous people are rarely perceived as intellectuals, Nahuas have long participated in the intellectual life of their own communities, and beyond.

# The IDIEZ Project

Founded in 2002 by John Sullivan, Angelina Belmontes Martínez, Urbano Francisco Martínez (Nahua, San Luis Potosí), and Delfina de la Cruz (Nahua, Veracruz), the Instituto de Docencia e Investigación Etnológica de Zacatecas (Zacatecas Institute for Teaching and Research in Ethnology, IDIEZ) is an urban research institute focusing on the revitalization of Nahuatl language and culture. The institute is associated with the Universidad Autónoma de Zacatecas and its U.S. non-profit counterpart Macehualli Educational Research. Its mission is as follows:

> We grant scholarships to indigenous university students in the Mexican city of Zacatecas, providing them with a monolingual space to teach and do research in older and modern aspects of their language and culture, and a multicultural space where they can dialogue with non-indigenous academics, as well as plan and implement projects designed to extend the practice of their way of life to all spheres of society.[1]

IDIEZ's location in the urban setting of the city of Zacatecas is an important aspect of the institute's profile. As one of the co-founders, John Sullivan, noted in a recent article, most indigenous language and culture revitalization efforts are taking place in rural areas, yet the majority of young indigenous people migrate to urban settings for school and/or work, and rarely return permanently to their rural communities.[2] More and more, indigenous peoples populate urban areas in Mexico, but cities are generally not welcoming to indigenous language and culture. IDIEZ provides a space where students and researchers can continue to practice and promote their language and culture in the city. The activities of the research community at IDIEZ explicitly demonstrate the critical and creative capabilities of the Nahuatl language, as well as the fact that indigenous languages can and should be vehicles for knowledge production in higher education settings.

Sullivan has stated that "every one of the students who has worked at IDIEZ has suffered systematic and continuous physical and/or psychological abuse coercing them to abandon their native language and culture."[3] IDIEZ has served as an antidote to these kinds of experiences. In a 2011 interview, Ofelia Cruz Morales (Nahua, Veracruz), a researcher at IDIEZ, reflected on her transition from viewing her language and culture as a liability to something in which she could express herself—as an indigenous person with her own language—freely and without fear:

> Cuando yo vi un, pues un gringo nos viene a decir esto: "lo que tú sabes, este es bonito, es hermoso,' yo dije "no es cierto, no es hermoso, no es nada." Entonces yo dije "no es cierto porque mis compañeros no me quieren, mis compañeros no me quieren con el simple hecho porque soy indígena, yo hablo el náhuatl." En IDIEZ nos hizo ver que no es cierto y ahorita sí yo puedo hablar con cualquier gente que venga y me queda viendo. No me importa lo ignoro pero antes no, yo sentía. Ahorita yo puedo hablar donde quiera y como yo quiera. Este cambio, es desde aquí del IDIEZ porque es allí donde yo comenzé a expresarme realmente lo que yo era, cómo era o sea mi idioma. Allí John nos dio un espacio donde nosotros podíamos hablar el náhuatl, pero a mi me costaba mucho trabajo hablarlo porque donde yo estudié en la Huasteca, nos prohibían hablar el náhuatl, entonces si nosotros hablábamos el náhuatl recibíamos un castigo. Yo tenía que pagar pero ¿para ese tiempo a donde agarraba dinero?[4]

> (When I saw, well, a gringo coming around saying this stuff: "these things you know [your language, your culture] it is good, it is beautiful." I said "that isn't true, it isn't beautiful; it's nothing." Then I told him "[what you say] isn't true; my classmates don't like me, my classmates don't like me for the simple reason that I am indigenous, I speak Nahuatl." At IDIEZ they helped me see that I was wrong. Today I can speak [my language] with anyone that comes along and sits there staring at me. I don't care, I ignore it. But before it really hurt. Now I can speak wherever I want and however I want. This change, it came from being

> at IDIEZ. It's there that I started to express really who I am, what I am like, or rather, [who I am through] my language. John [Sullivan] gave us a space where we could speak Nahuatl, but it was really hard for me to do because in the school in the Huasteca we were prohibited from speaking Nahuatl. If we spoke in Nahuatl we were punished. I had to pay [a fine]. But where [does a child] find money [to pay a fine]?)

The majority of her colleagues at IDIEZ share Ofelia's experience. As a group they are dedicated to eliminating or at least ameliorating the kinds of discrimination they suffered by ensuring a safe urban space for indigenous intellectual development and extending that space beyond the walls of the institute. Native-speaker teaching assistants, research assistants, and permanent instructors and research associates develop and teach culturally specific curriculum for year-round on-site and distance courses, as well as courses taught abroad. Indigenous and Western pedagogies and research methodologies are studied and practiced in tandem, as deemed appropriate by the members of the institute. Collaborative research projects between indigenous and non-indigenous scholars in an international network spanning North America and Europe are being forged and strengthened with each passing year.

The research collective at IDIEZ is currently designing a monolingual master's degree program in Nahua Studies through the Universidad Autónoma de Zacatecas to support indigenous scholarly development in the student's language and culture. To my knowledge, this is the first advanced degree program at a university in Mexico that utilizes indigenous language and/or cultural values as the vehicle and framework to study that language and culture. "Indigenous universities" in Mexico do exist (for example, the Universidad Autónoma Indígena de México in Sinaloa), but the extent to which these incorporate indigenous language, culture, or knowledge systems remains unclear. From what I can gather, institutions such as these have a majority indigenous-student body that utilizes Spanish to study primarily Western culture and knowledges. With this new degree program in mind, IDIEZ has been creating the kinds of monolingual reference materials necessary for a rigorous program of academic study (such as a grammar, dictionary, thesaurus, encyclopedia, etc.). Such resources—at least in a monolingual form—do not currently exist in Nahuatl. But not for long: a large-scale multiyear project that is nearing completion is that of a monolingual dictionary of contemporary Nahuatl (Huasteca Veracruz dialect). The creation of the monolingual dictionary has of course been done with an eye toward an end goal: to provide an important resource for advanced study of Nahuatl language and culture. But the monolingual dictionary project has also been a "didactic tool."[5] That is, the collaborative work between native and non-native speakers in identifying lexical items, agreeing upon definitions, and creating sample sentences has lead to creative and critical thinking in the native language. Thus, the very process of creating the dictionary has been one of recovery and revitalization.

CHAPTER 2

# *Writing Tlaxcalan Memories that Matter*

## Don Juan Buenaventura Zapata y Mendoza

Writing about the past is a highly selective task, one of remembering but also of forgetting (or silencing, in the words of Michel-Rolph Trouillot).[1] A written record of the social memory of a people, as ethnohistorian Stephanie Wood has argued, is similar to the production of an image, as it "is no less a product of careful selection, assemblage, and persuasive presentation."[2] The book you hold in your hands is the result of this very process—I have chosen to remember Nahua writings, a version of the past that has been silenced elsewhere. In doing so, I have necessarily omitted other stories to serve my particular purpose. In short, writing about the past implies assembling and recording *memories that matter* to the writer and to his/her intended audience.

Such was the task that occupied seventeenth-century Nahua noble and statesman don Juan Buenaventura Zapata y Mendoza, the author/compiler of one of the richest extant Nahuatl-language historical annals of the *altepetl* (city/state) of Tlaxcala.[3] The stories brought together would ensure that his descendants knew where they had come from and what their rights were as Tlaxcalan people. On the latter, his writing provides a window into the world of indigenous "negotiation within domination" and paints a dynamic picture of how Tlaxcalan elites—the embodiment of the altepetl—shaped and responded to the rapidly changing social and political landscape of colonial Mexico.[4]

Commonly referred to as *Historia cronológica de la noble ciudad de Tlaxcala*, Zapata's manuscript contains, as with other examples of Nahua annals, a yearly record of the altepetl territorial and political disputes, transfers of power, public works, and descriptions of natural/climatic phenomena.[5] Yet beyond these expected topics, our protagonist also left us with a detailed account of the cabildo's political activities during the seventeenth century, offering a vivid firsthand record of the Tlaxcalan elites' nuanced understanding of the relationships among colonial politics, religion, and the law. Specifically, Zapata's work details how Tlaxcalan elites promoted their political authority and rights and presents an image of skillful leadership in the challenging colonial context. Events gleaned from Zapata's manuscript exemplify what can be considered the discursive pillars of Tlaxcalan authority and rights during the seventeenth century: the assertion of pre-Hispanic noble lineage, loyalty to the Crown (first as military allies and later as administrators), and finally, faithful conversion to the Catholic religion. Records of the public performances found in Zapata's annals show each of the three discursive pillars deployed as critical tools in the affirmation and defense of the elite Tlaxcalan cabildo members' right (and by extension that of their indigenous subjects) to continue to enjoy their separate, privileged status established in the earliest days of European conquest and colonization.[6]

Presently housed at the Bibliothèque Nationale de France in Paris, Zapata's manuscript consists of 120 folios of Nahuatl alphabetic text.[7] The first 5 folios are a migration story entitled "Origen de la nación tlaxcalteca" ("The Origin of the Tlaxcalan Nation"), presumably copied from a pre-Hispanic document.[8] The remaining folios narrate a year-by-year account of events important to the Tlaxcalan confederation since its origins in 1310 through 1692, which had been compiled and edited from earlier texts (oral, pictorial, or alphabetic) and expanded upon by Zapata to include new histories accumulated and/or witnessed during his lifetime. He can rightly be called the primary editor of the manuscript as we see it today, as well as the "first author" of a large portion of the entries. That said, we also know that he did not have the final word. There were at least two additional hands involved in the text, both of whom appear to have taken over after Zapata's death. The first is his son, who very briefly picked up his father's work in 1691. The second is that of don Manuel de los Santos y Salazar, a family friend (and indigenous Franciscan priest) who more than likely acquired the manuscript from Zapata's son. Santos y Salazar added extensive marginalia and glosses, in both Spanish and in Nahuatl, as well as cover pages to the document.[9] Before moving to a closer examination of Zapata's intellectual legacy to future generations of Tlaxcalans, a brief discussion of the annals genre in general can offer an entry point to the broader context in which this text was crafted.

Many colonial-period Nahua intellectuals like Zapata demonstrate innovative methods of recording historical memories of their altepetl. Postconquest Nahua annals have much in common with the pre-Hispanic "historical" genre of the *xiuhpohualli* (*xihuitl*: year; *pohua*: to count). Yet as products of a time period when distinct cultures came into contact, they also give evidence of varying combinations of appropriation and modification—as well as rejection—of European technologies (Roman alphabet), style, language, and discourse. The xiuhpohualli consisted of year-by-year timelines of altepetl history, often painted on long strips of amate paper.[10] For each year, the *tlahcuiloh*, the writer/painter of the xiuhpohualli, provided the Mesoamerican calendar year-sign and accompanying pictograms representing key happenings of the polity. The altepetl origins, migrations, records of territorial and political disputes, transfers of power from one ruler to another, public works and celebrations, and natural/climactic phenomena were the predominant topics of the genre.[11] Scholars of the xiuhpohualli generally believe that the pictographs would serve as a guide for an oral recitation by specialized interpreters of the texts, the *tlamatinimeh* and/or *tlahcuilohqueh* (plural of tlahcuiloh).[12] According to Camilla Townsend, it is more than likely that these performances included several interpreters concurrently consulting several different xiuhpohualli, each repeating, or elaborating upon, a single topic.[13] It stands to reason that these oral performances then served to circulate, reproduce, and naturalize a certain kind of historical memory for the listeners of the interpretations, as the narratives were constructed by and for a specific ethno-political group.[14] The primary difference then between pre- and postconquest recordings of Nahua historical memory is that unlike pictographic histories such as the xiuhpohualli that would be interpreted in oral performances, annals compiled the oral *and* written altepetl histories into a single document using the Roman alphabet. Whether or not the annals were read aloud in a group setting, we do not know. However, there is substantial evidence that Zapata was in conversation with other annalists in his region, and that they copied each other's work. Krug and Townsend, for example, found that Zapata included the same pre-1538 data found in the other extant anonymous annals of the Tlaxcala-Puebla region.[15]

In contrast with the European-style monologic and episodic chronicles of the non-indigenous world, Zapata's manuscript maintained the polyvocal discursive style of the xiuhpohualli, as well as the year-count organization, and for the most part, a steadfast focus on topics related to the political and social life of the altepetl. On the issue of polyvocality, Townsend has argued that the test of the truth or legitimacy of the events recorded in the annals was their composite, polyvocal nature: Nahua histories demanded consultation, if not inclusion, of multiple sources and perspectives, especially if the event was deemed pivotal or controversial.[16] One of the more notable repetitions found in Zapata's annals, as Townsend has observed, are the two different versions of entries from the years 1519 through 1527, which deal specifically with the arrival of the Spaniards and the Catholic faith.[17] The first seems relatively benign, with a description of how the four lords of Tlaxcala spontaneously accepted baptism with the arrival of Hernán Cortés, as well as how the friars instructed the indigenous people in the new faith. The second version, however, portrays the indigenous lords requesting specific information about the religious practices of the European newcomers ("tlen quimomahuisotilia yn Caxtilan yn chritianos oncan omacia oquihtoque yehuatzin senquisca ychpochtli Santa Maria Asunpçion" [who do the Christians in Castile worship/honor? They replied, the Ever Virgen Santa María Asunción]) and details the violence that accompanied the cross, including zealous investigations of idolatry and the hanging of four nobles. As Zapata explains, "catca çan oquilihuiz temictiluya" (this is how things were; they [Spaniards] killed without reason). After these hangings, fear is the explanation Zapata offers for the rush to baptism on the part of indigenous people.[18] On which version is to be believed, historian Federico Navarrette has suggested a "last word" hypothesis in his study of Chimalpahin's annals.[19] For Navarrette, it seemed that the last of multiple versions of a story was presented as the most realistic. In this way, the annalist "guided" the reader/listener to a preferred understanding.[20]

As products of multigenerational collaborations and layers of texts, conversations, and personal experiences subject to future re-writes or modifications, the Nahua annals did not require a single authoritative voice. Therefore, most do not explicitly identify a specific author.[21] There are, however, exceptions to this rule, such as Hernando de Alvarado Tezozomoc (Tenochtitlan); Domingo Francisco de San Antón Muñón Chimalpahin Quauhtlehuanitzin, commonly referred to as Chimalpahin (Chalco); and our Zapata, who each give themselves away in their texts on several occasions. Nahua annalists—anonymous or not—were usually elite-class members of what Krug and Townsend have identified as a closed circle of intellectuals.[22] They tended to be well educated and politically active (or affiliated with the Church in some manner), and they were able to navigate both indigenous and Spanish cultures, in the political sense as well as in areas of language and culture.[23] Although the political life of the altepetl is the central concern of the genre, there is no indication that these texts were commissioned by a specific entity such as a *tlahtoani* or the cabildo. Instead, the annals seem to be "personal, unofficial enterprises" that are filled (in many ways delightfully) with subjective opinion and distinct biases.[24] Nahua anthropologist Luis Reyes García has also pointed out that the colonial annals were produced in a social context that placed high value on the individual's record of merit and service to his altepetl.[25] If we consider Zapata's centrality in altepetl political and religious activities—as recorded by his hand, in his annals—this manuscript can be read as a record of both the glory of the altepetl and that of the author. But this potential for bias should not deter us from considering this or other annals to be viable sources for cultural analysis. It is this very human quality of the genre that makes the annals such lively and rich sources from which to amass a better understanding of Nahua experience. As the Nahua annals are further studied, ideally we will learn more about why some annalists remained anonymous and others did not, and perhaps more importantly, we may be able to ascertain the annalists' motivations in taking on the daunting task of assembling and safeguarding the stories of their people.

If we were to imagine Zapata drafting his manuscript, he might be consulting the (now lost) annals of Tadeo de Niza, or contemplating the Lienzo de Tlaxcala in the cabildo hall.[26] Perhaps he is reviewing documents loaned to him by other Nahuas engaged in similar historiographical projects. Since his manuscript shows evidence of contact with (or even outright copying of) the "Anonymous Mexican" codex, the Anales de Tula, the Actas de Cabildo of Tlaxcala, as well as local church records, he may be poring through these documents in order to cull (or omit) the pertinent details of the story he wished to tell.[27] What is clear is that he seems to have consciously crafted a Nahua-centric history, using only Nahua sources, which stands in contrast to others, such as Chimalpahin, who drew widely from both Spanish and Nahua sources.[28] If the task at hand was to record memories that mattered to Zapata's beloved altepetl of Tlaxcala, for him only indigenous voices would do; style, structure, and sources belie a conscious preference for indigenous forms over European ones. His sense of "ethnic patriotism," as Townsend has called it, also extended into his lexical choices.[29] Both Lockhart and Townsend have noted that Zapata routinely avoided the infiltration of Spanish loan words commonly found in other Nahuatl-language texts of his time.[30]

A reinforcement of, or even a return to, indigenous intellectual practices that relied exclusively on Nahua sources and lexicon could be read as an overt assertion of intellectual sovereignty, a signal to those who might have had access to the text that Tlaxcalans had their own valid ways of producing and transmitting memory. At the same time, his use of alphabetic writing was a reflection of the context in which he wrote. Astute native leaders throughout New Spain quickly grasped that the documentation of pre- and postconquest indigenous land tenure, noble lineage, and tributary relationships (and the circulation of these documents) were requisite in securing privileges and acquiring political positions in colonial Mexico.[31] Since alphabetic writing was the official mode of communication for administrative dealings in New Spain, indigenous power brokers surely understood that it provided one of the primary means for entering the conversations of the political sphere. We cannot know if Zapata meant for his writing to be read only by Nahuas or if he assumed that his pages would one day be presented in a court of law as evidence of Tlaxcalan rights. That Zapata's annals were written in Nahuatl indeed suggests a Nahua audience, but does not exclude non-Nahuas since Nahuatl was a readily accepted administrative language and was regularly translated to Spanish for the courts. That Zapata seems to have been intent upon writing a Nahua-centric text in a Spanish-dominated context makes sense if we consider Tlaxcalans' long tradition of understanding themselves as distinct, unique, or special.

## Tlaxcala Is Special

The altepetl of Tlaxcala is well known for having routinely sought privileges as reward for their instrumental role as indigenous allies to Cortés in the conquest of the Aztec Empire, as well as the people's loyalty to the Spanish Crown. Diplomatic missions to Madrid began in 1527 when four high-ranking nobles from each of the Tlaxcalan sub-altepetl made a voyage across the Atlantic Ocean to petition and secure rights and protections.[32] Shortly thereafter, in August 1529, a royal mandate was issued stating that the Tlaxcalans would never be given in encomienda; they would not be obligated to provide tribute or draft labor to a conquistador.[33] Instead, Tlaxcala was to retain a direct tributary relationship with the Crown and was granted varying degrees of territorial autonomy as a *república de indios*. Additionally, Tlaxcalans were authorized to formally exclude all but elite Nahuas from their local government.[34] The Tlaxcalan cabildo, charged with serving both their indigenous constituents and the interests of the Crown, was elected from some 220 representatives of the indigenous noble houses of the four subunits of the polity. Bridging the political, economic, and religious spheres of New Spain, the primary responsibilities of the cabildo members—who, like Zapata, rotated through most, if not all, of the cabildo positions during their lifetimes—included labor organization, supervision of public construction, trade regulation, and the organization of religious ceremonies and rituals.[35] As formal representatives of Tlaxcala to outsiders (Spaniards, Church officials, other indigenous groups), the cabildo members served as key intermediaries representing, ideally, the interests of the altepetl before all others. Like other native intermediaries, it can be said that the Tlaxcalan cabildo members, borrowing Yanna Yannakakis's words, "held the colonial order in balance."[36] Zapata's text gives us a glimpse of the inner workings of this delicate dance, particularly the ways in which Tlaxcalan elites attempted to maintain control of their political and geographical territory, all the while bolstering Spanish hegemony.

Regardless of Tlaxcala's initial "exceptionalism" in the colonial order, by the seventeenth century the elite Tlaxcalans were at risk of losing their hard-won privileges and status, including their control of their cabildo. As the Spanish Crown consolidated power, tributary relationships were modified, and not in ways that were to the advantage of indigenous elites or their subjects. According to Charles Gibson, the renowned historian of Tlaxcala, shifting imperial policies and an increasingly powerful class of European and criollo colonists were the primary causes for why the once stubbornly independent altepetl slowly became subsumed into the "colonial scene."[37] During this time, the Nahua elite's political control of the Tlaxcalan cabildo was undermined as mestizos and Spaniards infiltrated the once all-indigenous political and physical territory of the city of Tlaxcala. Add to this the fact that the Crown's and Church's demands for more money, goods, and labor put the cabildo—the local collectors of tribute and organizer of labor—in an increasingly antithetical position in relation to the indigenous commoners they purported to serve.[38] At various times throughout the seventeenth century, these commoners questioned their loyalties to the cabildo, even going as far as openly rebelling against the Tlaxcalan elites on several occasions.[39]

It is during this time of instability and uncertainty that Zapata records his accounts of Nahua elites evoking, in public performances, the earlier-mentioned discursive pillars of Tlaxcalan political authority and rights: 1) they are heirs of the pre-Hispanic noble rulers; 2) they were, and continue to be, loyal military allies to the Crown; and 3) they are faithful Christian subjects of the Spanish Empire. Public spectacles such as religious fiestas, political oaths, and receptions for visiting dignitaries in seventeenth-century Mexico provided colonial subjects, including the Tlaxcalan elites, with the Geertzian "cultural frame" for "defining and advancing the claims of political authority."[40] Through the organization of and participation in such performances, native leaders conveyed—through an embodied, visual vocabulary—important information to their indigenous subjects regarding the allegiance of the altepetl to the Church and Crown, and elite-class cabildo members' powerful position in the colonial social hierarchy.[41] In her discussion of Spanish/criollo public performances aimed at asserting Spanish authority in the colonial context, Linda Curcio-Nagy maintains that "large-scale spectacle became one tool in an arsenal of colonizing agents that included coercive force, discriminatory laws, religious institutions such as the Inquisition, and economic power."[42] Yet Spaniards were not alone in recognizing the efficacy of such public displays. Indigenous subjects, including the Tlaxcalan cabildo, also utilized public spaces for negotiating relationships and identities in the new colonial order.

In reading Zapata's descriptions of public spectacles, Diana Taylor's theorization of performance draws our attention to "how performed, embodied practices make the 'past' available as a political resource in the present by simultaneously enabling several complicated and multilayered processes."[43] Complicated and multilayered indeed, as visible in the following examples from Zapata's manuscript, Tlaxcalan performances of loyalty to the Spanish Crown and Catholic Church were regularly combined with references to the past, functioning as often-contradictory political resources with which Tlaxcalan elites asserted authority while at the same time they confirmed their subjugation to the Crown.

## Performing Noble Lineage

*Historia cronológica* provides a year-by-year accounting of Tlaxcalan political successions from pre-Hispanic times through the late seventeenth century. This record provides evidence of an unbroken line of noble Tlaxcalan control of the territory, proof that Tlaxcalans never succumbed to colonizers—Aztec (Mexica) or European. A subtle, yet provocative, framing of Tlaxcala as always free and independent, this narrative serves to differentiate the Tlaxcalans from other Nahuas such as the Aztec (Mexica), now a conquered people. Thus this record not only naturalizes autonomy for Tlaxcalans but also bolsters petitions for privileges or special status. The assertion of autonomy, however, should not be read as rebellion against the Crown. The heirs of the pre-Hispanic *tlahtoqueh* (altepetl rulers) understood that their special rights were confirmed and secured by embracing a subordinate social position as vassals to the Spanish Crown.

Woven among the yearly reports of noble rule of the altepetl, Zapata records how cabildo members publicly performed their pre-Hispanic histories in postconquest times. These performances served to alert Spaniards and indigenous alike of their noble lineage, establishing their high rank in New Spain's social hierarchy. Such assertions took place at a time when the Spanish Crown was intent upon restricting privileges of both conquistadors and indigenous nobles. Romero Galván points out that in this context we see two related phenomena: first, the descendants of conquistadors began to develop a creole consciousness (a sense of "we are from here, and therefore should rule here"); and second, the indigenous nobles insisted upon reminding Spaniards (as well as their indigenous subjects) that they had *always* been here, and therefore should rule here.[44] Tlaxcala's justification and verification of privileges and rights rested primarily in written documents such as *cédulas* (royal decrees), jealously guarded in a locked chest in the cabildo hall. Hand in hand with this written record, public performance—processions to honor the king or other ranking dignitaries, religious celebrations such as Corpus Christi, or a saint's day—provided a forum for establishing and securing these rights in front of all ranks of colonial society: illiterate and literate, commoners and elites, and Nahuas and Spaniards alike.

In colonial-period public processions, it was common practice for indigenous nobles—and Tlaxcala is no exception—to wear clothing and other signs/insignias of pre-Hispanic social and political power, visibly linking themselves to the indigenous rulers of the past. On one hand, by appearing in Spanish political and religious processions dressed as pre-conquest lords, the Tlaxcalan elites of the colonial period affirmed subjugation to the Spanish Crown. That is, they sent a visual message conveying that their ancestors were now incorporated into Spanish ceremonies and rituals. On the other hand, these same actions announced hereditary rights to power in the new context.[45] Gibson saw processions with New Spain's indigenous elites dressed as the "four 'kings' of conquest times" as demonstration of a nostalgic attitude toward the past.[46] Likewise, in his analysis of similar processions in the Andean context, art historian Tom Cummins has read performances of pre-Hispanic Inka royalty as "resignation in the face of an irretrievable past."[47] Art historian Carolyn Dean, however, has offered another possibility. She has suggested that performances of royal Inka ancestry could have been deployed as a kind of "counterstrike" against threats to the political status of the descendants of the Inka noble lines.[48] Without discarding the "nostalgia" argument, I am inclined to agree with Dean, reading Tlaxcalan performances of pre-Hispanic royal ancestry in these processions as affirming noble Tlaxcalan continuity, unity, and authority, smoothing over the jagged edges of conquest. In the following section, I focus in on one such procession recorded in Zapata's annals wherein the four pre-Hispanic/conquest-era indigenous rulers of Tlaxcala (Xicohtencatl, Maxixcatzin, Tlehuexolotzin, and Citlalpopoca) are portrayed as ranking closest to, if not higher than, the king of Spain.

## *Aztaaxiluh* (The Forked White Heron Feather)

On January 17, 1677, all of Tlaxcala marked Charles II's ascension to the throne with an elaborate procession of common folk and dignitaries, carefully arranged according to rank, for their march through the streets of the altepetl. At the head of the procession on foot were the *macehualtin* (commoners), followed by Nahua political functionaries on horseback, and finally the Spanish and Nahua *gobernadores* on horseback as well. After these came a float that transported an indigenous man costumed as the young monarch, Charles II, flanked—on yet a higher level—by others portraying the four pre-Hispanic rulers, the tlahtoqueh. Each wore indigenous regalia, including the *aztaaxiluh*, the forked white heron-feather headdress often associated with the pre-Hispanic ruling classes and their important warriors (fig. 1).[49] Zapata writes, "nahui tlatoque quitlalique ymaztaaxiluh quitlamachcuique y huehuetque nahuitin tlacpac" (Above the king were the four rulers wearing the aztaaxiluh in imitation of the ancient ones).[50]

What is striking about this performance is first and foremost the double bind of calling up the memory of pre-Hispanic Nahua autonomy and authority and inserting it into the present frame of a procession honoring the king of Spain. Whereas the explicit reason for the procession appears to be the public expression of loyalty to the Crown, the positioning of the tlahtoqueh as not only closest to but also even higher than the king warrants further consideration. Was this simply a nostalgic reminiscence of past glories, or were Tlaxcalan elites attempting to project the image of equal (or greater) rank as that of the supreme ruler of the land? This staging becomes all the more interesting if we take into consideration that

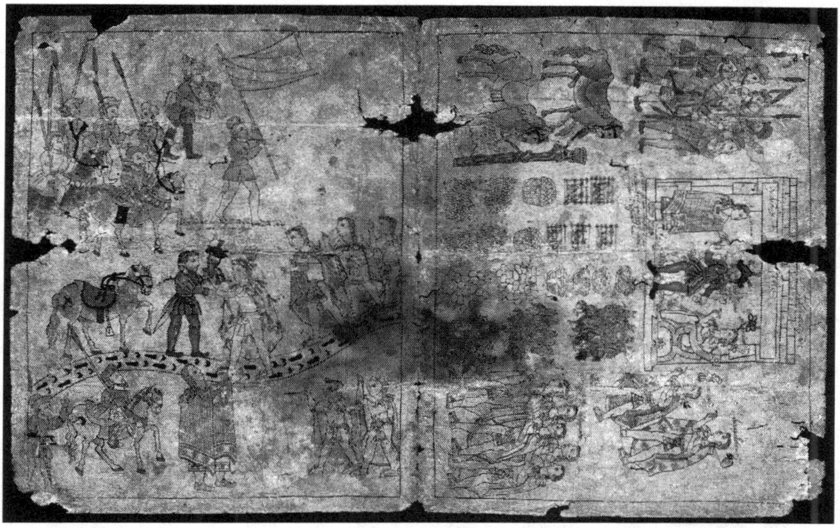

*Figure 1.* Xicohtencatl, wearing the *aztaaxiluh*, greets Hernán Cortés. Lienzo de Tlaxcala. Nettie Lee Benson Latin American Collection, University of Texas Libraries, The University of Texas at Austin.

at the time of this procession the collective political power of the heirs of the four tlahtoqueh was tenuous at best. The polity was not intact: mestizos had married into noble houses and used Spanish support to enter the once all-indigenous governing body of Tlaxcala. Around the time of this procession, in Zapata's annals we read how mestizos were disrupting the traditional rotational structure of the cabildo and, in his interpretation, were wreaking havoc. In referring to one particular troublemaking mestizo, Nicolás Méndez de Luna, Zapata calls him the "gobernador mictlan mextiço" (mestizo governor from hell).[51] "Mochi iymac puliuh." Because of him, Zapata writes, "everything was lost."[52]

Perhaps this performance was also a pointed barb at the mestizo infiltrators who, at least in Zapata's eyes, were the principal cause of strife in the cabildo and the community. Was this performance a tactical reminder to both Europeans and mestizos that the true "higher" authorities were the *pipiltin* (noble indigenous class), those who were there before all others, wearing the aztaaxiluh?[53] And was this message neutralized by the fact that the wearers of the aztaaxiluh, at least in this staging, signified power precisely because they rode closest to the foreign prince to whom they were subjugated? Considering the complex intercultural relationships of the time, it seems as if this performance satisfied the needs of many. In this single procession, the elites managed to embody all of the roles their intermediary position required while clearly announcing themselves as legitimate power brokers in New Spain's political hierarchy. We might also note that it is not only simply the visual performance (the content) of this procession that linked present to past but also the procession's physical occupation of the four quadrants of the altepetl that served as a meaningful sign to bolster noble Tlaxcalan claims of legitimacy and rights. In her book *For Space*, Doreen Massey has argued that space is an always-open and in-process configuration of interactions and multiple storylines and experiences, which she calls "simultaneity of stories-so-far."[54] An additional layer of the story—the construction of Tlaxcalan space—can be read in the procession of the four tlahtoqueh-impersonators marching counterclockwise through the streets of Tlaxcala. As they stopped and saluted the four directions, they repeated ancient Nahua practices of marking territorial boundaries and establishing possession. In this way, Tlaxcalan public performances such as this one also asserted, on indigenous terms, the configuration of the political and geographical territory under their control.

## Loyal Military Allies

The regular reminder of Tlaxcala's exceptional loyalty to the king and his agents by calling up the memory of their role as "first allies" was another performative strategy for advancing Tlaxcalan elite political authority and rights—at a time when these were anything but certain. Zapata, like the mestizo Tlaxcalan chronicler Diego Muñoz Camargo, makes no mention of the initial three-week battle between the Spaniards and the Tlaxcalans.[55] Nor does he record much in the way of interactions with Cortés. We might expect details of the battles that the Tlaxcalans fought as allies to Spain against the Aztecs (Mexica), perhaps heralding Tlaxcalan feats of bravery. The narrative on this topic, however, is terse and spare. In fact, "yn iquac poliuhque mexica" (then the Mexica were conquered) is the extent of the battle recorded in the entry for 1521.[56] Instead, it is Zapata's eyewitness account some 150 years later of a re-enactment of this "first" alliance with the Spaniards that takes up several pages of the manuscript. This episode stands out for its length and detail, as well as for being an exceptional example of Tlaxcala's strategic use of the past.

On February 15, 1670, Tlaxcalans gathered at the foot of the bridge into Tlaxcalan territory at San Juan Atlancatepec (a congregation of

Tepecticpac, on the outer ring of Tlaxcala on the road from Veracruz to Mexico City) for a scripted reception of the new viceroy. All present—from the elite cabildo members to the poor macehualtin—were costumed in the pre-Hispanic rough cloth or sack-like dress of the commoner. As the viceroy's caravan approached, the Tlaxcalan performers beat together sticks for a "quahuitl quihuihuicaque" or "recepción de palíos."[57] When the viceroy inquired as to the significance of the display, the Tlaxcalans responded, "timitzmohuiquilizque y capa timohuica" (we will follow you wherever you go).[58] They continued, "Hoticmatque y monetequipacholtzin ca yuhqui oquichiuque yn tachcoltzintzinhuan yn Marquez ynic oquitlanque yn izqui altepetl" (We have known your concerns. This is what our great grandfathers did when, along with the Marqués [Cortés], they conquered all of the altepetl). According to Zapata, the viceroy's reply was something along the lines of "yehuatzin ca huel oquimotlaçocamachitin yni tlatoli oquimitahuili ça neli amahuiztique tlaca yn atlaxcalteca yhuan yn amomahuiso yn amotemahuiztililiz anquinezcayotia ma totecuyo Dios amechmopili otlacauh yn amoyolutzin" (you are truly impressive people. Of course, you are Tlaxcaltecans. And your respect[ability] and the respect that you give is clear. May God our father keep you. You are most worthy).[59] By re-enacting the military alliance with Cortés in order to demonstrate loyalty to the viceroy, Tlaxcala offered a not-so-subtle reminder to the Spaniards of their indebtedness to their indigenous allies for their successes in New Spain. In addition, with a shrewd reading of the audience's desire for the display of a mass of submissive subjects—here no tlahtoqueh in sight—this performance persuaded the viceroy to voice mutual respect (as opposed to a hierarchical relationship), at least verbally confirming Tlaxcala's special status.

## Christian Subjects of the Spanish Empire

> "When the wars were over and armed heroes were no longer required, native leaders marched in as champions of the new religion."
>
> —Osowski, *Indigenous Miracles: Nahua Authority in Colonial Mexico*, 3.

Assertions of continuous control of their territory, reminders of their noble lineage, and regular allusions to their role as ally to Spanish conquistadors would not be enough to maintain Tlaxcala's autonomy and special status. Perhaps the most important resource at their disposal would be the regular public declarations of Tlaxcala's identity as faithful converts to the Catholic religion. Historian Edward Osowski has emphasized the crucial link between religious ritual and political negotiation in New Spain, reminding us that "only Christians had rights and protection under Iberian law: The Spanish world considered the possession of the 'true' faith a fundamental requirement for the political legitimacy of the indigenous leaders who were known to have descended from pre-conquest non-believers."[60] Here Osowski refers to the 1557 law that gave native leaders who had converted to Catholicism (or were descended from converts) swift access to the courts of law.[61] Thus, following Osowski, it can be said that each public display or performance of Christian faith provided the means by which the indigenous elites could rightfully access the political sphere and confirm their integration and status in colonial New Spain.[62]

The Tlaxcalan cabildo members regularly expressed their loyalty to the Crown (and confirmed their rights) through Catholic rituals performed in the public eye. The cabildo's sponsorship of religious celebrations such as the feast days of Tlaxcala's patron saint, Santa María de Asunción, and the elaborate Corpus Christi processions verified Tlaxcala's investment (both spiritual and financial) in the new order. Zapata notes the cabildo's contributions to what were considered "good works" by carefully recording the expenses and labor provided by the Tlaxcalans in order to build, outfit, and maintain the chapels and to celebrate Mass, high holy days, and other Catholic ceremonies. Throughout the most detailed portion of Zapata's annals (covering the years 1662–1688), we read of religious statues adorned and paraded through the altepetl, the forging and installation of massive church bells, receptions for visiting Church officials, and elaborate funeral processions for the king in absentia.

Beginning in 1651, the first year of Zapata's rotation as indigenous governor, the passages become increasingly detailed—especially those that treat religious duties organized and fulfilled by the cabildo—painting a picture of a community deeply embedded in the Catholic world. Events in the manuscript are regularly contextualized by the saint's day they happened to fall on (or near), and the vast majority of the entries from 1651 on center on religious ceremony and construction projects related to the Church. A pious man, in his first year as governor, Zapata makes a point to mention that he was responsible for the recovery of the mantle of Santa María de Asunción, hocked by the previous governor, don Gregorio Nacianceno, but now rightfully returned to the precious patroness of Tlaxcala: "yhuan hocçepa hocan yacuican nezqui yn imatotzin [ . . . ]. catca mochi nicquixtin don Juan Buenaventura Çapata de Mendoza gobernador jues" (and there, it appeared again her cloak [ . . . ]. It was I, don Juan Buenaventura Zapata y Mendoza, governor, who recovered it all).[63]

In the years that follow, Zapata provides extensive testimony of the cabildo members' public performances aimed at consolidating their relationship with the Crown and the Church. In 1662, he records the dedication and blessing of Tlaxcala's temple of San Francisco, recalling with great pride how Tlaxcalan nobles carried the effigy of Santa María de Asunción throughout the city with a golden key resting in her hands. The first resting point was the temple of San José, where the Blessed Sacrament (the Host, representing the blood and body of Christ) joined the procession. From San José they proceeded to the cabildo hall and on to the *zócalo*'s portals, strung with *xochimatlatl* or chains of flowers, for the occasion. Continuing on to the marketplace, the saint, the Host, and their Tlaxcalan entourage were met by the Franciscans carrying their statue of Saint Francis. Together, they marched to the chapel, where the golden key was ceremoniously taken from the patroness's hands to open the locked doors.[64] In this public procession, a particular version of state and Church—indigenous and Franciscan—was linked together by physically walking from the cabildo hall (elite rulers), to the *portales* (constituents), through the marketplace (economic center), and finally closing the circle at the church. Taylor has said that "embodied performances have always played a central role in conserving memory and consolidating identities in literate, semiliterate, and digital societies."[65] Processions such as this one from Zapata's manuscript show how the physical occupation of space and these "embodied performances" reminded and confirmed the "who" and the "what" of the Tlaxcalan altepetl for participants and observers alike. These public displays linking the Church, Crown, and native rulers highlight that the Tlaxcalan elites were, as Patricia Ybarra has observed, "experts at playing by the rules."[66] With this demonstration that they were faithful Christians, Tlaxcalans were guaranteed, at least in theory, the full protection of the law. This would, in turn, include the ability to negotiate with the Crown and her agents on behalf of their constituents regarding labor and tribute obligations and territorial boundaries.

Further passages from Zapata's manuscript give evidence of Tlaxcalans' commitment to their complex and at times contradictory role as Christian subjects of the Spanish Empire. This role is also manifest in the public events related to the death of King Philip IV and the subsequent succession of his son, Charles II. The Tlaxcalan cabildo's sponsorship of the funeral procession for King Philip IV, and the public oath to his heir in 1666, is one of the lengthier episodes of Zapata's manuscript. He took great pains in remembering and recording the details of this elaborate public performance of Tlaxcala's religious and political identity, with emphasis on how the cabildo garnered much approval from the royal court in Spain and solidified, if only for a time, Tlaxcala's privileged place in the social order. This episode illustrates how Nahua annals recorded the glories of the altepetl, as well as those of their author. Zapata likely had personal reasons for such careful attention to these events, since he played a prominent role in the organization and execution of the processions as a respected elder statesman.

It was not until May 29, 1666, that news of the death of King Philip IV reached Tlaxcala. Zapata recalls the first procession to announce the passing of their venerated ruler. All of the colonial subjects dressed for mourning in order to accompany the musicians, who had wrapped their instruments in mourning cloth, muting the sound, and the town crier, as the tragic news was announced throughout the streets of Tlaxcala. Following his usual habit, Zapata carefully notes the processional order according to rank and commented that all of the tlahtoqueh rode on horseback with the Spanish dignitaries.[67] Only high-ranking indigenous nobles and Spaniards had the legal right to ride horseback, and here Zapata rode among them, proudly representing Quiahuiztlan as a past governor.[68] One week after the announcement of the king's death, all of the *quauhxique* (carpenters) of Tlaxcala were called to build a catafalque in honor of their deceased ruler. They were also charged with the construction of outdoor platform stages upon which the cabildo members, priests, and Spanish dignitaries would make public oaths to the new representative of the Hapsburg monarchy, Charles II. Chosen by their noble peers, Zapata, representing Quiahuiztlan, and don Francisco Ruiz of Tepeticpac supervised the cabildo's material and labor contribution to the construction projects. In these passages he presents the precise measurements of the structure, the vast quantities of supplies procured, and the richly painted canopies erected for the occasion.[69] The catafalque, Zapata tells us, was placed inside "tocabillia" (our chapel), twenty-four *varas* long and fifteen wide (approximately sixty-six by forty-one feet), which he notes as even taller than the arches of the chapel, boasting three different levels.[70] On the third level of the catafalque was an altar with a "çitial," or a small chair/throne, upon which sat an image of Philip's son, the successor. Zapata describes the new monarch as "y piltzintl tohueytlatocatzin Carlos segodo yn ixiptlayotzin" (his [Philip's] young son, our great tlahtoani Charles II, his precious substitute).[71] Zapata's use of the term "ixiptlayotl" is provocative in that it can mean an "image, likeness, or representation," but it can also suggest "standing in for someone."[72] The king may have died, but the monarchy was alive and well, albeit now embodied by a young boy.

The public pledge of fealty to then five-year-old Charles II took place in Tlaxcala on August 15, 1666. On this auspicious day, the feast day of Santa María de Asunción, the pipiltin of Tlaxcala gathered first for a celebration of Christian Mass and then paraded the royal standard and a veiled painting of the young heir to the throne throughout the city, flanked by two indigenous kings-at-arms. Tlaxcalan and Spanish dignitaries alike marched from the cabildo hall, to the marketplace, toward Tecolostitlan and Quaquahxiuhtla, through the smaller market, and then back to the cabildo hall, proclaiming their allegiance to the Crown, again to the four directions of the altepetl. On horseback, Zapata and his fellow *comisario*, don Ruiz, went before the people carrying the "bastón," or ceremonial staff, which Ybarra notes is "generally associated with indigenous elders, who carry them as a sign of wisdom, authority, justice, and prudence."[73] Zapata tells us that he proudly swore loyalty to the Christian king at each of the resting points of the procession, standing above the people on the stages that had been constructed under his guidance. Fireworks were launched, after which he and Ruiz, each accompanied by a king-at-arms, threw coins to the crowds from silver platters. Later, at the doorway to the church of San José, the priests blessed the occasion with prayers and a public recitation of the hymn *Te Deum Laudamus*. Through this public spectacle, the Tlaxcalan cabildo members not only informed the indigenous masses of their expected allegiance to the new Christian king but also provided evidence of the elites' important position in the social-political order.

Several months after the oath ceremony, in October 1666, King Philip IV was symbolically laid to rest by the Tlaxcalans in yet another public ceremony that coincided with the viceroy's visit. Once more highlighting the Tlaxcalan elites' identity as faithful Christians, the cabildo members organized a funeral procession for the deceased ruler. Zapata describes the proceedings, which began in the cabildo hall. A golden crown wrapped in black cloth—standing for the body of the king—was placed on a red cushion, protected with an embroidered canopy. Beside the crown lay a scepter and a rapier arranged in the form of a cross. Zapata was an integral participant in this solemn event, charged with carrying the imperial crown through the streets of Tlaxcala to the catafalque inside the chapel of San Francisco. He conveys a sense of awe upon entering the chapel and gazing upon the resplendent structure: "Yn itech tobolu yuhqui ye comoniz y tecali mochi yztac çera yn tlatlaya" (On top of the catafalque it seemed as if all of the burning white candles would light the tomb on fire).[74] Zapata and other chosen pipiltin placed the cushion, the crown, the scepter, and the rapier in the catafalque and finished the day's events with the funeral vigil and finally a sermon in "laticopa," Latin.[75] The following day, Zapata writes, there were substantially fewer people on hand for continued funeral events, but he states that "we" (here he seems to be referring to cabildo members) again celebrated Mass and offered "Prayers for the Dead" at the sepulcher. Seven days later, the pipiltin again dressed in mourning to hear Mass for King Philip IV at the church of San José.[76]

Surely Zapata was pleased with his participation in these proceedings and considered himself an admirable example for his peers and subjects. His pride is palpable when he later writes that the cabildo members received a letter from the Queen Regent herself (Mariana of Austria, mother of Charles II), lauding the Tlaxcalans' extravagant displays of loyalty to her line:

> Axcan ypan xihuitl tonali lunes a 20 de febrero yhuan ypan xihuitl de 1668 años yn ohuala yn iamatzin y cartatzin toçihuatecuiyotzin reyna yn opan mehuiltitica Caxtillan yn oquihualmotlacuilhuilili yn inican pipiltin tlatoque tlaxcalteca hoquimomachitin yca çe amatlacuiluli yn queni nica oquimomahuizçotilique yn tohuey tlatocatzin ocatca torey ycan yn imahuizçotzin jura yhuan yn inetoquitzin horas ynic cotlayahualuloc yn omotlali quahutlapechtl yhuan tumulo acan iuhqui omochiuh ynic çenoya altepehuacan ynic çenoya auh yehuatzin ca huel oquimotlaçocamachiti y toçihuatecuiyotzin yn izqui tlamatl omochiuh oquimotili testimonio ynic oquihualmotitlanili yamatzin oquihualmomahuizçotili yn Tlaxcallan altepetl. [ . . . ] huel mochoquilique ynic mochitin tlatoque yn iquac quicaque yn icartazin.[77]
>
> (Today, the 20th of February in the year 1668, a letter arrived from our *cihuateuhctli* queen in Castile. She wrote to the pipiltin and the tlahtoqueh here in Tlaxcala. She had read in a written document how we had honored our great deceased tlahtoani and our king with the admirable oath and the funeral honors, for which a procession was made and a stage and a catafalque constructed; nowhere else in all of the lands was this done as [we did]. And she, our great cihuateuhctli, gave great thanks for all that we had done. She read testimony of this, which was the reason she sent this letter wherein she gave honor to the altepetl of Tlaxcala. [ . . . ] All of the tlahtoqueh cried when they heard the words of the queen's letter.)

For a time, at least, Zapata and the Tlaxcalan cabildo members had summoned the royal gaze through their public performances of Catholic ritual in honor of their king. They had again secured a favorable position in the evolving political scene of New Spain.

## "Yc mochi tlaqui" (With This, Everything Ended)

We might be initially drawn to read such performances in Zapata's manuscript as self-serving, aimed solely at protecting or bolstering the privileges only of the elites of Tlaxcala. However, we must remember that the indigenous nobles understood themselves to be the embodiment of the altepetl, and their well-being ensured that of their subjects. Furthermore, according to historian Susan Schroeder, "as long as the royal lineage of the rulership was intact, the conquered, or destroyed state could stay where it was, it could relocate, whatever; but it survived."[78] With this in mind, the preservation of the elite-class social and political control of the altepetl was integral to the continued autonomy, dare I say existence, of the Tlaxcalan people. From this angle, Tlaxcalan nobles such as Zapata can be seen as what Yannakakis has termed "gatekeepers," concerned with creating, preserving, and prolonging the survival of indigenous sociopolitical organization and autonomy.[79] Perhaps we are inclined to believe that the colonial-period Tlaxcalan elites had become, for all intents and purposes, undiscerning servants of the European colonizers, "statemakers" who made Spanish hegemony possible.[80] Yet we must not be hasty in equating honor and respect for the king, or the proclamation of Christian faith, with relinquishing autonomy or power, or happily agreeing to a subordinate position in colonial society. Instead, these seventeenth-century performances are examples of how Tlaxcalan elites deployed productive discourses to strategically and symbolically negotiate the social realities of both the elite class and the altepetl at large. They show us that indigenous people were not passive victims of Spanish conquest and colonization, but key players in shaping their own experience.

To be sure, Zapata's work is not to be taken as the one true history of Tlaxcala; this is only one version, coming from a man who was watching the power and the glory of his noble line fade. Putting pen to paper for the latter part of the manuscript, especially between 1678 and 1688, was likely a heartbreaking task for an aging man in that the noble rule of the cabildo was obviously falling apart. The old ways of the *pilli* rotating through the cabildo had ceased, and more mestizos joined the ranks of the municipal council. Zapata laments the election of the mestizo don Pascual Ramírez, representing Zapata's sub-altepetl Quiahuiztlan, as governor of the cabildo: "amo pili yn itech hoquizqui çan itlamozcalti totatzin frey Agostin de Artiaga" (he wasn't a nobleman, he was just someone that our father Agustín de Arteaga had taken in).[81] This same Ramírez would later be responsible for selling—without the permission of the pipiltin—important cabildo properties, including the portales, the *mesón* (inn), and the local jail.[82] What should have been a time to observe the splendid fruits of his life's labor was instead a sad ending for this Tlaxcalan patriot, who, in noting the sale of these properties, wrote succinctly in the margins of the manuscript , "Yc mochi tlaqui" (With this, everything ended).[83] For Zapata, his Tlaxcala had come to an end. Zapata's story ends, but that of Tlaxcala, of course, does not. In the later colonial period, the Tlaxcalan elites would attempt, with somewhat limited success, to restore noble indigenous rule to the altepetl. But the pillars of authority and rights that had served the noble class of Tlaxcala so well—performances of royal lineage, military alliances, and Christian conversion—began to falter during the eighteenth century with the transition from Hapsburg to Bourbon monarchs. The Bourbon Reforms frowned upon ostentatious public spectacles celebrating anything but the Crown, and their political policies were specifically aimed at unifying the state at the expense of local, independent political factions.[84] But Tlaxcala would—and did—find new ways to assert autonomy at the crossroads of politics, religion, and the law. Neither annexation to Puebla at the end of the eighteenth century nor the bitter divisions of the altepetl during the wars of independence from Spain would destroy what today is Mexico's smallest yet arguably most fiercely independent state, one that Zapata would surely recognize as home. Similarly, Zapata's legacy to Tlaxcalan people, and Nahuas in general, has endured; his manuscript is a rich testament to indigenous survival, cultural pride, and political finesse in times of crisis and change.

# Nonahuatlahtolnemilitzin (My Life in Nahuatl)

by Refugio Nava Nava
(written in Tlaxcala, February 2013)

Refugio Nava Nava is a Nahua from Tlaxcala. He holds a doctorate degree in anthropology from CIESAS, Mexico City, and is currently a professor/researcher at the Universidad Autónoma de Tlaxcala in Mexico. His research focuses on the maintenance and revitalization of indigenous languages, particularly his native language, Nahuatl. His publications include *Āmo polihuiz in totlahtol: No se perderá nuestra lengua/Ideologías, prácticas y retención del náhuatl en San Isidro Buensuceso, Tlaxcala* (2009), *Uitsilin* (2012), and *Malintzin itlahtol* (2013), and he contributed to the children's book *Adivinanzas Mexicanas: See tosaasaaniltsiin, see tosaasaaniltsiin* (2007), along with José Antonio Flores Farfán and others.

## Nonahuatlahtolnemilitzin

Nonemilitzin nicpanoltia nican noaltepetzin Tlaxcallan tlalli. Nican onimotlacatilihtzinoh huan cemihcac nican nimonemitia. Ihcuac neh onieya nicoconentzin tinochtin otitlahtoayah zan ce tlahtoltzin. Achto oticmatqueh itocatzin ocatca mexicano. Ihcon tehhuan otiquiliayah. Ihcon otictocayotiayah. Niman otechilihqueh quil oquipiaya occe itoca: Nahuatl.

Quenin zazoh tictocayotizqueh, ye nin totlahtol, ica nin totlahtoltzin otiquixmatqueh in cemanahuac, ica nin tlahtoltzin oticahcihcamatqueh in totlaixtlamachiliz.

Nehhuatl zan ce notlahtoltzin onicpiaya. Ica nahuatl oniczaloh itocah nochi in tlen oyiya nonahuac. Ihcon oniquixmat in tonaltzin huan in metztzintli. In tlalticpactl huan in ilhuicactl. Ica nahuatl onictocayotih in tepetl huan in atitlan, in milli huan in xochitl.

Ica nahuatl oniquixmat in paquiliztl huan in tlaocoxtl, ica nahuatl onitlatehuicaltih huan onitetlazohtlac, ica nahuatl onimocuicatih huan onichocac. Ica nahuatl onictocayotih in cocoliztl, in temohtiliztl, in celyotl. Ica nahuatl onipahpac huan onitlahuelmic. Ica nahuatl onicoch, onitlatehtemic huan oniihzac occe tonal. Nochi notlaixtlamachiliz ochihchihtoya ica nin tlahtol.

Ica macehualtlahtol onimahuiltiayah ihuan noyolicnihuan. Nochi oquipiaya zan ce itoca. Zan ce notlahtoltzin, zan ce nonemilitzin.

Tehhuan yoticmatiah quil oyiya occe tlahtol. Occequin tlacatzitzin, occequin conentzitzin omonohnotzayah ica caxtilantlahtol. Ihcuac in temachtihqueh ohuallayah ic nican oticcaquiyah quenin omonohnotzayah. Non tlahtol nohuihqui oquitequitiliayah in tepahtihqueh huan in aquihqueh ochanchihuayah occecan.

Ihcuac oticalaqueh temachtilcal otechilihqueh quil monequia timomachtizqueh in caxtilantlahtol. Nochtin in amoxmeh, nochtin in amameh oihcuilohtoyah ica non tlahtol. Ayec otiquittaqueh ce amoxtl ica nahuatl. Ayec oticmatqueh cox acah otlahcuilohuaya ica non tlahtol.

Otechilihqueh maticzalocan in yancuic tlahtol, maticpatlacan in totlanohnotzaliz. Amo otimoxihxicohqueh, amo otimocamachicauhqueh. Amo oticmatiah cox cualli nozo amo cualli oyiya. In tlen quema oticmatiah tehhuan ocachi otipahpactoyah intla timonohnotzayah ica nahuatl. Yenonic ompa temachtilcal oticanqueh in yancuic tlahtol nozo in tochan otimonohnotzayah ica mexicano.

Amo zan niman oticzalohqueh in yancuic tlahtol. Ohuehca, yolic omochiuh in tequitl. Ompa temachtilcal otechmachtihqueh in caxtilantlahtol nozo omonequia nochi tiquixmatizqueh occepa, nochi ticacihcamatizqueh opa. Ihcuac otipeuhqueh yetitlahtoah in caxtilantlahtol amo otimomatiah, amo otechnamiquia. Amo oticmachiliayah quemeh in totlahtol, amo otimotayah quemeh in tehhuan.

Ihcuac oniah hueyi temachtilcal onechmachtihqueh occe tlahtol itoca ingles. Occepa onipeuh in tlazaloliztl. Inic ce quizaloz occe tlahtol monequi ce quitzecoz in tlanahuatiliztl huan tlachihualiztl.

Axan yonichicauh, ye nitlacatl, yonimonamictih, yeniquinpiya noconehuan. Axan nicmati yeyi tlahtol huan mazqui nihueliti nimonohnotzaz ica in yeyi tlahtoltzitzin, ocachi nicacihcamati in nahuatl. Mazqui amo nimonohnotzah ica nahuatl, amo niquilcahua. Intla ninemi noaltepeh zan niman hualehuah nochi notlailnamiquiliz, nochi nonemiliz hualmahcoqui, nochi quipia zan ce itoca, zan nahuatl, amo nitlailnamiqui ica occe tlahtol. Zan niquinitta in tlachihualtzitzin huan niman niccahci imintoca ica nahuatl.

In occequin tlacatzitzin huan zohuatzitzih aquihqueh otimoizcaltihqueh tocepan nohuihqui amo quilcahuah nin tlahtol. Amo tihuelitih tiquilcahuazqueh pampa ica non chihchihtoc nochi in totlaixtlamachiliz. Tehhuan timonechocoah, timonohnotzah, timotlapohuiah ica tomacehualtlahtoltzin. In aquihqueh omotlacatilihtzinohqueh zatepan yocmo oquizalohqueh achto in nahuatl. Yehhuan opeuhqueh ica caxtilantlahtol. Occequih opeuhqueh ica in omemeh tlahtolmeh nozo oquincamacayahqueh huan oquinilihqueh in totlahtol amo oquipiaya ipatih. Oquinilihqueh ma cahuacan non tlahtol pampa tepinahtih in tla techcaquih ihcon timonohnotzah.

In tocnihuan amo acah oquinpalehui, amo acah oquinilih macamo cahuacah in totlahtol pampa ye non tehhuan, ye non tonemiliz, ye non tonelhuayotl, yenon tomahuizotl.

Nochi oticpolohqueh. Yoyolictzin in caxtilantlahtol otlatlan. In tehhuan amo oticmatqueh quenin monactia in caxtilantlahtol inemiliz. Omozohuac nochca. Yocmo omocac in totlahtol ipan imincamactzitzin in topilhuantzitzin. Oticcalaquihqueh in totlahtol ihtec in tochan, ompa omocehui, yocmo oquizaya ohtlipan, zan ompa omahmatzihtoya calihtic. Ompa omochixtoya, ompa oquichiz ce yancuic tlacueponiliztl.

Axan, occe tlamantli tictemoah, occe tonemac tiquicanhuia. Yoticahcicamatqueh in totlahtol quipia ipatih, ye ticmatih amacah techiliz tlen titlahtozqueh. Yen tehhuan tiquihtozqueh in tlen tlahtol ticanazqueh. Tiquicanhuizqueh in totlanequilitzin.

Yenonic yoticpehualtihqueh nin tequitzin. Yenonic titlahcuiloah, tiquinihcuiloah amameh, timocuicatiah, timonotzah nochca ica totlahtol. Yenonic ticyecoltiah in totlahtol occequin tlacatzitzin huan zohuatzitzin. Yenonic tochan timonohnotzah ihuan toconehuan ica mexicano.

Inic ticchicahuactizqueh in totlahtol monequi tipehuazqueh in aquihqueh quema ticmatih. Matimonohnotzacan nochcan, ma nochtin quimatican tehhuan ticpiya toaxcatlahtol, tehhuan ticpiah in tomahuizotl. Maticcuepilican in inahuatiliz, ipaquiliz huan itenehualiz in totlatzintli.

## My Life in Nahuatl

I live in my homeland, in Tlaxcalan territory. I was born here and I have always lived here. When I was a child we all spoke one language. First we understood our language to be called "mexicano." That is what we said, that is what we called it. Then they told us it had a different name, Nahuatl. Whatever you call it, it is our language. In this language I learned about the world; in this language we perceived and comprehended our culture, our knowledge.

I only spoke one language. In Nahuatl, I made sense of the world around me. I learned of the sun and the moon, the earth and the sky. In Nahuatl I gave names to the hills and the rivers, the maize field and the flowers.

In Nahuatl I learned what it was to be happy and to be sad; in Nahuatl I learned to curse and to speak of love; in Nahuatl I sang and I cried. In Nahuatl I learned of illness, of fear, and of loneliness. In Nahuatl I experienced happiness and I discovered anger. In Nahuatl I slept, I dreamed, and I woke the next day [with the sense that I had lived the best of times]. All of my experiences were built through this language.

In Nahuatl I played with my friends, and everything had one name. We had only one language between us; we had only one universe.

We knew that another language existed. Other people, other children, spoke Spanish. When the teachers came to our homes, we listened to them in that language, the one that the priests and the other people that lived far from us spoke.

When we started school they told us that we needed to learn Spanish. All of the books, all of the documents, were written in Spanish. We never saw a book written in Nahuatl; we never knew if anyone had ever written in Nahuatl.

They told us we had to speak this new language; we had to change our way of conversing. We did not resist this in school; we had no argument to present against this wave of ideas in favor of Spanish. We did not know if this change was good or bad. The only thing we knew was that our world was a happy one when we lived it in Nahuatl. Because of this, in school we used the new language, but in our homes we preferred our own.

We didn't learn Spanish quickly; it was a slow process. Even though they were teaching it in school, we had to learn about everything [the world] all over again. When we began to speak in Spanish, we didn't feel right. The language didn't work for us to create and express what we wanted to say. We didn't feel like ourselves in this [new] language.

When I went on to university studies I learned English. Once again I began the process of learning the world, since to speak a language one must connect experience with the words that describe them.

Now I am grown. I am married and have my children. I speak three languages and can converse in each, but it is in Nahuatl that I can truly express myself. Nahuatl is the root of my knowledge, and even if I am not speaking in my language, I have not forgotten it. When I am in my community, all of my memories are clear, all of my experiences are remembered, and they are remembered in one language, with one name, one name in Nahuatl. I cannot remember things in another language unless I consciously force myself to do so. Everything I see around me I name in Nahuatl.

My generation has not forgotten our language. We cannot forget it because all of our experiences were lived in it. We get together and speak [to each other] in our language. The generation after mine did not learn Nahuatl as their first language. They started out speaking Spanish. Others learned both but they were lied to and told that Nahuatl was of no value. They were told to stop speaking their language because it was an embarrassment.

No one helped my people. No one helped them see that they did not need to abandon their language. They did not need to abandon that which represented them, that which was their life, their roots, and their honor.

Everything was lost. Slowly but surely Spanish gained ground. We did not know how to stop it; Spanish spread nearly everywhere and became the primary form of communication for young people and children. Those of us that spoke Nahuatl hid it away inside our homes, where it stayed crouched and ready, waiting for a better moment to spring forth again.

Today we pursue a new ideal, a new destiny. We have won the right to say that our language has great value. We know that no one should prohibit us from speaking in Nahuatl. It is our right to decide which language we will live in. [We have learned how not to deny our way of life.]

Because of this we have begun this movement, we write, we publish books, we sing, and we speak in Nahuatl. Because of this we celebrate our language; because of this we share our language with other people. Because of this we speak Nahuatl with our children, and we work to make Nahuatl the language of our families.

Strengthening our language begins with those of us that still understand and speak it. We must use it everywhere, so that everyone knows that we have our own language and our own history. In this way we will give back to the people their voice, their happiness, and their capacity to name the world around them.

CHAPTER 3

# *Defending Indigenous Citizens When "Indians No Longer Existed"*

## Faustino Galicia Chimalpopoca

How does one legislate and govern in a pluricultural nation such as Mexico? Should indigenous lands be afforded special protections? What is the place of indigenous languages in Mexico? Questions like these, still pertinent today, are representative of the kinds of issues debated by nineteenth-century Nahua intellectual Faustino Galicia Chimalpopoca (or Faustino Chimalpopoca Galicia as he sometimes signed his name).[1] It is in the context of Mexico's transition from colony to independent nation that we turn to this Nahua public servant and scholar of his own language and culture. A political appointee in both liberal and conservative regimes (most notably in the Second Empire [1864–1867]), he regularly represented, or lobbied on behalf of, indigenous communities. Along with these political activities, Chimalpopoca was also a professor of law, of his native language Nahuatl, and of the Otomí language. Dedicated to the transcription and translation of scores of colonial-period Nahuatl texts, he authored a variety of didactic and religious works in both Nahuatl and Spanish. He was one of the most active scholars of the Nahuatl language and culture during the nineteenth century, yet scant consideration has been given to his multifaceted career.[2] In this chapter I advocate for a reconsideration of his not insignificant contribution to the political and intellectual landscapes of nineteenth-century Mexico, as well as Nahuatl Studies in general.

Nineteenth-century Mexico is rarely considered a hotbed of Nahua intellectual activity, and as discussed in the introductory chapter of this book, original texts written in the Nahuatl language from this time period are few and far between. This does not mean that Nahuas ceased acting as intellectuals, or that they put down the pen for that matter. Instead, it is a reflection of two interrelated issues of the historical moment: 1) the creation of the juridical category of "citizen" in the newly independent Mexican nation; and 2) the declaration of Spanish as the republic's official language.[3] First, in establishing independence from Spain, *criollo* politicians had essentially erased ethnic identities by deeming residents in Mexican territory "citizens" with newly enacted laws. Whereas the process of ethnic compression that began in the early colonial period—varied attempts at converting highly stratified and heterogeneous indigenous groups into one generic mass of "Indians"—had been only moderately successful, the elimination of ethnic identification in favor of national citizenship theoretically disappeared indigenous people, enveloping them into the nation. This legalized disappearance often gives a false sense of silence or inactivity from indigenous fronts due to the fact that indigenous people are identified (and self-identified) to a considerably lesser degree. Secondly, with Spanish as the language of administrative dealings, Nahuatl (and other indigenous languages) became all the more peripheral, with written creative work in indigenous languages virtually nonexistent. Instead, in the nineteenth century, indigenous intellectuals oftentimes worked in the dominant language. Chimalpopoca is no exception; along with Nahuatl, many of his writings are in Spanish. How do we reconcile the idea of a politician/scholar who often wrote in the Spanish language with that of a Nahua intellectual? There is nothing antithetical between the two positions: Chimalpopoca's activities and language choices, as we will see, are a sign of the times.

## Formative Years at San Gregorio

Like Antonio del Rincón, the early colonial-period Nahua grammarian discussed in an earlier chapter, Chimalpopoca is said to have been descended from Texcocan nobility.[4] Little is known of his childhood, except that he was a student at El Colegio de San Gregorio around 1810. Founded by the Jesuits in 1586, San Gregorio was originally designed to provide secondary education to indigenous males from prominent families.[5] Similar to other schools operated by the religious orders, the primary goal was to prepare (mostly Indian) students to serve as teachers and models of Christian and

Spanish behaviors in their own communities. Along with general instruction (reading, writing, arithmetic), indigenous students were provided a conservative Catholic religious upbringing. Throughout the colonial period, San Gregorio was a renowned center for the training of *padres lenguas*, priests who spoke and studied indigenous languages. Indian students were regularly encouraged to continue to speak their languages (along with Latin and Spanish), since the European and criollo priests needed native-speaker teachers and informants to better tend to their indigenous flock, and to root out heresies. The school was known to have amassed what was considered one of Mexico City's most magnificent collections of indigenous-language documents, with a large majority of the texts in Nahuatl.[6] We can assume that Chimalpopoca, like the other students, had access to the vast repositories of indigenous-language documents housed at the library of the school.

While San Gregorio was not under the auspices of the Jesuits during Chimalpopoca's attendance (they had been expelled from Mexico in 1767), the educational model of the school still shared many similarities with the earlier Jesuit mission. During the early nineteenth century, as the Mexican nation struggled for independence, San Gregorio slowly shifted from its focus on forming "good" governors (according to Catholic/Spanish norms) of the Indian sphere of society to an emphasis on the education of emissaries of the new nation's ideals. San Gregorio's new mission was to create public servants who were "útil a la patria y capaz de enfrentar los retos del progreso y la modernidad" (useful to the nation and capable of meeting the challenges of progress and modernity).[7] The young Indian men were instructed in authorized behaviors, groomed to serve as role models to their communities and to embody a new dogma based on nation building and capitalism. During Chimalpopoca's formative years, San Gregorio's curriculum straddled a novel blend of scientific, humanistic, and moral-religious education.[8] This educational experience is reflected in his political profile as a conservative Catholic who took a scientific approach to solving social problems, availing himself of what he considered to be the best of both worlds.

## Independence? The Juridical Erasure of Indians and the Dispossession of Land

An important aspect of Chimalpopoca's intellectual profile is the role he played in mediating between indigenous and non-indigenous groups during intense political instability. Mexico's attempts to move from the old colonial structure to that of an independent nation were anything but smooth. Politicians attempted to organize the nation according to the needs of the capitalist market, shepherding the uneven and chaotic transfer of power from landowners, military personnel, ranchers, and merchants to city councils, and state and national government officials.[9] The constant clash and power-grabbing of the two major political groups, the conservatives and the liberals, was the product of a bitterly divided political sphere. The conservatives were "strongly Catholic, Spanish, and landed," whereas the liberals were "largely anti-clerical, pro-republic, democratic, and anti-Spanish."[10] The conservatives believed that the new nation ought to maintain traditional (European) structures and values, embodied by the Church and monarchy. The liberals, however, had diagnosed Mexico's problems as stemming from these very traditions.[11] A time of change for criollos and mestizos, it was even more so for indigenous people by virtue of the fact that the nineteenth century heralded not only their legalized disappearance but also the dispossession of their communally held lands.

In 1821, conservative Mexican army general Agustín de Iturbide announced the Plan de Iguala, which established the "Three Guarantees" of the colony-turned-independent empire under his rule. The Plan stated that the republic would be Catholic, independent from Spain, and based on equality for all (hence the slogan Religión, Independencia y Unidad [Religion, Independence, and Unity]). Specifically, the Plan de Iguala "declared that all Mexican nationals were citizens, without further distinctions."[12] In its most positive light, Iturbide's declaration can be seen as attempting to eliminate the deeply ingrained colonial social structures that had created a highly stratified society based on difference. The result of the Plan de Iguala and declarations and constitutions that followed, however, can be summed up by liberal politician José María Luis Mora's famous 1824 claim that "por la ley no existen indios" (legally, Indians don't exist).[13] Taking into consideration the magnitude of such legislation, it is worth remembering that while independence movements in the early nineteenth century were often invoked in the name of the poor and the indigenous, there is no indication that indigenous people were consulted as these declarations and constitutions were drafted.[14] They were not included in the debates that imposed upon them their new identity as "citizens," although they would soon need to respond to the changes this implied.

With this new legal personality, the few protections afforded indigenous people under Spanish colonial rule were eliminated.[15] These had ranged from the continued right to hold communal lands to exemption from military service and the Inquisition.[16] The Spanish Crown had earlier established such protections after having decided—not unproblematically—that Indians were minors before the law. Now, as Mexican citizens, this minor status was removed. However, as Guillermo Bonfil Batalla reminds us, whereas the juridical designation changed, the hierarchical social structure did not.[17] Now the Indian was expected to negotiate this new place in society with less formal protection as well as with all of the inherited baggage of the colonial experience. Economic, political, and social marginalization of the indigenous population continued as before. To be sure, the declaration of equal rights for Indians did not result in the experience of equal rights.

The rights of citizenship codified in the independent nation's founding documents often proved out of reach for most Indians. At various intervals between the 1824 and 1857 constitutions, many Mexican states revoked the basic civil rights of domestic servants and the illiterate.[18] As Moisés González Navarro writes, "No necesitaban estas leyes mencionar por su nombre a los indios, para directamente anularlos en la vida política (It was unnecessary to mention Indians explicitly in these laws in order to directly annul their participation in political life).[19] The nature of Indian experience (servitude and limited access to education, resulting in illiteracy) inherited from the colonial period often made it impossible, or at the very least challenging, for many to access new constitutional rights as citizens. In this climate one needed a clear understanding of the slippery legal terrain in order to identify, circumvent, or eliminate the barriers to equal enjoyment of rights. This is where intellectuals like Chimalpopoca would have become increasingly important in defending and promoting the rights of marginalized communities as they were, with little warning, made to play by new rules. In order to secure their place in the nation, indigenous communities and their representatives needed to exhibit an extraordinary amount of ideological flexibility, what Guy Thomson has termed "political bilingualism."[20] Chimalpopoca demonstrated this flexibility with his deployment of both conservative-religious and liberal-scientific discourses in order to effect social change. An example during his earlier career can be seen in his participation in the debates surrounding the administration of San Gregorio in newly independent Mexico.

The conservative and liberal viewpoints of national politics were played out in the halls of Chimalpopoca's alma mater San Gregorio between 1828 and 1834, where he was by that time serving as a member of the faculty. Tensions mounted as the school's stakeholders—indigenous students and faculty, and interested government representatives—argued over how this particular institution, founded as a Catholic school, should function in an independent republic. San Gregorio collected rents from a range of properties, including the Hospital Real de los Naturales; the haciendas of San José Acolman, Tetespan and Ixtapan; the Coliseo (Mexico City's principal theater); and more than thirty urban fincas.[21] This income had allowed the school to maintain and develop the earlier-mentioned library and to provide scholarships ensuring the education of Indians (and now occasionally criollos and mestizos) who would have otherwise been unable to pay tuition. By 1828, the independence-era laws aimed at stripping the Church of its once considerable power brought questions of corporate land ownership to the forefront. The problem for San Gregorio was that the Spanish Crown had ceded properties to the school as a religious corporate entity that conformed to the old laws, the Leyes de Indias, for the specific purpose of funding the educational needs of Indians. With disentailment, or the dissolution of corporate property ownership, it was no longer clear who owned the school (the Church?), who should administer it, and who should benefit from its substantial holdings. For the most part, both conservative and liberal factions of the indigenous intellectual elite at San Gregorio agreed that the properties of San Gregorio should remain with the school, with profits dedicated to supporting the education of Indians. Conservatives such as Chimalpopoca and his colleague (and former classmate) Francisco Mendoza y Moctezuma argued that indigenous people should hold the rights to the San Gregorio properties, and both were vehement in their wish to see indigenous control over what they thought was, and should continue to be, an indigenous institution.[22] They complained that they did not need outsider supervision and argued that they were perfectly capable of managing San Gregorio themselves: "El Colegio permanece como si necesitacemos todavía de esos guardadores que dan las leyes a los que no pueden defenderse por sí mismos" (The Colegio continues as if we still needed those guardians that make laws on behalf of those who are incapable of defending themselves).[23] With this campaign, they made a strong case for distinct and exclusive rights based on their indigeneity, ironically the hallmark of colonial policies that legislated separate spheres for Indians and non-Indians. At the same time, these indigenous intellectuals rejected the idea of their supposed helplessness, as "children who need shepherding," which was the very foundation of the colonial laws and societal structure. They did not advocate a return to an idealized past; instead, they lobbied for a new indigenous-state relationship that recognized the indigenous rights established during the colonial period but rejected the legal framework that had viewed indigenous peoples as minors before the law.

There was also much discussion regarding the type of education that students of San Gregorio should receive. Would San Gregorio hold to tradition and serve primarily Indian students with a curriculum that included religious instruction? Or would the school, as some would have it, be open to all citizens and be scoured of any trace of the Jesuits? Was the idea of a separate education for Indians in agreement with Indians' new legal status as "equal" citizens? Chimalpopoca and other conservatives were in favor of a continued adherence to the moral-religious instruction inherited from the Catholic fathers. Demonstrating a "traditionalist" stance in regard to the role of religion and the value of indigenous languages in the curriculum, his camp also thought that the rector should be a Catholic priest fluent in an indigenous language.[24] Not all Nahua intellectuals of the time were in agreement. Chimalpopoca's childhood schoolmate, and candidate for the rectorship of San Gregorio at the time, Juan Rodríguez Puebla represented the liberal point of view.[25] Like Chimalpopoca, Rodríguez Puebla was a Nahua educated at San Gregorio and later became faculty. In sharp contrast to Chimalpopoca's deeply religious conservative front, Rodríguez Puebla's camp wished to facilitate the integration and assimilation of the Indian to dominant cultural norms in a strictly non-religious atmosphere. Rodríguez Puebla eventually attained the rectorship and moved the school toward his secular vision. Chimalpopoca continued to teach at San Gregorio during Rodríguez Puebla's administration, but was soon otherwise occupied in matters of education at the citywide level.

In 1849, Chimalpopoca served as the president of the Comisión de Instrucción Pública (Board of Public Education) in the conservative "monarquist" *ayuntamiento* (city council) of Mexico City. At the time, the nation was perpetually on the brink of disintegration, and the fighting between Indians and criollos/mestizos in the Caste War of Yucatán (1847–1901) was a constant reminder of this instability. Politicians and government officials in the Mexican capital desperately sought viable solutions to unite the citizenry. Chimalpopoca's version of good public policy had room for both science and religion, tradition and innovation:

> La ciencia, las costumbres y la religión son los tres grandes e importantes poderes por los que indudablemente se cría, alimenta y crece el bien de la sociedad. Por el contrario, la ignorancia, la falta de moralidad y el carácter impío, derramando el mas activo veneno de la corrupción

> en todos los corazones de los mortales no tienden sino al incendio, la ruina y la destrucción.[26]
>
> (Science, traditions, and religion are the three great and important powers from which undoubtedly the good of society is cultivated, nurtured, and augmented. On the other hand, ignorance, lack of morality, and ungodliness, spreading the most active poison of corruption in all mortals' hearts, lend themselves only to hellfires, ruin, and destruction).

He seemed to embrace both the "enlightened" scientific approaches of the independence era and the foundational discourses of religion and Christian morality harkening back to the colonial period. In this spirit, Chimalpopoca implored the board to create a normal school for teachers in Mexico City in order to regulate public education, suggesting the Lancasterian models already being employed in Oaxaca, Zacatecas, and Guadalajara.[27] While this project was on far too grand a scale for the council to implement, he was able to successfully secure two hundred pesos for the purchase of school supplies for the girls' schools in the city. Reminding us of his religiosity and pro-indigenous language stance, he also lobbied for religious materials to be printed in Nahuatl and distributed throughout Mexico City.[28]

In addition to teaching and local politics, Chimalpopoca was also an attorney and property administrator of indigenous communal holdings. In these roles he would continue to be engaged with issues related to indigenous autonomy and rights as citizens, especially involved in fighting the systematic dispossession of communally held indigenous lands. In the process of becoming "full and equal citizens," many Indians in Mexico suffered a debilitating blow with land disentailment codified in the 1856 Ley Lerdo. This liberal-sponsored law deemed "corporate" land purchase or administration as illegal, forcing the Church to "disentail" or dissolve its real estate holdings, the base of the Church's power and the source of its funding. The Ley Lerdo not only affected the Church but also was seen as an "all out assault" on indigenous villages.[29] Whereas Indian lands were previously held in common, the disentailment process revoked communal holdings and redistributed land to individuals.[30] If in its most positive manifestation the Ley Lerdo was aimed at creating opportunities for individual proprietorship of "fallow land," it was interpreted as explicit aggression toward the traditional spatial and financial organization of Indian communities. Therefore, the disentailment legislation triggered a scramble for the organization and defense of indigenous property rights.

Speculators waited like vultures, swooping up land that—if not properly protected—was forced into sale.[31] During the colonial period, Indian barrios in Mexico City had been organized and administered as communal structures called *parcialidades*. After the passage of the Ley Lerdo, attempts were made to force Indian parcialidades to cede their lands to the city. These communities needed savvy administrators who understood the complicated and shifting legal terrain. As an attorney fluent in the intricacies of both colonial- and independence-era legal canons, Chimalpopoca was such a person. He became the official *administrador de bienes* (property administrator) in 1855 for the Indian barrio of San Juan (Tenochtitlan) in Mexico City.[32] The role of administrador was especially important during the disentailment process when decisions needed to be made as to how and when lands were held corporately, who owned them, how they could be distributed, and whether or not they could be sold. He was also responsible for regulating community properties and waters, and for managing San Juan's funds for civil and religious obligations (weddings, baptisms, burials, charity for the poor, patron-saint fiestas, public works, scholarships, etc.). Andrés Lira tells us that Chimalpopoca personally received complaints and requests for financial assistance from the people of San Juan at his home at #3 Plazuela de Loreto.[33] During Chimalpopoca's tenure as property administrator for San Juan, no land was unwillingly relinquished, which perhaps explains why he was also later asked to represent the barrios of Santiago (Tlatelolco), Nonoalco, and Magdalena Salinas when city officials attempted to dispossess them of their lands as well.

Criollos and mestizos probably had mixed feelings about Chimalpopoca's management of San Juan and other Indian parcialidades. In light of Indian rebellions across the nation, this stubborn entrenchment of Indian land tenure and the adept management by Chimalpopoca was, as Lira suggests, more than likely perceived as problematic, if not threatening.[34] But Indians too may have looked warily at Chimalpopoca since he seemed to move quite comfortably in the criollo/mestizo sphere. He managed to maintain an active presence throughout the lurching changes of governments—liberals, 1856–1857; reactionaries, 1858–1861; liberals, 1861–1863; and the Second Empire, 1864–1867.[35] As the ideal go-between, he measured and mediated government demands along with the needs of the Indian communities. With his knowledge of both Indian and non-Indian customs, and his in-depth understanding of both the old and new legal systems, Chimalpopoca was able to protect Indian interests, all the while promoting his own ideas of the progress of the nation. Nowhere would this be more evident than in his activities as a collaborator and political appointee of the Second Empire (1864–1867).

## The Second Empire

On October 31, 1861, Spain, England, and France agreed to threaten joint military intervention in Mexico in response to liberal Benito Juárez's refusal to pay foreign debt.[36] Historian Jan Bazant explains that "it soon became clear, however, that Napoleon III had ulterior motives and designs for Mexico. Hence Britain and Spain withdrew their forces, leaving the enterprise to the French."[37] The French military intervention—often intentionally glossed over in Mexican historiography as an embarrassing hiccup in the trajectory of the nation—led to the crowning of Archduke Maximilian of Habsburg as the emperor of Mexico. Maximilian's brief reign as emperor of the so-called Second Empire began in April of 1864, and lasted only through June of 1867, when he was executed, and Juárez's liberal regime resumed control of the government.

Marking the apex of his power as a public figure, Chimalpopoca was an indefatigable presence in the Second Empire. He served as personal teacher and interpreter of the Nahuatl language to Emperor Maximilian and as president of the Junta Protectora de las Clases Menesterosas (Council for the Protection of the Impoverished, JPCM). This prominence in the short-lived Second Empire conceivably explains why Chimalpopoca has a very minimal presence in published historical narratives of nineteenth-century Mexican politics. Both Mexican and foreign historiography have regularly remembered collaborators of the Second Empire as a group of traitors.[38] For example, liberal politician José María Iglesias painted the conservatives as "monstruos criminales" (criminal monsters) whose project was "antinacional y estúpido" (against the nation and stupid).[39] Iglesias opined: "No hay entre ellos una sola persona de recomendables antecendentes; todos son asesinos, salteadores, modelo de cinismo y de ferocidad [ . . . ] Para juzgar de la popularidad de la invasión francesa, basta saber que han salido del fango todos sus aliados" (There isn't a one of them with decent backgrounds; they are all assassins, highway robbers, models of cynicism and ferocity [ . . . ] To judge the popularity of the French invasion, let's just say that all of its allies crawled out of the mud).[40] After the fall of the Second Empire, many collaborators were executed or exiled, and they were often victims of character assassination.[41] Chimalpopoca's punishment was that of being portrayed in the annals of Mexican history as just another inconsequential member of Maximilian's entourage. Yet he was much more than a "hanger-on" in the imperial court. His constant presence in the emperor's closest political circle shows him working tirelessly to improve the lives of marginalized citizens, in particular his Indian brethren.

In 1863, one year before Maximilian began his brief reign, a group of public figures gathered as the Asamblea de Notables (Assembly of Notables). Chimalpopoca is listed in the ranks of its 215 members.[42] At their initial meeting it was agreed that Mexico should be a monarchy, and Maximilian was their chosen ruler. The decision to support a foreign regime was, for many of the Asamblea, a painful one, but they felt that in the present state of near-anarchy, the only solution was to pin their hopes on Maximilian.[43]

By this time Chimalpopoca seems to have become more conservative and even more vocal about his view on the place of religion in government. Whether as a consequence of his years of dealing with the assault on Church and Indian land holdings, or maybe in reaction to the 1857 constitution, which failed to declare Catholicism as the national religion, Chimalpopoca's version of good governance placed religion at its center. We see this in a speech he gave in both Nahuatl and Spanish on October 1, 1863, as a representative of the Asamblea de Notables. Reportedly speaking before a crowd of five million, he urged indigenous people to support the crowning of Maximilian as emperor. Printed on October 4, 1863, in a Mexico City newspaper, Chimalpopoca's speech highlights his view that religion was integral to the betterment of the nation:

> MAC[E]HUALTZITZINTINÉ, ÍHUAN MOCHTIN ALTEPEME,
> In yectlatocayotl in quì paleuhtoc ìn huei altepetl Francia, cenca mo centilana mexica tlalpan. In huel nelli Tota zin Dios oquimo tlaocoltilli in to huey tonetequipachol, ìhuan yehuatzin oquînmìxpololtilli ìn huexcatlotoque, qui milhuia impíos. Ipampa ca immanel ìnìque oqui tlatlallique miec yaotlacencahualiztli, ochollòque ìhuan cholotihui, inayac quì palehuiz ìtlacuamanaliz, ìtlacemitoliz, ìhuan ìhuey iztlacatil.
>
> Ipampa inon xìmo yolchìcauhtzinocan, ihuan xicmo chìhuilican queme miectin ìquizayampa in tonatiuh, ìhuan mìctlampa altepeme quichîuhticate, omo cen màcocque ìhuicpa in tlahueliloc demagogia ìhuan momoztlae qui hualtitlanilia in Regencia inecenpa tlatol, ic machiltiloz itetlacamatiliz. In Imperio omacoc ipampa to teoyolicanemiliz anoce to Relìgion îpampa inon, àmo ximo mauhtitzinocan, ximacoctzinocan. Yuh quìnin ìhueca tlachieliztzin in To teuìco Dios quimocne liliz ìn to netequipachol.[44]

(INDIANS AND ALL PEOPLES OF THIS LAND,
The good rulership supported by the great nation of France, expands throughout the Mexican territory. The righteous and true God Our Father has shown mercy and compassion for our suffering and has confounded the blasphemous and ungodly ones. Because even though they have accumulated many weapons, they have fled, and continue to flee, without honoring their promises, revealing their illegitimacy.

Because of this, you must strengthen your hearts, and raise your voices in protest as have the other nations of where the sun rises [the East] and toward Mictlan [the North], sending away demons and demagoguery. Every day they send messages to the Regency, with which they make known their obedience to the empire that commands here once again. They have embraced the empire because of our spiritual way of living, our Religion. Do not be afraid. Stand Up. God watches from afar and will relieve us of our misery.)

If the choice to support a foreign regime was for many a move toward national reconciliation, for Chimalpopoca it may have seemed like a long-awaited vindication of his own religious beliefs. For even though Maximilian was influenced by European liberalism, at least he was Catholic. In this short speech, Chimalpopoca portrays the empire as chosen by divine wisdom; the military prowess of the liberals is no match for the unseen, yet omnipresent, hand of God. Below I reproduce Chimalpopoca's Spanish-language version of this speech, which yields very subtle differences from the original Nahuatl proclamation. These variations demonstrate his ability to utilize the appropriate discourses of the distinct culture/language groups:

RAZA INDIA Y PUEBLOS TODOS,
El gobierno de órden, protegido por la gran nacion francesa, va cundiendo con inesplicable velocidad por el vasto territorio mejicano. El Señor de los ejércitos, no hay duda, apiadado de tanto padecer nuestro, ha confundido al impío y blasfemo. Porque no obstante haber acumulado éste tantos aparatos de guerra, él ha huido y sigue huyendo, sin que le valgan tampoco tantos engaños, promesas y mentiras.

Por tal motivo, cobrad aliento é imitad cuanto antes á tantos pueblos del Oriente y Norte que en gran masa se pronuncian contra la malhadada y destructora demagogia, dia á dia mandan á la Regencia sus actas en que patentizan su libre y espontánea adhesión ó reconocimento al Imperio, que la Asamblea de Notables ha restablecido. La causa de éste

> es justa; porque es la de la religion, y por lo mismo no debeis titubear en seguirlo, y porque veo que por medio de él la adorable Providencia Divina mejorará nuestra suerte.[45]
>
> (TO THE INDIAN RACE AND ALL PEOPLES,
> The government of order, protected by the great French nation, spreads with inexplicable speed across the vast territory of Mexico. The God of armies, without a doubt, has taken pity on our suffering, and has confounded the ungodly and blasphemous ones. Because even though they have accumulated so many weapons of war, they have fled, and continue to flee, with no concern for all of their deceptions, promises, and lies.
>
> Because of this, gather your strength and follow with haste the example of all of the great masses of people in the East and the North who have stood up against the ill-fated and destructive demagoguery, that day after day send declarations in which they express their free and spontaneous support and recognition of the Empire, reestablished by the Asamblea de Notables. The Empire's cause is just, because it is that of religion. Because of this you should not hesitate to support it, and because I believe that through the Empire, adored Divine Providence will improve our future.)

In the Nahuatl version, imperial government is represented with the term "yectlatocayotl," which can be translated as "good rulership," whereas in the Spanish it is "el gobierno de órden," or "the government of order." In these different phrasings, Chimalpopoca appeals to both Indians and non-Indians in the crowd. Indians might have understood good rulership as being treated fairly, and non-Indians were desperate for an end to the violence that often sprang from unresolved agrarian struggles. Whereas both speeches evoke God as favoring his cause, in the Spanish version Chimalpopoca offers a more militaristic discourse of "law and order." In the Nahuatl version he declares that the empire "commands again" ("inecenpa tlatol") and that others are proclaiming their "obedience" to this ruler ("ic machiltiloz itetlacamatiliz"), a perhaps nostalgic reference to a seemingly better past. However, in the Spanish version, appealing to others in the crowd more than likely versed in the discourses of the independence movement, Chimalpopoca frames support of the empire as "free and spontaneous." Finally, the Nahuatl version closes with a promise that the empire will relieve the suffering of Indians in the present day, whereas the Spanish speech projects the long-term progress of the nation into the future, promising a better tomorrow.

Chimalpopoca expertly read his public and was able to promote the empire as being in concert with the concerns of both cultures. This brief bilingual and bicultural speech is evidence of Chimalpopoca's nuanced understanding of the preoccupations of the divided and pluricultural nation. From where he stood, religion and foreign leadership would solve the nation's most pressing problems. He would have the opportunity to put his theories into action once Maximilian was installed as emperor.

Chimalpopoca was at Maximilian's and his wife Carlota's sides in May 1864 when they were greeted enthusiastically by a large contingency of Indians in Naranjal, Veracruz, on their way to the capital of the nation. He translated the welcoming words offered by the indigenous *alcalde* to the newly arrived emperor: "No mahuistililoni tlatocatziné, nican tiquimopielia mo icno masehual conetzitzihua" (Our great and honorable Emperor, here we are your poor Indian children). Through Chimalpopoca, Maximilian replied: "Cenca no huey paqueliz, no tlazo pilhaune, in anhualmicaque cetilizca ipampa amo altepelzin [*sic*]" (I am very pleased, my dear children, to receive you as representative of your altepetl).[46] Why such an eagerness to accept an outsider as ruler, and to do so returning to the role of children no less? For one, with Maximilian indigenous people were presented the possibility of restructuring unequal social and political relationships that had most certainly not improved since the declaration of independence from Spain.[47] As historian Erika Pani has observed, the progressive erosion of indigenous political and territorial rights that began with the eighteenth-century Bourbon Reforms at the tail end of Spanish hegemony was only accelerated by the recent independence-era legal reforms.[48] But a new ruler offered the hope of addressing these issues. In situating themselves as children of the monarch, the indigenous people of Naranjal evoked their colonial-period identities as wards of the Crown and minors before the law. Whereas it may seem odd to wax nostalgic for colonial times, it appears to have been in some ways preferable to the new reality of citizenship without voice, and also without land. In an effort to recover both, indigenous politicians suggest a willingness to make certain concessions, such as willfully inserting themselves into a subordinate role in the paternalistic indigenous-state relationship.

Maximilian did not disappoint the hopeful masses. In a letter written to King Leopold (May 12, 1865), he insisted that "the best are and continue to be the Indians; for their sake I have just passed a new law which creates a council concerned with aiding them, attending to their wishes, complaints, and needs."[49] The council he spoke of in the letter, the JPCM, was established April 10, 1865, and was comprised of five council members, with Chimalpopoca appointed by the emperor as president.[50] Along with reviewing and resolving the complaints of the most impoverished citizens of Maximilian's empire, the council was also charged with suggesting measures to aid in the improvement of basic education, facilitating access to education for all citizens, and distributing uncultivated lands to the poor. Since the JPCM was an "órgano de consulta y no de decisión" (of a consultative nature, not a decision-making body), we might be led to believe that the council was "only for show" or a token offering to the poor.[51] However, the JPCM was one of the very few commissions appointed by Maximilian to have enjoyed nearly unlimited and direct access to the emperor. Pani saw Chimalpopoca's appointment as president of the JPCM as logical. He had already been named *visitador de pueblos de indios* by the emperor and also had substantial experience dealing with land issues.[52] His "political bilingualism" made him the ideal candidate to assess the challenges at hand and recommend viable legislative solutions that could potentially satisfy multiple sectors of society.

Sometimes interpreted as romantic, utopian, and paternalistic, Maximilian's stated objective in the creation of the JPCM was to ensure that Indians had the same sort of political access—ideally leading to better social and economic opportunities—that non-Indian citizens of the empire enjoyed. We would be incorrect, however, in interpreting this as a move to provide special treatment or protections to Indians not afforded to other citizens, as in the colonial period. These measures were instead designed to ease the incorporation of the Indian into the nation. As opposed to the liberal position that Indians themselves were impeding "progress" and national unification, Maximilian's view was that the real issue at hand was the woeful poverty and general experience of inequality that the majority of Mexicans suffered on a daily basis. That this majority was indigenous was a secondary issue. In fact, as Pani states, "la junta no defendía lo que hoy podríamos llamar 'derechos indígenas,' sino los derechos de los indígenas como ciudadanos—comunes y corrientes—del imperio" (the council did not defend what today we might call "Indian rights," but instead the rights of Indians as ordinary citizens of the empire).[53] Following Pani's interpretation, while Maximilian's politics could be considered "sensitive" to Indian issues, this was more in terms of reconciling liberal principles with the very real problem of the marginalization of a massive portion of the population.

An overwhelming majority of the approximately 4,800 pages of 272 complaints submitted to the JPCM were registered by Indians, and they dealt with problems such as working conditions, and land and water issues.[54] In the short two years of the JPCM's existence, besides reviewing each and every one of the complaints they received, the council also managed to open a maternity hospital and an orphanage.[55] Beyond this, the JPCM was also responsible for the preparation, under imperial orders, of some of the most progressive legislation of the time dealing specifically with workers' rights, agrarian reform, and education.[56] In the first year of the JPCM's operation, Chimalpopoca gave a summary to the emperor detailing the council's activities, including its work on suggested legal reform:

> El primer trabajo de la Junta fue ocuparse de un proyecto de ley sobre reglamento del trabajo de los operarios de campo. Otro sobre colonización, otro de instrucción secundaria a los indígenas. Se ocupa actualmente de formular un proyecto de ley sobre instrucción primaria que comprenda todos los pueblos del Imperio.[57]
>
> (The first task that the Junta concerned itself with was a project on a law dealing with workplace regulations for farm laborers. Another has to do with colonization [land distribution and resettlement], and yet another with secondary education for Indians. Right now we are working on a law regarding elementary education for all peoples of the Empire.)

After receiving recommendations from the JPCM, on November 1, 1865, Maximilian called into effect the first two laws: the Ley Sobre la Libertad de los Trabajadores de Campo (Law on the Freedom of Farm Laborers) and the Ley para Dirimir las Diferencias Sobre Tierras y Aguas Entre Pueblos (Law to Resolve Land and Water Issues Between Pueblos). In the Ley Sobre la Libertad, Maximilian proclaimed debt peonage illegal, stating that regardless of debt accumulated to the *hacendado*, workers were free to come and go as they pleased. The law canceled debts over ten pesos, regulated work hours, instated child labor restrictions (possibly the first child-labor law in Latin America), prohibited physical punishment of workers, and essentially dissolved the practice of the "company store," mandating the opening of markets at the hacienda.[58] The Ley para Dirimir Diferencias Sobre Tierras y Aguas Entre Pueblos established an administrative framework to put an end to the seemingly endless lawsuits between landowners and indigenous communities over land and water.[59] This legislation "recognized the legal character of the pueblos so that they could defend their interests and reclaim rights to their land and water."[60] The following year, again based on proposals set forth by the JPCM, Maximilian instated the Second Empire's agrarian reform laws: the Ley Sobre Terrenos de Comunidad y de Repartimiento of June 26, 1866 (Law for Community Lands and Their Distribution) and the Ley Agraria que Concede Fundo Legal y Ejido a los Pueblos que Carezcan de Él of September 16, 1866 (Agrarian Law for the Distribution to Pueblos that Lack Community Lands). These laws were aimed at, according to Enrique Krauze, "not only the restoration of the land to its rightful owners but the donation of land to those villages in greatest need."[61] They would clearly benefit indigenous communities.

If legislation from the empire seemed favorable to indigenous communities, this was because Indians were actually being afforded the same consideration as non-Indians. These laws did not, however, promise any kind of protection or promotion of indigenous custom or culture in terms of land. In fact, nothing in Maximilian's political behavior or legislations suggests anything more than them being directed toward improving the life of all Mexican citizens. Chimalpopoca's collaboration with the empire, including his (co)authorship of the above-mentioned laws, offers an idea of his evolving notions of Mexican citizenship. Whereas his earlier activism in the San Gregorio debates suggested a separatist outlook reminiscent of the colonial hierarchy, at this point in his career he seems to be more invested in an "integrated" idea of citizenship that promised Indians equal footing (which might include land restitution in a chronically unfair system).

The problems tackled by the JPCM and the solutions they offered were not popular, particularly with the landed class. Chimalpopoca and the other members of the JPCM were subject to regular attacks by journalists and public intellectuals.[62] Liberals and conservatives alike were distressed by Maximilian's law that protected workers from hacienda-owner abuses. According to Robert Duncan, liberals felt that Maximilian's labor reforms "interfered with the freedom of contract," and conservatives were unhappy with any meddling with what they conceived of as their traditional right to control their workers as they saw fit.[63] Regardless of public criticisms, we can imagine that Chimalpopoca was pleased with seeing his ideals turned into public policy. But this satisfaction would be short lived. Maximilian's laws were tossed out with the emperor in 1867.

Chimalpopoca's only surviving child, Concepción Chimalpopoca Oscoy, recounted her father's experience after the emperor's execution: "Cuando entraron los liberales, buscaron a Faustino Galicia Chimalpopoca para fusilarlo, pero se ocultó en un sótano; saquearon la casa y rompieron los muebles. Allí habían ocultado las alhajas más costosas de muchas iglesias" (When the liberals came to power, they searched for Faustino Galicia Chimalpopoca to execute him, but he hid in the basement; they looted the house and broke the furniture. They [the imperialists] had hidden some of the most important treasures of the churches [in our basement]).[64] All of Chimalpopoca's properties were confiscated, and it is rumored that he went briefly to France to escape persecution. Like many other collaborators of the empire banished from public intellectual life, Chimalpopoca went to work at the National Museum in Mexico City.[65] There is also evidence that he returned to his work as an attorney defending indigenous land claims, but his prestige and political power had vanished. It might be that during these final years of his life, impoverished and shunned by society, he saw his efforts as having been in vain. It is important to recall, however, that some fifty years later the same basic tenets of the Second Empire agrarian reforms developed by the JPCM—restitution and land grants—would be the cornerstones of twentieth-century reforms.[66] Therefore, discussions of agrarian reform and indigenous rights in Mexico are incomplete if we do not consider Chimalpopoca's (and other JPCM members') pioneering activities during the Second Empire.

As if it were not enough, the political sphere is not the only area where Chimalpopoca labored: he was also a professor and scholar. Over the years he held formal teaching appointments at the Colegio de San Gregorio, where he taught Nahuatl and law; was Professor of Nahuatl at the University of Mexico (1858–1865); and was Professor of Nahuatl and Otomí at the Seminario Conciliar del Arzobispado (1866–?). He was also regularly involved in the restoration, transcription, and translation of colonial-period indigenous-language documents and carried out linguistic studies as a member of the Sociedad Mexicana de Geografía y Estadística (Mexican Society for Geography and Statistics, SMGE).

Members of the SMGE—Mexicans, foreigners, liberals, and conservatives alike—followed the lead of other nations such as Germany, England, France, and the United States and turned to scientific methods to compile and analyze the fragmented data that qualified and quantified who and what the Mexican nation was, and would become. Embarking on a massive inventory project dealing with the state of the economy, agriculture, industry, and commerce, they sought to understand the people—physically, morally, and culturally—who inhabited the territory.[67] Chimalpopoca appears as a member of the SMGE beginning in 1850 as an honorary associate, and he is listed from 1854 through 1865 as a member.[68] Along with other supporters of Maximilian, he was removed from the society's membership list with the fall of the empire, but reappeared on the roster in 1871, this time as an honorary member.

The SMGE was responsible for the first systematic attempts to collect and organize data on the indigenous peoples and languages of the newly independent nation. The linguistic and ethnographic studies carried out by the SMGE were particularly concerned with the "calidad, origen y diversidad del universo amerindio" (quality, origin, and diversity of the Amerindian world) in order to provide a scientific evaluation of the historical trajectory of the Indians.[69] Through linguistic research, nineteenth-century intellectuals believed they could reconstruct the history and evaluate the evolutionary progress of specific groups of indigenous peoples. They hoped to calculate the perceived value to the metanarrative of the nation that indigenous pasts could lend. At the same time, it was assumed that the accumulation of data regarding distinct languages/cultures would allow for comparative work so as to arrive at an understanding of the "progress" of indigenous development. For his part, besides authoring two philological studies published in the *Boletín de la Sociedad Mexicana de Geografía y Estadística*, Chimalpopoca also regularly participated in group projects commissioned by the SMGE, including the ambitious Comisión de Investigación de Idiomas y Dialectos Aborígenes (Aboriginal Languages and Dialects Research Commission).

Upon first approach, the SMGE members' intense preoccupation with indigenous languages suggests a vindication of indigenous languages and culture. The SMGE research agendas, however, were not in any way geared toward the promotion or revitalization of indigenous language. Instead, they were tools in the service of the study of antiquities. Case in point, the majority of the SMGE members analyzed colonial-period documents as their sources, as opposed to actually speaking with the Indian population of their present day.[70] What did Nahua intellectuals such as Chimalpopoca think about the projects of the SMGE? Did they believe that their language was something of the past, useful only for linguistic studies? A Spanish-language tract written by Chimalpopoca offers a clue to his disposition on the matter. While this document is undated, we can safely assume that it was written some time between 1852 and 1867 when Chimalpopoca was a member of the Comisión de Investigación de Idiomas y Dialectos Aborígenes, since he specifically mentions the directives of this committee. My sense is that it was either a draft destined for publication in the *Boletín* or a speech he intended to deliver (or perhaps delivered) to the SMGE:

> Señores,
> Grande sentimiento me causa la ignorancia en que me encuentro de no conocer el suelo que piso y en el que tanto tiempo perdido La Providencia Divina ha conservado mi existencia, y tanto mas se aumenta mi pena, cuando que veo que cada dia si no se han acabado completamente, se

ban disminuyendo en gran manera los elementos que me podian dirigir, aunque por tradicion al conocimiento de tantos tesoros y preciosidades que oculta en su seno Mexico.

Porque por desgracia nosotros los mex.(icanos) desde que mal entendimos, que ya eramos libres y podiamos vestir pantalones, no solo no debiamos hablar la lengua mexicana sino obvidarla del todo; por que ¿qué se diria de un Señor de pantalon hablando en tal idioma? Lo siento en extremo porque la verdadera historia de mexico esta marcada en su idioma o en la lengua náhuatl.

Ademas, nos alentamos, si no nos atrevimos, al desprecio de la propia lengua (india, desde) que cierta vez se mando en Tolocan, que nada se enseñase en tal idioma sino todo en el puro castellano y ved aquí, que no encuentro a quien preguntarle ¿cómo debo pronunciar el nombre que es la materia de las investigaciones que está encargada de ejecutarlas la comicion cientifica, para decir yo en la inteligencia de la naturaleza de lo que se trata. Podre decir:

¿Cacahuamilpa? No se, porque veo que uno de los componentes del nombre es *cacahuaca* verbo que significa hacer mucho ruido, hacer grande destemplanza.

¿Cácáhuámilpa? Viene el verbo cácáhua q[e] significa ir dejando por partes, o poco a poco algo como depósito o como vulgarmente se dice *deposadera*.

¿Càcahuamilpa? Se presenta el verbo càcahua que significa soltar completamente, o irse separando poco a poco.

¿Cacahuamilpa? Veo en el compuesto el nombre *cacahuatl*, que significa lo que se dice hoy *cacao*, o arbol de cuyo fruto se hace el chocolate.

¿Chachahuamilpa? Se hace ver en él, el nombre chachahuatl que significa lirón, y chachahuamilpa da a entender lugar en que hay abundancia de estos animales.

¿Çacahuamilpa? Veo en él el nombre zacahuitztli que significa grama y zacahuamilpa quiere decir lugar que abunda de grama. Ademas ignoro tambien si el lugar en q[e] se halla la grieta o cueva es el que tiene tal nombre o la misma cueva.

Con tal ignorancia mal haria yo decir magistralmente que cacahuamilpa quiere decir lugar en que se dan muchos cacahuates, cuando este nombre castellanizado se expresa en el mexicano con el de tlaliacahuatl fruto que es de dentro de la tierra. O como un anticuario satisfecho de su inteligencia dijo que el nombre Acamapic, primer emperador mexicano, queria decir boca fruncida estaria bonito el primer magistrado con su boca fruncida. Mas espero que las observaciones que haga con empeño la comisión me den el verdadero nombre de cacahuamilpa para saber cual es un objeto o cual es su notabilidad.[71]

(Gentlemen,
It causes me great pain the ignorant state in which I find myself, of not understanding the land upon which I walk, and thinking of all of the time I have wasted that Divine Providence has conceded me. My sorrow only increases when I see that the sources I could consult with have, if not come to an end, are diminishing greatly. This is so even in light of our tradition to study all of the treasures and precious things concealed deep in the heart of Mexico.

Because unfortunately, we Mexicans, thinking that since we were free and we should wear gentlemen's [European-style] pants, we misunderstood in thinking not only should we not speak our native language, but that we should also forget about it. What would the people think of a man in [gentleman's] pants who spoke *that* language? I am so saddened by this because the true history of Mexico is marked in her language, in Nahuatl.

Moreover, we encourage the disdain for our own language that at one time was the language of Tlalocán, and we no longer teach in the language, instead everything is in Castilian. So now I cannot even find anyone to whom I could ask how I should pronounce the name of the things that the scientific commission is researching, in order to speak knowledgeably on the subject. Should I say:

Cacahuamilpa? I do not know because I am seeing one of the components of the word *cacahuaca*, a verb that means to make a lot of noise, excessive disruption.

Cácáhuámilpa? This comes from the verb *cácáhua* that signifies to go leaving pieces, or little by little depositing something, or as is commonly said *deposadera*.

Càcahuamilpa? Here we have the verb *càcahua* that signifies to let go completely, or to go along separating little by little.

Cacahuamilpa? Here I see a compound with the word *cacahuatl*, which means what today we call *cacao*, or the tree whose fruit we use to make chocolate.

Chachahuamilpa? In this one we see the word *chachahuatl*, which means dormouse, and thus chachahuamilpa implies a place where there is an abundance of these animals.

Çacahuamilpa? Here I see the word *zacahuitztli* which means a kind of plant/grass and *zacahuamilpa* means a place where there is an

> abundance of this plant. I'm not even considering if the place where this plant is found is the crevice or the cave that has this same name or if it is the cave itself.
>
> With this ignorance I would be remiss to say, with any authority, that cacahuamilpa means a place where there are many *cacahuates*, when this castilianized word expressed in Nahuatl actually refers to *tlaliacahuatl*, or fruit from underground. This would be akin to the situation when that aficionado of antiquities, smug with his intelligence, said that the name Acamapic, first Nahua emperor, meant frowning mouth. [Because] it would be convenient to have the first leader with a frowning mouth. I only hope that the observations that the Commission strives to record provide me the true name of cacahuamilpa in order to truly know which object is which, and to understand its properties.)

Chimalpopoca begins with a falsely modest appraisal of his ignorance regarding the nature of the world around him and the history of the people and land he inhabits. In pointing out the lack of sources to successfully carry out his research, he may be implying that along with archival materials, indigenous people themselves are the bearers of knowledge. He laments that independence-era society in general has silenced these living, breathing libraries with assimilative practices. The consequences of the theories and practices of nation building, which have at their heart a sense of radical incompatibility between (civilized) nations and (barbarous) indigeneity, are evident in the second paragraph with his correlation between being "free" Mexicans and the need to cease speaking and learning native languages ("no solo no debiamos hablar la lengua mexicana sino obvidarla del todo"). Freedom, in Chimalpopoca's eyes, has come with the high price of the derision or elimination of native language. Adding insult to injury, the de-Indianized national personality of Mexico has left his patria with an inaccurate and only partial understanding of its past and present.

Most of Chimalpopoca's colleagues involved in the commission—including esteemed luminaries such as José Fernando Ramírez, Manuel Orozco y Berra, Joaquín García Icazbalceta, and Alfredo Chavero—would have agreed with his statement that "the true history of Mexico is marked in her language, in Nahuatl." This was the very basis of many linguistic studies, to understand the past through language. At the same time, very few would have said that this meant indigenous languages ought to be protected and encouraged, or that Indians of the present day ought to be consulted. In fact, most members would have followed their colleague

Francisco Pimentel, who wrote in the 1860s that in order to unify the nation, Indians would need to "forget their customs and even their language, if that were possible."[72] In general, indigenous languages were thought to be, like the colonial documents in which they were studied, a thing of the distant past that should be mined for data and then promptly archived.

Chimalpopoca went against the grain in denouncing the trend of Spanish-only education, arguing that as native speakers "disappeared" into the Spanish language and dominant (Western) culture of the nation, the scientific commission's project—and ostensibly the good of the nation—was in jeopardy. Furthermore, in the phrase "what would the people think of a man in pants who spoke *that* language," he succinctly brought to the forefront one of the key issues at hand: language discrimination. *That* language is conceived of—by the general public and by Indians as well, who had internalized the constant message of indigenous inferiority—as subordinate to Spanish. At the time, indeed through the present day, indigenous languages—often incorrectly categorized as dialects—were thought to have been less developed than those of European origins. This erroneous idea was set forth to explain and confirm indigenous cultures' supposedly lagging position on the evolutionary scale of progress. Yet Chimalpopoca counters this conception of indigenous languages as lacking in complexity with his discussion of a single word—cacahuamilpa—in the Nahuatl language. His lengthy display of his deep understanding of the language underscores his argument that the native speaker is the authority in these matters, and it would serve the commission well to recognize him/her as such. If they truly wished to understand the Mexican nation, scholars needed to address how policies that imposed Spanish and attitudes that denigrated indigenous languages were responsible for the disappearance of important knowledges. By the end of the speech, Chimalpopoca has made a compelling case for reconsidering policies of the day and demonstrated a scientific rationale for linguistic and cultural plurality.

## Transcriber, Translator, Author

A brief review of the documents bearing Chimalpopoca's mark as transcriber and/or translator—found in the Archivo Histórico of the Biblioteca Nacional de Antropología e Historia in Mexico City, the Bancroft Library at University of California at Berkeley, the Newberry Library in Chicago, the Lilly Library at Indiana University, the New York Public Library, the

Benjamin Franklin Library in Paris, and the British Museum, to name a few—show that he worked with an immensely varied corpus of texts.[73] Examples include historical-mythological narrations (such as the *Anales de Cuauhtitlán* or *Códice Chimalpopoca*, to be discussed shortly); pictographic representations pertaining to ritual time, ceremonies, and natural cycles; cantos/lyrical poetry; ecclesiastic translations from Spanish to Nahuatl for evangelization purposes (including catechisms, prayers, loas, and theater); land titles and transactions (both pictographic and alphabetic); historical annals from the Tlaxcala-Puebla region (including those surely consulted by don Juan Buenaventura Zapata y Mendoza: see chapter 2); anonymous letters to the king of Spain; toponym studies related to Texcoco; tribute lists; philological studies; Techialoyan codices; an original historical account (in Spanish) of El Colegio de San Gregorio; a Latin treatise on logic translated to Nahuatl; a (possibly original) Otomí grammar; and a variety of texts dealing with the Virgin of Guadalupe.[74] Besides this transcription and translation work, Chimalpopoca is also author of several original texts. True to his Catholic roots, one of his first publications was a catechism in Nahuatl, the "Devocionario para oír misa en lengua mexicana: Dedicado a los indios" (1848). *Silabario Mexicano* (written and circulated in 1849; published in 1859) is a manual for teaching Nahuatl literacy, which includes a brief introduction to the Nahuatl alphabet, several vocabulary words based on syllable length, and *huehuehtlahtolli*-style texts that detail the proper comportment of boys and girls, including personal hygiene. "Disertación hispano-nahua-latina sobre el origen y modo de contar de los indios nahuacenses" (1858) explains in Spanish (implying an audience of non-native speakers) the complex method of counting in the Nahuatl language. Chimalpopoca published three more original texts of note in 1869. Two were geared toward non-native speakers: *Epítome o modo fácil de aprender el idioma náhuatl o lengua mexicana*, a grammar, and *Vocabulario correcto de la lengua mexicana*, a glossary. The third, *El centavo de Nuestra Señora de Guadalupe*, is a short pamphlet in Nahuatl and Spanish addressed to "No macehual icnihtzitzihuane"/"Hermanos mios los indios" (My fellow Indians), in which he sought donations to support the worship of the Virgin Guadalupe. In spite of this lengthy record of scholarship, Chimalpopoca's work with colonial-period Nahuatl-language texts has rarely been celebrated.

If Chimalpopoca's political activities have generally gone unnoticed, his name is quite familiar to those who study pre-Columbian and colonial codices. In honor of his attempt at the first transcription and translation of the *Anales de Cuauhtitlán* (1570) and *Leyenda de los Soles*

(1558), the French Mesoamericanist Charles Étienne Brasseur de Bourbourg renamed this important set of Nahuatl-language texts as the *Códice Chimalpopoca*.[75] One of the most vocal critics of Chimalpopoca's work has been the highly regarded scholar of Nahuatl, Ángel María Garibay, who complained that the so-called *Códice Chimalpopoca* was not a codex nor did it benefit from the "menos que mediocre" (less than mediocre) translation provided by Chimalpopoca.[76] Regarding Chimalpopoca's version of the *Relato de las Apariciones Guadalupanas*, published by Jesuit historian Mariano Cuevas (1879–1949), Garibay said that the translation is "infeliz," or unfortunate.[77] He suggested that it was "su impericia de la lengua de los documentos que quiso usar, lo dejó tranquilo en su crédito al cacareado Chimalpopoca, cuyas fantásticas traducciones han hecho un caos en la investigación antigua" ([Cuevas's] lack of facility with the language of the documents that he attempted to use that led him to trust the translations of the over-esteemed Chimalpopoca, whose bizarre translations have made complete chaos of the research of classical documents).[78] Garibay's critiques are repeated in many other publications. For example, in the prologue, "Estudio previo," to the 1960 edition of Manuel Orozco y Berra's *Historia antigua y de la conquista de México*, Garibay states:

> La adoración casi se daba a peritos de la lengua, del tipo de Chimalpopoca Galicia, a quien su carácter de instructor imperial de Maximiliano en esta lengua no quitó la ignorancia de la lengua antigua en sus fuentes genuinas y mucho menos eclipsó su manera fantástica de traducir. Este juicio duro alguna vez espero hacer de conocimiento publico, bien matizado y comprobado con hechos.[79]

> (There was a great deal of fawning over experts in the language, like Chimalpopoca Galicia, who, even though he was imperial instructor of Nahuatl to Maximilian, couldn't hide his ignorance of the classical language in genuine documents, much less conceal his bizarre translations. Some day I hope to publically make known concrete proof in support of this harsh judgment.)

Whereas Garibay never published this promised evidence to support his diagnosis of Chimalpopoca's translation skill (or lack thereof), he did offer a token of generosity in regards to Chimalpopoca's grammar, *Epítome o modo fácil de aprender el idioma náhuatl o lengua mexicana* (1869). He deemed it "bastante útil" (very useful).[80] To be fair, Garibay was not alone in his general distaste for the work of Chimalpopoca. Framed as a corrective to Chimalpopoca's earlier transcription and translation of the *Códice Chimalpopoca*, Gumersindo Mendoza and Felipe Sánchez Solís published their own revised translation (under the title *Anales de Cuauhtitlán*) in 1885.[81] They explained that the new version was necessary because Chimalpopoca's translations, in their estimation, were extremely problematic. They offered a three-column comparison for the reader to decide: the first column contained the original Nahuatl transcription, the second Chimalpopoca's translation, and the third their new and "improved" translation. In support of their critiques, they cited José Fernando Ramírez's assessment of Chimalpopoca's work with several other documents, specifically accusing Chimalpopoca of disorganization and questionable translation skills:

> En copias de este género es muy importante marcar la procedencia como garantía de su autoridad. La llevan todas las que sacaron bajo mi inmediata inspección; mas faltan en las que, durante mi residencia en Europa, sacó el Lic. Faustino Galicia, a quien ocupé como copiante y traductor, no obstante el especial encargo que le hice. Circunstancias inopinadas han impedido suplir este descuido, bien que por lo que toca á la autenticidad de los originales no hay duda.—Téngola respecto á la fidelidad de la traducción, quizá porque mis conocimientos en la lengua mexicana son muy limitados. Procede mi desconfianza de la dureza que se nota en la version, y de las varias enmiendas que se han hecho por mis indicaciones.[82]
>
> (In copies of this type of document it is very important to note their origins in order to guarantee authenticity. All of the copies that I personally inspected have this information; this information tends to be missing, however, on those that the Lic. Faustino Galicia completed while I was away in Europe (I hired him as a transcriber and translator), even though I was very specific about this issue. Unexpected circumstances have made it impossible to remedy this error; however, there is no question as to the authenticity of the originals that these copies were made from.—I cannot say the same of the translation, perhaps because my skills with the Mexican language are limited. My concern stems from the fact that this version is a rough draft, and note the various amendments made per my suggestions.)

Ramírez elaborated on his doubts about the translation, stating that "el Lic. Galicia [Chimalpopoca] es sumamente aficionado y propenso a las versiones metafóricas, y he notado que frecuentemente no convienen con los símbolos" (Licenciado Galicia is extremely enthusiastic with and prone to metaphoric interpretations, and I have noted that his translations do not always agree with the symbols).[83] Suffice it to say that general consensus was that Chimalpopoca's translations were at times less than satisfactory.

Yet Mendoza and Sánchez Solís would not be immune from criticism either. Primo Feliciano Velázquez took them to task in his 1945 edition of the *Códice Chimalpopoca: Anales de Cuauhtitlán y Leyenda de los Soles*. He faulted the pair for giving the false impression that the first and third portion of the *Anales* have the same author, and he pointed out where their version omitted letters and subverted letter order in certain words, and how they suppressed entire lines of the original manuscript, leaving the general public with access to less than half of the original document.[84] In Velázquez's eyes, their translation was much, much worse than Chimalpopoca's: "No podían ser tan enormes los yerros de Galicia Chimalpopca, *nahuatlato* que mamó el idioma y ennobleció más su progenie con su educación literaria y científica" (xv) (Galicia Chimalpopoca, a native-speaker scholar of Nahuatl who ennobled his progeny with his literary and scientific education, could not possibly have made the kinds of errors as those [of Mendoza and Sánchez Solís]). He also affirmed that while Mendoza and Sánchez Solís had claimed that Chimalpopoca's translation was given to them as a "complete" translation, this clearly was not the case—it was more than likely an initial rough draft that they had been dealing with. That said, Vázquez classified his project as building upon and revising all of the previous translation efforts:

> Los traductores de que hemos hablado, sin medir la estatura de un Carochi o de un Olmos, dieron pruebas de conocer el *náhuatl* y merecen justamente nuestro respeto; con todo, cuantas veces creemos deber alejarnos de su sendero, lo hacemos, explicando, eso sí, en una o muchas notas la causa de nuestro desvío, persuadidos de que tanto provecho se obtiene de los aciertos del maestro, como de sus descuidos o yerros, que a nadie faltan. Hay que espigar aún en los campos por donde expertos segadores han pasado.[85]
>
> (The translators we have discussed, while not comparable to a Carochi or an Olmos, proved to be knowledgeable in *nahuatl* and deserve our respect; when I have found it necessary to deviate from their translation I have done so, clearly explaining my reasons with one or many notes. I

believe that we can benefit as much from the accuracies of our teachers as their oversights and errors—none of us is immune. We need to continue to return to the areas where experts have passed.)

That Velázquez's rationale for this new translation was significantly less critical of Chimalpopoca than the Mendoza and Sánchez Solís edition is more than likely due to the simple passage of time. Mendoza and Sánchez Solís were both prominent anti-imperialists, which begs the question as to whether their publication of Chimalpopoca's rough draft in the guise of a complete translation (prefaced with Ramírez's charge of sloppiness) was perhaps part of the ongoing defamation of collaborators of the Second Empire. But for Velázquez, the impassioned political dramas of the Second Empire and its aftermath were of little importance. He hardly had reason to belabor Chimalpopoca's errors, some sixty-five years after the man's death.

My aim in revisiting critiques and revisions of Chimalpopoca's scholarly work is not meant to be apologetic, nor to defend his language proficiency or translation abilities. Instead, it is to suggest that the time has come to consider the fact that without Chimalpopoca's curatorial efforts—salvage, recovery, and (yes, sometimes questionable) transcriptions and translations—many of the Nahuatl sources that we work with today would have been lost, stolen, or destroyed. The sheer volume of documents that bear his rubric make clear his commitment to preserving what he considered to be Mexico's cultural patrimony. And while his translations may have indeed at times been fanciful, we must consider that (as he mentions in his speech on the possible translations of cacahuamilpa) he did not seem to be surrounded by other native-speaker colleagues with whom he could consult. Add to this the fact that the written sources he worked with represented dialects from a variety of regions over a greater than two-hundred-year span. Read in this light, we might consider his efforts as imperfect but important—if not invaluable—intellectual contributions to the study of Nahuatl-language texts and Nahua culture today. The combination of Chimalpopoca's unpopular political decisions led to him being nearly erased from historical memory, and public criticism (deserved or not) of his overall linguistic abilities, particularly related to the *Códice Chimalpopoca*, have nearly succeeded in characterizing his work as inconsequential. Yet I hope to have shown that revisiting the career of this highly active politician and scholar offers a unique perspective of how one particular Nahua participated in modernity as an indigenous intellectual, notably at a time "when Indians no longer existed."

# *Tlapepetlaca (Lightning Strikes Again and Again)*

by Victoriano de la Cruz Cruz
(written in Warsaw, Poland, January 2013)

Victoriano de la Cruz Cruz (fig. 2), a native speaker of the Nahuatl language, was born in Tepoxteco, Chicontepec, Veracruz. He holds a master's degree in Indoamerican Linguistics from the Centro de Investigaciones y Estudios Superiores en Antropología Social (Center for Research and Advanced Studies in Social Anthropology, CIESAS) in Mexico City. He has worked at the Instituto de Docencia e Investigación Etnológica de Zacatecas (Zacatecas Institute for Teaching and Research in Ethnology, IDIEZ) since 2003 and recently served as the assistant director of research at the Instituto Nacional de Lenguas Indígenas (National Institute of Indigenous Languages, INALI) in Mexico. He is currently completing his doctoral studies at the University of Warsaw, Poland, where he teaches Nahuatl language and culture, and is a research assistant in the project "Europe and America in Contact: A Multidisciplinary Study of Cross-Cultural Transfer in the New World Across Time," financed by the European Research Council. His areas of interest include languages in contact, Nahuatl syntax and morphology, and Nahua worldview as reflected in the language.

*Figure 2.* Victoriano de la Cruz Cruz. Courtesy of the author.

## Tlapepetlaca, Tlapepetlaca

Mohmoztlah tlaneci, mohmoztlah tiotlaquilia, mohmoztlah ticochih, mohmoztlah timayanah. Nochi cenyohui. Zan totlahtol ayohcanah quennopa quipano. Mohmoztlah miquih miaquin macehualmeh, mohmoztlah tiquilcahuah, mohmoztlah ayohcanah ticnequih tizanilozceh. Amo nicmati tlen pano ipan tonemiliz huan ipan totzontecon.

Nechillia nonanan: "mohmoztlah tiquixtlapachoah quence nocon, mohmoztlah niquixtlapachoa notecon huan mohmoztlah miaquin macehualmeh quiixtlapachoah inintlahtol pampa amo ipatiuh." Nototatah micquiya huan notonanan nimantzin quiahxiliti huan nimantzin moahcizceh. Mohmoztlah techhuahcaittazceh, mohmoztlah techpannextizceh quen ticmictiah inintlahtol, ininixtlamatca huan quen tictzohtzontequih, tiquixtzacuah huan ticcuechoah inintlahtol. Miac noicnihuan quipinahuiah totlahtol, noteixmatcahuan quintlahtlacoltiah inintatahhuan, quintlahtlacoltiah inintotatahhuan pampa amo quinnextilihqeh. Huanquinon,

¿Acquiya quipiya tlahtlacolli? ¿Tlen amo quinecqui quicacqui zo tlen amo quinecqui tlahtohqui? zo ¿melahuac coyotl amo quinmacac manoh ma mohmoztlah tlahtocan?

Tlalli choca, tlalli mocuezoa, tonanan tlalli pinahua pampa mohmoztlah tipannehnemih huan amo ticmanahuiah yon amo quitlepanittah ininconehuan, ichamancahuan, cintli ayohcanah eli. Tlahuel monequi ticcaquizceh huan ticpohuazceh tlen techcahuilteuhqueh huahcapameh huan tototatahhuan. Inihhuantin melahuac ixtlamatinih melahuac tlachiyanih. Yeca naman nicnequi nimechilliz tlan ce acahya nocca quinpiya itatahhuan huan itotatahhuan xiquinillican ma mechnextilican. Pampa zan innihhuantin huelizceh mechnextiliah. Zan xictlapocan cualli inmonacaz huan iuhquinon nimantzin inquimatizceh huan inmomachtizceh inin yehyectzin tlahtolli. Iuhcatzan miac macehualmeh huan coyomeh axcanah quinequih ma titlahtocan, axcanah ma tiquintlacaquilican, iuhcatzan techpinahtiah axcanah ma timahmahuican. Miac xihuitl panotoc quemman ahcicoh ipan totlalhui caxtilcameh huan tototatahhuan quimocuitlahuihqueh totlahtol huan naman tlahuel monequi ma ticcencuililican pampa titlacatinih tlen ni tlalli. Tonelhuayo huan toxic motoctoc ipan millah huan nechca tlixictli. Iuhcatzan ticpanquizah ipan ceyoc tlalli ma tichuicacan totlahtol huan totlallamiquiliz huan amo ma tictlatican. Ayohcanah timoyoyontiah quen tototatahhuan zan quena monequi ma tichuicacan totlahtol.

Tlamemelatzticah huan ma tenticah totlahtol. Zampa ma ticatequican, ma ticchamanaltican tonelhhuayo huan zan iuhquinon cueponiz totlahtol quen ce pilcintzin huan quen ce pilxochitzin.

## Lightning Strikes, Again and Again

Every day the sun rises, every day the sun sets. Each day we sleep, each day we are hungry. Everything continues. But with our language it is different. Every day many people die, every day we forget our language, now every day we don't want to speak in our language. I don't understand what we are doing with our lives, what we are thinking.

My mother says: "Each day I turn my big clay bowl upside down; each day I turn my small clay bowl upside down [this marks the end of my day]. And many people do the same with our language, because they say it is of no use." My grandfather has died and my grandmother will soon be with him. Every day they will watch us from afar; they will watch how we kill their words, their thoughts. They will watch how we destroy and look down upon their words, how we turn them upside down like the clay bowls and jars at the end of day, marking the end. Many of my people are ashamed to speak their language, my family members blame their parents, and they blame their grandparents for not teaching them. Who is to blame? The one who did not want to listen or the one who did not want to learn? Maybe the other one, the *coyotl*, who prohibited us from speaking our language?

The earth cries, she is saddened. Our mother earth is ashamed of us because every day we walk upon her and we do not defend her. Nor do we respect her children, her tender shoots; we, like *maíz*, no longer grow. We must listen to and read what we have inherited from our ancestors, from our grandparents. They are truly the ones who know, truly the wise ones. Because of this I say to you my fellow *macehualmeh*: if your parents and your grandparents are still with you, ask them to teach you. Because they are the only ones who can teach their knowledge, their words. Just open your ears and you will learn quickly, you will know this beautiful language. Even though so many indigenous and non-indigenous people don't want us to speak our language, you must ignore them. Even if they act as if we are an embarrassment, we have nothing to fear. So many years have passed since the Spaniards arrived, and all through this time our ancestors, our grandparents, have cared for and protected our language. And we must now continue because we are of this land, we were born here. Our roots and our umbilical cords are buried in the milpa and next to the fire ring. Even when we move to the cities, we must take our language and our knowledge; there is no need to hide these things. We do not wear the same clothing as our grandparents, but we must wear our words.

Our language agonizes and suffers. Let us give her water so her roots may once again become green, so our language will blossom again like maíz, like a flower.

CHAPTER 4

# *Knowing, Speaking, Teaching, and Writing*

## Doña Luz Jiménez

In 1997, the Museo Casa Estudio Diego Rivera y Frida Kahlo in Coyoacán (Mexico City) hosted an unusual exhibition—the focus was not on a particular artist, style, or movement. The show was instead organized around the female indigenous model who had inspired the most prominent artists working in twentieth-century Mexico. Throughout the gallery were paintings, drawings, photographs, and sculptures of the iconic Nahua woman who for artists such as Diego Rivera, David Alfaro Siqueiros, Fernando Leal, Jean Charlot, Tina Modotti, and Edward Weston had embodied the "spirit" of Mexico.[1] Today, her image can be found in museums around the world, and she is an omnipresent figure in the murals of Mexico City's public buildings, including the Palacio Nacional, the Colegio de San Ildefonso, and the Secretaría de Educación Pública.

The woman is nearly always portrayed stoically, silently working: tending to her child, grinding corn, or selling flowers (figs. 3 and 4). As Erica Segre has observed in her study of twentieth-century Mexican art, such artistic renderings convey the sociopolitical ideals of the time, particularly with regard to proselytizing a certain kind of *mexicanidad*.[2] The images tell us something of the artist's interpretation of what was valued or desired in terms of female indigeneity, and Mexican-ness in general. These representations of indigenous motherhood and domestic work can shed light on the mindset of the producers and perceived consumers of these images, but very little of that of the woman depicted. This particular indigenous

*Figure 3.* Diego Rivera, *The Flower Seller*, 1926. Doña Luz Jiménez, model. Honolulu Museum of Art, gift of Mr. and Mrs. Philip E. Spalding, 1932.

*Figure 4.* Unknown/Leopoldo Aguilar, Luz Jiménez and Mexican Painter Manuel Rodríguez Lozano at the Escuela de Pintura al Aire Libre de Coyoacán, ca. 1922. Jean Charlot Collection, University of Hawaii at Manoa Library.

woman, however, was not just a malleable medium for artists, nor was she silent. She was doña Luz Jiménez, a prolific storyteller and one of the few published female Nahua writers in postconquest history.[3]

Like the 1997 Coyoacán exhibit, this chapter centers in on doña Luz Jiménez, but the gaze will be reversed and the medium exchanged.[4] As opposed to asking how artists utilized her likeness to reflect upon and create a sense of the Mexican nation, I will consider how doña Luz looked back at twentieth-century Mexico in her testimonial writings and short stories produced in collaboration with Mexican anthropologist Fernando Horcasitas: *De Porfirio Díaz a Zapata: Memoria Náhuatl de Milpa Alta* (1968, Nahuatl/Spanish) and *Los cuentos en Náhuatl de doña Luz Jiménez* (1979, with Sarah O. de Ford, Nahuatl/Spanish).[5] Because her published work was often mediated by outsider academics such as Horcasitas (to my knowledge all except for two stories in the short-lived Nahuatl language newspaper *Mexihcatl Itonalama*), a review of her life and writing also returns the gaze to the academy, prompting an evaluation of the nature of collaborations between people separated by race/ethnicity, class, and gender.[6] Since my own work is caught precisely in this tangle, I will also address some of the ethical considerations related to my collaboration with Nahuas. The chapter closes with a reflection on reading doña Luz's work with Nahuas today in Reading Circles.

* * *

Julia Jiménez González (doña Luz) was born in 1897 in Milpa Alta, the second eldest of six children.[7] Her early childhood was a relatively typical one as the daughter of subsistence farmers in a rural indigenous community. However, her life was radically changed by two major events: 1) government-sponsored assimilative education for Indian children; and 2) the violence and displacement wrought by the Mexican Revolution. The recollection of these experiences—along with her knowledge of traditional lifeways and narrations of local myths, legends, and didactic and comical tales—are the primary topics found in the publications stemming from her collaboration with Horcasitas.

Doña Luz met Horcasitas at anthropologist Robert Barlow's home in 1948 and continued to work with him for nearly twenty years, until her death in 1965. Along with assisting Horcasitas in his courses on modern Nahuatl at the Universidad de las Américas in Mexico City, doña Luz regularly narrated her memories and tales in Nahuatl while Horcasitas transcribed her words by hand. After their sessions, he (or his former students Thomas Ford or Sarah O. de Ford) would read the transcription aloud, and doña Luz would make any necessary corrections before providing a Spanish-language version of the story through the same process. Horcasitas tells us that both before and after their sessions doña Luz regularly made additional comments, in Spanish, about the stories, which he includes as bracketed "asides" in the texts. These bracketed items were not translated back to Nahuatl, since doña Luz died before this task could be completed.[8] My sense is that Horcasitas avoided providing his own Nahuatl translation, which he was perfectly capable of doing, in order to avoid invading doña Luz's Nahuatl space. Since one of his stated aims in publishing these materials was to produce what he considered to be authentic didactic materials for his Nahuatl courses, Horcasitas's (non-native) translations would have potentially interfered with this goal.[9] In addition, in the introduction to the *Los cuentos* collection, Horcasitas and O. de Ford note that they regularly resisted the urge to polish doña Luz's texts (Nahuatl or Spanish) because her words offered important data to anthropologists and linguists interested in "rural" Spanish or Spanish spoken by non-native speakers and indigenous peoples.[10] But these are not simply captured words. Doña Luz had an active role in the construction of the messages she chose to convey (and what she chose not to convey). Yet it would be disingenuous to suggest that Horcasitas did not have a hand in the final outcome of these texts. Surely he guided the conversations to topics he was interested in (the Mexican Revolution, for example). He also supervised the posthumous publication of the texts, which included arranging the stories in *De Porfirio Díaz* in a somewhat chronological fashion and organizing those in *Los cuentos* according to genres he assigned them. He also wrote introductory paragraphs for the *De Porfirio Díaz* stories (marked as his own intervention by a distinct italic font) and created titles for all of the texts in both collections. This is without a doubt a joint endeavor, but the knowledge—the intellectual content—of these texts is attributable only to doña Luz.

## Reading Doña Luz Jiménez

The twenty-three stories in *De Porfirio Díaz a Zapata* offer some of the precious few—perhaps the only—published Nahuatl-language texts that narrate the firsthand experience of assimilative education for Indians in early twentieth-century Mexico and the Mexican Revolution. This collection has been categorized as both an *autobiografía/memoria* (autobiography/memoir) and as a *testimonio* (testimonial). Whereas autobiography and memoir denote a personal or individual recollection, testimonio—in the

Latin American literary sense—is indicative of a collective representation and collaborative enterprise. It is tempting to read the text as an autobiography or memoir, especially since doña Luz refers to herself throughout as "NiLuz" or "I, Luz." Yet we must consider that in Nahua culture identity is triangulated, always in relation to others. For example, to identify or introduce my friend Delfina, it is more appropriate to call her *inan* Jacqueline (Jacqueline's mother) than by her individual name. If I ask who a particular man is, say someone we encounter on the road, a common answer would be *itah* Manuel (Manuel's father), as opposed to calling him by his name, Porfirio.[11] It is thus only in the sense of Maurice Halbwachs's assertion that "autobiographical memory is always rooted in other people" that we might consider *De Porfirio Díaz* to be an autobiography.[12] Frances Karttunen has also pointed out that doña Luz does not discuss her personal life after the revolution; because of this Karttunen has read the *De Porfirio Díaz* collection as "more a history of a community than of a person."[13] Yet Horcasitas makes clear that this is not "a history in the usual sense of the word."[14] Doña Luz's writing is instead a subjective retelling of the past from a perspective that has been regularly excluded from the official histories of dominant culture: that of a poor indigenous woman.

Along with autobiography and memoir, *De Porfirio Díaz* is often associated with the testimonio genre. Texts falling under this rubric tend to be first-person narratives of a poor and/or illiterate individual that are recorded (and often edited) by a sympathetic interlocutor, usually an academic.[15] Doña Luz alerts us to this very format in the story entitled "The Village I Remember": "Iqui in, temachtiani, niauh nimitztlanonotzaz inin tlatoli itech naltepeuh ihuan nonemiliz" (And so, professor, I am going to tell you a few words about my village and my life).[16] Latin American testimonio has been theorized by, among others, literary scholar John Beverley. According to Beverley, the individual story in testimonio can stand for the history or experience of a people, the personal as a window to the collective.[17] This framing of the "I" of testimonio as a "we" is in concert with Miguel León-Portilla's assertion that "correspondió a doña Luz ser portadora de la palabra de un pueblo que se creía silenciado para siempre, 'los indios,' los nahuas" (It was doña Luz's lot to be the carrier of the story of a people that we had thought silenced forever, that of "the Indians," the Nahuas).[18] The individual/collective construction of her narrative is evident in the story "The Men of the North": "¡Ay maestro, si usted supiera lo que pasó cuando Zapata nos abandonó! El pueblo de Milpa Alta no se lo sabrá perdonar." (If only you knew, professor, all the things that happened to us when Zapata abandoned us! The people of the village will never forgive him for leaving us in the hands of the enemy).[19] She speaks of an "us," but this traumatic event dramatically shifted her personal trajectory as well; the community and the individual in doña Luz's stories are intertwined.

The importance of the testimonio of her childhood years before the Mexican Revolution can not be underestimated in that her words offer a rare view of how theories of racial politics in twentieth-century Mexico trickled down to real-world practice. At the turn of the century, Indians in Mexico and their way of life were considered barriers to progress and a hindrance to Mexico's successful entry into the capitalist market system. The "order and progress" theme of the Porfirian state (1876–1880, 1884–1911) was based on, in varying degrees, adherence to the ideas of positivism (Auguste Comte) and Social Darwinism (Herbert Spencer).[20] Intellectual elites debated how and why it was that Mexico lacked order and progress, and arrived at the conclusion that the fault lay with the Indian population. According to T. G. Powell, "progress" during the Porfiriato would be achieved by modernizing "backward Mexico through economic development programs."[21] Indians were singled out as this "backward" component of society; they were not just *a* problem; they were *the* problem. Mexico's "backwardness" (read: Indian-ness) was hypothesized as resulting from a wide variety of biological, environmental, behavioral, and dietary reasons that needed to be changed or eliminated for the good of the nation and presumably for that of the Indian as well.[22] Historian Mary Kay Vaughan refers to Porfirian economic and social reforms as having the ultimate goal of "transform[ing] the behavior patterns of an entire population in order to create a modern labor force."[23] Subsistence farming, practiced by doña Luz's father and other *milpateños*, was thought to be particularly unproductive. In order to enter and compete in the capitalist market, the Porfirian solutions were two-fold. First was the planned colonization of "unoccupied, uncultivated lands," which were, we can assume, quite occupied by indigenous people and simply not cultivated in the desired fashion.[24] Second, and pertinent to a discussion of doña Luz's experience, was to change the Indian through education.[25] According to Vaughan, the national school system was charged with the mighty task of creating a citizenry committed to the ideals of capitalist productivity.[26] As seen in doña Luz's writings, these desirable behaviors, practices, and beliefs would be instilled on a daily basis, through force.

Justo Sierra, minister of public education, 1905–1911, insisted that "obligatory public instruction was necessary to national survival and growth—to the development of production, the unification of the country, and the maintenance of political order."[27] Sierra believed that the key to improving the "Mexican race" was biological and cultural mixing. In his view, mixing would filter out all of the negative aspects of the Spanish or mixed "races," tempering them with an influx of indigenous blood that would, in a strange sort of alchemy, remove Catholic dogma, greed, and the perpetuation of social stratification and discrimination, while leaving intact other desirable attributes.[28] In his mind, the main problems with Indian people were their lack of education and their diet. He believed that once they had more access to education (and less to chili peppers), they would better themselves.[29] It should not go unnoticed that education was now being extended to everyone—wealthy, poor, mestizo, Indian, men, and women. But what was the price of this "opportunity"?

In doña Luz's stories, we learn of how students were recruited to attend the free-yet-obligatory school. She recalls the day that all of the men in the village were rounded up, jailed, and interrogated:

> Quintitlaniz tla quintitlanizque inpilhuan tlamachtilcalco. Aquen otlanaquiliaya quititlaniz ipilhuan tlamachtilcalco oquincacahuaya. Ihaun tlen oquitoaya amo oquipiaya tlen tzauhtazque ce metztli. Ihuan oquimilhuiaya: "¿Quezqui cocone nanquimpia? ¿Nanquititlanizque tlamachtilcalco?" Occequi oquitoaya: "Amo nicpia cocone; zan nocnehuan." "¡Can nozo xiquilhui motatzin ma quintitlani tlamachtilcalco! ¡Amotla tlaxtlahuazque!"[30]

> (They were asked if they were willing to send their children to school. Those who answered "yes" were freed. And those who claimed that they did not have any children were locked up for a month. They were questioned: "How many sons and daughters do you have? Are you going to send them to school?" Some answered: "I do not have any children—just brothers and sisters." "Well then, tell your father to send them to school. It won't cost them a cent!")[31]

Free education was, as we might imagine, not quite free. To begin with, a child who attended school all day was no longer contributing to the important work in the cornfield or the household. Add to this the fact that each student was required to exchange his or her traditional indigenous clothing for Western garb—shoes, stockings, and dresses. In "Los buenos maestros" ("The Good Teachers"), the families of the school-age children are made to purchase stockings to hide the girls' legs. The teachers explained that this was to ensure that boys couldn't look up their skirts as they climbed the stairs to the second floor of the schoolhouse, a perhaps unintentional imposition of the sexual tensions of the dominant culture. Also, indigenous families were instructed that boys ought never to go barefoot. The parents wondered how they could comply with these orders when they had no money. The school principal's response to these concerns is a threat: "Tlacamo nantlanentocazque ticchihuazque que ye quezqui xihuitl: namechtzacuazque. ¡*Solo* [*sic*] iqui on namotitizque quename nantlaneltocazque!" (If you do not follow our orders, we will do what we did some years ago. We will put you in jail. That seems to be the only way you will learn to obey us!).[32] Obligatory education included pressuring indigenous families—under threat of jail—to earn and spend cash money, a forced integration to the new capitalist order. For the very poorest children, clothes and shoes arrived from Mexico City. The families were gathered together, and the children were called up on a stage and made to dress and put on the shoes right then and there, a humiliating spectacle for all to see.[33] In "A Proper Way of Life," we read how adult dress was monitored and modified as well, with a local judge threatening jail for indigenous men who continued to wear white cotton homespun pants. The judge's words menace: "I have already told you that I do not want you to wear those short white pants. I want the people of this village to learn how to live in a better way."[34] If the adults did not yield and change their dress, doña Luz tells us, they were jailed for one month.[35]

The modification of physical appearance was but one element of the assimilative educational process. The imposition of the Spanish language and the denigration of the native language were also key strategies for molding young Indian girls and boys into their desired forms. In thinking back to her early childhood in Milpa Alta, doña Luz notes that her parents spoke both "macehualcopa" (Nahuatl) and "caxtilancopa" (Castilian). She adds: "En esa época, no como ahora, nadie se avergonzaba de hablar el mexicano. Muchos no sabían el castellano" (It was very different in those times. No one was ashamed to speak Nahuatl. Many people did not even speak Spanish).[36] This particular brand of education would teach the children to be embarrassed about indigenous ways. With "progress" came language discrimination, which is prevalent even to this day, often resulting in fear of speaking one's native language in public. This was a common theme in our Reading Circles meetings. Most participants reported a long-term sense of shame in speaking a native language, had at one point lied about being a native speaker of his/her language, and felt that they had been discriminated against when it became known that they were indigenous or when they were heard speaking their language. At school, doña Luz tells us, "Oquintlatolmachtiaya caxtilancopa ihuan telpochtiazque nozo ichpochtiazque quimatizque quenemizque ihuan tlen quichihuazque" (We were taught to speak Spanish and to know how to live a proper way of life. We were prepared to grow up as well-behaved young men and women).[37] Learning to live a proper way of life, according to these stories, basically entailed de-Indianization: different clothing, a different language, and different activities. Doña Luz refers often to these proper versions of Indian children as "palomaxtoton" (little white doves); whether she meant to imply that the Indian children had indeed become white is not clear, but the association of white and proper is not lost.

Proper living also included daily bathing. If a young girl arrived to school without first bathing, she would suffer the mortifying punishment of being groomed by the boys. Doña Luz tells us, "Ican tepinauhtin quename pipiltoton otetzcuazhuiaya oteamohuiaya" (It was a terrible shame to have the boys comb and wash one's head).[38] This demeaning practice was enough to quickly encourage daily bathing, but the preposterousness of all that this entailed is revealed in one short phrase: "Ompa Milpa Alta amo onyeya atl" (There was no water in Milpa Alta).[39] The teacher's instruction to send the children to school freshly bathed was not necessarily well suited to the realities of Milpa Alta. Fathers of school-aged children woke at four o'clock in the morning to go to the next village, Nochcalco, for water each day in order to comply with the teachers' wishes. We can imagine why these parents might have hesitated to send their children to the school. The financial burden of buying clothing and shoes, or the mighty task of securing water, would be sufficient deterrent, let alone the fact that many families were surely content with their own ways. Yet the teachers would badger those who did not immediately send their children to the school, insinuating that to do otherwise was to neglect the present and future well-being of the Indian children:

> "¿Amo namechtlacoltia quenamehuan nanquipano? Tla nanquimatizquia amatl achi occe cuali tequitl nanquipiazquia? Huel miac namechilhuia itech xitlachacan inimequez cocone. Namehuan nanhuehuetizque ihuan namopilhuan amo namechequictazque ipampa amo cuali omomachtique."[40]
>
> (Are you not ashamed at the way in which you are spending your lives? Are you not sorry for yourselves? If you knew how to read and write, you would have a much better position in life. I insist that you look out for

your children. You will grow old, and your children will turn their backs on you because you did not give them an education.)[41]

The descriptions of the pressures brought to bear on indigenous families to send their children to the school are peppered with terms that connote obedience, such as "otlaneltocaya" (translated as "had decided to obey" in *Life and Death*)[42] and "titlaneltocazque" (we will obey or be converted). These terms suggest that adherence to the dominant culture norms was clearly in process, if not almost complete. In "The Good Teachers," we learn how Milpa Alta residents finally relented:

> Ye yiman on yomohtaya que melahuac nochtin chantlaca otlaneltocaya queni ca yazque cocone tlamachtilcalco. Aihmo ca oyaya nian tzatzapaltic nian tzoyo. Iqui in ica yomomelauhta, momelauhtaque chantlaca. Aihmo onyeya nian tetzacoz. Nian aihmo, tetzacuiloya ipampan aihmo mohuicaya *pantalón*. Nochtlacatl yoquipiaya ipantalon ihuan cuali icoton. Nian tequixtililoz *multa*. Anca nochtin piltzitzintin quen palomaxtoton tzicuintihue ompan tlamachtilcalco.[43]

> (By that time, it was clear that the people had decided to obey and were willing to send their children to school. Almost none of the children were ragged or dirty. They had taken the good path and gave an example to the people of the village. Men were no longer arrested or taken to jail for wearing trousers [white cotton *calzones* worn by rural Indians]. By this time, every man had his good [proper European-style] trousers and a good shirt. They were no longer fined, because all the children ran off to school like little white doves.)[44]

Doña Luz's use of the word "yomomelauhta"—translated in the text as "the good path" and having at its root the verb *melahua*, meaning "to straighten something out"—highlights her own internalization of the constant message of Indian-ness being something that needs to be fixed, or improved upon (in the direction of European or mestizo norms).[45]

In exchange for leaving behind indigenous ways, the schoolmaster promised a better future for indigenous children: "quizazque coconentoton noihqui temachtiquez nozo totopixque nozo *licenciados* ihuan occequi cuacuali tequitizque cana occeni" ([the school will] turn out children who will become teachers or priests or lawyers. Others may have to find work far away from the village).[46] In this phrase we see a classic example of the Porfiriato's recipe for Indian integration and acculturation to dominant culture:

"education, migration, and occupational shifts."[47] Regarding occupational shifts, Karttunen makes an important observation regarding the kind of education that the girls in doña Luz's school received: "Girls were taught not only lessons from school books, but also drawing, dressmaking, embroidery, and how to bake wheat bread—skills to set them apart from their Indian mothers."[48] This kind of training was aimed at disrupting and fragmenting traditional indigenous social patterns while ensuring that the young Indian women were prepared for their new place in the capitalist economy, obviously in the service sector—dressmaking and baking do not make a lawyer.

After reading about the harsh strategies of public education in Milpa Alta, it might come as a surprise that doña Luz herself did not resist going to the school. On the contrary, she was desperate to attend so that she could learn to read and write: "Nichocaya coza ipampa onicnequia nicmatiz tlen quitoa amame, inon tlacuiloltin" (I cried because I wanted to know what was written on the papers).[49] Worn down by doña Luz's relentless begging, her mother managed to enroll her even though she was younger than the other children, promising the schoolmaster that hers was no ordinary child: "Coza quitequipachoa momachtiz. Ye quiixmati tepitzin *letras*" (She likes to learn. She already knows a few letters).[50] With a sense of nostalgia, doña Luz told Horcasitas, "He visto mucho malo y mucho bueno en mi vida, pero lo que más me gusto fue cuando yo era chiquita y comencé a ir a la escuela" (I have seen many good things and many bad things in my life, but what I loved most was when I was a little girl and started going to school).[51]

Five years into her formal education, doña Luz's school days ended abruptly with the unexpected arrival of the Mexican Revolution to Milpa Alta. She begins her story of the war by saying: "Amo otlaculaoc oncan techtlanahualiz quename ye huitz atlatlacamamaniliztli. Amo otimatiaya hueyi quiahuitl ihuan de tlacatecolotl" (The heavens did not thunder to warn us that the tempest was coming. We knew nothing about the storms nor about the owlish wickedness of men).[52] Then a thirteen-year-old girl, doña Luz witnessed the massacre of nearly all of Milpa Alta's men, her father included, at the hands of the federal army. In a single sentence she sums up the horror: "Opanoya ce aca oquinequia panoz in ihpac mimiquez" (If we wished to walk in the street we had to walk over corpses).[53] This is not a partisan story: federal troops and Zapata's rebel forces are portrayed as equally violent and exploitative. She recounts her home being burned to the ground by the Zapatistas, as it was near the federal barracks. In her story "Zapata's Lieutenant," we also learn of folk hero Emiliano Zapata's men raping the village girls: "Noihqui oquinmichtequia ichpocame. Otlanonotzaloya que oquinhuicaya ica cuauhtla inca omahuiltiaya. Aihmo ce tonali ohualaya intlac itatzitzihuan. Oixpolihuia ica cuauhtla. Cox oquicuaya tecuani nozo oquintocaya, amo machia" (They also carried off girls. People said that they took them to the woods and raped them there. These maidens were abandoned forever in the woods, never to return to their homes. No one knew whether they were devoured by wild animals or whether the Zapatistas murdered and buried them there).[54] Some eight months after the massacre, the remaining inhabitants of Milpa Alta—mostly widowed women and their children—were forcibly removed from the village by federal troops. Doña Luz, her mother, and her siblings emigrated to Santa Anita Zacatlalmanco on the south side of Mexico City. In narrating how the Carrancistas forced her people to leave Milpa Alta, she tells us that times were quite desperate: "Ihuan iqui on omonemili oncuan ica panozque tepilhuan ihuan tatatin amo motequipachozque ica tomin" (They had but one thought—that of keeping their children and [parents] alive without starving for need of money).[55] *Milpateña* women sold whatever they could in the city to survive: corn, firewood, tortillas, or homemade foodstuff. Others worked as servants or begged in the street.[56] Doña Luz's commodity was that which the schools had tried to erase, her Indian-ness—her physical appearance, her language, and her cultural knowledge.

According to family lore, once in Mexico City she entered and won an Indian beauty contest, Izcalichpochtzintli. At around this same time she saw a Help Wanted sign that advertised work for live models at the open-air painting schools in Mexico City. Doña Luz's grandson Jesús Villanueva Hernández has vivid memories of his grandmother telling this story over and over again: how she was so grateful for those few years of schooling that had given her the ability to speak and read Spanish, enough so that she could read the Help Wanted sign. No longer a schoolgirl, she transformed herself into "Luciana" the model and began posing for the painters at the Escuela de Pintura al Aire Libre de Chimalistac and the Escuela de Pintura al Aire Libre de Coyoacán.[57] There she met Mexican artist Fernando Leal and French muralist Jean Charlot (who later became *padrino* [godfather] to doña Luz's daughter), both of whom went on to produce a large corpus of art with doña Luz as the subject. In a 1971 interview, Charlot remembered doña Luz's extraordinary ability to consciously portray, communicate, and mediate her identity as an Indian woman:

> There is a whole image there that she projected. Now many of the other girls *could* put their village clothes on and pose with a pot on their shoulders, but they didn't do it, so to speak, to the manner born. And Luz

> had one thing that was important: she could do it both naturally, as the Indian girl that she was, and know enough so that she could imagine from the outside, so to speak, what the painters or the writers saw in her, and she helped both see things because of that sort of double outlook she could have on herself and her tradition.[58]

This innate capacity to physically communicate—or translate—her culture would make her a favored model of artists in Mexico for decades. Yet neither doña Luz nor her descendants have ever owned any of the myriad paintings, sculptures, or photographs in which she appears. In any case, there probably would have been nowhere to keep them; at one point doña Luz lived in what was actually a large packing crate.[59] At the same time, she did not seem to be much concerned about possessing any of the artwork. Family members remember her saying: "They paid me for my time, no? And if I want to look at what they made of me, why there I am, all over the walls of the National Palace. Why should I need to own a picture of me, when it is there for me and anyone else to see, free?"[60] In stating "what they made of me," it is as if she had separated herself from the images using her likeness, or that she viewed these paintings as a fantasy far removed from her own daily life. Ironically, it is the quotidian experience of indigenous people that the artists were attempting to capture or portray. The model, however, apparently did not see this connection in the works. Several paintings and photographs show her posing nude, which was (and is) considered scandalous for a Nahua woman. This brings to mind the classic Mexican film *María Candelaria* (1944) starring Dolores del Río, which portrays an indigenous community's rejection and subsequent murder of the female Indian protagonist as her punishment for posing nude for artists. We can imagine that disrobing for artists was not something that doña Luz would have readily shared with the community of Milpa Alta, whether out of embarrassment or real danger. I asked her grandson Jesús Villanueva Hernández what the family had thought of her work with the artists. He replied that neither doña Luz's mother, nor any other person in Milpa Alta for that matter, knew that she was a live model. Milpateños may not have known the nature of her work, but they surely knew that doña Luz had some sort of a relationship with the Mexico City artists and intelligentsia. Karttunen recalled that when she and R. Joe Campbell visited Milpa Alta, community members told them that they remembered Diego Rivera sending a car to fetch doña Luz when he wanted to work with her in Mexico City. Rivera also loaned the money to cover Luz's daughter Concha's wedding expenses and made a grand show of forgiving the loan as his wedding gift.[61]

In addition to her work as a model, to support her family doña Luz took on whatever odd jobs she could cobble together, such as cleaning, cooking, caring for children, and designing and selling textile handicrafts.[62] Modeling and domestic work put food on the table, but they were not her true calling. She yearned to become a teacher and applied to the *maestros rurales* (rural schoolteachers) program.[63] Sadly, her application was rejected, which makes the fact that she is the model for Diego Rivera's painting *La maestra rural* (1932) a seemingly cruel injustice. In the meantime, through her connections in the art world, doña Luz began to meet prominent anthropologists, linguists, and writers, who, like the artists she was posing for, were fascinated with indigenous cultures. Karttunen explains that "interest in folklore that had developed in Mexico [ . . . ] looked to its indigenous roots for inspiration and values. [Anthropologist Franz] Boas and his many colleagues were ever ready to collect what in Nahuatl are called *zazanilli* (animal fables, moral tales, and the like), and doña Luz was able to provide them endlessly."[64] Thus, it is with the academics and scholars she finally took up the coveted mantle of teacher, leading them through the intricacies of her language and culture. Along with her decades-long relationship with Horcasitas, we know that she collaborated regularly with U.S. author and anthropologist Robert Barlow, narrating folktales in Nahuatl.[65] The extent of her influence in Barlow's work, however, is not entirely clear as he followed the protocol of his time, only citing doña Luz once.[66] In a story about the Day of the Dead published in *Estudios de cultura náhuatl*, Barlow is listed as the author of the text and doña Luz as the informant: "la señora en calidad de informante lo narró a Barlow" (the female informant narrated the story to Barlow).[67] We might bristle at the term "informant" today, as it implies a ready-to-order source for extraction as opposed to a collaborator or knowledge producer in his/her own right. Yet this was the accepted terminology of the time used to refer to the generally anonymous, often socially marginalized, person or persons who supplied the knowledge utilized in anthropological or linguistic studies. The elimination of an informant's name was (and often still is) common practice in these fields. Anonymity, in its most positive light, can be seen as protective, and it is oftentimes at the request of the collaborator. But anonymity also denies recognition of the scope of the collaborator's intellectual contribution. Who is the knowledge producer? (S)he who sought out the story and transcribed it, or (s)he who is the source of the experience and knowledge under consideration? In my view, both. That is, all anthropological and linguistic studies of/with indigenous peoples that are traditionally understood to be solely the result of the intellectual labor of the academic can and should be re-read as the intellectual work of indigenous peoples as well.

The mere mention of the informant's name in academic publications during this time period was highly unusual. Therefore it is intriguing that along with Barlow's nod to our protagonist, doña Luz is also credited by Benjamin Lee Whorf in his 1946 article "The Milpa Alta Dialect." These anomalous instances of public recognition perhaps suggest that Barlow and Whorf understood the complexity of doña Luz's task as well as the skill she demonstrated. Along with a broad base of knowledge related to her culture and language, her work required stamina, patience, and intellectual curiosity. Lest the reader think I am arguing that doña Luz (or other so-called indigenous informants for that matter) are intellectuals solely because of their working relationships with outsider intellectuals or interventions in the lettered sphere, let us return to Fixico's discussion of native geniuses, whom he calls "keepers of traditional knowledges who have insightful life experiences and who possess gifts of special insights to life."[68] Doña Luz Jiménez's intellectualism was grounded first and foremost in the local reality of her community and her lived experience, and bolstered by the fact that she was capable of sharing this knowledge with outsiders.

While Barlow and Whorf mentioned doña Luz specifically as their source, in other instances she was not identified at all. In her book *Idols Behind Altars* (1929), Anita Brenner refers to "what she was told in Milpa Alta." Doña Luz and Brenner had a close bond as *comadres* (Brenner was godmother to doña Luz's daughter Concha and was at doña Luz's bedside when she died), and Brenner regularly accompanied doña Luz to Milpa Alta along with other artists and writers. We can therefore safely assume that doña Luz was her primary source of information. From personal letters between doña Luz and Jean Charlot, we show that the friendship with Brenner was strained at times, precisely for the fact that doña Luz did not receive authorial credit or the promised profit from her stories published in Brenner's children's book, *The Boy Who Could Do Anything and Other Mexican Folktales* (1942).[69]

After all was said and done, more often than not doña Luz was viewed as a source of knowledge, but not a knowledge producer: she was raw material for artists, a vessel of information to be mined by anthropologists, or even just a cook who told stories, but rarely an intellectual equal. This experience was often coupled with limited or minimal financial compensation for her work. While doña Luz seemed to have had a hand in the making of many careers, she remained impoverished nearly her entire life. Her letters to Jean Charlot over several decades reveal a constant struggle to make ends meet while piecing together modeling and academic work, and they attest to her clients regularly failing to pay, or paying her late for her services. Nevertheless, she seemed to relish her interactions with the intelligentsia of Mexico City. In a letter to Charlot (April 20, 1948), she expresses her gratitude to him for having made these relationships possible: "No sabe compradito cuán agradecida estoy de parte de Ud. pues es Ud. Quien me enseña a vivir más mejor en mi vejez. Eso de tener roces con personas cultas y no tontas, por eso le pido a Dios que lo cuide y bendiga sus preciosos niños y mamá" (You have no idea *compadrito* how grateful I am, since it is you who has taught me how to live better in my old age. Being able to be around educated people and not stupid people, for this I ask God to protect you and to bless your precious children and mother). Karttunen interviewed doña Luz's daughter Concepción (Concha) and asked her if she thought her mother preferred her work with the artists or with academics. Concha's response was that "what she liked was being with people from whom she could learn [ . . . ]. That was the delight of her life"[70] (fig. 5).

*Figure* 5. Anonymous, Doña Luz Jiménez, 1964. Col. Fondo Documental y Fotográfico Luz Jiménez.

## Showing the Path through Story

In addition to her recollections of assimilative education and surviving the Mexican Revolution, *De Porfirio Díaz* also includes stories related to ceremonial practice, medicine, legends, myths, localized Nahua culture of Milpa Alta, and narratives of cultures in contact. While these stories can be entertaining, they are much more than a way to pass the time. They are the carriers of vital knowledges about doña Luz's community's understanding of itself in relation to the natural and supernatural world, passed down orally through the generations. They lead the listener (or now the reader) to contemplate who they are and where they have been, and by extension they have the capacity to inform future decisions. Sto:lo scholar Jo-ann Archibald has called this "storywork": in her view, indigenous stories prompt us "to think deeply and to reflect upon our actions and reactions."[71] Dian Million (Tanana Athabascan) has argued that indigenous stories are in fact *theories* in that "they posit proposition and paradigm on how the world works."[72] Similarly, Heidi Stark (Turtle Mountain Ojibwe) understands indigenous stories to be "methods that teach us how to survive in an ever-changing environment."[73] With these approaches in mind, I read doña Luz's stories as intellectual work: they inform, guide, and explain the world and our place within it.[74]

In her story of the legend of the mountain Iztaccihuatl (White Woman) that looms over the Valley of Mexico, we learn how the great mountain Popocatepetl (Smoking Mountain) falls in love with the shepherdess Malintzin. She rejects his proposal of marriage: "Nian tehuatl, nian amaca; niaz nichociz. Tinechixotiz" (Neither you nor anybody else. I am going to sleep, and you will watch over me).[75] Later, a Catholic priest arrives and, seeing Malintzin alseep, commands her to rise. Malintzin replies: "Axan xinechehuacan tla nanchichicahuaque" (If you feel so strong, why do you not try to lift me?).[76] The priest is no match for Malintzin, who declares that she will remain with Popocatepetl as Iztaccihuatl, the mountain. She will watch over her people and ensure that they honor the old ways by making pilgrimages to her partner (but not husband), the great Popocatepetl. Besides the representation of land as a powerful feminine presence, we could also read resistance to Christian influence in this tale: Luz's story reminds us that as long as the great mountains are there, the old ways will continue. Nahua reverence for the spirits that are (or reside in) the mountains, and pilgrimages to both honor and petition them, are recurring themes found throughout doña Luz's texts.

"The Miraculous Lord of Chalma" explains ceremonial obligations related to pilgrimages to Chalma. One of the most-visited pilgrimage sites in Mexico (second only to the Basilica of Our Lady of Guadalupe in Mexico City), Chalma's pilgrims pay homage to "The Black Christ" in a shrine built on top of that of the pre-Hispanic God of the Cave, Ozoteotl (an avatar of Tezcatlipoca, or Smoking Mirror).[77] A tale of the syncretic blending of pre-Hispanic and Catholic rites, in this story doña Luz recalls how first-time pilgrims dance in front of the cypress trees adorned with offerings of braids, hats, and little bags of umbilical cords. After the dancing, the pilgrims attend Mass in the Catholic Church.[78] This lengthy recollection of her own pilgrimage to Chalma is a reminder of the persistence of the indigenous practice of sacred pilgrimages to caves and hills, including the elaborate preparations, the physical demands, and the state of clarity and intention required to carry out the ceremonial obligations. On this last issue, doña Luz says that "ahquen amo ca iyolo oyaya Chalma tlalhuiquixtiz tla itla oquipanoaya ipan tepetl" (he who goes to Chalma without a full heart may be in danger on that hill).[79] Doña Luz's description of pilgrimage to Chalma holds significant similarities to pilgrimages and ceremonial rituals throughout Nahua communities today; I was in fact given the same warning to go with a full heart as I embarked on my own first pilgrimage up a small mountain near Chicontepec, Veracruz, in honor of Chicomexochitl (7-Flower). Not surprisingly, this particular story resonated with many in the Reading Circles, as the practices described are regular occurrences in their own communities of origin to this day.

The second collection of doña Luz's work, *Los cuentos en Náhuatl de doña Luz Jiménez*, also includes stories related to ceremony, among many other topics. The original Nahuatl texts are accompanied by a Spanish-language version (both by doña Luz) and are divided into six categories: 1) "Relatos cosmogónicos y etiológicos" ("Cosmogonies and Etiologies," seven stories); 2) "Relatos de lo sobrenatural" ("The Supernatural," twelve stories); 3) "Cuentos moralizadores" ("Moralizing Stories," four stories); 4) "Acontecimientos locales" ("Local Tales," three stories); 5) "Cuentos de hadas" ("Fairy Tales," eight stories); and 6) "Cuentos cómicos" ("Comedic Tales," eleven stories). According to doña Luz, the stories were, for the most part, the kind that elders would tell to children and young people.[80] All of the stories are didactic in nature, similar to the *huehuehtlahtolli*, or elder discourse speech, found, for example, in book six of the sixteenth-century Florentine Codex. To give an idea of the richness of this relatively untapped source of cultural wisdom, I will comment briefly on selected stories by doña Luz found in this collection; however, an exhaustive analysis of the entire corpus awaits.

"In tlaltihpactli" ("El mundo" ["The World"]) includes several versions of the origins of human beings. One confirms a Nahua cosmogony of gender complementarity—the first people sprang from an egg that God (in this case "toteotatzin" or "Dios Nuestro Padre" [God our Father]) tossed up into the air from which man and woman simultaneously emerged. Another is that we were made from two stalks of corn. Yet another version blends Nahua and Christian beliefs: God made man out of mud then pulled out his own (God's) rib to make woman. The story "Teotl" ("Los dioses" ["The Gods"]) alerts us to the existence of paired supernatural beings in male/female aspects in the Nahua pantheon. This same story treats seven layers through which the dead pass, echoing the colonial-period sources that report specific afterlife destinies for those who died in combat, for women who died in childbirth, and for children.[81] The mountain Iztaccihuatl appears again twice in this collection. The first story, "Zazanili ipampan Iztaccihuatl I" ("Cuento sobre la Mujer Blanca I" ["Story of the White Woman I"]) is marked as one passed down through the generations: doña Luz begins by saying, "Tocoltzitzihuan omontlanonochiliaya" ("Nuestros abuelos contaban . . ." [Our grandparents used to tell us that . . .]).[82] In this story treating sacred landscape, she explains pilgrimages to the caves and mountains, in this case the great mountains, to petition for the rain needed to ensure a good corn harvest. "Zazanili ipampan Iztaccihuatl II" ("Cuento sobre la Mujer Blanca II" ["Story of the White Woman II"]) is another version of the story of Popocatepetl and Iztaccihuatl. In this telling, Iztaccihuatl is the daughter of Moctezuma, who is loved by a young man named Chimalpopoca. Moctezuma is enraged by Chimalpopoca's desire for his daughter and turns them both into mountains. The twist in this story is that the mountains/lovers are then charged with protecting the Indians from the "caxtilteca" (Spaniards, mestizos, non-Indians). Moctezuma says, "Amo nihnequi hualazque caxtilteca nozo cuitlaxcoliztaque. Amo nihnequi aca quinchochohtiz macehualtin" (No quiero que venga la gente capitalina, la gente de panza blanca. No quiero que nadie haga llorar a los indios [I don't want the city-folk, the white-bellied people, to come here; I don't want anyone to make the Indians cry]).[83] The spirits of the caves and mountains not only regulate life-giving rain but also serve as protective barriers and spaces of refuge against the invaders.

Twelve stories in *Los cuentos* were specifically grouped by Horcasitas as dealing with "the supernatural"—God walks among the villagers, young girls are bewitched by the Lord of Chalma, tricksters shift shapes, outsiders (termed "árabes") cast spells for non-payment of goods, deals are made with the devil, and a village woman uses mystical powers to harm others. To Western ears these stories are magical, fantastic, or other-worldly. Yet in Nahua culture, the liminal veil between what Western cultures consider other-worldly and of this world is quite porous. For Nahuas these didactic tales are not impossible ghost stories; they deal with logical, everyday circumstances. They teach the younger generation right behaviors and warn of the perils of incorrect actions in situations that can and will occur. The lessons gleaned range from ensuring that one provides for the dead to being aware of the borders of safe and unsafe spaces, from how to avoid being cheated to forging appropriate interpersonal relationships. They encapsulate some of the most important teachings of what the Reading Circles called *cualli nemiliztli*, or the good life.

"Mihcatzintli ihuan ce cihuatl" ("El muerto y la mujer" ["The Dead Man and a Woman"]) reminds the listener of the obligation to honor and tend to the dead. An impoverished widow goes begging in the streets in order to feed her children. Disappointed with the meager twenty-five centavos she collects, she takes the offering to the church and prays for all of the dead who have been forgotten. Her prayers are moving to one of these poor souls, the deceased patriarch of a rich local family. He instructs the woman to go immediately to the home of his son with a note that he has written. The unworthy son who has neglected the needs of his father's soul in the afterlife is evicted, and the home and its contents are given to the woman and her children. "Zazanili ipampan tetlachihui" ("Cuento sobre la bruja" ["Story About the Witch"]) presents the life of Porfiria Cuetzpalin, who casts spells on those in the community who refuse to loan her things. A neighbor's illness is the result of Porfiria's curse, a sickness that could not be cured by Western medicine. Only another "tetlachihui" or local curandero could help the poor woman. It is cualli nemiliztli to honor one's elders, as seen in the story "In coli, in piltontli ihuan in tatapatli" ("El abuelo, el niño y la cobija" ["The Grandfather, the Boy, and the Blanket"]). In this story, a son decides to evict his father, who has become a "burden," from the family home. The elderly man does not know where to go and requests permission to sleep at least one night near the house, but outside. He asks for a blanket to guard him from the night chill. The son sends his own young son (the grandson) to the stable to find a horse blanket for the grandfather. The boy returns with the blanket cut in two: "Amo nihmacaz nochiuh. Nimitzmopililiz icac tehuatzin timohuehuetiliz. Yehuatl on ica timoquimilotzinoz que nocoltzin" (No se la daré todo. Guardaré [la mitad] para cuando tú estés viejo. Con ella te cobijarás como mi abuelo [I won't give him all (of the blanket). I will keep half for you for when you are old. With this you will cover yourself, just like my grandfather]).[84] The son sees the errors of his ways and invites the elder back into the home. Stories such as these are entertaining, but they also encode a sort of handbook for social behavior: do this, don't do that.

Many of the stories in the *Los cuentos* collection are called *zazanili*, or tales, and often include the term "tlanonotzaloya" (it was told that . . .), which marks the texts as anonymous or collective knowledge. Doña Luz as an individual does not take credit as the creator of original stories in the *Los cuentos* collection. Nor does she usually figure as a character in the zazanili. However, in one, "In demonio ihuan macuili cihuantoton" ("El demonio y las cinco niñas" ["The Devil and the Five Little Girls"]), doña Luz herself is a protagonist. She recalls a day when she and her fellow milpateña classmates were playing outside the school. While they had been told repeatedly to stay close to the school and warned not to go into the woods, the little girls did not obey ("pipiltzitzintin amo otlaneltocaque").[85] The girls were gone long enough to cause concern, and after some frantic searching on the part of the teachers, the five youngsters finally reappeared. All were sobbing, terrified of the devil they had encountered in the woods, whose eyes burned like fire. Doña Luz, like a good student, had not entered the woods, but had stayed behind to study. Later, when she told her parents what had happened, they explained that the woods were where the devil took the souls he had captured and should at all costs be avoided. Bad things indeed happen in the woods. If we recall, this is where Zapata's men took milpateña women to rape them during the revolution. In "Zazanili ipampatzinco comaletzin itocatzin Quiliofas" ("Cuento de la señora llamada Cleofas" ["The Story of Comadre Cleofas"]), murderers learn the lesson that they cannot hide their crimes. After robbing and murdering the widow Cleofas, two young men are eventually brought to justice when a chilacayote squash appears in the field with the face of the missing woman. Village authorities place a burning ember in the "mouth" of the woman's image on the squash, and it begins to speak. It identifies the assassins, who are then sentenced to death, and leads the widow's surviving children to the place where she had hidden all of her money.

The teachings in these stories are not always such somber affairs. Many are quite comical and evoke laughter at the expense of the outsider. In "Ce gachupin ihuan ce ahuacatl" ("Un español y un aguacate" ["A Spaniard and an Avocado"]), the Indian teases a Spaniard who doesn't know how to eat an avocado. The Spaniard approaches the Indian and asks him how one would go about eating this strange new fruit. The Indian takes the meat of the avocado for himself, gives the Spaniard the skin and the seed to eat, and escapes before the Spaniard realizes he has been duped. "Ce gachupin ihuan ce macehuali" ("Un español y un indio" ["A Spaniard and an Indian"]) again portrays the Indian getting the best of the Spaniard, but the Spaniard is at fault because he is greedy. The Spaniard arrives in Milpa Alta and sees an Indian man scraping at the ground with a stick, presumably to get rid of "jicotes" (hispanized *xicohtli*, or bumblebee). When asked what he is doing (in Spanish, which the Indian doesn't understand), the Indian replies in Nahuatl (which the Spaniard doesn't understand), "minax," which is translatable as "they sting."[86] The Spaniard hears "minas," as in mines (gold or silver perhaps), gives the Indian his horse and pistol as compensation for the "mines," and tells him to run along; the mines belong to him now. The Spaniard begins to scrape the dirt, which of course upsets the bees, which sting him in the face and eyes. The Indian is long gone, all the richer for the Spaniard's horse and pistol. In these two tales the Indian takes on the role of the trickster, the knowing subject who makes his way through a dangerous and unfair world by his wits. James Scott has read trickster tales as the "veiled cultural resistance of subordinate groups."[87] As tricksters, the Indians of doña Luz's stories win small victories in a chronically unjust society. These were some of the favorite stories of the Reading Circles.

## Reading with Nahuas

Reflection on doña Luz's experience with the academy has brought to the forefront issues related to my own research, particularly related to how academics and indigenous people (not mutually exclusive categories) can collaborate in an equitable manner. This is not a new concern: in his essay "Research, Redskins, and Reality," Vine Deloria Jr. continues the critiques developed in his now-classic *Custer Died for Your* Sins (1970) of the unequal relationships between the academy and indigenous people. Similar to doña Luz's experience, Deloria points out that these relationships have long been marked by both the denial of indigenous intellectual protagonism and the lack of appropriate remuneration.[88] Likewise, Maori scholar Linda Tuhiwai Smith's seminal work *Decolonizing Methodologies: Research and Indigenous Peoples* (1999) offers a sweeping view of the implications and obligations of researchers working with indigenous peoples and their cultural heritage sources. She suggests a series of guiding questions for intercultural research, including the following:

Who defined the research problem?
For whom is this study worthy and relevant? Who says so?
What knowledge will the community gain from this study?
What knowledge will the researcher gain from this study?
What are some likely positive outcomes from this study?
What are some possible negative outcomes?
How can the negative outcomes be eliminated?
To whom is the researcher accountable? What processes are in place to support the research, the researched and the researcher?[89]

Taking into consideration the directives articulated by indigenous intellectuals such as Deloria and Tuhiwai Smith, I have been ever mindful of the risks and responsibilities of this project. Equally, I have been concerned with the potential benefit of my work to the individuals with whom I have worked and the communities in which I have studied. A laudable model for productive and ethical scholarship has been anthropologist Keith Basso, who worked with the Western Apache on intellectual projects by and for the people that were never published for the academy. I have similarly sought ways to make meaningful contributions to my colleagues and their communities. Yet even the best-intentioned collaborative projects can go—sometimes comically—awry. Several years ago, Victoriano de la Cruz Cruz (Nahua) and I worked with a series of elders in two rural Nahua communities in Veracruz to record their life histories and other stories in Nahuatl. One of the major concerns of the older generation was that the children no longer spoke Nahuatl. They lamented the fact that even though the local elementary school was supposed to be bilingual (Nahuatl and Spanish), the children had no texts in Nahuatl and they were not taught to read or write in their native language. Victoriano and I proceeded to transcribe the elders' stories and distributed them for use in the school. We were both so pleased—Victoriano in that he was doing something in his own community to contribute to the revitalization of his language and culture, and I for providing what seemed to be an important service to a community that had welcomed me so warmly. Yet in this extraordinarily impoverished community, where so many of the people are consumed with much more pressing issues such as staving off hunger, Nahuatl-language literacy is not the first, nor even the second, priority for many. This can be attested to by the "toilet paper" provided for me on a return visit: a set of the collected stories and transcriptions stacked neatly next to the latrine.

There is no one set of theories or practices that can, in every instance, appropriately or adequately mediate such relationships. Therefore, I have attempted to develop, through ongoing conversations with Nahua colleagues and community members, a set of always-in-process guiding principles and questions that we regularly revisited. These principles and questions center on the idea of "bridging."

1. *Bridging People*: How can we cultivate intercultural collaborations wherein we all experience ourselves as interlocutors and co-creators of new collaborative knowledges? How can the process be mutually beneficial on personal and professional levels, including, as Vine Deloria Jr. has suggested, fair recognition and compensation? What kinds of practices promote an open exchange of ideas? In the case of the Reading Circles (more on this shortly), it was important to begin our meetings by identifying our strengths and interests and to articulate what we could both *learn from* and *contribute to* the group. As I learned about Nahuatl language, culture, and the nuances of Nahua rhetoric from my colleagues, I offered techniques of textual analysis and paleography, as well as database navigation skills necessary to identify primary and secondary sources.
2. *Bridging Sources*: How can we connect Nahua cultural heritage sources (and research on the same) with Nahua communities? In working with Nahua colleagues and communities, I have been acutely aware of my position as an outsider with access (at least to written texts in the archives and libraries) and of Nahua people's lack of access to these same sources. With this in mind, I have focused on not only distributing copies of available texts but also sharing practical information about how one might go about finding these texts on their own (how to enter the archive, how to navigate online databases, etc.). Another important issue related to bridging communities and their cultural heritage sources is that of creating curricula at all levels of public education (primary through university) that include and highlight indigenous voices. The authors and texts treated in this book are meant to contribute to such a project.
3. *Bridging Knowledges*: How can we provide training and mentorship in scholarly research to Nahua community members so that they may go on (if interested) to participate autonomously in the scholarly conversation that is so often dominated by non-Indians? At the same time, how can Nahua ways of knowing inform our collaborative research process? Maori scholar Linda Tuhiwai Smith explains that "the responsibility of the researcher and academics is not simply to share surface information (pamphlet knowledge) but to share the

> theories and analyses which form the way knowledge and information are constructed and represented."[90] This has meant teaching and practicing methods of analysis in the Reading Circles and providing training and access to equipment and software, as well as creating forums for native speakers to disseminate their work, for example at national and international conferences. Moreover, it has implied considering how Nahua practices of knowledge production—often experiential and collective—could guide our process.

As I mentioned in the introduction, on one of my first visits to a small rural Nahua community where I have worked, an elder suggested that as an outsider researcher I could pay my debt to the community by writing about—telling a story about—the policies and practices that located (and maintained) his community and indigenous people in general in subordinate social and economic positions in Mexican society, and to return this knowledge to the youth of his community. Sharing Luz Jiménez's work in Reading Circles was an attempt to begin to honor this obligation.

## Reading Doña Luz Jiménez with Nahuas

Anthropologist Edward Bruner has observed that "meaning is always in the present, in the here-and-now, not in such past manifestations as historical origins or the author's intentions."[91] Taking this into account, I was interested in the meaning for Nahuas that might emanate from a reading of doña Luz's work today. Literary scholar Allen Carey-Webb's discussion of reading testimony in the classroom hinted at the possible outcomes that reading doña Luz's work could have in the Nahua community: "As published validation of the lives and experiences of people that might otherwise be unknown, testimonials send the message [ . . . ] that all lives are important, that their own experiences may be worthy of serious attention and academic analysis."[92] Could seeing oneself in text really influence how a marginalized individual or group perceived their reality? What would this act of reading oneself, of recognizing oneself in printed texts do for native speakers of Nahuatl?

Ours was not the first time that native and non-native speakers have come together to read doña Luz Jiménez's work. León-Portilla's Seminario de Cultura Náhuatl at the Universidad Nacional Autónoma de México previously read and commented on doña Luz's texts in the 1980s. In describing the responses of native-speaker participants of this group,

León-Portilla notes that many heard echoes of their parents' and grandparents' stories, where others reported personal experiences similar to those of doña Luz: "La lectura ha sido revivir la memoria de lo que fue su pueblo [ . . . ] Es—así lo dicen—como ver en un espejo algo de uno mismo y reencontrarse" (Reading [doña Luz's text] was akin to reliving the memory of what their community used to be [ . . . ] It was—they say—like looking at themselves in the mirror and finding themselves again).[93] In terms of the impact of these readings, León-Portilla was of the mind that doña Luz's texts significantly influenced contemporary Nahuatl writers as a kind of cultural touchstone: "Para saber más acerca de sí mismos, pensar y enriquecer la memoria de lo que han sido y ver lo que son ahora, estos relatos han venido a ser algo como su Biblia" (To learn more about themselves, to think and enrich the memory of their people's past and present, these stories have come to be almost like a Bible).[94] Some of the native-speaker participants such as Librado Silva Galeana and Francisco Morales indeed went on to become renowned writers of contemporary Nahuatl literatures.

Our Reading Circles took place during the summers of 2008, 2009, and 2011 at the Instituto de Docencia e Investigación Etnológica de Zacatecas (Zacatecas Institute for Teaching and Research in Ethnology, IDIEZ), a non-profit research institute in Zacatecas, Mexico, where indigenous and non-indigenous students and scholars research Nahuatl language and culture. Like doña Luz, the participants have all worked and lived in multiple languages and cultures. They had also made the decision, based on varying combinations of intellectual curiosity and necessity, to leave their rural communities and move to the city. Again, like doña Luz, they have been able to make a living based on their "Indian-ness" by acquiring employment that not only allows but also promotes their language. Over the course of several weeks, we met daily in the afternoons for one or two hours to read doña Luz's words out loud and to discuss linguistic, literary, and thematic aspects of the texts. Many of our Reading Circles meetings focused on stories related to doña Luz's educational experience, specifically "La escuela" ("The School"), "Muy propio y muy correcto" ("The Proper Way of Life"), "Los buenos maestros" ("The Good Teachers"), and "El centenario" ("The Centennial"). While separated by nearly one hundred years, the Reading Circles participants and doña Luz share remarkably similar experiences with the public education system in Mexico. Regardless of Mexico's official rhetoric that espouses bilingual, bicultural, or even intercultural education, generally, education in indigenous communities continues to be an epistemologically and physically violent experience. For the Reading Circles participants, reading doña Luz brought forth many painful recollections of being punished and ridiculed for speaking their native language in school, in some cases not more than five years ago. The women in the Circles all recalled being punished by being "knuckle-knocked" in the head and being charged one peso per Nahuatl word that escaped from their lips (fines were kept in a large glass jar on the teacher's desk in the front of the room). They remembered boys being sent outside in the broiling noontime sun and made to hold a rock over their heads for an hour each time they were caught using their language. As with doña Luz's experience, they had been told that it was for their own good, that these punishments were to "help them get ahead," by getting rid of their "backwardness." At school they were taught that there were evolved languages and primitive languages (indigenous languages bore, of course, the primitive label), that sooner or later their language would disappear anyway, and that if they maintained their native language they would be permanently inhibited from learning Spanish and "successfully" integrating into society. Abelardo, who hailed from a different (although nearby) community than the other participants, claimed that he had heard of these kinds of punishments, but that he had not seen or experienced them at his school. All of the other participants found this to be quite odd (in fact, some did not believe him), since they all lived in the same general vicinity and most agreed that these punishments were a near-daily event. Several days later Abelardo brought up the topic again and revealed what he believed to be the reason that the children in his community were not punished: they simply didn't speak their language in school. "They knew better," he said. They had already internalized the lesson. Indeed, his community is considered by other neighboring villages to be one of the more "de-Indianized" enclaves. Other communities even go as far as to say that those from Abelardo's village are no longer *macehualmeh* (indigenous), but instead *coyomeh* (non-Indians, outsiders) now. In some ways it might seem that the public school system had succeeded in Abelardo's community, that the work of de-Indianization was complete. But not quite, since here he was working as an intellectual in his own language, questioning what he had been taught in school, and through doña Luz's words recognizing his own individual struggles and cultural survival. Doña Luz ends her tales in *Life and Death* by saying, "Nican yotlan notlatol ipan Momochco Malacateticpac" (Here ends my story about Milpa Alta).[95] Little did she know that it might only be the beginning or that her memories and tales of nearly one hundred years ago would today contribute to Nahuatl intellectual discovery in the twenty-first century.

## One Hundred Years, Two Hundred Kilometers (Bridging People and Texts)

Each member of the Reading Circles had a personal copy of doña Luz's texts, but access to her words and ideas did not come easily for all. I close this chapter with some observations on what I believe to be two of the more important results of our Reading Circles meetings: the identification of issues that impede Nahua access to and understanding of Nahua texts, and some of our tactics for bridging native speakers and their cultural heritage resources.

In terms of mutual intelligibility, most native speakers of Nahuatl today can understand, to a variable extent, the thirty-some other spoken regional variations. But what of the written word? I had assumed that in the same way a native speaker of English could muddle through older English texts—Shakespeare or a King James Bible, for example—a Nahua could do the same with ease. I was mistaken. While the Reading Circles participants share a common language and cultural matrix with doña Luz, they are separated by not only one hundred years but also two hundred kilometers (all participants originate from the Huasteca region of the state of Veracruz).[96] They speak and write in a dialect of the Nahuatl language that has changed along a distinct trajectory. Doña Luz's texts come to us in a form that might be considered a Central Valley Milpa Alta variation of Nahuatl, which maintains many similarities with written colonial-period texts, including similar preterit and future suffixes, lexicon, and even orthographic conventions (chosen, to be clear, by Horcasitas). Because of this, reading doña Luz's texts initially presented some challenges to the group, particularly for those who had little experience with colonial texts, or written Nahuatl for that matter.

A major challenge, one that I had frankly underestimated, was that the majority of the Reading Circles participants were not accustomed to reading or writing in their own language. This has to do with the fact that indigenous-language literacy skills are almost never taught in the public school system in Mexico. For the most part, the idea of "bilingual-bicultural" education continues to stand for the practice of using the indigenous language in the classroom only to transition the student to Spanish reading, writing, speaking, and thinking. Because of this, most Reading Circles members had only begun to read and write in Nahuatl since commencing their work and study at IDIEZ. Whereas one of the participants had been reading, writing, and studying the grammar of her language for at least eight years, others were novices, one participant with as little as two months of regular study and practice. For our Reading Circles this meant that very few had the skills necessary in order to identify and bridge differences between their own dialect and doña Luz's. Those who had minimal or no previous training specifically in colonial orthography, basic grammar, or the individual peculiarities of resources (dictionaries, grammars) were, in a word, lost. We set doña Luz's texts aside and spent several days discussing interrelated issues that were potentially creating barriers to understanding and enjoying these texts—unfamiliar orthographies and lexical items, preterit and future suffixes that in some ways were different from those employed by the group—before finally navigating the major dictionary sources available. After a few days, we returned to doña Luz. The difference was astounding, to say the least, and all participants were able to participate fully in the reading and discussion process.

On the first issue of unfamiliar orthographies, whereas there is no single standardized Nahuatl orthography, we can identify two major orthographic conventions (with extensive internal variations): 1) colonial orthographies that were developed and employed by the religious orders in the early sixteenth century and utilized for nearly five hundred years; and 2) those introduced by linguists and anthropologists in the early twentieth century, employed regularly for at least the past seventy years. The Franciscan missionary-linguists were responsible for the earliest orthography devised to represent the Nahuatl language. Based on Spanish and Latin, their system did not account for contrastive vowel length or glottal stops. The Jesuits noted the deficiencies of this system (see chapter 1 on Antonio del Rincón) and began to mark contrastive vowel length and glottal stops with a diacritical system, but outside of the great Jesuit grammarian Horacio Carochi's circle, this practice was never institutionalized.[97] Native speakers tended toward the Spanish-based (Franciscan) orthography and did not regularly mark long and short vowels or glottal stops.[98] Thus, a somewhat standardized Spanish/Latin-based orthography with occasional diacritical markings has been employed for hundreds of years in Nahuatl alphabetic texts. It was not until the early twentieth century that a different (although equally non-standard) orthographic system influenced by North American structural linguistics was introduced to the scene by linguists, many associated with the Wycliffe Bible Translators Summer Institute of Linguistics. This system has been called in turns a "practical" orthography—which begs the question of "practical for whom"—and a "contemporary" orthography, which suggests that it is the orthography of the present, which in a sense it is, but not for everyone. For example, many, but not all, contemporary Nahua writers, such as Natalio Hernández Hernández and Librado Silva Galeana, regularly employ what could be called a modified colonial orthography.[99] For our purposes here, I'll simply call this "practical" or "contemporary" strand a "newer" one.

For some Nahuas, these newer orthographies provided the means with which to reject the oppressive dominant culture. For example, in order to less resemble colonial Spanish orthographic conventions, *qu*, *c*, and *z* were exchanged for *k* and *s*, although many of the digraphs from the colonial orthographies were sometimes retained in these modified orthographies (e.g., *tl*, *qu*, *hu*, *tz*, *ch*, *tz*).[100] Nahua cultural promoter and playwright Ildefonso Maya Hernández (see chapter 5) at one point even went as far as to completely reject the Roman alphabet and invent his own orthographic system to represent the Nahuatl language (it never quite caught on). In terms of adjusting orthographies as an ideological or political move, others have suggested a calculated return to colonial orthographies since they are seen as related to "purer" or "better" versions of the language (associated with "high Nahuatl" of the noble class of the early colonial period). This is not the place to dissect these issues or their corresponding (and at times internally conflicted) ideologies of nationalism and peoplehood, but suffice it to say that there is a wide array of opinions on how and why the Nahuatl language should be written.[101] At any rate, the two strands of orthographies have existed side by side for nearly one hundred years now, with the newer orthographies gaining wider dissemination throughout the twentieth and twenty-first centuries.

Most Reading Circles participants reported having seen their language written (prior to working at IDIEZ) in the newer orthography, for example in the few grade-school primers that occasionally circulated in their communities or on geographical markers in or around their places of origin.[102] Colonial orthographies (including the one that is employed in most of doña Luz's texts) tend to include the following graphemes: *a*, *c*, *ch*, *cu*/*uc*, *e*, *h*, *hu*/*uh*, *i*, *l*, *m*, *n*, *o*, *p*, *qu*, *t*, *tl*, *tz*, *x*, *y*, *z*. Newer orthographies tend to include these: *a*, *k*, *ch*, *ku*, *e*, *j*, *i*, *l*, *m*, *n*, *o*, *p*, *s*, *t*, *tl*, *ts*, *u*, *w*, *x*, *y*. Therefore, participants whose primary exposure to their written Nahuatl language was through the newer orthographies might have expected to read "koauitl" for firewood (as it is written in Ildefonso Maya Hernández's play *Ixtlamatinij*), but instead encountered "cuahuitl" in doña Luz's text. This was not a major barrier per se, but the group had to keep in mind that reading Nahuatl texts demands a certain amount of flexibility and a basic understanding of the possible ways in which the sounds of their language might be represented. The participants had varying levels of facility with colonial orthographies since IDIEZ has taken to teaching and writing with a modified colonial orthography (its orthography does not mark vowel length, but does include the *h* for the glottal stop). The rationale for IDIEZ's use of this particular orthographic convention has been explained in the following manner:

> Hueliz tiquitztoc ceyoc piltlahcuiloltzin tlen motequihuia ipan amoxtli tlen primaria. Huahcauhquiya macehualmeh peuhqueh tlahcuiloah ica piltlahcuiloltzin: quipiya ce centzontli huan epohualli xihuitl. Quihcuilohqueh miyac amatl huan amoxtli. Tohhuantin ticnequih tictequihuiczeh piltlahcuiloltzin tlen huahcapameh, pampa iuhquinon tihueliz ticpohuaz nochi tlen quihcuilohqueh ininhuantin, huan nouhquia tihueliz ticcuamachiliz mas cualli queniuhqui motecpantoc tlahtolli tlen nahuatl.[103]
>
> (It is possible that you have seen different letters [orthographical conventions] in grade-school books. Nahua people began writing a long time ago: some four hundred and sixty years ago. They wrote many documents and books. We want to use this same orthography of the old ones because in this way you can read everything that they wrote, and you can learn/understand better how Nahuatl words are structured [grammar]).

While I am sympathetic to this position, and strongly advocate teaching the skills necessary to access nearly five hundred years of Nahuatl writing, we cannot overlook the fact that newer orthographies have been regularly used over the past hundred years not just by linguists, anthropologists, and state agencies but also by many contemporary Nahua writers and intellectuals (including Ildefonso Maya Hernández; see chapter 5). Furthermore, it cannot be stressed enough that indigenous peoples' often-anonymous voices are the sources of knowledge that appear in the linguistic and anthropological studies and most (if not all) of these studies employ the newer orthographies.[104] My concern is not which of the two major orthographies should be used today; it is instead how to ensure native-speaker access to Nahua-authored and Nahuatl-language texts (which implies both major conventions). We would do well then to consider training in the basics of newer orthographic conventions in addition to those that spring from the colonial tradition. In the Reading Circles we discussed the history and general properties of these two conventions and addressed the various peculiarities of both. We began to note patterns in doña Luz's Nahuatl that helped decode what for some—especially those new to

IDIEZ, with minimal Nahuatl-language literacy—had initially looked like a foreign language. Through these discussions we established some of the similarities and differences between doña Luz's orthography and those that the participants had seen and/or used in their communities of origin or at IDIEZ. This in turn led to interesting conversations led by native speakers regarding how their language ought to be represented. Should contrastive vowel length and glottal stops be marked in Nahuatl writing? Are the newer orthographies the way of the future, or is there something to be gained by building off of tradition (i.e., using the colonial orthographies)? Is it even necessary to standardize a Nahuatl orthography? These are important questions for native speakers to answer, and in our Reading Circles the group began to ponder these issues.

Reading the texts out loud was an important strategy for our group. This was a challenge in and of itself for Nahuas unaccustomed to reading written texts in their language, but it helped make connections between sound and possible orthographic representations. By reading out loud we were also able to clarify what were initially unfamiliar lexical items. For example, the terms below marked as "unknown" by the group during silent readings seemed more familiar once they were spoken aloud and considered in the context of the sentence:

"oyecoya" ([they] had arrived) = *ahcicoya* (Contemporary Huasteca Veracruz [CHV])
"yiman" (then) = *niman* (CHV)
"cuicaya" ([they] had not worn [the shoes]) = *huicaya* (CHV)
"iqui" (in this way) = *ihquinon* (CHV)

Reading out loud was a fine strategy for deciphering many of the terms that did not, on paper, make sense to the group. But there were plenty that even when verbalized did not find correlation with the lexicon of the participants. For these we relied upon the major dictionary resources available to us (Alonso de Molina's *Vocabulario en la lengua castellana y mexicana* [1555–1571], Rémi Siméon's *Diccionario de la lengua nahuatl o mexicana* [1885], and Frances Karttunen's *An Analytical Dictionary of Nahuatl* [1992]). These rich resources, however, require at least minimal knowledge of colonial orthographies (since two of the three were produced before the twentieth century and all use a colonial or modified colonial orthography). Many of our readings led to discussions of "doña Luz wrote this way, but we [the native-speaker participants] would write it this way." We began to compile a list of orthographic, lexical, and grammatical variations of dialects of Nahuatl separated by space and time, creating a bridge between doña Luz and her readers.

One issue we encountered had to do with the differences between the two dialects in forming the preterit tense. Our main challenge wasn't so much recognizing the subtle distinctions (this came quickly), but how to reconstruct the modified preterit verb stem to its present-tense form, since it is the present-tense verb stem that is found in the major resources. We availed ourselves of Lockhart's reconstruction strategies in *Nahuatl as Written* as well as his clear explanations of how to best utilize the major dictionaries mentioned above (Molina, Siméon, and Karttunen) as we searched for the definitions of new or unfamiliar terms.[105] The group discussed how Molina, for example, employed certain orthographic conventions, cited verbs in their present-tense forms, and alphabetized and organized entries in a particular, if not peculiar, fashion. Siméon's text shares similarities with but also differs from Molina, especially in the way he grouped the possible uses of a word under one main heading. Karttunen's dictionary is unique in attesting contrastive vowel length and glottal stops and in using separate sections for words beginning with *ch*, *cu*, *tl*, and *tz*. Since at the time all of the Reading Circles participants were in some capacity contributing to a monolingual dictionary and grammar of contemporary Nahuatl in the Huasteca Veracruz region (one of the major projects at IDIEZ; see a brief description between chapters 1 and 2), this experience demonstrated to them that they were joining an ongoing tradition of dictionary making—one that they could follow, or from which they might break. We made a conscious effort to use all three sources simultaneously as an exercise in familiarizing ourselves with the general organization of each. Even when we came across the term we were looking for in the first source, we still insisted on consulting the other two as well. Our study of the dictionaries was by no means exhaustive, but at the very least provided the opportunity for practice and reflection as related to reading and writing in Nahuatl in the past and the present.

A final observation on the issue of orthographies: Abelardo de la Cruz and I worked together outside of the Reading Circles, translating two of the essays that doña Luz had contributed to *Mexihcatl Itonalama*, both of which employed the newer orthographic convention. Since Abelardo had some experience with orthographic variations and grammar, our main challenge with these texts had to do with doña Luz's lexicon. One might think this would have been a non-issue; as unfamiliar terms were identified, we should have been able to simply look them up in one dictionary or another. Yet the only major dictionaries and grammar resources that might assist a Nahua from today's Huasteca in understanding a Nahua from the Central Valley more than one hundred years ago require a basic knowledge of the modified colonial orthographies, not to mention Nahuatl morphology. In order to use these resources, we had to identify the root word or verb stem as it was presented in the newer orthography and then re-write it to its potential colonial form, hoping to find this "new" term in one of the dictionaries. This was excellent practice for navigating orthographies and resources, but was not always successful. Whereas the development of more sophisticated dictionary and grammar resources that use the newer orthographies might seem to be the solution here, again if native speakers are to access centuries of intellectual work in their own language, we cannot ignore the importance of instruction in colonial orthographies. In the meantime, if the goal is repatriation of knowledges, we might consider how we can teach, read, and write in both colonial and newer orthographies. This might seem like a naïve charge to take up an unwieldy task, but our Reading Circles' success in accessing doña Luz Jiménez's storywork is proof that it can be done and that native speakers are certainly up to the challenge.

TLEN NAMAN 4

# *Cihuatequiuh (Women's Work)*

by Sabina Cruz de la Cruz
(written in Zacatecas, Mexico, and New Orleans, United States, January 2013)

Sabina Cruz de la Cruz (fig. 6) is a native speaker of Nahuatl from Tecomate, a small community outside of Chicontepec, in the Mexican state of Veracruz. She completed an undergraduate degree in law in 2007 at the Universidad Autónoma de Zacatecas. Focusing on federal labor law, her thesis was entitled "Discriminación desde la ley" (Legalized Discrimination). As part of her studies, she also translated federal labor laws into Nahuatl. At present she is a research associate at IDIEZ, where she teaches Nahuatl language and culture in Mexico and abroad, and she concurrently contributes to the IDIEZ monolingual dictionary project. She is also completing a master's degree in education with an emphasis in history. Her area of expertise is indigenous primary and secondary education.

## Cihuatequiuh

Na notocah Sabina Cruz de la Cruz. Nicpiya cempohualli huan mahtlactli xihuitl, nihuallauh pan ce pilaltepetzin itocah Tecomate; Chicontepec, Veracruz. Notatahhuan nocca yoltoqueh. Nicpiya macuilli noicnihuan, tlen cihuameh na nitepipi, nicpiya ce nomimi. Nimomachtih, nochi tlamachtiliztli pan Tecomate hazta telebachillerato. Teipan niyahqui pan altepetl tlen Mexco nitequitic pan calli tlahco xihuitl pan

*Figure 6.* Sabina Cruz de la Cruz. Courtesy of the author.

xihuitl tlen 2000, cualli nitequitic. Zampa notatah tlahuel techillihyaya ma timomachtican. Huanquinon nomimi ya achtohui yahqui Zacatecas huanya ce imachicniuh notatah, ya quipalehuih ma calaqui pan caltlamachtiliztli. Huacca na nicnehnehuilih axcanah nicnequi nitequitiz zan pan calli, notatah tlen techillia nopa tlahuel cualli para tohhuantin, axcanah titlaihyohuizceh.

Teipan na niahcico nican pan Zacatecas. Achtohui nicchiuhqui examen, tlahuel nimahmahuiyaya pampa nimoilliyaya axcanah nicalaquiz pan nopa caltlamachtiliztli tlen Leyes. Huan quemman nechillihqueh quena nicpanoltih examen tlahuel niyolpacqui huan notatahhuan nouhquiya. Peuhqui nimomachtia, tlahuel ohuih nicmachillih pampa axcanah nochi niccuamachiliyaya tlahtolli ica español, na nochipa nizaniloh nahuatl pan nopilaltepeuh. Pero iuhcatza nimomachtihtiyahqui pan cequin semestre nimocauhqui huan zampa nicchiuhqui huan queuhquinon niquizzato.

Quemman nimomachtiyaya pan eyi semestre peuhqui nechtemoa ce tlacatl huan axcanah mexicano, na axquemman niquitztoya huanya nizaniloh ce tonatiuh huan peuhqui nechnohnotza nahuatl, na axcanah nicnequiyaya nicnanquilliz ica nahuatl. Peuhqui huanya nizaniloa. Teipan nouhquiya peuhquiya nizaniloa ica náhuatl. Zan ayicanah niyohuiyaya pan Instituto de Docencia e Investigación Etnológica de Zacatecas (IDIEZ), nechtemohqui miac hueltah, nouhquiya yahqueh nechtemoah cequinoqueh notequixpoyohuan pampa quinequih ma nicalaqui huanya inihhuantin. Ce tonatiuh, na nicnehnehuilih quenque ce acahya tlen axcanah ichan Mexco, ya quinequi quimatiz huan quinequi techzancehcotiliz huanya ya. Nicnehnehuilih huan teipan niquillih quena niyaz, niyahqui, nicamatqui nochi, queniuhqui tequitih ica nahuatl, na nicmatiyaya nizaniloz huan axcanah nicmatiyaya queniuhqui moihcuiloa ce tlamantli. Naman na nitequiti pan Instituto de Docencia e Investigación Etnológica de Zacatecas (IDIEZ). Nouhquiya nicmachillih quentzin ohuih pero niman nihuelqui nitlahcuiloa ica nahuatl.

Teipan peuhquiya niquinmachtia momachtianih tlen Estados Unidos pan verano, tlahuel nicamatqui nopa tlamachtiliztli. Hazta naman nichuica chicueyi xihuitl nitequiti nican, nouhquiya ni tequitl quichihua ma tiyacan pan Estados Unidos, na niyahtoc omeh hueltah ce semestre niontlamachtia pan Universidad tlen Tulane, New Orleans, Louisiana, ica naman eyi pan xihuitl 2013 niitztoc zampa. Nouhquiya tlen itztoqueh pan IDIEZ yahtoqueh pan Estados Unidos pampa naman mochihua tlamachtiliztli tlen verano nepa. Nicpenzaroa ni tequitl tlahuel yehyectzin huan cualli, tlahuel hueyi ica techhuicatoc totlahtol, hueliz niquihtoa totlahtol yoltoc axcanah mictoc.

Monequi ma titlamachtican ica totlahtol nochimeh macehualmeh. Huan axcanah zan coyomeh tlen momachtiah huan quichihua inintequiuh. Niquihtoa quena hueli, nihuallauh ce pilaltepetzin, nizaniloa huan naman nitequiti/nitlamachtia ica nahuatl. Nouhquiya nizaniloa castilla huanya noicnihuan, nizaniloa nahuatl huan castiyah huan quemman niyauh niquinpaxaloah notatahhuan Tecomate nouhquiya nizaniloa nahuatl. Ce tlamantli tlen maz nechpactia, tlamantli tlen mochihua nocca; ce ilhuitl mochichiquilhuia, quemman monamictiah, momapacah, mochihua cencah; nopa quihtoznequi yoltoc tonemiliz.

Nopa ce hueyi tequitl tlen mochiuhtoc haztah naman tlen nonemiliz. Nocca polihui miac tlamantli tlen hueliz mochihua ica totlahtol. Naman nicnequi niquittaz ma oncah tlamachtiliztli ica nahuatl ica nochimeh macehualmeh huan pan tomexco, tlahuel monequi mochihuaz ni tequitl. Niquihtoa tlahuel monequi ma mochihua ni tlamachtiliztli ica náhuatl ica nochimeh macehualmeh, maz ica pipilmeh pampa ininhuantin huelizceh quichihua para axcanah ma polihui totlahtol, ma quimatican canin huallohuih.

Naman nouhquiya niquihtoz, na nimomachtia nomaestría pan altepetl tlen Zacatecas, nocaltlamachtican itocah Centro de Actualización del Magisterio en Zacatecas (CAMZ), nimomachtia "Educación Histórica," nichuica ce xihuitl huan tlahco nimomachtia nocca nechpoloa tlahco xihuitl tlamachtiliztli huan nouhquiya monequi nictlamiz notesis pan julio tlen 2013 tlen ica nimotitularoz huan itocah "La enseñanza del náhuatl para el fomento de la identidad nacional." Ni tlamachtiliztli nouhquiya nicmachillihqui ohuih quemman nicpehualtih, miac chantequitl, nitlapohuaz miac, oncac tonatiuh niquihtohqui ayoccanah nimomachtiz. Quemman niquihtohqui ayoccanah nimomachtiz, huanya nizaniloh John Sullivan huan peuhqui nechtlaillia ica tlamachtiliztli, nechillih ya nechapoyaroa ica ni maestría. Huan queuhquinon nicnehnehuillih quena melahuac tlen nechillih, huanquinon niccencuillih nimomachtia. Tlahuel niyolpactoc iuhcatza ohuih tlen nicchihualtoc pan nonemiliz, maz ica tlamachtiliztli pero naman nicmati quena nihueli nicchihuaz tlen nicnequi huan nouhquiya ica notequiuh.

## Women's Work

My name is Sabina Cruz de la Cruz and I am thirty years old. I come from a small community called Tecomate (Chicontepec, Veracruz). My parents are still alive. I have five siblings. I am the oldest of four sisters and we have one older brother. I completed all of my studies from primary school through high school in Tecomate. After that, in 2000, I went to Mexico City where I worked as a domestic servant for six months. My father again urged my siblings and me to continue our studies. First my older brother went to Zacatecas where he stayed with my father's cousin. He helped my brother get into the university. Then I thought to myself: I don't want to spend my life working in a house as a servant. The advice my father gave was good for us: If we studied, he told us, we wouldn't suffer.

So not long after that I arrived here in Zacatecas. First I took the entrance examination. I was really afraid because I didn't think I would be admitted to the law school. And when they told me I had passed the exam, I was so happy, my parents too. I started to study. It was really hard because I didn't understand all of the words in Spanish. I had always spoken Nahuatl in my community. But I went along studying for several semesters, and I managed to stay in school and kept moving ahead.

During my third semester, this man [John Sullivan, co-founder of IDIEZ] started coming around looking for me. He wasn't a Mexican and I hadn't seen him before. I talked to him one day and he started talking to me in Nahuatl, but I didn't want to respond to him in Nahuatl [I didn't want him to know I spoke it]. But then I started to talk with him and I started to speak Nahuatl with him. But I still didn't go to the Zacatecas Institute for Teaching and Research in Ethnology (IDIEZ) [where he worked]. He came looking for me many times, and so did some of my friends who worked at the institute to recruit me to work with them. One day I thought to myself, "Why does this person who isn't even from Mexico want to know about us, and why does he want us to work with him?" So I went to check it out. I went to the institute, and I liked how they were all working in Nahuatl. I knew how to speak in my language, but didn't know how to write it. Now I work there. It was hard at first but it didn't take long to learn to write in Nahuatl.

Next I started to teach Nahuatl to students from the United States that came to study with us during the summer; I really like that class. I have been working at IDIEZ now for eight years and with this job we also go to the United States. I have already taught two semesters at Tulane University in New Orleans, Louisiana, and now I am here again for the third time. My colleagues at IDIEZ have also traveled to the United States to teach because we are doing the summer classes there now. I think that this work is beautiful and good. Our language has taken us to faraway places. I can say that our language is alive; it has not died.

I think it is really important that we *macehualmeh* (Nahuas) study in our own language, that it isn't just the *coyomeh* (outsiders) that study it or research it. I know we can do it. I am from a small village, I speak Nahuatl, and I work in my language and teach in my language. I also speak Spanish. With my siblings I speak Nahuatl and Spanish, and when I go to visit my parents in Tecomate, I speak Nahuatl. Another thing that makes me very happy are the ways in which we still practice our culture: Xantolo [Day of the Dead] and Lavamanos [a ritual kinship ceremony between parents and godparents]. These are things we do today just as we did long ago, and this to me is an indication that our culture is alive.

This is the work that has been carried out so far in my life. There are so many things we have yet to do with our language. Now I want to see classes taught in Nahuatl for indigenous people, and here in Mexico. We need this. I say we need classroom instruction for all indigenous people [of all ages] in our language, but even more so for children because they are the ones who will ensure we do not lose our language. They must not forget where they come from.

Right now I am completing my master's degree in education (history) in Zacatecas, at the Centro de Actualización del Magisterio en Zacatecas

(Zacatecas Center for Continuing Education in Teaching, CAMZ). I have been studying for a year and a half now, and I have half a year to go of classwork and then I will write my thesis by July of 2013. My thesis is entitled "Teaching in Nahuatl for the Development of National Identity." The master's program was hard, too, when I started: a lot of homework and reading. One day I said to myself, "I can't do this, I am going to quit." When I decided to quit I talked to John Sullivan about it. He gave me some good advice, and he promised to help me and support me through the process. So I thought about it and I said to myself, "You know what? He's right; I can do this," so I kept going. I am very happy even though things have not been easy for me, especially with my studies. But I know today I can do anything I put my mind to, in my life and in my work.

CHAPTER 5

# *Performing the Recovery of Indigeneity*

Ildefonso Maya Hernández

Many of the previous chapters focused on Nahua intellectuals who have lived in or near Mexico City, the cultural capital of the Mexican nation. In this chapter we move to the predominantly indigenous Huasteca region of Mexico during the latter half of the twentieth century. Our protagonist is Ildefonso Maya Hernández (1936–2011), a Nahua bilingual-bicultural educator, playwright, artist, and activist who spent the majority of his lifetime in Huejutla de Reyes, Hidalgo.[1] Regardless of his chosen medium, the main topics of Maya's large corpus of intellectual work depict the challenges faced by indigenous people in Mexico today, and the recovery and celebration of Nahua knowledges and culture. While Maya was an accomplished painter, boasting over 140 large-scale murals scattered throughout the states of Veracruz and Hidalgo, as well as countless works on canvas, this chapter centers primarily on his work as writer and director of open-air theater through an analysis of his play *Ixtlamatinij* (*The Learned Ones*, [1987] 2007). Considered by Maya to be one of his finest works, *Ixtlamatinij* takes on the controversial topic of the state co-optation of indigenous people as agents of assimilation to dominant culture in their roles as bilingual-bicultural teachers. A state-trained bilingual-bicultural teacher himself, Maya's critique of the theories and methods of this educational model stems largely from firsthand experience within the system. I close this chapter with attention to his work as a modern-day *tlahcuiloh*—writer and painter of what he entitled *Ama Tlanamaquilistli*, or *Pages/Books of Knowledge*.

## Meeting Maya, Master Storyteller

In 1953 Ildefonso Maya wrote a grammar of the Nahuatl language, entitled "Nauatl gramatical." In the opening pages, he introduces himself to the reader and establishes his subjectivity in relation to dominant culture:

> Mi nombre es Piltat, mi lengua materna es el nauatl o mexkatl, porque la ranchería en donde yo nací, que se llama Chahuatlán, Municipio de Ilamatlán, Ver., todos hablamos el nauatl o mexkatl, porque todos somos indios y aunque yo ya no vivo en mi tierra, sigo hablando el nauatl o mexkatl, que me enseñaron mis padres. [ . . . ] Esta modesta aportación que pongo en sus manos, es para que conozcan y aprendan no como dicen el dialecto nauatl, sino como la lengua nauatl, que como tal, está al nivel de cualquiera de las lenguas modernas de nuestro tiempo, como: el inglés, Alemán, Español, Ruso, Italiano o Frances. Advierto de que se trata de una lengua viva y de uso ordinario. A los hombres y a las mujeres que habitamos a este país: México, sepa que habemos más de tres millones de indios que usamos la lengua nauatl o mexkatl; a pesar de la imposición oficial del uso del español, que a saber claramente el castellano sí es dialecto del español de la península Ibérica. Insisto y me resta ofrecer esta pequeña obra para que aprendan el nauatl o mexkatl que realmente es la lengua nuestra que no hay que dejar perder nunca, como perdí mi nombre de Piltat y que hoy me llamo: Ildefonso Maya Hernández, aunque nunca ha sido de mi conformidad. Perdí mi nombre; pero la lengua que me enseñaron mis padres, la seguiré usando, aunque hable inglés, Italiano, Español, Kiliua, Tsoji, Pipil, Ña,Ñu porque el Nauatl o Mexkatl es mi primera lengua. IKA NOCHI NO YOLO, KIA KEJ NI MECH ON YOLMELAUA, TLASKAMATIJ GRACIAS.[2]
>
> (My name is Piltat and my native language is Nahuatl or Mexcatl because in the village where I was born, Chahuatlán, in the municipality of Ilamatlán Veracruz, we all speak Nahuatl or Mexcatl, because we are all Indians. And although I no longer live there, I still speak Nahuatl or Mexcatl, the language my parents taught me. [ . . . ] This modest contribution that I present to you is so that you may know and learn how the language Nahuatl (not a dialect like some say) is equal to any of the modern languages of our time such as English, German, Spanish, Russian, Italian, or French. Nahuatl is a living language that is used every day. To the men and women who live in this country Mexico: you should know that we are more than three million Indians that

speak Nahuatl or Mexcatl, even in the face of the official imposition of Spanish (and truth be told, Castilian *is* a dialect of the Spanish of the Iberian Peninsula). It remains for me to give you this humble work so that you can learn that Nahuatl or Mexcatl is actually our true language and that we ought never to lose it in the same way I lost my name, Piltat. Today my name is Ildefonso Maya Hernández, even though I have never approved of it [having this name imposed upon me]. I lost my name, but I will continue to use the language my parents taught me—even though I can also speak English, Italian, Spanish, Kiliua, Tzotjil[?], Pipil, and Ñahñú—because Nahuatl or Mexcatl is my first language. WITH ALL MY HEART, I TELL YOU ALL OF THIS IS TRUE. THANK YOU THANK YOU.)

One of Maya's main concerns, as evidenced above and elsewhere in his work, is the legacy of colonialism in the present day, particularly the ways in which indigenous people and their languages have been marginalized. In this introductory paragraph to his grammar, he offers a corrective to "official" history and rejects the commonly held yet erroneous belief that his language is a dialect. Maya's use of the Spanish language to critique its imposition exemplifies Fernando Ortiz's well-known concept of *transculturation*, the strategic give and take of cultural elements. In discussing transculturation, Mary Louise Pratt has maintained that "while subjugated peoples cannot readily control what emanates from the dominant culture, they do determine to varying extents what they absorb into their own, and what they use it for" (6). Maya's use of the tools of dominant culture to critique and contest marginalization in the earlier days of his career foretells the nature of his work in the following decades.

I had the opportunity to meet with El Profesor, as everyone affectionately called him, on various occasions in 2008, 2009, and 2010 at his home in Huejutla de Reyes. Prior to my first visit, I spoke with him briefly on the telephone to arrange the interview. After establishing the date I would arrive, I inquired as to how I would find his home (which also served as the Centro Cultural de la Huasteca Hidalguense [Hidalgo Huastecan Cultural Center], a local museum of sorts). Maya told me to go to the *zócalo* (main plaza) and simply ask anyone I came across if they knew where El Profesor lived. This seemed like folly, but I soon learned that indeed nearly everyone in Huejutla knew where to find him. And most held strong opinions about this outspoken and at times controversial public figure; the majority loved him to a fault, some found him to be exasperating, and still others were simply not quite sure what to make of him or his work.

The taxi drivers of Huejutla professed effusive adoration for Maya. Nearly every taxi driver I encountered not only knew El Profesor but also credited him with what in some cases seemed like miraculous feats. Maya cured one fellow's alcoholism, helped another kick a drug habit, and taught one to read and still another to paint. Maya had great admiration for the taxi drivers as well. Much to the chagrin of local bureaucrats, instead of following provincial Mexican custom that demands obsequious homage to politicians and other power brokers, Maya was notorious for thanking taxi drivers whenever he was in front of a crowd or had a microphone in his hands. He was always keen to recognize the men who had chauffeured him around the region, whether it was to teach Nahuatl to nuns and priests or to visit the local "house of ill repute," where he taught reading, writing, and typing skills to prostitutes. On several occasions the *taxistas* had pooled their money together to bail Maya out of jail, once when he was incarcerated for being a bit too overt in his critique of political corruption in a mural he was painting. Apparently, the town council of Huejutla, the sponsor of the mural, did not take well to being parodied in such a public forum. Maya also had an affectionate following of a group of twenty-five homosexual men whom he instructed in the art of making piñatas so that, I was told, instead of being referred to as *los putos* (the "fags"), they would be known as *los de las piñatas* (the fellows who make the piñatas).

When I stepped out of the taxi at his home, I found El Profesor sitting—as he did most days—in the shade of his home's doorway in the company of his wife Felipa and their scrappy rat terrier Cachito. He looked me up and down, grunted, and struggled out of his chair. Stooped and dependent on a cane to walk, Maya's body seemed tired, but his eyes still twinkled with mischief and his mind and tongue were sharp. He was known to be funny and sarcastic with all whom he encountered, and I would not be an exception. After silently inspecting me for several minutes, he invited me to sit down next to him and to turn on my tape recorder ("You people love to record things," he said, "so turn the thing on!"). And then he began to spin his tales. I was barely allowed a word in edgewise, and when I did have the occasional opportunity to ask a question, he answered monosyllabically and then returned to whatever topic he found more suitable. Maya was happy to talk, but he was in charge. Whether his stories were fact or fiction, one cannot be sure. What became clear, however, is that I was in the presence of a master storyteller. He spoke of being a *mozo*, or servant, for Frida Kahlo and Diego Rivera as a youth: "Frida era hoooorr-rrrible, fea, fea, fea. Su cara, su carácter, su pintura: horrible" (Frida was horrible, ugly, ugly, ugly. Her face, her personality, her painting, all of it horrible); of how he was awarded a scholarship that made it possible for him to finish his secondary education and another that sent him to the University of Washington in the United States for undergraduate education; of taking acting classes at Bellas Artes in Mexico City; of playing bit parts in movies with Mexican film star María Félix: "nunca tenía roles importantes, pero me reconocieron por morir bien" (I never held important roles, but I was known for being good at dying); and finally of being flown in a helicopter to the presidential residence, Los Pinos, during José López Portillo's term, and calling the president a "*cabrón*" for leaving him waiting all day without having been offered food or water. Maya mused about his large-scale popular theater productions that he insisted brought the grown men in the audience to tears, he pondered his struggles with the Catholic Church and his own spirituality, and he reflected on his native language, which included a lengthy presentation of a new Nahuatl orthography of his own invention that he was sure would catch on—alas, it never did. Some of his stories were so incredible that I began to wonder if he wasn't pulling my leg, or at the very least having a bit of fun with his captive audience. However, over the course of our meetings, I have decided that if anyone was capable of doing all of these things, it was surely Ildefonso Maya.

He read love poems aloud that he wrote over fifty years ago; reminisced about his travels in the Mexican Republic, Europe, and the United States; and discussed working with indigenous peoples of western Mexico on his first assignment as a bilingual schoolteacher. Much like many of his fellow indigenous bilingual-bicultural educators, Maya was first assigned to a region where his native language, Nahuatl, was not spoken. He spent a great deal of time talking about the primary reason he has been so prolific (some three hundred [mostly unpublished] plays, boxes of poetry, stacks upon stacks of drawings, and of course, the paintings and the murals): it was his belief that God wanted him to celebrate, revitalize, and promote Nahua culture. Maya avoided alcohol; he said it was a "childish distraction." He was too busy "telling the truth as God orders," a truth heavy with social, political, and cultural criticism. His interests were broad, dealing with a spectrum of issues that affect indigenous communities in Mexico, including conflicts between mestizo and indigenous cultures; the role of the Catholic Church in Mexican society; traditional indigenous religious life and ceremonies; race, ethnicity, class, and gender; education and language; urbanization; politics, especially economic policies; and land reform.

One of Maya's stories stood out as particularly emblematic of his style of social commentary. According to Maya, for most of its existence Huejutla had been a relatively small town with limited or at least difficult access to larger cities. Daily life changed significantly in the early 1980s once a paved highway was built, connecting Huejutla to the larger town of Pachuca (120 kilometers away) and the nation's capital, Mexico City (230 kilometers away). The conveniences of "modern" living and the rapid exchange of goods and ideas, as well as the social ills that Maya associated with the metropolis (drugs, increased crime, and rampant consumerism) flowed freely into this once-sleepy provincial town. Maya's initial artistic response to the arrival of the highway was a charcoal drawing of the peaceful city center being surrounded by a giant serpent. Several years later, along with dozens of the schoolchildren he taught at the local secondary school, he built a massive serpent (in the fashion of Chinese New Year dragons) complete with a papier-mâché head with fiery eyes, a gaping mouth, and sharp fangs. As part of a dance performance of the Bonampak Ballet in the public square, Maya brought this serpent, spanning some sixty-five meters and supported by over one hundred young people. As he tells it, spectators watched curiously, perhaps uncomfortably, while the students/performers entered the mouth of the serpent to take up its skeleton structure. After the serpent had "devoured" most of Huejutla's school-age children, it undulated around the main plaza. Finally, after encircling the plaza and the onlookers, the serpent stopped and stayed silently immobile for several minutes. Without warning, the serpent began to shake violently and opened its fanged mouth to "vomit" out a man dressed as a priest holding hands with a tall white foreigner, both smiling innocently. The highway, in this rendering, ate the innocents of the town, with the only return being the "gift" of priests and foreigners.

Maya's work is anything but subtle. While a devout Catholic, his work is nonetheless highly critical of the Church. One of his more provocative drawings portrays a congregation of pious Indians in prayer, a dog on top of the altar eating the Host, and a priest oblivious to both, lazily gazing out the doorway. He proudly brought this drawing out at the end of our last visit in response to yet another one of my questions he had no intention of answering. In presenting the drawing he said: "You have come here with your list of questions, but you already know the answers. Any human being, regardless of the language they speak, knows deep down what is right and wrong, and any human being is capable of understanding my work. I don't hide anything; you don't need me to walk you through the meaning of my work. You will see what you are capable of seeing, and that is enough." He paused for a moment and then, always the mischief-maker, said: "But seriously . . . if you can't figure this one out [referring to the drawing], you must be really stupid."

In our conversations he referred often to his fascination as a child with the storytellers of his community, as well as an acute awareness from a very young age of the performative nature of both Catholic and indigenous religious ceremonies. He recalled that his very first popular theater production was when he was a seven-year-old boy playing the priest in a "play" he had organized, in which he led the village children to the river. At the head of the procession, he carried a large wooden cross fashioned out of sticks found in the woods. Even though Maya benefited from classical theater training at Bellas Artes in Mexico City during his early twenties, and was a professed aficionado of Greek tragedies and Shakespeare, he intentionally distanced himself from Western and classical theater in his own productions. In his desire to present a faithful reproduction of indigenous quotidian experiences and the problems of their communities, Maya left behind what he characterized as the "false world" of stage, panels, and scrims and instead took most of his productions to the street (or water well, or thatch hut). If the setting of the play was the river, that is precisely where it was staged. Besides lending a sense of urgency and authenticity to the production, he reminded me (with a wink and a smile), "It's a lot cheaper that way."

In order to set the stage for a close examination of one of Maya's most widely performed and critically celebrated plays, *Ixtlamatinij*, I offer a closer look at bilingual-bicultural education and the recruitment of indigenous teachers for this program. As an indigenous bilingual teacher himself, Maya undoubtedly gleaned parts of the storyline from his personal experience and observations in the communities in which he worked.

## Bilingual-Bicultural Education in Late Twentieth-Century Mexico

In Mexico, the public school system is widely recognized as an agent of sociocultural integration, with its principal goal the creation of a sense of belonging to the nation.[3] Through the uniform curriculum, the citizenry learns and practices the habits of the dominant culture's ideal citizen. At school, "correct" social behaviors are taught and enforced, while those deemed undesirable are eradicated. In *Proyectos étnicos y proyectos nacionales* (1983), Stefano Varese has outlined how this "creation of a sense of belonging" via Mexican public education has been a contradictory process for the state and has also had devastating effects in indigenous communities. Varese's study shows how nationalism as inculcated through the state's educational apparatus is actually at odds with the neoliberal capitalist model. The problem lies in the fact that while the educational model of the 1970s and 1980s purported to culturally and linguistically integrate and assimilate peripheral/minority cultures, the maintenance of these communities as marginalized sectors of the population—as on-demand low-salaried laborers and self-sufficient subsistence farmers when their labor was not needed—was essential to the function of this particular economic system.[4] It follows then that the integration and assimilation process must remain incomplete. Varese also explains how assimilative education has created a series of negative outcomes for indigenous communities. As it imposes an approved "Mexican" version of subjectivity, it (intentionally or not) has done so at the expense of indigenous ways of learning and knowing. Therefore, this educational model tends to create a formal opposition between what is framed as "legitimate" Western knowledge and "backward" indigenous knowledge. By extension, it separates what is taught at school from the quotidian experiences of indigenous students, essentially removing the family and indigenous community from their roles as legitimate educators.[5] Even so, Jorge Hernández Díaz has called our attention to the way in which state-sponsored assimilative education has paradoxically provided the very means with which indigenous communities and their leaders could contest the dominant-culture system.[6] Through formal education, indigenous citizens have learned to navigate the framework of the hegemonic order and acquire the tools—such as the language of dominant culture—necessary to effectively negotiate their social, political, and economic positions in Mexican society.

As discussed in the earlier chapter on doña Luz Jiménez, the educational policies of early twentieth-century Mexico were aimed at the transformation of the indigenous citizenry into a certain kind of de-Indianized subject. Language, dress, profession, and consumption patterns were targeted areas of modification. The 1930s heralded the government's renewed interest in indigenous culture and language, but the underlying rationale continued to be facilitating the assimilation of the Indian to a "civilized" way of life.[7] On the whole, twentieth-century public education for indigenous citizens of Mexico can be characterized as hostile to indigenous ways of knowing/being, especially in regards to language. By the 1970s and 1980s, however, a slight shift is evident. The general policy of the explicit eradication of indigenous languages transitioned to (an albeit weak) state-sponsored promotion of indigenous languages in the classroom as part of what came to be known as the bilingual-bicultural educational model.[8] In this model, the mother tongue serves as a bridge; once the indigenous student has a basic command of Spanish, the indigenous language is progressively eliminated from the curriculum. In support of this program, in 1978 the Federal Ministry of Education created a specific subsection dedicated to overseeing the elementary education of indigenous children, the Dirección General de Educación Indígena (Department of Indigenous Education, DGEI). The DGEI was also responsible for selecting and training indigenous bilingual-bicultural educators to serve in primarily monolingual (indigenous-language) communities.[9]

Since the very beginning of the bilingual-bicultural project of the DGEI, indigenous recruits have been notoriously ill equipped in both preparation and resources.[10] Most were sent for training to the Dirección General de Capacitación y Mejoramiento Profesional del Magisterio (Department of Training and Professionalization of Teachers, DGCMPM), which claimed to prepare indigenous teachers for both "regular service" (for non-indigenous students) and "bilingual-bicultural service" (for indigenous students).[11] Already at a distinct disadvantage from their mestizo counterparts (who more often than not had received a higher-quality education prior to their enrollment in the program), indigenous bilingual teachers were asked to do twice the amount of work during their training periods. They were given extra materials, beyond those required for the "regular service" training, that they were to study on their own. As opposed to focusing on issues of pedagogy, or perhaps advanced study in Spanish (the bilingual teacher's *second* language), the obligatory extra materials encompassed a broad range of highly complex topics: legal information to assist communities in questions of the law; linguistics to better understand the general properties of the indigenous language; tactics for community development; and anthropology.[12] After graduating from the program, the indigenous teachers were expected to serve rural indigenous schools not only as educators but also as ad hoc lawyers, linguists, social workers, and anthropologists. Add to this the fact that more often than not they were sent to serve in a community that did not utilize his/her own indigenous language.

It could be argued that the inadequate pedagogical and Spanish-language training of the recruited indigenous teachers was aimed at ensuring the reproduction of what postcolonial theorist Homi Bhabha has called "a particularly appropriate form of colonial subjectivity."[13] That is, indigenous bilingual educators were afforded the kind of education that assured a citizenry that was *nearly* the same as the dominant other, but not quite.[14] This mimicry, or incomplete performance if you will, codifies the subordinate role of Indians in Mexican society: assimilation to dominant cultural norms does not mean becoming equal; it means becoming less Indian, more manageable or governable, all the while continuing to accept belonging to an inexpensive labor force that is self-sufficient when not needed (such as subsistence farmers). The educational system, then, can be read as molding Indians into "authorized versions of otherness" in order to ensure continued subordination under the guise of limited inclusion.[15] Some of the general premises of the bilingual-bicultural teacher program—creating employment, providing training, and teaching students in a supposedly culturally sensitive manner—are all on paper quite laudable. The actual practices of this program, however, reveal serious flaws. For by accepting an often desperately needed job, the indigenous bilingual-bicultural teacher becomes an agent of the state, asked to participate in and even promote his/her own cultural and epistemological annihilation in the classroom.

Late twentieth-century manifestations of attempts to manage and coopt indigenous subjects have been effectively couched in terms of celebrating multiculturalism. Anthropologists such as Peter Wade, however, remind us that "celebrating multiculturalism" should be considered a red flag in that it is often used as a method to avoid social unrest, as "a tactical manouevre for coping with protest."[16] Charles Hale has observed this phenomenon in Guatemala as a "menacing political project"; in his view, neoliberal multiculturalism "promotes the cultural rights of indigenous peoples while perpetuating their economic and political marginalization."[17] Susan Rippberger echoes Wade and Hale in stating that "the rhetoric of pluralism may act as a façade to disguise a continuing inequitable structure or to delay reform."[18] In this light, the timing of the bilingual-bicultural model of education of the 1970s and 1980s should give us pause in that it correlates closely with a sharp uptick in social unrest in Mexico. Was the bilingual-bicultural teacher training and educational reform aimed at creating a cadre of indigenous collaborators who could potentially neutralize current and future rebellions? Were indigenous communities proffered a false sense of inclusion by acknowledging cultural—but notably not economic or political—rights?[19] Is it simply a coincidence that the Huasteca Hidalguense—where Ildefonso Maya was eventually sent as a bilingual-bicultural teacher and where he wrote and staged his many open-air theater performances, including *Ixtlamatinij*—was known to be one of the most "violent and conflict-ridden parts of Mexico"?[20]

According to anthropologist Frans Schryer, the initial financial support for Maya's theater productions came from the office of Hidalgo's governor Guillermo Rossell de la Lama (1981–1987), in exchange for his work as a cultural mediator between Nahuas and mestizos during the prolonged agrarian struggle in the region.[21] Promoted as cultural revitalization events, Maya's open-air plays were regularly staged in what were considered "trouble spots."[22] It was no secret that the very government agencies and leaders who were working to "contain peasant unrest or channel it to an officially approved direction" were responsible for funding these performances.[23] Thus, many in the town of Huejutla remember Maya's role on the political stage during this time as suspect; some townspeople (all of whom requested anonymity) even went as far as calling him a puppet of the state (similar to what Hale and Millamán have described as an *indio permitido*, an "authorized" indigenous subject).[24] Others, however, recalled the ways in which Maya's plays explicitly challenged the state and prompted audience members to do the same, as in a Boal-like "theatre of the oppressed."[25] Maya avoided discussing the politics of this time period with me, but was careful to mention on more than one occasion that he had resigned his privileged position as director of the regional office of the Instituto Nacional Indigenista (National Indigenist Institute, INI), due to "ideological differences."

## *Ixtlamatinij* (*The Learned Ones*)

Ildefonso Maya's play, *Ixtlamatinij* (*The Learned Ones*), was written and first performed in Nahuatl in 1987. Recently, in 2007, it was published as a trilingual version in an anthology of Mexican indigenous theater, *Words of the True People/Palabras de los seres verdaderos*.[26] A play in two acts, the first scene opens with a Nahua family reuniting for the annual celebration of Xantolo (Day of the Dead) in a Huastecan village. Tensions flare when one of the sons, Epitacio, a bilingual-bicultural teacher, returns to his community having internalized the dominant culture's discourses of "progress" and Indian inferiority. His disdain for his own culture and his attempts to coerce his parents into becoming more mestizo and less Indian cause a rift between the family members, threatening to destroy the unity of the family. By highlighting the embodied performances of ethnic identities—specifically ceremony, language, and dress—*Ixtlamatinij* goes to the heart of one of the major challenges in Mexican indigenous communities today: how to respond to extraordinary pressure from dominant culture to leave behind one's indigenous identity. Furthermore, the play calls into question how the imposition of other (non-indigenous) identities—ostensibly aimed at bringing peoples together—actually diminishes the possibility of family/community/national unity.

In the opening scene, the grandfather, Juantsi, lights beeswax candles and places good ears of corn and tamales on the Xantolo altar. [27] Nichaj, the mother, brings the incense that will carry the offerings and prayers in its smoke to the spirit world, leading the *ánimas* (souls/spirits of the deceased) home. Tachoj, the mute brother of Kosej (Nichaj's husband), offers a song from his "kokouilotl" whistle. As with most Nahua ceremonies, each person offers something—prayers, flowers, incense, animals, foodstuffs—or if one has nothing material to offer, there is always the simple offering of work (such as tying together strings of flowers), dance, or a song from a homemade whistle. Soon the candles begin to flicker, announcing the arrival of the ánimas.[28] Akostij, the elderly *curandero* (healer) and brother of Juantsi, enters and offers incense to all corners of the room while Juantsi invites the souls of the deceased to join them by saying: "Nikaj tij tlaliya to yolo, to tlalnamikilis uan to chikaualis. Xij selikajya tlen timech tenkauiliya [ . . . ] xitlakuakaj, xikajkokuikaj ni tlauili, ni popochtili, ni sempoal xochitl tlen san tlemach amechpaktia."[29] (Here we give our hearts, our integrity, and our strength; receive what we are offering to you [ . . . ] feel worthy and eat beneath these candles, this incense, these flowers that please you so.)[30] Like the ánimas, the grown children who have migrated from the community for work will return home for this annual celebration.[31]

Xantolo, closely associated with Todos Santos or Day of the Dead, is a Nahua ceremonial activity that takes place each year in late October and early November. During this time, Nahua families come together to welcome the ánimas of their deceased ancestors to feast, as well as to renew and solidify kinship relationships in the living community with the exchange of gifts. To prepare for Xantolo in the Huasteca, families build altars in their homes, including an arc made of *limonario* leaves strung with *cempohualxochitl* flowers, providing a gateway between the spirit world and the present material world. In the process of preparing to receive the ánimas, one is drawn to remember individuals, the extended family, and the community. The play's audience will recognize this preparation and remember their own Xantolo celebrations and their own departed loved ones and living relatives who return to the community. In this way Xantolo is one of the keys to the continuity of indigenous cultural memory in that the act of remembering—who we are, where we have been, what has happened to us—is ritualized. Xantolo as the context for this play is highly relevant as it is this ceremony that reminds the indigenous community of the ways of knowing, being, and speaking that the bilingual education program is attempting to eliminate.

The return of both the living and the dead for Xantolo to a specific geographical space is likewise a significant element of the play. In the Huasteca, and throughout Mesoamerica, important spirits dwell in the surrounding hills and mountains.[32] For indigenous peoples whose religious life is connected to sacred landscape, land holds learned lessons and cultural memory. Keith Basso's work with the Apache (particularly his classic *Wisdom Sits in Places* [1996]) has centered on how land and the stories associated with geography teach and re-teach indigenous knowledge. The landscape not only serves as coordinate for getting to and from different places but also literally coordinates the people: the stories inscribed in the land and the retelling of these stories (either verbally, or simply remembering them silently in passing) continually invoke memories and knowledge. Add to this the fact that geography is not as easily erased as other forms of knowledge: you can burn a book or prohibit languages in certain environments, but it is more difficult to move a sacred hill or make a mountain chain disappear. It is true that indigenous place-names can be replaced, but the change of a name on a map does not assure that the previous name will be erased from the memories of those who have walked the land and lived upon it. In this way, as Guillermo Bonfil Batalla has observed, indigenous-language place-names serve as firm reminders of the past: they are "stubborn reserve[s] of knowledge and testimony."[33] The annual celebration of Xantolo—which includes this return to a place/space/knowledge—interrupts and complicates assimilative projects aimed at erasing indigenous culture.

## Performances and Discourses of Civilization and Progress

Much of Mexico's twentieth-century policies on education for indigenous people have been geared toward what the Secretaría de Educación Pública (Secretary of Public Education, SEP) has characterized as "overcoming the evolutionary distance which separates the Indians from the present era."[34] It was not uncommon to attempt to bridge this "evolutionary distance" with material signs of the so-called civilized culture. Recruited as a bilingual teacher and subsequently trained to teach this particular brand of progress, *Ixtlamatinij*'s Epitacio arrives home ready to instruct his family on the proper and authorized version of Mexican identity. One of the principal lessons he has internalized through his training is that in order to improve their quality of life, Indians must change; at the very least, they must adopt the outward signs of dominant culture. As the bearer of this message, Epitacio (standing for the state) is highly critical of his family's ceremonial activity (which he calls "fanaticisms"), their language, and their dress. Oftentimes, as we will see is the case for Epitacio, those placed in a position to promote the assimilation of their own people exhibit self-hatred.[35] Building off of Albert Memmi, Frantz Fanon, and Homi Bhabha, Diana Taylor has described this in terms of an internalization of the colonizer's definition of the other as inferior, a debilitating byproduct of exclusion and domination.[36] In his introduction to the play, Maya speaks to this phenomenon in Nahua culture, as well as its ramifications:

> Ni ti maseualmenj timo pinauaj pampa tij matij axtij piaj tlanmamikilistli kej kaxtiltekamej. Tij tlamielkajkejya to maseualtlalnamikilis, yejeka timoluiya ayok tij pia chikaualistli tlen ika tech xayak nextia, timo uiuipolojkejya; yon ayok tij piaj topatij; pampa kaxtiltekamej tech tlami ixpolojtiauijya, kejuak ayok tleno tinesij; yejeka uajkema ti kalakij tlamaxtiloyaj uan ti peuaj timochtiaj ti tlapouaj uan ti tlajkuiloa, timoluiaj, ti peuajya timotsontlananaj, pampa tij konanaj ti ixtlamatij kej kaxtiltekamej; ijkinoj ti peuaj timo ueyi nekij, pampa kejuak tij kajtiauiyajya maseualistli; uakinoj tij konanaj tikin pinajtia uiuimaseualmej, pampa tojuantij tij kajtiauiya maseualiatli uan ayok tij tlepanitaj yon tleno, timo koyonekij uan ti peuaj timo sisiniya.[37]

> (We Indians are *ashamed* of being Indians because we think we lack the wisdom and culture of the Spaniards. We have already *forgotten* our traditional Indian culture and wisdom. Thus, we have lost the strength of the culture that represented us; we have lost it through our own *ignorance*; we have lost our values. Since the Spaniards and now the mestizos have defeated us, we feel we no longer count for anything. Therefore, when we begin to *learn to read and write in school*, we feel superior because we think we are being liberated; we become uppity because we feel we are shedding our Indian-ness. We then begin to make fun of Indians as being dumb; having shed our ignorance, *we no longer have respect for anything*; we begin to believe we are mestizos or Spaniards, and *we transform ourselves into violent individuals*.)[38]

In the play, the character of Epitacio carries this learned self-hatred and demonstrates how the assimilative discourses (and practices) of the bilingual education model—for which he is now the agent—can create conflict in indigenous families. Upon arriving to the family home, Epitacio tells his brother Nicolás, the son who has stayed to farm the family parcel of land, all about what education and bettering oneself means:

> Epitacio: Pa que veigas lo qui hace el istudio, asina se sopera ono. Asina dejas de ser indio, ignorante, uigüi como los animalitos. [ . . . ] Palabra, carnal, que ser hijo de un indio es pior, me arde la cara de vergüenza haber nacido de unos ignorantes cualquiera, siento refeo que me miren mis cuates, los di razó, que yo suy hijo de unos indios.[39]
>
> (Now you see where study can get you. That's how you better yourself. That's how you stop being an Indian—ignorant and dumb like an animal. [ . . . ] I swear, brother, being the son of an Indian is the worst thing. My face burns from the shame of having been born to some ignorant nobodies; I feel terrible when my friends "of reason" see that I'm the offspring of Indians.)[40]

In his study of the effects of colonization, Albert Memmi hypothesized that "memory is not purely a mental phenomenon. Just as the memory of an individual is the fruit of his history and physiology, that of a people rests upon its institutions. [ . . . ] [The colonized] often becomes ashamed of these institutions, as of a ridiculous and overaged monument."[41] Epitacio's disdain for religious ceremonial life in the indigenous community is apparent when he arrives home and ridicules the abundance on the altar left for the ánimas when the family is so impoverished—"Bread dolls for those dying of hunger," he scoffs.[42] Here, Epitacio repeats the state discourse of blaming Indian poverty on the excesses of their religious ceremonies, as opposed to a series of other social, political, and economic factors. There is no question that an enormous amount of time, energy, material goods, and money are dedicated to religious ceremonies in Nahua communities today. The maintenance of a reciprocal relationship with the spirit world is paramount to many Nahuas, and therefore that which is sought (abundance, for example) is also offered to spirits/deities in ceremony. Epitacio's disgust at seeing food on the altar when he knows that his family is often hungry and impoverished stems from his acceptance of mestizo cultural values, as well as selective forgetting of the logic behind the lavish offerings. Upon surveying the tamales, chocolate, flowers, candles, and saints' images on the altar, he states, "Hay que combatirlos pa quitar el banatismo como dice el koyotlakatl" (We've got to fight all of this to put an end to fanaticism, *as the mestizos say*).[43] He then begins to make fun of his grandfather Juantsi, who dances, having donned a ceremonial mask. Nicolás, normally deferent to Epitacio, defends the tradition and tells his brother to leave the elder alone: "Ya ves ques el costompre, que Xantolo osamos máscaras" (You know it's our custom to use masks for Xantolo, our Day of the Dead feast.)[44] Epitacio is enraged and launches into a tirade against all things he associates with Indian-ness:

> Epitacio: Qué costombres ni qué costombres, tudo lo viejo ya pasó, ya no vale nada, hura hay que ver como se livierte ono, la música, las cirfezas, los cuates. Pa que chingaos venemos si no es pa livertirnos con estos pinchis indios; hay qui docarlos, qui hablin la castía, ma timo koyonekikaj on. Pa eso arroyamos los billetes cada quincena, pa gastarlo dándonos gusto, pa eso suy mayestro, pa tombar tudo lo indio y déjemos de estar judidos, pota, carnal, tuvía no empezamos.[45]
>
> (Don't talk to me about customs! The old ways are history now; they're worthless. These days a man has to have fun: music, beer, and buddies. What would be the point of coming here if we couldn't make fun of these damned Indians? We must educate them; teach them to speak Spanish. We must believe we are "people of reason," friend. That's why we roll up a wad of bills every payday: to spend on a good time. That's why I'm a bilingual teacher: to do away with everything that's Indian so we're no longer screwed. Damn, brother, we've got a long way to go.)[46]

Here Epitacio not only distances himself from his indigenous identity ("these" damned Indians; we must educate "them") but also describes the correct identity performance, that of mestizo culture. This correct performance includes special music (which he later describes as decidedly not indigenous), beer instead of pulque (a traditional fermented maguey beverage), and cash earned as a wage laborer. Epitacio's training has not provided him with the means to offer finite solutions to centuries of asymmetrical power relations that have resulted in indigenous marginalization or, using his term, being "screwed." Instead, he has been groomed to believe (and to teach others) that the difficult living conditions, including extreme poverty and discrimination, are the fault of the Indian community for choosing the incorrect cultural model. We learn more about the dominant culture's discourse of civilization and progress through Epitacio's criticism of ceremonial dances, such as the Ueuejme or Danza de los Viejos (Dance of the Elders), and the Cuanegros:

Epitacio: La docación nos va a sacar de las uigüeras de los viejos; qué xayacate, ni qué las danzas, hayi más mejor, muchis cusas que la música de viento y la de fiolín; hay que bailar sí; pero con el conjonto y traer una mi chamaca bailando hasta que el cuerpo guante, en lugar de andar tlatsinteuijtinemis con esa pinchi mósica concacaj, concacaj concaj conca conca concacaj concacaj.[47]

(Bilingual education is going to save us from the old people's foolish ways. What good are these masks and these dances? There are much better things than flute and violin music; sure, we have to dance, but to a band and with a girl until the body gives out—not moving our rears to that damned music that goes *concacaj, concacaj, concacaj, concacaj, concaj, concacaj, concacaj.*)[48]

In asking "what good are these masks and these dances?" Epitacio demonstrates that he has internalized the discriminatory view toward indigenous embodied practices that serve as public performances of resistance and memory. The Cuanegros dance, for example, challenges dominant culture's notions of history with a re-enactment of racial and social struggles in Mexico. To dance the Cuanegros, indigenous men in the Huasteca disguise themselves as European conquistadors and African slaves who play out a conquest/courtship ritual to win the hand of an indigenous woman.[49] The Spaniard, as opposed to being portrayed as powerful, is inept, and the woman refuses both suitors; this performance surely strays far from the state's ideal narrative.

## Language

Epitacio: Carnal, no se te olvide que yo soy maestro y me tienis que me respetas; porque yo ya no soy igual que ustedis que son indios,
ura yo soy mayestro pa enseñar a que se duquin los pinchis crías,
se civilicen, a que sepan utras cusas de la coltora nacional; que leyan en castiano,
que hablin como los "de razó."[50]

(Brother, don't forget that I'm a teacher and you must respect me.
I'm no longer equal to you Indians;
I'm a teacher now and I teach the damned kids to become civilized,
to learn new things about our national culture; to read in Spanish,
to speak like those "of reason.")[51]

Like ceremonial rituals and dance, language (chosen or imposed) can be read as a performance of cultural/ethnic identity, marking membership in, and exclusion from, a particular segment of society. Epitacio's lines above show how his bilingual-bicultural teacher training has fostered an antagonistic relationship with his own identity as an Indian, as well as with "the damned kids" he teaches. As a conduit of national culture, the bilingual teacher's role during the 1970s and 1980s (and in many places still to this day) was to eradicate markers of indigeneity and to teach indigenous peoples how to perform a role that the nation finds acceptable. The bilingual-bicultural teacher thus became the vehicle for the circulation, internalization, and eventual reproduction of the ideals of the nation, conveying the narratives and signs of what Benedict Anderson has called the "imagined community."[52] Anderson frames the nation as an imagined community due to the fact that for the most part "members of even the smallest nation will never know most of their fellow members, meet them, or even hear of them, yet in the minds of each lives the image of their communion."[53] This imagined twentieth-century Mexican nation as taught through the educational system was to be comprised of Spanish speakers with an agreed-upon common history, ideals, and goals. The fact that there are more than sixty-four indigenous languages in Mexico—and each language community holds distinct understandings of origins, historical events, knowledges, and so on—has complicated the effective transmission and acceptance of the desired narrative. Maya's play brings to life the storyline of attempts to change indigenous populations through the elimination of the native language and the imposition of Spanish. He draws us in to the linguistic landscape of late twentieth-century Mexico with a vivid representation of language use, languages in contact, and language as cultural capital in indigenous communities today.

Language use—Nahuatl or Spanish—in Huastecan Nahua communities during the latter portion of the twentieth century was, and in many cases continues to be, gendered. Mirroring actual Nahua communities, the female protagonists in the play, Nichaj and Tilaj, are primarily monolingual Nahuatl speakers. The men, on the other hand, are bilingual with varying degrees of Spanish proficiency. Up until recent decades, formal education for female children was minimal, resulting oftentimes in monolingualism (indigenous language only) among Nahua women. While today this is changing dramatically, in the past it was rare for women to leave their communities in search of work. Because of this they had little contact with Spanish speakers, which made proficiency in the second language unnecessary.[54] Indigenous males, however, have regularly had more access to formal education and also have had more contact with Spanish speakers in their work life. Nahua men must have a minimal level of Spanish proficiency in order to carry out pertinent business in local government offices (traditionally staffed by non-indigenous people), to negotiate with a regional hacienda owner if they are looking to hire themselves out as a *peón* or day laborer, and if they leave the community (as do Epitacio and Cirilo in the play) in search of other sources of employment. In both the Nahuatl and Spanish versions of *Ixtlamatinij*, this same situation is reflected in the mono- to limited bilingualism of the women and more clearly bilingual speech from the men. The level of Spanish fluency (or lack thereof) exhibited in male speech in the play corresponds directly to each character's educational experience and his interactions with the mestizo population.[55]

Nicolás and the elder men who live in the community speak either Nahuatl or a hybrid Nahuatl-Spanish ("Nahuañol") that suggests limited education or at the very least infrequent use of Spanish. Because Nahuatl utilizes digraphs and consonants that Spanish does not, and Spanish has consonants and vowels that Nahuatl does not, mispronunciation and hypercorrection are common markers in the non-native Spanish language of Nahuas.[56] Maya's play offers a marvelously accurate representation of Nahuatl and Spanish in contact in the Huasteca. Throughout the Nahuatl and Spanish versions of the play, we see the following examples:

1. letter substitution in loan words that include consonants not used in Nahuatl (for example, *b* since Nahuatl does not use the letter *f*, "*el banatismo*" for *fanatismo*, fanaticism; and the use of *t* instead of *d*, "*ofrenta*" for *ofrenda*, altar);[57]
2. hypercorrection (such as an overuse of *f* in words that really should be *b/v*, "*festido*" for *vestido*, dress; "*cirfeza*" for *cerveza*, beer) and incorrect Spanish vowel pronunciation ("Tó ansina respetas tudo, tiveras bueno genti mi muchacho" [Tú así respetas todo. De veras es buena gente mi muchacho]);[58]
3. invented words adapted from oral Spanish (for example, *liveras* instead of *de veras*, truthfully, really; *fiero* instead of *feo*, ugly);
4. fluid code-switching ("Nejlia, ni ti intios tech pinajtia; ya ni me lu digas osté, ya xi tech elcaua carnal" [Nahautl > Spanish > Nahuatl > Spanish]);[59] and
5. Spanish loan words that have been "nahuatlized" with the "oa" suffix of Nahuatl verbs (for example, *emborracharoa* > *emborracharose* [for the Spanish *emborracharse*, to get drunk] or *mo vestiroa* [for the Spanish *vestirse*, to dress oneself).

The protagonists all show varying degrees of Spanish-language proficiency. While Cirilo prefers Nahuatl, he speaks impeccable grammatically correct Spanish acquired during his military service. Epitacio, the teacher, has a tragically weak command of Spanish grammar, pronunciation, and vocabulary that contrasts sharply with Cirilo's prowess in the brothers' second language. Why would military personnel be better educated than public school teachers? Earlier I suggested that the educational system in Mexico has been set up in a way that creates Indians who were nearly mestizo, but not quite. If this is the case, it is not necessary (it would, in fact, be detrimental) to provide indigenous teachers such as Epitacio or his students with adequate tools necessary to be equals in the sociopolitical landscape. The military, with other mechanisms to ensure subordination and obedience, has no need to deny indigenous recruits a higher-quality education.

As in the past, today in Mexico indigenous languages are generally stigmatized and their use in public often invites discrimination. The Spanish language, on the other hand, denotes power. Beyond affording the opportunity to "read" experience and performances of social identities through language use in this play, Maya also tells us something of the perceived cache and power status of Spanish, and how this has been internalized by Nahuas. In *Ixtlamatinij*, it is more the form—the act of speaking Spanish, the linguistic performance—than the accuracy of the language that is important. Epitacio speaks a nearly incomprehensible Spanish riddled with grammatical errors, and it doesn't really matter; he is still seen as a bearer of the cultural sign of non-indigenous superiority. Nicolás, the brother who has stayed in the community to farm, is in awe of his brother Epitacio's Spanish-language abilities and wants to be like him: "Tiveras tó soyis cofró, kualtsi tij yecoua nompa castia" (You really are smart! What beautiful Spanish you speak!);[60] "Tó como mayestro, kenkiluiyaj, moneki menseñas tudo lo que sabes osté, pa que yo tampién lu vas decir ansina" (You as a bilingual teacher, as they call you, should teach me everything you know, so I can talk just like you).[61] The use of Spanish communicates something, but it isn't necessarily the content of the words. It is instead a sign of power, although one that only functions within indigenous communities. The "beautiful Spanish" Epitacio has been trained to impart as a bilingual-bicultural teacher may have weight with non-native speakers, but is nearly unintelligible to a monolingual Spanish speaker. Outside of the indigenous community, Epitacio remains in his assigned subordinate role as the "not quite mestizo" subject.

Along with abandoning indigenous languages, authorized versions of Indians as Mexican citizens also require a costume change. For his part,

Epitacio has taken to wearing boots, although he complains that they are painful to wear, perhaps referring to the fact that the costume of his new identity is ill-fitting. He wants his parents to wear shoes as well, insisting that this will somehow transform them into mestizos. How can slipping on a pair of shoes signal a different identity? Anthropologist Alan Sandstrom reminds us that "in the past, officials needed a quick measure of 'Indian-ness,' and they settled on the criterion of footwear as one distinguishing feature. People who wear shoes are mestizos; those who don't are Indians."[62] Along with shoes, Epitacio brings a plastic bag full of clothes that he asks Nicolás to take to his parents. In the same way that the state has co-opted Epitacio to carry the message of Indian inferiority, he now turns to his brother to do the dirty work of telling their parents that they need to change:

> Nicolás: Papá uan taua ma, puncase lo que lis traigo; porque no carnal Pitacio, ax kineki an mech miraros kej intios, semejante fiero an mo vestiroa, uan inki itajya nompa to Pitacio, yaja mayestro; uan siej ki pia ueruensa totatua nemi ikxikatsa uan sa de calzoncio. Yejeka kijtoa, aprisa ximo camiarokaj ika ni yektli pantaloj uan ni festido uan ni sepatos, uakinon kemaj uajkej asis to Cirilo, uste vas estar como in lecenciao, uan taua ke de probesura.[63]
>
> (Papá, and you, mamá, put on what I've brought you, because my brother Pitacio doesn't want to see you looking like Indians; that Indian clothing you wear is really ugly. You know that our Pitacio is a bilingual teacher, and it embarrasses him for you to go around barefoot and wearing breeches. So he says you should change into this nice pair of pants, this dress, and these shoes. Then, when our Cirilo arrives, you'll look like a lawyer and you'll look like a schoolteacher.)[64]

Epitacio's conflation of a certain kind of dress with "civilization" is reminiscent of Chiapas governor Victórico Grajales's "Campaign to Civilize Through Dress" in the 1930s, a policy that forbade indigenous languages and burned traditional clothing in the name of civilization.[65] The logic of Epitacio's arguments (when we quit wearing these clothes, we will be different) reflects the kind of preparation the bilingual-bicultural program provided for its recruits, but Epitacio's internalization of this message is the result of the colonial condition. On the receiving end of century after century of the message of Indian backwardness and inferiority, Epitacio now embodies the self-hatred that Maya spoke of in his introduction. But not all Indians have learned to view their own culture negatively. In fact,

Nichaj—a Nahua woman with little or no formal education—is disappointed with the contents of the plastic bag and is appalled that her son wants her to dress in a fashion she considers unpalatable: "Na kilt, me quieris me vistes xilona, san tlemach fiero, cuchina ni merias, san tech keskuayo kekeloa" (He wants me to dress like a mestizo woman, as ugly as they look. These no-good stockings just tickle my legs).[66] She complains, but complies in order to please her son.

Cirilo arrives to find his parents uncomfortably costumed in Western clothing and wonders aloud if they will be "playing" non-indigenous people in the Cuanegros dance. He sees his own parents' traditional clothing as "mejor, mucho más bonito" (better and much prettier).[67] He demonstrates his solidarity with the indigenous community's traditional ways by stating that he wants to look like his parents and will wear the traditional *cotón* shirt for his visit. He leaves briefly to pay his respects to other community members, as is customary, at which time Epitacio arrives home, drunk. Juantsi, the elder, disapproves of the change of clothing, telling the family: "Nejlia an mech uiui ita ne koyotlakatl, axtlatlepanita; namej in tsijkolojtinemise kej totolimej. Pubre no nieto, kineki mech tlalis: kej lencenciao uan kej pubresura, san tlen kuetsona; yon axkimati ken mech chiuas, siquiera borlas uan borlas" (That guy 'of reason' is really making fools of you; he doesn't respect you. Now you're going to go around limping like turkeys [in the shoes]. My poor grandson, he wants to turn you into a lawyer, and you into a schoolteacher. This is really serious; he's gone overboard; he can no longer figure out what to do except to make fun and more fun).[68] When Epitacio drunkenly demands that everyone put on the clothes, Juantsi calls a halt to the process. The tension builds as Epitacio breaks with prescribed Nahua social behavior that insists upon respect for all elders:

> Epitacio: Osté te callas, viejo. Tó ya no tienis remedio, to agüelo, ya no soplas; ya timo chingaro on; pero estos cabronis son mis jefes y no vuy a permitir que sigan de indios atrasados, si tienin que mejurar, tienin que dejar el pinchi calzón y la nagua, vestir como los de razón, punerse zepatos y hablar en castiano. [ . . . ] Tienin que cambiar; se tienin que vestir como los de razón y dejar de andar como los indios. Si quierin que los respete les diga papá . . . y quierin ustedis decirme hijo, antuns si tienin que puner la ropa que les cumpré.[69]
>
> (You shut up, old man! There's no hope for you, grandfather, you're worn out, you're worthless now, you bastard. But these sons of bitches are my parents and I'm not going to let them go on like backward Indians. They

have to better themselves; they have to give up their damned breeches and skirts and dress like people of reason, put on shoes, and speak Spanish. [ . . . ] You must change; you must dress like people of reason and quit going around like a couple of Indians if you want me to respect you and call you my parents. And if you want to call me "son," you must put on the clothing I bought.)[70]

Cirilo returns home to witness Epitacio's threats to the elders, and the brothers begin to argue:

Cirilo: Yo lo único que entiendo es que esa no es la forma de mejorar a nuestros padres. Cambiarlos, hacerlos que se pongan ese vestuario que no es de ellos, que hablen la lengua que no es la suya y presionarlos con la amenaza de desconocerlos, no es lo más correcto de tratar a nuestros padres; esto es una falta de respeto muy grande.[71]

(All I know is that this isn't the way to better our parents—by changing them, making them put on someone else's clothes, making them speak a language that's not theirs and pressuring them with the threat of disowning them; that's not the proper way to treat our parents. You're showing a huge lack of respect toward them.)[72]

In this brief exchange, two very different versions of what is considered appropriate behavior are evident, particularly in regards to the meaning of "respect." On one hand, throughout the play Epitacio (standing for state-sponsored national culture) demands respect based on his association with what he perceives to be a superior cultural model. He believes he deserves the respect of others because he has acquired the behaviors, national language, and dress that denote participation in the capitalist economic system. On the other hand, Cirilo frames respect in terms of deference to elders and adherence to traditional Nahua culture as manifested in ceremony, language, and dress. The argument escalates:

Cirilo: ¿Estás loco? Pues mira. Quiero que sepas que yo me siento muy orgulloso de haber nacido de ellos y de que sigan visitendo su ropa tradicional y hablando la lengua de nuestros antepasados. Y también quiero que sepas que no me gusta nada lo que tú pretendes hacer con ellos. Eso que tú quieres hacer es una tontería, una locura; o eres un tonto o de plano estás trastornado al humillar y maltratar a nuestros padres de esta forma.[73]

(Are you crazy? Look, I want you to know that I feel very proud of having been born to them, and that they still wear the same clothing and speak our grandparents' tongue. I also want you to know that I don't like what you're trying to do to them at all; it's stupid, it's crazy. You're either an idiot or you're just plain crazy, humiliating and mistreating our parents like this.)[74]

Epitacio: Yo no soy on tuntu, soy maestro pa docar a los intios, pa sacarlos del atraso en que stán, abrirles los ojos y que ya no sigan en la ignorancia y en el banatismo, estoy aquí pa qui se civilicin. Y sabes que si alguien respeta y sabi algo, ese suy yo.[75]

(I'm not an idiot; I'm a teacher who teaches Indians in order to pull them out of their backwardness and open their eyes so they don't continue in their ignorance and fanaticism. I'm here to civilize them. And you know that if anyone is respectful and knows something, it's me.)[76]

At this point Epitacio draws his knife and lunges toward his brother. Nichaj, the mother, attempts to stop the fight, and Epitacio accidentally cuts her, symbolizing the epistemological violence caused by the state's (Epitacio's) deployment of discourses of progress and civilization into indigenous communities. The local police are called to take Epitacio away until he sobers up and the community authorities can decide what to do about this turn of events. By morning he has had time to reflect on what has transpired, and he is ashamed and repentant.[77]

Before Epitacio is returned to his family home by the local authorities, Cirilo gathers the family together and asks the family to forgive and forget what happened the night before:

Cirilo: Quiero pedirles un favor, quiero que todos olvidemos lo que aquí sucedió el jueves pasado, que mi hermano Epitacio no se sienta culpable, ni avergonzado de lo ocurrido y para el bien de todos, si es que como dice mi hermano que ya está arrepentido de todo y reconoce que es un error lo que él pretendía hacer, vamos a darle la oportunidad de que se sienta con confianza, que se sienta contento para que volvamos a estar unidos como antes lo habíamos estado.[78]

(I want to ask a favor: I would like for all of us to forget what happened last Friday [*sic*]. Please. May my brother Epitacio not feel guilty or ashamed of what happened, for the good of all; that is, if he's as sorry as he says he is, and recognizes that what he tried to do was wrong, let's give him the chance to feel at ease. Let's make him feel good so we can be together again as we were before.)[79]

Through Cirilo, Nahua families in the audience are asked to not let this all-too-familiar experience divide and destroy their communities. The restoration and maintenance of balance—a key element of Nahua cosmovision—trumps bruised egos and egregious behaviors. Indeed, for the sake of the integrity of the family and the community, at times one must forget instead of remember.

Epitacio returns to the family home on his knees, wearing his traditional cotón shirt and begging forgiveness in the Nahuatl language. His return to traditional dress and his first language symbolize his return to the indigenous community. Balance in the family is restored as the errant son reconnects to traditional ways, and the play concludes with the united family continuing the Xantolo ceremony. Although the family claims "all is forgotten," every time the arc is erected to welcome home the living and the dead, this story will be remembered. Epitacio's family will remember that particular year at Xantolo when their ties were nearly broken. Memory, while strategically selective, is also pernicious.

## The Performance After the Performance

Through the realistic protagonist, setting, and topic of *Ixtlamatinij*, Maya has stated that he hoped audience members would recognize themselves on the stage, prompting them to reflect on similar dramas being played out in their communities. Two principal aims of the performance, according to El Profesor, were to encourage post-performance discussion regarding problems in the community and to inspire reflection on the positive aspects of Nahua culture.

The play has been performed dozens of times in Veracruz and Hidalgo Huastecan municipalities and smaller outlying indigenous communities for audiences comprised of both indigenous people and mestizos. Over the years, Maya recruited both native speakers of Nahuatl and non-native speakers to perform. Generally, the actors have been both secondary school children and community members without professional training, and only occasionally semiprofessional actors. Some of the non-native-speaker actors, as theater scholar Adam Versényi reports, have been encouraged by their participation in the play to return to a Nahuatl linguistic proficiency that had become lost to them. By performing in Nahuatl, the student-actors "become capable of crossing the cultural boundaries erected to cut them off from their heritage."[80] Thus, participation in and of itself is a resistive or recuperative move orchestrated by El Profesor. Versényi tells of his experience attending a staging of the play in 2005 and the striking performance that came afterwards:

> After the play concluded, the school's vice-principal introduced each of the twenty by name, delivering a brief description of our titles and backgrounds. Each of us was then invited up to the podium to give commentary or critique upon the work we had just seen. It quickly became clear that, with exception of Don [Frischmann] and myself, everyone else so honored was a former student of Maya. Each person now held a position of importance at either the municipal, state, or national level in areas ranging from politics to labor to culture. Each person who spoke had, as a child, acted in one of Maya's plays or performed traditional dances he had been taught by Maya, and all of them credited Maya for inspiring their pride in traditional Huasteca cultural forms and for providing them with the self-confidence and dignity necessary to have achieved their current positions. By their very presence, these men and women belied the path taken by those described in Maya's introduction to the play more than anything present in *Ixtlamatinij* itself.[81]

These performances-after-the-performances are very public displays of indigenous survival and rejection of the forces of assimilation, demonstrating that it is not necessary to give up one's own identity in order to survive and prosper. In fact, recourse to their own traditions via their participation in Maya's productions has provided the personal motivation and strength for many to successfully maintain their own culture while participating actively in dominant culture as well. I read this play in the Reading Circles with five native-speaker colleagues, each of whom has seen these same kinds of scenarios played out in their own communities. There was some disappointment expressed by the group regarding the ending. They had hoped to see what happened after Epitacio returned home, in his cotón, speaking his language. What happened in his classrooms after the Xantolo celebration was over? Did Epitacio continue to honor his own culture in the face of constant discrimination? Was he able to maintain his position as a bilingual-bicultural teacher or was he forced to resign? These, after all, are the very questions that these young Nahua intellectuals are grappling with on a daily basis. What this sequel looks like is up to them, and just as Maya hoped, the reading of this play has given them food for thought.

*Ixtlamatinij* could be summed up by a few of the choice words and phrases from Maya's introduction: Ashamed. Forgotten. Ignorance. Learn to Read and Write in School. We No Longer Have Respect for Anything. We Transform Ourselves into Violent Individuals. If his lament is clear in the introduction, the path to cultural recovery is also evident at the end of the play, as well as this "performance after the performance": Pride. Remembered. Knowledge. Learn to Know at Home. Respect Everything. Be Who We Really Are, Indians. It is only after this painful experience that this family, particularly Epitacio, learns this. But that is the way to wisdom in Nahua culture, since to be a "learned one," an intellectual, implies knowledge acquired through personal experience.

## The Return of the *Tlahcuiloh*

In the same way that Ildefonso Maya's masterful critique of bilingual-bicultural education is thanks in large part to his own personal experience as a bilingual-bicultural educator, his experience of living and working in various Nahua communities is the source for his four *Ama Tlanamaquilistli* (*Pages/Books of Knowledge*; figs. 7–10), painted codices with Nahuatl and Spanish text. Maya, it could be argued, is a modern-day *tlahcuiloh*. Long before the arrival of Europeans to today's Mexico, Nahua people had a highly specialized class of intellectuals responsible for recording the knowledge of the people, known as the tlahcuiloh or the *tlahcuilohqueh* (plural): the painter, the scribe. He, or possibly she, was the keeper and the painter/scribe of a vast store of knowledge on religion and ceremonies, histories, laws, customs, geography and land tenure, flora, and fauna.[82] The tlahcuiloh had an acute understanding of Nahua cosmovision and its symbolic representations.[83] He practiced and perfected the art of painting/recording/writing relationships with the spiritual and natural world, as well as relationships with other peoples, on folded screens or accordion-like tracts of amate (tree-bark paper), on animal skins, or on cotton cloth (*lienzos*).[84] After conquest, the production of these *amoxtli* (codex-like "books") continued, often in a hybrid fashion—sometimes on European paper or perhaps employing a combination of pictographs with alphabetic script. Most of the amoxtli produced before

*Figure 7.* Ildefonso Maya Hernández, *Ama Tlalnamaquiliztli* (*Pages/Books of Knowledge*). Title page for *Quen Tiyolque* (*Origins of Man*), first of four bilingual twentieth-century codices.

*Figure 8.* Ildefonso Maya Hernández, *Ama Tlalnamaquiliztli* (*Pages/Books of Knowledge*). Title page for *Quen Timonempolohque* (*How We Ruined Ourselves*), second of four bilingual twentieth-century codices.

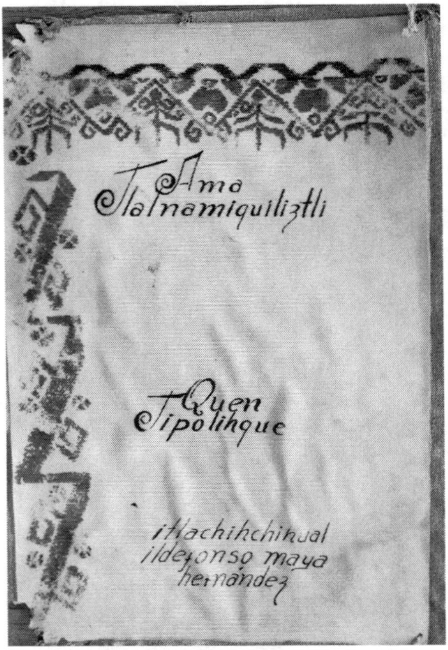


*Figure 9.* Ildefonso Maya Hernández, *Ama Tlalnamaquiliztli* (*Pages/Books of Knowledge*). Title page for *Quen Tipolihque* (*How We Perished*), third of four bilingual twentieth-century codices.

*Figure 10.* Ildefonso Maya Hernández, *Ama Tlalnamaquiliztli* (*Pages/Books of Knowledge*). Title page for *Quen Techcoltzahpilocuepque* (*How the Ancient Birds Returned to Us*), fourth of four bilingual twentieth-century codices.

European contact were destroyed during the initial years of conquest, as they contained information considered to be heretical. The genre fell into decline after the first century of the colonial period, due to the hegemony of the Roman alphabet and the strategic suppression of the indigenous intellectual classes. In spite of this, the old practices were not completely forgotten. For his part, Ildefonso Maya has returned to the codex-style painted books as a move to recover and redesign indigenous discursive and material communication tools.[85]

Mounted on goatskin tracts and painted on Japanese linen, each of Maya's four accordian-like amoxtli consists of one title page and thirteen additional pages. All carry the title of *Ama Tlalnamiquiliztli*, with distinct subtitles related to each book's contents, and they can be read as a cycle or individually. The books, in many ways similar to the Aztec Leyenda de los Soles (Legend of the Suns), convey stories of creation and destruction specific to Nahuas of the Huasteca.[86]

### *Book 1: Quen Tiyolque (Origins of Man)*

The first book opens with the Great Spirit springing from a mass of circular orbiting energy and descending to Earth to plant the sacred corn. The Spirit chews and softens the kernels from this sacred corn, making dough with which to mold humans, men and women. When all of the kernels of the great cornstalk are masticated, the creation of humans is said to be complete. The Great Spirit then attaches a small corncob to our chins and teaches us that this will be our sustenance: "Ixihcuaca ni cintli yaha anmechyolitihtiaz!" (Eat this corn, it will give you life!) (fig. 11).

At the Great Fire we learn that we can speak to each other and understand each other, and that by kissing and with the mixing of our breath, we are to multiply. We live happily. We sing and paint, dance, and cover ourselves with flowers as we populate the earth.

### *Book 2: Quen Timonempolohque (How We Ruined Ourselves)*

This book speaks of human demise due to greed and sloth. By eating excessively from the corncob attached to our chins (our sustenance), the cob falls away and now we must labor for our food. We begin to cultivate corn in the milpa. Angered by his lazy creations, the Great Spirit pulls his

*Figure 11.* Ildefonso Maya Hernández, *Quen Tiyolque* (*Origins of Man*). Ica chicuace (fol. 6).

eyes out. One of the eyes falls to earth, now resting in the Coatzacoalcos River in Veracruz.[87] This was a time of toil; besides the work of cultivating corn, women now must carry children for nine months before birth (as opposed to the earlier mixing of breath for reproduction) (fig. 12).

*Quen Timonempoloque* includes information on Nahua rituals associated with childbirth, such as the practice of burying the child's umbilical cord with a deeply rooted plant where the child was born, symbolically tying the child to the land. One panel discusses the forty days of seclusion after childbirth, and the mother and child's ritual bath upon reintegrating with society. Finally, the book closes with scenes of hunger and aging. It is no longer possible to cultivate corn because the soil is depleted. The people look to the Moon for direction.

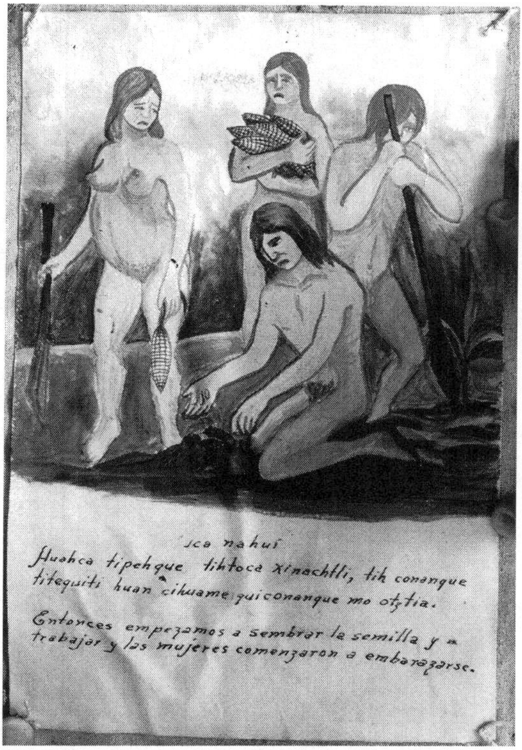


*Figure 12.* Ildefonso Maya Hernández, *Quen Timonempolohque* (*How We Ruined Ourselves*). Ica nahui (fol. 4).

## *Book 3: Quen Tipolihque (How We Perished)*

This book tells the story of man's relationship with Rabbit and the Moon, as well as a variation of the myth of the great flood. In this telling, a man cuts down the forest to make room for his milpa, and each morning he returns to find that the trees stood as they did the previous day, before he cut them down. After several days of the same events, the man hides, waiting in the dark of night to discover the secret of the miraculous grove. At midnight a giant rabbit springs from the moon and, by urinating on the trees, restores them. The man jumps from his hiding spot, threatening to kill the rabbit for tricking him. The rabbit explains that he is the bearer of the secret message of the Moon: he knows that there will soon be no more

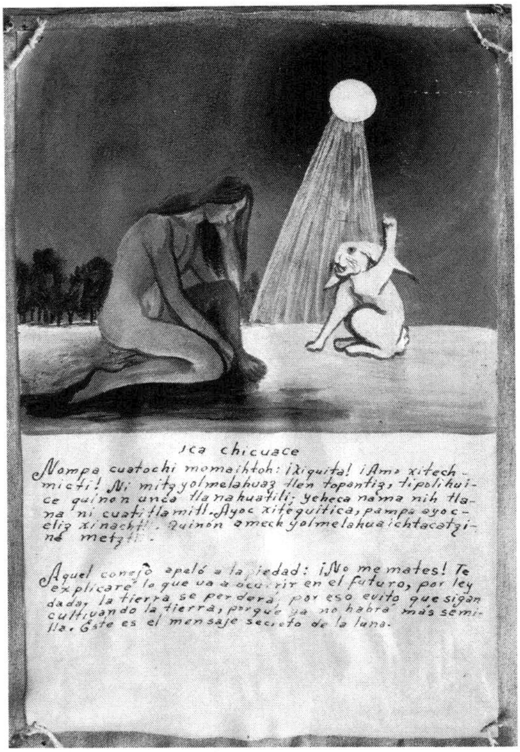


*Figure 13.* Ildefonso Maya Hernández, *Quen Tipolihque* (*How We Perished*). Ica chicuace (fol. 6).

seeds, and that this world was coming to an end. The rabbit promises to explain how mankind can be saved, in exchange for his life (fig. 13).

The rabbit directs the man and his family to build a wooden house, and as a great storm begins, they are instructed to enter the house with his animals, with fire, and with corn seeds. The storm and rains commence, flooding all of the land, the hills, and the mountains with water. The book ends on the last day of the great flood, with the little house bumping the ceiling of the sky.

### *Book 4: Quen Techcoltzahpilocuepque (How the Ancient Birds Returned to Us)*

This book opens with the end of the flood, and because of the rising waters, the little house is close enough to the moon for the rabbit to jump there and make it his home. As the waters recede, the man sees all of the dead animals and, quite hungry, lights a fire to make a meal out of the rotting meats. The smoke from the fire bothers the Great Spirit. Thinking he had exterminated man with the flood and confused as to the source of the smoke, the Great Spirit sends a series of birds to survey the situation. In this book we learn how birds came to repopulate the earth after the flood. Instead of returning to the Great Spirit, each winged messenger stays to feast on meat with man. The hummingbird is the only bird to return with his report and is therefore rewarded for his work by being made even more beautiful. Man, on the other hand, is punished. The Great Spirit decapitates all of the surviving humans and reattaches their heads to their buttocks, turning them into monkeys. Only one man escapes the Great Spirit's wrath, since he had already turned himself into a man-buzzard by eating all of the putrefying meat. The book ends with the young man-buzzard and his female dog turning into humans by beating the female dog on the ribs (fig. 14). They find corn seed they had hidden before the flood, and the cycle of life begins once again.

* * *

The knowledge recorded in Maya's books are ripe for analysis on multiple levels, from the textile patterns on the first pages and pigment choices to the mythical content of the stories and the Nahuatl lexical and orthographic choices, as well as his translations into Spanish. I will comment only briefly on the ideological underpinnings of the *Ama Tlanamaquilistli*, as well as some of the pedagogical possibilities of the books.

First, Maya recorded knowledge utilizing the genres that he regularly insisted all belong to Nahuas: the painted images linked to pre-Hispanic practices, and Nahuatl and Spanish language, both written in alphabetic script. Together, they remind the reader that Nahua communities utilize a variety of visual knowledge systems, as well as multiple languages. Maya's use of more than one sign system is a strategically inclusive move. For example, similar to the pre-Hispanic *tlamatinimeh* (the wise interpreters of the ancient painted books), the elders in primarily rural indigenous communities may not read and write the Roman alphabet, but they do not need a written gloss to interpret the paintings; they have heard these stories passed from generation to generation. For the elders, the books can be used to confirm local knowledge, elicit new variations, entertain, and teach or confirm a range of topics including cultural knowledge. They can also be utilized for teaching alphabetic literacy in either language. Besides elders in Nahua communities, Maya's intended audience is Nahuas removed from their language, returning *to* their native language, Nahuatl (reterritorializing). For them, the amoxtli are what second-language acquisition

*Figure 14.* Ildefonso Maya Hernández, *Quen Techcoltzahpilocuepque* (*How the Ancient Birds Returned to Us*). Ica mahtlactli huan ome (fol. 12).

specialists would call "content-rich" didactic tools. Nahuas relearn their language and their culture simultaneously. Additionally, Maya's amoxtli can teach native speakers about the historical changes of their own language. If one is unaware of, for example, how vowels have elided over time (from o-u-a-e-i-then disappearing) or how glottal stops have been marked, eliminated, or exaggerated in specific regional variations, Nahuatl writing from outside of one's own region—there are more than thirty dialects of Nahuatl today—can be challenging, even for the native speaker (see more on this issue in chapter 4 on doña Luz Jiménez). By using Maya's texts to discuss these properties, the native speaker is able to not only more readily access his or her own cultural patrimony but also gain the necessary skills to work with a larger corpus of intellectual production of Nahuas spanning temporal and geographical areas. If we turn our attention to the Spanish translations of each screen, the amoxtli can likewise be employed to teach Spanish proficiency, without removing a Nahua student from his or her own culture. In Maya's deployment, Spanish is not "foreign"; it is simply one of many communication tools available to Nahuas. The pictographic/Nahuatl/Spanish amoxtli as text for learning the Spanish language offers an alternative to mainstream Spanish texts that are culturally removed from indigenous experience in Mexico. The move to embrace both Nahuatl and Spanish in indigenous communities has also been endorsed by Nahua poet Natalio Hernández Hernández. In a brief yet poignant statement at the 1998 Congreso de las Academias de Lengua Español (Conference of the Academies of the Spanish Language), Hernández claimed the Spanish language for indigenous people: "axcan tihmati melahuac timoyolchicahua, melahuac miac timotlapielia, ipampa tiquinpia miac tlatolme tlen totlalnantzin ihuan cachopin tlahtoli tlen noihqui totechpohui" (today we truly know our hearts are full, we truly have many things to watch over [we are rich], because we have many languages from our precious land and the *gachupín* [Spanish] language that also belongs to us).[88]

Through *Ixtlamatinij*, Maya critiques the problems caused by the integration and assimilation projects of the state, particularly those that, through the educational system, reinforce colonial relationships of inequality. He also offers a solution to the conundrum of national integration, as visible in the *Ama Tlanamaquilistli*: he shows how multiple sign systems and ways of knowing can work together, as opposed to being contradictory, and offers an inclusive vision for the future of Mexico, indigenous and non-indigenous alike.

## CONCLUSIONS AND BEGINNINGS

# *Reading and Writing Nahua Space*

It is written that in 1591 an elder of the Nahua village of San Matías Cuixinco in the Central Valley of Mexico called his people together to tell a very important story and to have this story recorded in alphabetic script. The elder explained how Cuixinco lands were founded and defended in pre-Hispanic times by the ancestors of the people gathered. He spoke of how Spaniards later confirmed these territorial boundaries when the people of Cuixinco accepted the Christian faith and agreed to pay tribute to the king of Spain. The story goes that on this particular day, at the time of the alphabetic rendering and public witnessing of this story, the people of Cuixinco were guided through their land. At certain intervals the group paused to announce a place-name along the community's border, to weave grasses and stack small piles of stones, and to feast and to sound trumpets. They told—and perhaps even re-enacted—stories of events that had taken place at each location, looking back to battles and peacemaking between peoples, or encounters with gods and saints. With this walk through the land (whether it actually took place or was through the mind's eye, we cannot know), and through story, the people were bound to this space and simultaneously this space was bound to the people.

The elder is explicit about his motivation for re-telling and now writing the stories of Cuixinco's past and present. He warns of a sure and dangerous future: Spaniards were coming for their lands:

> Sepan que en acompañandose Con los que traen el sombrero encasquetado, Y sus espadas debajo del brazo quienes tambien andan a caballo en Juntandose Con los Susodichos Y Comiendo de los que ellos Comen

> Seran Perdidos porque estos pretenderan quitarles sus tierras y pegu-Jales diziendo que Se las Vendan Y Con este pretexto Se Yran apoderando dellas, Y Se las Yran quitando poco a poco. [ . . . ] esto es lo que digo Y declaro lo qual Se ponga por escripto Y en toda forma para que Se Sepa Y Assi mesmo Saved hijos mios que os doy la forma para poder Saver hablar Y Responder en la defensa de Vuestras tierras Y Sepais donde Caen los linderos Y los podais defender ante la Justicia.[1]
>
> (Know that by accompanying those that wear helmets and carry swords, those that also ride horseback, by gathering with them and eating what they eat, you will be lost because they will try to take your lands from you and regulate them, saying that you should sell them to them. Under these pretexts they will take control of the lands and they will take them from you little by little. [ . . . ] This I say and declare, that which is written down properly in order that you understand. And in this way you should know my children that I give you the way in which you will be able to speak and respond in defense of your lands, and so that you know where the borders are and so you can defend them in a court of law.)

The elder insists that with the knowledge encoded in the stories he tells, his people and their descendants will have all that they need in order to protect themselves and to ensure that they are recognized as the legitimate, rightful custodians of their territory. With this new written record, they will also have the requisite paper trail to prove it to outsiders. This paper trail is today known as the primordial title of San Matías Cuixinco, a set of four Nahuatl-language documents and their Spanish versions written perhaps as early as 1591, but more than likely at a later date during the seventeenth century.[2]

As Stephanie Wood has explained, primordial titles are not—as the moniker misleadingly implies—legal titles to land.[3] They are instead "informal community histories," alphabetic (and at times pictographic) texts written by indigenous communities, in indigenous languages, primarily during the seventeenth and eighteenth centuries in a context of indigenous *congregación* (forced relocation) and *composición* (legalized distribution and titling of lands).[4] The narratives brought together in the primordial titles are meant to offer proof of why a community is deserving of legal title that they do not currently possess. Robert Haskett has observed that the primordial titles can be read as "an intellectual reaction to conquest and colonial subjugation."[5] From this perspective, these writings are important sources of indigenous thought, teachings, and self-representation in a time of crisis. The audience of most primordial titles seems to be first and foremost the indigenous community.[6] The elder narrator in the title of Cuixinco, for example, repeatedly calls for his audience's attention by saying, "Xicmocaquiltican nopilhuane" (listen [to this] my children). But we know that many of these types of documents were also presented to the Spanish courts. The primordial title of Cuixinco was in fact translated from Nahuatl to Spanish in 1702, and submitted to the courts to protest the fact that the Hacienda of Atempan had wrongfully taken a portion of their land.

The dozens of extant Mesoamerican primordial titles scattered throughout national and local archives are a diverse corpus, yet tend to be recognizable by the kinds of stories they contain. They may include recollections of the community both before and after the coming of the Spaniards. Many recount the peoples' origins, with an emphasis on the heroic feats of their ancestors, as well as the acceptance of the Catholic faith, choosing of patron saints, and construction of churches. Most depict interactions and dealmaking with important Spanish dignitaries, and more often than not, they include elders dispensing advice and warnings to their people. Detailed descriptions of the territorial boundaries of the land in question are a mainstay, and these geographical details are nearly always accompanied by what James Lockhart has called "ritual signatures"—the earlier-mentioned performances of possession such as naming and altering the landscape in a small way, or sharing a meal and playing musical instruments along the way.[7] Both the stories within the primordial titles and the documents themselves mark indigenous presence at a moment when these communities were at risk of being subsumed, erased, or fragmented. Through story, and through alphabetic writing, the elder of Cuixinco instilled in his people the knowledge that they had a history in that place, and that they deserved a future there as well.

In many ways this book has followed the example of the elder of Cuixinco. Whereas his stories followed the contours of Cuixinco land and social memory, I have extended an invitation to explore the borders of Nahua intellectual territory. Along with my Nahua colleagues, I have set about to acknowledge, listen to, read, and write about the stories of Nahua intellectuals and writers who have created this vast and ever-changing space. Geographer Doreen Massey has argued that space can be conceived of as "constituted through interactions" and is "always under construction."[8] That is, spaces are created and undone, renovated and imagined, through ongoing relationships and stories. Space, according to Massey, can be thought of "as the sphere of multiplicity of trajectories" where there is constant flux and movement, and ample room for all of our stories and lives.[9] With this understanding of space, this book commences a transhistorical and multidisciplinary re-thinking, re-reading, and re-writing of *Nahua space*, crisscrossing through and within Mexican space. By focusing on the written word, intertwined with oral traditions and embodied knowledges, I have dipped into certain historical moments in order to demonstrate that Nahuas have long availed themselves of the technology and practice of writing, both before and after conquest. Like the primordial titles, this book marks indigenous presence. To be more precise, it marks Nahua *intellectual* and *written* presence in modernity. In doing so, one of my aims has been to call into question why this presence has long been ignored and undervalued by dominant culture, and hidden from Nahua people.

Having left aside the tasks of quantifying degrees of Nahua assimilation and resistance to dominant culture and loosened the stranglehold of rigid categories and definitions of indigeneity—of expectations—I have offered examples of how certain Nahuas made their voices heard through the written word. As we have traveled through Nahua intellectual territory, we have seen how Nahuas thought and wrote about their language and culture; how they pushed to fashion and assert self-rule in the colonial context; and how they defended their right to lands and to live, worship, speak, and dress as they saw fit. For Nahuas, alphabetic writing over the centuries has been a vehicle for both the support and critique of institutions and practices, indigenous and non-indigenous alike. It has been deployed to teach younger generations about who they are and what is theirs, and also to engage outsiders. Today, as seen in the writings of Refugio Nava Nava, Victoriano de la Cruz Cruz, and Sabina de la Cruz, alphabetic writing continues to be used to reflect on the past, the present, and the future and to tell stories of survival, strength, and hope. Refugio's, Victoriano's, and Sabina's concerns are remarkably similar to those of their intellectual ancestors, even though they have exchanged red and black ink on amate paper for Microsoft Word and a laptop. To be sure, Nahuas exchange ideas in and about their language and culture in cyberspace as well, with Facebook and Twitter serving as lively meeting spaces for Nahuas in the city and the countryside, in Mexico and abroad.

With the example of Nahua priest and grammarian Antonio del Rincón, I argued that as opposed to being passive receivers of an imposed European technology, Nahuas have appropriated and adapted alphabetic writing for their own purposes. That Rincón's purpose for writing was to support rather than resist the imposition of the Catholic faith is troubling for some. Knowing that his activities have rubbed some the wrong way simply reminds us of the dominant culture's propensity for categorizing and assigning permissible (palatable?) identities to indigenous peoples. Those who were openly defiant or even covertly resistant of the Spanish imperial project have received the lion's share of critical attention. But there were myriad indigenous responses to conquest and colonization; Rincón's intellectual project—regardless of his ideological slant—deserves equal consideration. Finally, we cannot overlook the fact that even though it was not the initial impetus for its creation, texts such as Rincón's grammar—and others produced by and for the religious orders in the early colonial period—are today key resources for Nahuas as they move to recover and revitalize their language.

We know that Europeans wrote copiously about their experiences and observations of the colonial world. But Nahuas did so as well. My attention to don Juan Buenaventura Zapata y Mendoza's historical annals illustrated how Nahuas have both recorded and performed the events—real, imagined, or selectively fashioned—that held meaning for them. Written in Nahuatl, his annals were undoubtedly destined for future generations of Tlaxcalans that they might remember the grandeur and distinction of their line. They also convey the adaptability and resourcefulness of Tlaxcalans in protecting and promoting their autonomy and traditional governing system—with uneven success—in the new colonial order. Zapata's intellectual legacy is indeed a story of Tlaxcalan pride, but equally one of survival in a hostile and rapidly changing world.

I have insisted that a narrative of Nahua intellectualism and writing should not be restricted only to individuals working in his/her native language. In my treatment of Faustino Galicia Chimalpopoca, I emphasized that even while the practice of writing in the Nahuatl language diminished during the nineteenth century, Nahua intellectuals such as Chimalpopoca forged ahead, oftentimes utilizing Spanish as well as, in his case, Nahuatl, Otomí, and Latin. Working in several languages—including the language of the colonizer—made it possible for Chimalpopoca to successfully protect indigenous communal properties, lobby for and craft legislation in favor of indigenous rights, and promote the value of his native language in public spaces. If we release the expectation of Nahua intellectual work as being carried out exclusively in the Nahuatl language—especially in contexts where the native language was prohibited or would be ignored—we are presented with new ways to listen to indigenous voices.

In my reading of doña Luz Jiménez's stories, I advocated for a reframing of the so-called indigenous informant as a knowledge producer in his/her own right. This reconsideration goes directly to the heart of the questions of who an indigenous intellectual is and how we define indigenous intellectual work. If we are thinking indigenous intellectualism *from* Nahua culture, we accept that knowledge is transmitted through stories. This position follows Margaret Kovach (Plains Cree/Saulteaux) who writes that in indigenous communities there is an "inseparable relationship between story and knowing."[10] Where else, then, to seek examples of Nahua intellectualism than in the words of a master Nahua storyteller? How else, then, to create new knowledge with Nahuas today than to sit together in the Circles, reading and exchanging ideas?

The *teyolia*, or life force, left the body of Ildefonso Maya Hernández in June 2011, but it burns bright in a very large corpus of plays, short stories, codices, and paintings. It was my great joy and honor to sit with El Profesor over the years, and to have listened to and learned from him. With a focus on a very small portion of his work, I considered his uncanny ability to portray the legacy of colonialism and coloniality in Nahua communities and his equally impressive sensitivity to the linguistic landscape that surrounded him. His intellectual career also sheds light on how state projects of indigenous assimilation unwittingly provided the tools and networks with which Nahuas and other indigenous peoples have recovered their dignity, demanded their rights, and imagined a different future.

I did not choose these texts and their authors intending to demonstrate diversity within this particular ethno-linguistic group throughout the past five centuries. However, the respective life stories, the issues these individuals concerned themselves with, and the genres they employed to express themselves all point to the heterogeneous nature of Nahua interests and intellectual activities. If one were to ask what it has meant to be a Nahua intellectual and writer in postconquest Mexico, these accounts defy any stereotypes and refuse categorization. The Nahuas in these pages are of royal lineage and of humble origins. They have lived in the city and in the countryside, among Spaniards and isolated from them. They were priests, politicians, teachers, storytellers, and playwrights. They collaborated with indigenous and non-indigenous power brokers, collectors of antiquities, academics, artists, and rebels. They were conservative Catholics, adherents to traditional customs from long before the Spaniards arrived, and proponents of melding the two traditions together. They knew how to read the intricacies of Spanish colonial and Mexican constitutional law, as well as those of the natural world. Nahua experience over the centuries, as read in these chapters, disrupts any notion of indigenous peoples in Mexico as a monolithic or singular entity.

The diverse nature of Nahua intellectualism and writing does not mean, however, that we cannot identify common threads. For one, it should not go unnoticed that Nahua writing has been overwhelmingly dominated by Nahua men. An urgent task is to ask ourselves (and the archives) if we have overlooked instances of female Nahua writing or if we ought to be focusing elsewhere to learn more of women's contributions to the intellectual legacy of Nahua people. We must, of course, consider the factors that may have impeded women's ability to speak, to write, and to be heard in various historical moments. For example, from its earliest introduction to Nahua territory, alphabetic writing was a gendered and classed affair—the Catholic priests reserved reading and writing only for young indigenous men of noble descent. Common sense would suggest the patriarchal order established in the colonial period and replicated through the present day as sufficient explanation for the limited presence and/or visibility of women in Nahua intellectual territory. But then how are we to explain the conspicuous absence of Nahua women in today's vibrant community of female indigenous-language writers in Mexico including Irma Piñeda (Zapotec), Celerina Sánchez (Mixtec), and Mikeas Sánchez (Zoque), to name a few? As we continue our exploration of Nahua intellectualisms and writings, the identification and analysis of factors both within and exterior to Nahua communities that have prohibited, limited, or encouraged female and/or male Nahua intellectual work over the centuries deserve careful and sustained attention.

We also note the continued presence of colonial structures and relationships of inequality long after the official end of the colonial period. As evident in these writings, being indigenous in postconquest Mexico has consistently meant being socially, politically, and economically marginalized. At the same time, for the most part the intellectuals treated in this book were able to earn a living without having to abandon his/her own language and culture. Today this is almost unheard of; not long ago, Victoriano de la Cruz Cruz mentioned that he was at a loss to identify more than one or two places in his country where "mi lengua me daría de comer" (my language could feed me [provide me with a living]). As more and more young Nahuas migrate to urban centers in search of work, they are forced to assimilate to dominant cultural norms in order to avoid discrimination and secure employment. In this context, programs and research institutes like the Zacatecas Institute for Teaching and Research in Ethnology (IDIEZ) are becoming increasingly more important in that they provide the much-needed safe urban spaces for the study and development of indigenous languages and cultures, as well as the rare employment opportunities that do not require the rejection of native culture.

Is Victoriano's comment a grim diagnosis, or is there still reason for optimism? Recent activities at global and national levels signal a positive shift in the areas of indigenous political, social, economic, and cultural rights, including the 2007 United Nations Declaration on the Rights of Indigenous Peoples and Mexico's 2003 passage of the Ley General de Derechos Lingüísticos de los Pueblos Indígenas.[11] The Ley General specifically provided for the recognition and promotion of the pluricultural and multilingual makeup of Mexico. Article 7 of the law promises that "las lenguas indígenas serán válidas, al igual que el español, para cualquier asunto o trámite de carácter público, así como para acceder plenamente a la gestión, servicios e información pública" (indigenous languages will be valid, in the same manner as Spanish, for any matter or proceeding of a public nature, in order [for the citizen] to have complete access to the formalities and services of public information). Whereas article 10 guarantees the right to legal representation and courtroom proceedings in the indigenous language, this has been nearly impossible to put into practice. Monolingual (Spanish) mestizos tend to dominate social service positions, and attorneys and judges who are fluent in one of Mexico's 68 languages or 364 regional variations are few and far between. The creation of positions that insist on bilingualism as a condition of public service in predominantly indigenous areas would be a step toward complying with the new law. Intercultural multilingual curriculum designed to prepare indigenous (and non-indigenous) people for such positions in local, state, and federal government or in the legal system would potentially increase professional opportunities for Nahuas and other indigenous people in their native languages. This, of course, would require the integration of the Nahuatl (or other indigenous) language and culture programming at the level of higher education, a substantial shift of educational ideology and infrastructure. The 2003 Ley General also mandated the creation of the Instituto Nacional de Lenguas Indígenas (National Institute of Indigenous Languages, INALI), a federal entity charged with promoting the revitalization, preservation, and development of indigenous languages; improving the general public's knowledge of indigenous cultures and languages; and assisting with the implementation of public policy at the federal, state, and local levels.[12] Nevertheless, the gap between theory and practice often seems insurmountable. As I was explaining the 2003 law (in 2010) to an elder in the Huasteca, he interrupted me to say that I was naïve to think that such laws—those that benefit indigenous people—had been or would be acted upon: "Estas leyes nunca llegan a estas partes" (these types of laws never make it here). The actual impact of these global and national initiatives in Nahua communities remains to be seen.

In the epigraph that opened this book, Abelardo de la Cruz (Nahua) summed up what is an all-too-common experience for indigenous people in Mexico (and around the globe) today: he had been denied evidence of how indigenous peoples had engaged the world—and the word—around them as thinking, reasoning beings. He had been told explicitly and implicitly that people like him lacked intelligence and therefore had little or nothing to contribute to their local, national, or global communities. In our Reading Circles, however, Abelardo and his fellows encountered the writings of other Nahuas across the ages and saw people whose ingenuity and creativity ensured their individual survival as well as that of their community, language, and culture. And he began to see and believe that he too possessed these same qualities. I am convinced that the recovery and repatriation—the re-territorialization—of these stories to Nahua communities has empowering, generative potential. My albeit brief experience has shown that awareness of, and access to, Nahua writing is a key element of language and cultural revitalization projects in Nahua communities and can foment future Nahua intellectual work. The intellectuals treated in this book, for example, have already come to figure prominently in the teaching and research agendas of the Nahuas who sat with me in the Reading Circles. Antonio del Rincón, don Juan Buenaventura Zapata y Mendoza, Faustino Galicia Chimalpopoca, doña Luz Jiménez, and Ildefonso Maya Hernández presently serve as guideposts for the identification of Nahua intellectuals that can and should populate this narrative of Nahua space. Our task now is to explore further the networks in which they circulated as we continue to think, speak, read, and write about other Nahua intellectuals and writers like them. For this is not simply an old story waiting to be told. It is also the beginning of a new one.

# Notes

## Introduction

1. I use the terms *indigenous, Indian, Nahua, native,* and *native speaker* interchangeably. The question of appropriate terminology to be used in discussing peoples indigenous to the Americas is much debated and to date unresolved. Knowing that Christopher Columbus did not arrive at the Indies, and thus the people he encountered were not "Indians," for many it is problematic to continue to use the term Indian. At the same time, "Indian" (or *indio* in Spanish) is commonly used both within and outside of native communities for a variety of reasons. For example, Nahua playwright Ildefonso Maya Hernández (see chapter 5) preferred the term *indio,* as opposed to *indígena,* since, as Adam Versényi states, it served "as a constant reminder of the stupidity of the colonizing Spaniards who, believing they had reached the West Indies, called the inhabitants of the Americas 'Indians'" (445). The ideal, of course, is that each person is identified in the terms that they themselves use. Within their own communities and in their own language, present-day native speakers of the Nahuatl language often call themselves *macehualmeh* (common peoples), which distinguishes them from the *coyomeh* (literally, coyotes: generally people of European or mixed descent, whites, or outsiders). My use of the term "Nahua" as opposed to *macehualmeh* is due to the fact that *Nahua* is widely understood and utilized by both indigenous and non-indigenous communities, as well as among the general public and academic specialists. Finally, the method I have used in identifying specific individuals in this book as Nahuas is that he/she has been identified or self-identifies as such in the available literature.

2. The recovery and critical analysis of indigenous intellectual work and engagement with the written word in the Americas is an emerging field of study. Pioneering works along these lines include Warrior, *Tribal Secrets* and *The People and the Word,* as well as Montejo, *Maya Intellectual Renaissance.* See also Gutiérrez, *Nationalist Myths and Ethnic Identities;* Warren and Jackson, *Indigenous Movements, Self-Representation,*

*and the State in Latin America*; Rappaport, *Intercultural Utopias*; and Zapata Silva (ed.), *Intelectuales indígenas piensan América Latina*.

3. Lockhart, *Nahuas and Spaniards*, 2.

4. The term "Aztec" here refers to the Triple Alliance of Tenochtitlan, Tlatelolco, and Tlacopan. See López Austin's entry "Aztec" in *The Oxford Encyclopedia of Mesoamerican Cultures*, 68–70.

5. Pizzigoni, "Conclusion."

6. It is difficult to place a number on exactly how many individuals speak Nahuatl today, as sources vary greatly (INEGI, 2005: 1.3 million; Montemayor and Frischmann, 2:xiv, 2.5 million). It is thought that many native speakers decline to identify themselves as such to census takers due to discrimination.

7. P. Deloria, *Indians in Unexpected Places*, 4.

8. Camp, *Intellectuals and the State in Twentieth-Century Mexico*, 33.

9. Zapoteco Sideño, personal communication, July 25, 2011.

10. Fixico, "Call for Native Genius and Indigenous Intellectualism," 45.

11. Molina, *Vocabulario*, II:126r.

12. Ibid., II:52v.

13. Regarding active-action noun stems with *–liz*, see Andrews, *Introduction to Classical Nahuatl*, 356–362.

14. Molina, *Vocabulario*, II:48r. The incorporation of *ixtli* to *tlamatini* is not necessarily a recent phenomenon. Juan Cohuatl, a leader of Teolocholco Ocotelulco Tlaxcala, is called an "istlama" (wise man) in the 1556–1557 census. Gibson, *Tlaxcala in the Sixteenth Century*, 119.

15. Karttunen, *An Analytical Dictionary of Nahuatl*, 121; Karttunen and Lockhart have also noted in their study of the polite Nahuatl speech of the sixteenth century in the Bancroft Dialogues that *ix-* "by itself often has to do with presence, perception, wisdom" (*The Art of Nahuatl Speech*, 54).

16. Karttunen, *An Analytical Dictionary of Nahuatl*, 104, 275.

17. Boone, "Introduction: Writing and Recording Knowledge," 3.

18. Ibid., 15–20.

19. Ibid., 24–27. See also Graña-Behrens, "*Itz'aat* and *Tlamatini*."

20. Some of the known Nahua collaborators of Bernardino de Sahagún—intellectuals in their own right—include Antonio Valeriano (Azcapotzalco), Alonso Vergarano (Cuauhtitlan), Martín Jacobita (Tlatelolco), and Andrés Leonardo (Tlatelolco).

21. *Códice Matritenses de la Real Academia de la Historia*, VIII:118r–118v, quoted in León-Portilla, *La filosofía náhuatl*, 327 (translation to English, León-Portilla, *Aztec Thought and Culture*, 10–11). The description of the tlamatini in the Florentine Codex by Bernardino de Sáhagun and his collaborators (as transcribed and translated to English by Charles E. Dibble and Arthur J. O. Anderson) is quite similar to the earlier one found in the *Códice Matritenses*. I have chosen the *Códice Matritenses* version due to the fact that I prefer León-Portilla's translation of this fragment to the Dibble and Anderson version. For me, León-Portilla's more literal translation evokes imagery that is important in approaching the poetics of Nahuatl texts, especially metaphorical speech.

22. Boone, *Stories in Red and Black*, 25.

23. Boone, "*In Tlamatine*," 13.

24. Graña-Behrens, "*Itz'aat* and *Tlamatini*," 27.

25. León-Portilla, *Aztec Thought and Culture*, 22–23. Since the publication of his book *La filosofía náhuatl* in 1956, León-Portilla's framing of the activities of Nahua tlamatinimeh as philosophy has been subject to criticism, with some suggesting that his use of the Western term/concept "philosophy" is decontextualized, and thus misrepresents, Nahua social functions (Mignolo, "Philosophy and the Colonial Difference," 80). James Maffie's *Aztec Philosophy*, published in 2013, promises to revive this debate.

26. Sahagún, *Coloquios y doctrina cristiana*, 138–141.

27. León-Portilla, *Aztec Thought and Culture*, 18–19.

28. Sáhagun, *Florentine Codex*, book 10, 28.

29. Boone, *Stories in Red and Black*, 24.

30. Rabasa, *Tell Me the Story of How I Conquered You*. Nahuatl is a gender-neutral language; therefore, tlahcuiloh could be interpreted and translated as "he" or "she." However, there are few identified female tlahcuilohqueh in extant sources. See the *Códice Telleriano-Remensis*, which includes an image of the wife of Huitzilhuitl, a Mexica ruler, as a tlahcuiloh (folio 30r). The *Codex Cardona* also includes an image of one María Bartola, poised with pen in hand. See Bauer, *The Search for the Codex Cardona* and Wood, "The Search for Answers about the Cardona," 391.

31. Along with his own scholarship, including the classic *The Nahuas After the Conquest*, James Lockhart's legacy in particular is visible in the network of high-profile scholars of postconquest Mesoamerica who either completed doctoral studies under his direction or employ "New Philology" methods often associated with him (Robert Haskett, Caterina Pizzigoni, Matthew Restall, Susan Schroeder, Lisa Sousa, Kevin Terraciano, Camilla Townsend, and Stephanie Wood, among others). This method holds as its basic premise that the very best way to study a culture is to utilize "sources created by the people themselves, in their own language, revealing their outlook, their rhetoric, their genres of expression, the intimacies of their lives, above all their categories" (Lockhart, *Of Things of the Indies*, 350). See also Lockhart, Sousa, and Wood, *Sources and Methods for the Study of Mesoamerican Ethnohistory*, http://whp.uoregon.edu/Lockhart/.

32. Rama, *The Lettered City*; Rappaport and Cummins, *Beyond the Lettered City*, 3–4.

33. de Certeau, *The Practice of Everyday Life*, 30.

34. On Bourbon Reforms and their effects on indigenous languages in Mexico, see Yannakakis, *The Art of Being In-Between*, 161–191.

35. While it has long been assumed that administrative documents were no longer written in Nahuatl after the very early 1800s, Miriam Melton Villanueva and Caterina Pizzigoni's essay "Late Nahuatl Testaments from the Toluca Valley" analyzes recent discoveries of mundane documents written in Nahuatl from the Toluca Valley dated through 1825.

36. See a listing of contemporary indigenous language writers in Mexico today at the website for Escritores en Lenguas Indígenas A.C., http://www.nacionmulticultural.unam.mx/eliac/menu/02escritores.html. Adam Coon's in-progress dissertation entitled "Iahqui Estados Onidos" offers an in-depth study of later twentieth- and early twenty-first century literatures in Nahuatl.

37. Restall, Sousa, and Terraciano, *Mesoamerican Voices*, 19. Miriam Melton Villanueva's dissertation, "The Nahuas at Independence," illuminates the transition from Nahuatl to Spanish in administrative documentation in Nahua communities.

38. Borah, "Race and Class in Mexico"; Cox, *The Red Land to the South*, 6; Gutiérrez, *Nationalist Myths and Ethnic Identities*, 3. See also *Cuéntame* (Tell Me About It; http://cuentame.inegi.org.mx/), an educational website for children operated by INEGI, Mexico's national institute for geographic and demographic data collection. According to the page related to speakers of indigenous languages, "un elemento muy importante que los distingue y les da identidad, es la lengua con la que se comunican" (an important element which distinguishes [indigenous peoples] from others, and that which gives them their identity is the language with which they communicate). http://cuentame.inegi.gob.mx/poblacion/lindigena.aspx?tema=P.

39. Chacón, "Contemporary Maya Writers," 14.

40. Bonfil Batalla, *Utopía y revolución*, 22.

41. See Field, "Blood and Traits." For an introduction to race and ethnicity in Latin America, see Mörner (ed.), *Race and Class in Latin America*; Cope, *The Limits of Racial Domination*; Wade, *Race and Ethnicity in Latin America*; and Carrera, *Imagining Identity in New Spain*.

42. O'Brien, *Firsting and Lasting*, xxii.

43. S. Ortiz, "Towards a National Indian Literature," 10.

44. Justice, "Seeing (and Reading) Red," 106. See also Justice, *Our Fire Survives the Storm*, 11–13.

45. Moraña, Dussel, and Jáuregui, "Colonialism and Its Replicants," 2.

46. Mignolo, *The Idea of Latin America*, 11.

47. Quijano, "Coloniality of Power, Eurocentrism, and Latin America," 533.

48. Ibid., 537.

49. Ibid., 541.

50. Montejo, *Maya Intellectual Renaissance*, 162.

51. Ibid.

52. Hernández Ávila and Varese, "Indigenous Intellectual Sovereignties," 84.

53. Gramsci, *Selections from the Prison Notebooks of Antonio Gramsci*, 12; Roseberry, "Hegemony and the Language of Contention," 358–361.

54. Roseberry, 361.

55. See, for example, Greenblatt, *Marvelous Possessions*; Mignolo, *The Darker Side of the Renaissance*; and Gruzinski, *La colonización de lo imaginario*.

56. Chacón, "Contemporary Maya Writers," 63.

57. Brooks, *The Common Pot*, 254.

58. Round, *Removable Type*, 224.

59. Ibid.

60. Lopenzina, *Red Ink*, xi.

61. Ibid.

62. Hernández Hernández, *In tlahtolli, in ohtli, la palabra, el camino*, 97.

63. de la Cruz, "*Reflexiones sobre la escritura y el futuro de la literatura indígena*," 487.

64. Ibid., 488.

65. Ibid., 489.

66. Consider, for example, the bilingual Nahuatl-Spanish novels by Crispín Amador Ramírez (Nahua, San Isidro Atlapexco, Hidalgo): *El infierno del paraíso* (2005) and *El tiempo no abortó/Tonali Amo Tlanki* (2008), analyzed in my colleague Arturo Arias's recent essay, "Nahuatlizando la novelística."

67. Quoted in Rappaport, *Intercultural Utopias*, 167.

68. Frischmann, "The Indigenous Word in Mesoamerica," 19–20.

69. Besides the earlier mentioned studies by Salomon and Niño-Murcia, Brooks, Round, and Lopenzina regarding debates on orality and literacy, see Finnegan, *Literacy and Orality*, 12–13; Womack, *Red on Red*, 12–16; Konkle, *Writing Indian Nations*, 28–29; Weaver, *That the People Might Live*, 21–26, 40–42; and Ong, *Orality and Literacy*.

70. Townsend, "Reading Symbolic and Historical Representations in Early Mesoamerica," 185.

71. Cornejo Polar, *Escribir en el aire*, 13–14.

72. On contemporary Mexican indigenous literatures, see Montemayor and Frischmann's important three-volume anthology, *Words of the True Peoples/Palabras de los seres verdaderos*, treating indigenous prose, poetry, and theater. Each volume includes the work in the original indigenous language and is accompanied by a Spanish and English translation.

73. For more on "experience" as an analytical framework, see Scott, "The Evidence of Experience" and Ireland, "The Appeal to Experience and Its Consequences."

74. Warrior, *The People and the Word*, xxiii.

75. Ibid., xx.

76. Ibid., xiv–xv.

77. Mallon, "Introduction," 2.

78. V. Deloria, *Custer Died for Your Sins*; Mihesuah (ed.), Introduction to *Natives and Academics*; Mihesuah and Wilson (eds.), *Indigenizing the Academy*; Tuhiwai Smith, *Decolonizing Methodologies*.

79. Mallon, "Introduction," 2.

80. Mendieta, "Remapping Latin American Studies," 294. The literature of postcolonial theory, subaltern studies, and post-Occidental theory is vast. For an introduction, see Said, *Orientalism*; Spivak,"Can the Subaltern Speak?"; and Guha, *Subaltern Studies Reader*. In conversation with the previous texts, but with an eye toward Latin America, see Latin American Subaltern Studies Group, "Founding Statement"; Beverly, *Subalternity and Representation*; Mignolo, *The Darker Side of the Renaissance*; and Moraña, Dussel, and Jáuregui (eds.), "Colonialism and Its Replicants." See also Coronil, "Beyond Occidentalism."

81. Latin American Subaltern Studies Group, "Founding Statement," 10.

82. Rabasa and Sanjinés, "Introduction," vii; Beverley, "Writing in Reverse," 274.

83. The following Nahua students and researchers who participated in Reading Circles and individual (formal and informal) interviews welcome comments and inquiries: Abelardo de la Cruz de la Cruz (abelardouaz@gmail.com); Delfina de la Cruz de la Cruz (celiyaz.2003@gmail.com); Ana Delia Cruz de la Cruz (delia_266@hotmail.com); Catalina Cruz de la Cruz (caty020@hotmail.com); Sabina Cruz de la Cruz (sabi476@hotmail.com); Ofelia Cruz Morales (ofecruz_12@hotmail.com); Eduardo de la Cruz Cruz (chavalon_8603@hotmail.com); and Victoriano de la Cruz Cruz (tepoxtec03@hotmail.com). Note that many participants share similar surnames; the Cruz and de la Cruz surnames were bestowed on scores of Indian communities by the Catholic Church. Abelardo de la Cruz de la Cruz and Victoriano de la Cruz Cruz are siblings (although they have variations in their surnames), as are Catalina, Sabina, and Ana Delia Cruz de la Cruz.

84. Rappaport, *Intercultural Utopias*, 83.

85. Hale, *Engaging Contradictions*, 4.

86. Ibid., 88. Over the past several decades, researchers in social sciences and the humanities have become increasingly more aware of the need to renovate ethnographic practices characterized by the authoritative monologues that simultaneously objectified the "other" being described and silenced their intellectual contribution. In an effort to depict more accurately the construction of knowledge as one of negotiation and dialogue in the field, anthropologists such as James Clifford have argued that the dialogic process should be more transparently reflected in the written ethnographic texts themselves. See Clifford, "On Ethnographic Authority." Rappaport suggests, however, that we need to move beyond issues related to the writing of ethnographies and pay more attention to what it is anthropologists are actually doing in the field. For Rappaport, it isn't how the dialogues that take place in the field are represented in scholarly publications that should be our main concern; it is the nature of these dialogues as they occur.

87. Tuhiwai Smith, *Decolonizing Methodologies*, 35.

88. Thiong'o, *Decolonizing the Mind*, 3.

89. Tuhiwai Smith, *Decolonizing Methodologies*, 16.

90. Warren and Jackson, *Indigenous Movements, Self-Representation, and the State in Latin America*, 3.

91. Freire, "Creating Alternative Research Methods," 30.

92. Rabasa, *Without History*, 11.

93. Wright, *Lectura de náhuatl*, 40.

94. Taylor, *Theatre of Crisis*, 34.

95. Ibid., 35. Inés Hernández Ávila also refutes Taylor's observation here in her essay, "The Power of Native Languages and the Performance of Indigenous Autonomy."

96. Karttunen, *Analytical Dictionary*, xii.

97. Spivak, "Roundtable," 720.

## Chapter 1

1. Guzmán Betancourt, "La política lingüística de la Compañía de Jesús en Nueva España," 386.

2. Decorme, *La obra de los jesuitas mexicanos*, 251.

3. Yannakakis, *The Art of Being In-Between*, 14–15. Following Irene Silverblatt, Yannakakis notes the difference between nineteenth-century understandings of "race" as a biological phenomenon and colonial-period "racial thinking" that is more a calculus of lineage/descent and legal categories. Silverblatt, *Modern Inquisitions*, 17.

4. Gibson, *The Aztecs Under Spanish Rule*, 153. The term *peninsulares* refers to Spaniards born in Europe, but residing in the colonies (in this case, New Spain). *Criollos* refers to those born to Spaniards, but in the colonies. On the shifts in social stratification in the early colonial period, see also Nutini and Isaac, *Social Stratification in Central Mexico*, 39–43, and Pérez Rocha and Tena, *La nobleza indígena del centro de México después de la conquista*.

5. Yannakakis, *The Art of Being In-Between*, 14. *Indios* were protected from slavery (although given in encomienda and repartimiento), exempt from the Inquisition (yet

subject to investigations by ecclesiastical prosecutors, or *provisores*), allowed to exercise political autonomy (to the extent that it did not contradict Crown policy), issued legal title to communal land holdings, and provided a separate juridical apparatus, the Juzgado General de las Indias.

6. Ibid., 15. By the mid-seventeenth century, colonial anxieties over race and place would find their full expression in an elaborate caste system (*sistema de castas*), which proposed to codify some forty different categories of "racial" mixtures in New Spain. On the caste system in New Spain, see Cope, *The Limits of Racial Domination*, and Carrera, *Imagining Identity in New Spain*.

7. On the pivotal role of the native intermediary in colonial society, see Yannakakis, *The Art of Being In-Between* and Charles, *Allies at Odds*.

8. Yannakakis, xii–xiii.

9. Burkhart, *Holy Wednesday*, 59.

10. Adorno, "Cultures in Contact," 33.

11. P. Deloria, *Indians in Unexpected Places*, 7.

12. Pérez de Ribas, *Corónica y historia religiosa de la Compañía de Jesús de México en Nueva España*, 130.

13. Karttunen, "La contribución del trabajo de Antonio del Rincón a la lexicografía náhuatl del siglo XX," 396.

14. Menegus and Aguirre, *Los indios*, 32–33; Martínez Baracs, *Un gobierno de indios*, 352.

15. See Guzmán Betancourt, "Antonio del Rincón." Rincón is mentioned briefly in Zambrano, *Diccionario bio-bibliográfico de la Compañía de Jesús en México*, 2:606, 611–613 ("Carta anua de 1594"); 3:227, 7:138. See also Real Junta de Temporalidades, 48r, Archivo General de la Nación, Mexico City. Most sources note that Rincón was descended from the kings of Texcoco. I am grateful to the staff at the Biblioteca José María Lafragua at the Benemérita Universidad Autónoma de Puebla, particularly the director, Manuel E. de Santiago Hernández, for exceptional patience as we searched to no avail for our elusive protagonist in their holdings related to the Colegios San Jerónimo and Espíritu Santo in Puebla. It is my understanding that this may be explained by the fact that many of the earliest documents related to the Jesuits in Puebla are now held in the Biblioteca Nacional de Chile in the Fondo Toribio Medina. It remains to be seen if more information regarding Rincón will appear in that location, or perhaps in Rome.

16. Florescano and Malvido, *Ensayos sobre la historia de las epidemias en México*, 187.

17. See Schwaller, "The Expansion of Nahuatl as a Lingua Franca."

18. Errington, *Linguistics in a Colonial World*, I:39.

19. Burkhart, *Slippery Earth*, 12.

20. *Códice Ramírez*, 188.

21. Lopes Don, "The 1539 Inquisition and Trial of Don Carlos of Texcoco in Early Mexico," 580; Duverger, *La conversión de los indios de Nueva España*, 111.

22. Ibid., 111.

23. Regarding the case of don Carlos Ometochtzin, see *Proceso inquisitorial del cacique de Tetzcoco*; Lopes Don, "The 1539 Inquisition and Trial of Don Carlos of Texcoco in Early Mexico"; Gruzinski, *The Conquest of Mexico*; Rabasa, *Franciscans and Dominicans Under the Gaze of the "Tlacuilo"*; and Greenleaf, *Zumárraga y la Inquisición mexicana*.

24. Gruzinski, *The Conquest of Mexico*, 19.

25. Gibson, "Aztec Aristocracy in Colonial Mexico," 173–174.

26. Nagel Bielicke, "Un acercamiento a la vida de Antonio del Rincón," 448; Sánchez Vásquez, "Síntesis sobre la Real y Pontificia Universidad de México," 294.

27. Menegus and Aguirre, *Los indios*, 58.

28. I am indebted to Father Joseph Weiss, Ph.D., S.J., at St. Thomas More Catholic Community in St. Paul, Minnesota, who patiently assisted me in mapping out Rincón's trajectory and helped me better understand the gaps or silences in the documented trail.

29. Nagel Bielicke, "Un acercamiento a la vida de Antonio del Rincón," 448.

30. Osorio Romero, *Colegios y profesores jesuitas que enseñaron latín en Nueva España*, 26.

31. Zubillaga, "La provincia jesuítica de Nueva España," 78; Decorme, *La obra de los jesuitas mexicanos*, 22; Alegre, *Historia de la provincia de la Compañía de Jesús de Nueva España*, 287n; Palomera, *La obra educativa de los Jesuitas en Puebla*, 25–39; and Montiel Bonilla, "La fundación de los colegios jesuitas en Puebla," 31.

32. Nagel Bielicke, "Un acercamiento a la vida de Antonio del Rincón," 448–449.

33. Ibid., 449.

34. Ibid., 450.

35. For important insights regarding the differences between the Franciscan and Dominican orders, particularly how each order's approach to evangelization can be linked to divergent understandings of "the concept of *habitus*, the place of the senses in the acquisition of knowledge, and the relationship between mind and language," see Rabasa, *Franciscans and Dominicans Under the Gaze of a "Tlacuilo,"* 21–22. Ricard, *The Spiritual Conquest of Mexico*, discusses the Franciscan, Dominican, and Augustine orders at length. Kobayashi, *La educación como conquista*, addresses the relationship between Franciscan evangelization and education of Indians. For the Dominican order, see Fernández Rodríguez, *Los dominicos en el contexto de la primera evangelización*. See also Díaz Balsera, *The Pyramid Under the Cross*; Burkhart, *The Slippery Earth*; and Gonzalbo Aizpuru, *Educación y colonización en la Nueva España*.

36. Some suggest that the intention of evangelization in indigenous languages was to ensure that the majority of Indians remained linguistically isolated, further ensuring that they would be separated from the bad influence of the Spaniards. Or perhaps it was shrewd job protection on the part of the friars; if the Indians could not speak Spanish, the religious men would always be necessary to bridge both worlds. Ricard, *The Spiritual Conquest*, 52.

37. Heath, *Telling Tongues*, 15.

38. Ibid., 8.

39. Ibid., 13. See Hernán Cortés's October 15, 1524, letter to Charles V in *Cartas y relaciones de Hernán Cortés al emperador Carlos V*.

40. Ibid., 14. See *Recopilación de Leyes*, lib. VI, tít. I, ley 18, 1550 ("Que donde fuere posible se pongan escuelas de la lengua Castellana, para que la aprendan los Indios"). See also *Recopilación de Leyes*, lib. I, tít. XXIII, ley 11, 1535 ("Que sean favorecidos los Colegios fundados para criar hijos de Caciques, y se funden otros en las Ciudades principales"). This decree would be repeated in 1540 by Charles V (and again by Philip II in 1579, and Philip III in 1618 and 1619).

41. For more on the uneven installation of Spanish as the language of empire in the early colonial period, see Juan Lodares's essay "Language, Catholicism, and Power,"

where he argues that linguistic heterogeneity, differences in Crown theories and practices in terms of linguistic policy, and expansion of the Spanish language correlating with the Spanish Empire's decline (as opposed to the Spanish language as technology of unilateral domination) were the defining characteristics of the time. See also Binotti, "La 'lengua compañera del imperio.'"

42. Heath, *Telling Tongues*, 19–20. See "Al provincial de la orden de Santo Domingo de la Nueva España: Que procure como todos los religiosos de su orden enseñen a los indios la lengua castellana, Valladolid 1550" in García, *Documentos inéditos ó muy raros para la historia de México*, 15:106–108.

43. Ibid.

44. Examples of the double-edged sword of education for Indians can be found in Pérez Rocha and Tena, *La nobleza indígena del centro de México después de la conquista*, which offers examples of forty early colonial documents written by Indians of New Spain (in Latin, Castilian, and Nahuatl), demanding restitution and privileges, many addressed to King Charles V and King Philip II.

45. Fuchs, *Mimesis and Empire*, 20.

46. Pellicer, "Oralidad y escritura de la literatura indígena," 29; Gonzalbo Aizpuru, 58.

47. Schwaller, "The Expansion of Nahuatl as a Lingua Franca." See *Recopilación de Leyes*, lib. I, tít. VI, ley 30, 1574, 1578 ("Que los Clerigos y Religiosos no sean admitidos à Doctrinas, sin saber la lengua general de los Indios, que han de administrar"). See also Philip II's 1565 order, "A los prelados de Nueva España: Que procuren que los clerigos curas sepan el idioma de sus feligreses, Buengrado, 1565" in García, *Documentos inéditos ó muy raros para la historia de Mexico*, 15:163–165.

48. Heath, *Telling Tongues*, 26; Cédulas Reales, vol. 47, Archivo General de la Nación, Mexico City.

49. Heath, *Telling Tongues*, 26.

50. Foucault, "Two Lectures," 98.

51. Guzmán Betancourt, "La política lingüística de la Compañía de Jesús en Nueva España," 386.

52. Heath, *Telling Tongues*, 22–23.

53. Lockhart, "Introduction," 6.

54. Poole, "Church Law on the Ordination of Indians and *Castas* in New Spain," 637.

55. Ibid., 640.

56. See Philip II's letter "Al Arzobispo de Mexico: Que por ahora no de las ordenes a los mestizos, sino solo a personas de reconocida suficiencia, El Pardo, 1578" in García, *Documentos inéditos ó muy raros para la historia de México*, 15:215–216.

57. Poole, "Church Law on the Ordination of Indians and *Castas* in New Spain," 642–643.

58. Quoted in ibid., 641.

59. Ibid., 643.

60. Quoted in ibid., 644. Poole also states that it is unclear to what extent the Franciscans and Jesuits participated in the conversations related to Indians and the priesthood at the Third Provincial Council (650).

61. Ibid., 638–639.

62. Ibid., 639. The ambiguity of the Third Provincial Council's rulings is expertly described and analyzed by Poole, 643–649. For further reading on the issue of the

ordination of Indians during the colonial period, see Álvarez Mejía, "La cuestión del clero indígena en la época colonial"; Menegus and Aguirre, *Los indios*; and Llaguno, *La personalidad jurídica del indio*.

63. Osorio Romero, *La enseñanza del latín a los indios*, v.

64. Poole, "Church Law on the Ordination of Indians and *Castas* in New Spain," 641, 650.

65. Ibid., 637.

66. The eighteen extant colonial Nahuatl grammars and dictionaries are as follows: Grammars: Andrés de Olmos, 1547; Alonso de Molina, 1571; Antonio del Rincón, 1595; Diego de Galdo Guzmán, 1642; Horacio Carochi, 1645; Agustín de Vetancurt, 1673; Juan Guerra, 1692; Manuel Pérez, 1713; Antonio Vázquez Gastelú, 1726; Carlos de Tapia Zenteno, 1753; José Agustín Aldama y Guevara, 1754; Ignacio de Paredes, 1759; Joseph de Carranza (17??); Jerónimo Tomas de Aquino Cortés y Zedeño, 1765. Dictionaries: Alonso de Molina, 1555; Bernardino de Sahagún, 1590; Anonymous, 1590; Anonymous, 1598. For further information on these grammars and dictionaries, see Fountain, "Colonial Linguistics in New Spain," and Aguirre Beltrán, *Lenguas vernáculas*.

67. The Olmos grammar was known to have circulated since 1547, but it was not actually published for the first time until 1875 by Rémi Siméon. For a detailed analysis of Olmos's extraordinary texts and pioneering efforts in ethnographic/linguistic matters in New Spain, see Baudot, *Utopia and History in Mexico*, specifically chapters 3 and 4.

68. Mignolo, *The Darker Side of the Renaissance*, 54.

69. Fountain, "Colonial Linguistics in New Spain," 264.

70. One example is don Pablo Nazareo de Xaltocan, who wrote a lengthy letter in Latin to King Philip II demanding restitution and privileges reflecting his rank as a noble Indian. The text, with translation to Spanish, can be found in Osorio Romero, *La enseñanza del latín a los indios*.

71. Garibay, *Llave del Náhuatl*, 122.

72. Baudot, *Utopia and History in Mexico*, 225–234.

73. Regarding Molina's unparalleled two-part Spanish-Nahuatl/Nahuatl-Spanish dictionary, see Clayton and Campbell, "Alonso de Molina as Lexicographer."

74. Schwaller, "A Catalogue of Pre-1840 Nahuatl Works Held by The Lilly Library."

75. Karttunen, "La contribución del trabajo de Antonio del Rincón a la lexicografía náhuatl del siglo XX," 391.

76. For extensive analysis of Nebrija and the early Nahuatl grammarians, see Esparza Torres, "Nebrija y los modelos de los misioneros lingüistas del náhuatl."

77. Lodares, "Language, Catholicism, and Power"; Mignolo, *The Darker Side of the Renaissance*, 50.

78. Olmos, "Arte para aprender la lengua mexicana," 9.

79. Molina, "Argumento" in "Arte de la lengua mexicana y castellana."

80. Rincón, "Prologo al lector" in *Arte mexicana compuesta por el padre Antonio del Rincón*.

81. In Molina's prologue to his *Arte*, he begins by saying that the language *lacks* letters (*b, d, f, g, r, s*) (34). My assertion that Molina sees alterity, but perhaps not lack, has more to do with his global comparison of Nahuatl to Latin in terms of structure. Regarding the issue of lack of letters (seen repeatedly in colonial grammars), I believe this speaks more to the grammarian's audience (non-native speakers) who will attempt

to come to terms with the new language by making correlations with their own, than to a kind of sinister Eurocentrism. Indeed, perhaps the native speakers of Nahuatl found Castilian and Latin to have a lack or excess of letters, in comparison with their own. Rincón echoes Molina in saying, "Estos no tienen seis letras nuestras que son. B. D. F. G. R. S. ni tampoco vsan la. v. consonante, ni las dos. ll. al modo del español" (62) (They do not have six of our letters, which are the b, d, f, g, r, s; nor do they use the "v" or the "ll" as in Spanish). This, in my estimation, is simply a marker of a non-indigenous audience for his work.

82. Fountain, "Colonial Linguistics in New Spain."

83. Rincón, "Prologo al lector" in *Arte mexicana.*

84. See Garcilaso de la Vega, *Royal Commentaries of the Incas*, 51, 79–81.

85. Ibid., 5, 51. Garcilaso describes how by being unaware of this nuance of the Quechua language, the process of identifying (and thus extirpating) idolatrous behavior was often based on limited or incorrect (uninformed) information related to this issue of pronunciation: "The Spaniards attribute many other gods to the Incas because they are unable to distinguish the times and idolatries of the first age from those of the second. Moreover they are not well enough acquainted with the language to be able to ask for and obtain information from the Indians, and their ignorance has led them to attribute to the Incas many or all of the gods the latter removed from the Indians they subjected to their empire [ . . . ]. A particular source of this error was that Spaniards did not know the many diverse meanings of the word *huaca*. This, when the last syllable is pronounced from the top of the palate, means 'an idol,' such as Jupiter, Mars, or Venus [ . . . ]. Because of these very various meanings, the Spaniards, who only understood the first and main sense of 'idol,' think that the Indians regarded as gods everything they called *huaca*" (76–77). As the knowing subject, Garcilaso explains in three continuous pages the many meanings of the word *huaca* (79–81).

86. On Rincón's diacritic system, see Smith Stark, "La grafía del náhuatl de Antonio del Rincón."

87. Olmos, "Arte para aprender la lengua mexicana," 7.

88. Molina, "Arte de la lengua mexicana y castellana," 55. Note that Rincón more than likely had access to Molina's grammar, as the glossary portion of the *Arte mexicana* follows Molina's unique system of citing verbs. Regarding Molina's system, see Lockhart, *Nahuatl as Written*, 153–154.

89. In the very first sentence of Carochi's *Arte*, he notes his intellectual debt to the first three grammars and to Rincón: "Aviendo salido à luz tres Artes desta lengua, sufficientes y doctos, en particular del P. Antonio del Rincon que cõ tanto magisterio la enseña parecerà superfluo este" (14) ("After the publication of three learned and sufficient grammars of this language, particularly that of Father Antonio del Rincón, who teaches it so masterfully, this one may appear superfluous" [15]).

90. Karttunen, "La contribución del trabajo de Antonio del Rincón," 403.

91. *Códice Matritenses de la Real Academia de la Historia*, VIII:118r–118v, quoted in León-Portilla, *La filosofía náhuatl*, 327. Translation to English from León-Portilla, *Aztec Thought and Culture*, 10–11.

92. Las Casas, *Bartolomé de las Casas: A Selection of His Writings*, 142–146; my emphases. The original Spanish version of the *Apologética historia sumaria* can be found in Las Casas, *Obras escogidas de Fray Bartolomé de las Casas*, 4:434–437, 439–441, and 445.

93. Alegre, *Historia de la provincia de la Compañía de Jesús de Nueva España*, 278.
94. Errington, *Linguistics in a Colonial World*, 27.

## Tlen naman 1

1. www.macehualli.org.
2. Sullivan, "The IDIEZ Project," 145.
3. Ibid., 140.
4. Interview, May 26, 2011.
5. Sullivan, "The IDIEZ Project," 142.

## Chapter 2

1. Trouillot, *Silencing the Past*, 26–28.
2. Wood, "Introduction," 5.
3. A noble son of Quiahuiztlan, one of the four sub-altepetl of Tlaxcala (along with Ocotelolco, Tizatlan, and Tepeticpac), don Juan followed the expected sociopolitical trajectory of a high-ranking member of the Tlaxcalan noble class. He served in a variety of political positions in the indigenous cabildo (municipal council) of Tlaxcala, including *regidor* (council member), *alcalde* (judge), *gobernador* (indigenous governor), treasurer, and notary. Townsend, "Don Juan Buenaventura Zapata and the Notion of a Nahua Identity," 153.
4. I take the phrase "negotiation within domination" from Ruiz Medrano and Kellogg's excellent volume, *Negotiation Within Domination*.
5. The manuscript has only begun to circulate again outside of the archive somewhat recently, with Luis Reyes García and Andrea Martínez Baracs's transcription of the Nahuatl text, Spanish translation, and critical introduction (Zapata y Mendoza, 1995). Ethnohistorian James Lockhart has identified Zapata's annals as the standout of the later years of the Nahua annals tradition, for both the quantity and quality of his treatment of Tlaxcala's past and for the level of detail as it relates to seventeenth-century Tlaxcalan politics (Lockhart, *The Nahuas After the Conquest*, 391–392). Camilla Townsend has carried out the most in-depth analyses of Zapata's life and work, and she is presently completing the first systematic and comprehensive analysis of the annals genre. Both Lockhart and Townsend have pointed to the groundbreaking, yet unfortunately interrupted, dissertation work of Frances Krug on the Tlaxcalan-Puebla annals as being important for their research on Zapata and the annals genre in general. See Krug and Townsend, "The Tlaxcala-Puebla Family of Annals."
6. See Kranz, "Visual Persuasion." Reading the Tlaxcalan pictorial genre's framing of Tlaxcala as deserving of rights and privileges, Kranz's study focuses specifically on the *Lienzo de Tlaxcala* and images from Tlaxcalan chronicler Diego Muñoz Camargo's manuscript.
7. Manuscript in Paris: Méxicaine 212, collection E. Eug. Goupil, Ancienne Collection J. M. A. Aubin, Bibliothèque Nationale de France. Reyes García and Martínez Baracs note that other copies of this manuscript in Mexico may also be found in the following locations: one copy at the Biblioteca Nacional de Antropología e Historia (BNAH), Colección de Francisco del Paso y Troncoso, leg. 50; one copy at Centro de

Investigaciones y Estudios Superiores en Antropología Social (CIESAS) in Mexico City; and two copies in the city of Tlaxcala—one with recently deceased Tlaxcalan intellectual and muralist Desiderio H. Xochitiotzin (1922–2007) and the other with Tlaxcalan writer and teacher Isaías Bello. I have consulted the BNAH manuscript, but cite the Reyes García and Martínez Baracs critical edition (1995). Translations to English are my own.

8. Zapata y Mendoza, *Historia cronológica de la noble ciudad de Tlaxcala*, 38.

9. Regarding don Manuel de Santos y Salazar, see Townsend's introduction to *Here in This Year*, 21–40, as well as the introduction to Zapata's manuscript by Reyes García and Martínez Baracs, *Historia cronológica de la noble ciudad de Tlaxcala*, 27–29. See also Lockhart's assessment of Santos y Salazar's contribution to Zapata's text in *The Nahuas After the Conquest*, 592–593, n. 53.

10. Boone, *Stories in Red and Black*, 197.

11. Ibid.

12. Lockhart, *The Nahuas After the Conquest*, 376; Townsend, *Here in This Year*, 11–12.

13. Townsend, "Glimpsing Native American Historiography," 632–635.

14. Lockhart, *The Nahuas After the Conquest*, 378.

15. Krug and Townsend, "The Tlaxcala-Puebla Family of Annals," 6.

16. Townsend, "Glimpsing Native American Historiography," 627.

17. Townsend, "Don Juan Buenaventura Zapata and the Notion of a Nahua Identity," 161. Zapata y Mendoza, *Historia cronológica de la noble ciudad de Tlaxcala*, 96–107.

18. Zapata y Mendoza, *Historia cronológica de la noble ciudad de Tlaxcala*, 102–103, 104–105.

19. Navarrette, "Chimalpain y Alva Ixtlilxóchitl," 108.

20. Ibid.

21. Lockhart, *The Nahuas After the Conquest*, 376.

22. Krug and Townsend, "The Tlaxcala-Puebla Family of Annals," 3. It should be noted that after 1577, the compilation, editing, and authoring of postconquest annals was being carried out at a time when writing about the indigenous past or possessing such documents was prohibited by the Crown. That the annals genre thrived in an atmosphere of censure is not surprising, however, as we know that one of the hallmarks of colonial law in New Spain was that "legislative iteration mean[t] noncompliance" (Lockhart, "Introduction," 6).

23. Lockhart, *The Nahuas After the Conquest*, 376.

24. Ibid., 376, 378.

25. Reyes García, *Anales de Juan Bautista*, 14.

26. Martínez Baracs, "Historiadores de la segunda mitad del siglo XVII en Tlaxcala," 111.

27. Krug and Townsend, "The Tlaxcala-Puebla Family of Annals," 7–10.

28. Townsend, "Don Juan Buenaventura Zapata and the Notion of a Nahua Identity," 156–160; Martínez Baracs, "Historiadores de la segunda mitad del siglo XVII en Tlaxcala."

29. Townsend, "Don Juan Buenaventura Zapata and the Notion of a Nahua Identity," 155.

30. Ibid., 154–156; Lockhart, *The Nahuas After the Conquest*, 392. Zapata was also careful to note when a priest heard confession or preached in the Nahuatl language. See 96–97 and 422–423 of his manuscript, *Historia cronológica de la noble ciudad de Tlaxcala*.

31. Florescano, *Memoria mexicana*, 374–375; Ruiz Medrano, *Mexico's Indigenous Communities*, 31–32.

32. For versions of the alliance with Cortés and subsequent petitions for privileges based on service, see, for example, Gibson, *Tlaxcala in the Sixteenth Century*, 26, 158–169; Lockhart, Berdan, and Anderson, *The Tlaxcalan Actas*, 2; Baber, "Empire, Indians, and the Negotiation for the Status of City in Tlaxcala," 24; and Ybarra, *Performing Conquest*, 14–15.

33. Baber, "Empire, Indians, and the Negotiation for the Status of City in Tlaxcala," 23–24. Those familiar with Gibson's seminal work on the history of Tlaxcala might note a discrepancy in Baber's timeline, who cites "first privileges" as being awarded in 1529. In Gibson's work, he states that the 1527 delegation did not appear to be successful and that the year 1535 marks "the first authenticated cases of royal privilege in the history of Tlaxcala" (*Tlaxcala in the Sixteenth Century*, 164–165). Baber, however, notes that Gibson did not work in the Spanish archives, which is where she found evidence of earlier privileges.

34. See *Recopilación de Leyes*, lib. VI, tít. 1, ley 42, 1585 ("Que los Gobernadores de Indios de Tlaxcala sean naturales").

35. Lockhart, Berdan, and Anderson, *The Tlaxcalan Actas*, 1.

36. Yannakakis, *The Art of Being In-Between*, 3.

37. Gibson, *Tlaxcala in the Sixteenth Century*, x–xi.

38. Martínez Baracs, *Un gobierno de indios*, 321–352.

39. Ibid., 321–376.

40. Geertz, *Local Knowledge*, 143, quoted in Curcio-Nagy, *The Great Festivals of Colonial Mexico City*, 3.

41. Ramos, "Succession and Death," 185–186.

42. Curcio-Nagy, *The Great Festivals of Colonial Mexico City*, 3.

43. Taylor, "Performance and/as History," 68.

44. Romero Galván, *Historiografía novohispana de tradición indígena*, 352–353.

45. Curcio-Nagy, *The Great Festivals of Colonial Mexico City*, 50.

46. Gibson, *Tlaxcala in the Sixteenth Century*, 14.

47. Cummins, "We Are the Other," 222–223.

48. Dean, *Inka Bodies and the Body of Christ*, 98.

49. Nicholson, "A 'Royal Headband' of the Tlaxcalteca," 73–75.

50. Zapata y Mendoza, *Historia cronológica de la noble ciudad de Tlaxcala*, 550–551. Reyes García and Martínez Baracs render aztaaxiluh as *aztaxilotl* in the Spanish translation, which they define as the braided red-and-white headdress with feathers worn by the nobles of Tlaxcala. More than likely, aztaaxiluh refers to the *aztaxelli* (the forked white heron feather itself, as opposed to the braided red-and-white headband). Justyna Olko, a specialist in royal/noble Nahua insignias, noted that she has not seen attestations of aztaxilotl in extant documents, whereas references to aztaxelli are plentiful (personal communication, May 2012). Olko has written extensively on the aztaxelli in her book *Turquoise Diadems and Staffs of Office*, 139–143. Zapata does, however, use the term aztaxilutl, which he cites as being exchanged during the *xochiyaoyotl* or *guerras floridas* (ritualized wars aimed at capturing, enslaving, and finally sacrificing enemy combatants) with Huexotzinco Huitilhuacan (124–125). This variation (aztaxilutl as opposed to aztaxelli) is perhaps specific to Tlaxcalan Nahuatl.

51. Zapata y Mendoza, *Historia cronológica de la noble ciudad de Tlaxcala*, 510–511.

52. Ibid.

53. Following Michel de Certeau, I use the term *tactic* to suggest the different ways that people negotiate within a context of domination. See de Certeau, *The Practice of Everyday Life*, 34–39.

54. Massey, *For Space*, 9.

55. Ybarra discusses the Tlaxcalan's intentional omission of the battles before the alliance between the Spaniards and the Tlaxcalans (*Performing Conquest*, 16). See also Gibson's discussion of these events (*Tlaxcala in the Sixteenth Century*, 15–27). As a counterpoint to Tlaxcalan versions, Spanish soldier Bernal Díaz del Castillo devotes several pages in his chronicle to these battles: see his *Historia verdadera de la conquista de la Nueva España*, chapters 62–65. Townsend notes that Zapata more than likely had access to Muñoz Camargo's Spanish text, but there is no evidence that he used Muñoz Camargo's history to construct his own; in fact, several dates differ between the two ("Don Juan Buenaventura Zapata and the Notion of a Nahua Identity," 160).

56. Zapata y Mendoza, *Historia cronológica de la noble ciudad de Tlaxcala*, 132–133.

57. Ibid., 444–445.

58. Ibid.

59. Ibid.

60. Osowski, "Indigenous Centurions and Triumphal Arches," 81.

61. *Recopilación de Leyes*, lib. VI, tít. 7, ley 1, 1557 ("Que las Audiencias oigan en justicia à los Indios sobre los Cacicazgos").

62. Osowski, *Indigenous Miracles*, 1–6.

63. Zapata y Mendoza, *Historia cronológica de la noble ciudad de Tlaxcala*, 292–293.

64. Ibid., 320–321.

65. Taylor, *The Archive and the Repertoire*, xvii.

66. Ybarra, *Performing Conquest*, 3.

67. Zapata y Mendoza, *Historia cronológica de la noble ciudad de Tlaxcala*, 362–363.

68. Regarding indigenous nobles being afforded the privilege of riding horseback, see Gibson, *The Aztecs Under Spanish Rule*, 155.

69. Zapata y Mendoza, *Historia cronológica de la noble ciudad de Tlaxcala*, 364–367.

70. Ibid., 364–365.

71. Ibid.

72. Karttunen, *An Analytical Dictionary of Nahuatl*, 115; Molina, *Vocabulario*, II:46v.

73. Ybarra, *Performing Conquest*, 8.

74. Zapata y Mendoza, *Historia cronológica de la noble ciudad de Tlaxcala*, 372–373.

75. Ibid.

76. Ibid.

77. Ibid., 394–395.

78. Schroeder, "Writing Two Cultures," 26.

79. Yannakakis, *The Art of Being In-Between*, 221.
80. Ibid.
81. Zapata y Mendoza, *Historia cronológica de la noble ciudad de Tlaxcala*, 566–567.
82. Ibid., 634–637.
83. Ibid., 636–637.
84. Lockhart and Schwartz, *Early Latin America*, 347.

## Chapter 3

1. Andrés Lira has suggested that Chimalpopoca changed the order of his last names depending on the politics of the time (*Comunidades indígenas frente a la ciudad de México*, 269). That is, if the government in power was sympathetic to indigenous issues, he placed the surname Chimalpopoca first; if not, he led with Galicia.
2. Schwaller, "A Catalogue of Pre-1840 Nahuatl Works Held by The Lilly Library," 83.
3. The move toward Spanish as hegemonic language for all subjects of New Spain is evident before independence, as early as the eighteenth century. In 1769, for example, the archbishop of Mexico, Francisco Antonio de Lorenzana y Buitrón, made clear his favor of teaching the Spanish language to natives (*Cartas pastorales*, 47). See Yannakakis, *The Art of Being In-Between*, 172–178, regarding colonial language policy in general and the late eighteenth-century shift toward enforcing Spanish language use in particular.
4. Sepúlveda y Herrera, *Catálogo de la Colección de Documentos Históricos de Faustino Galicia Chimalpopoca*, 11.
5. Schmidt-Díaz de León, "El Colegio Nacional de San Gregorio," 157.
6. See Soberón Mora, "San Gregorio, un colegio transcolonial," for a discussion of the holdings of the library at San Gregorio, 149–159.
7. Schmidt-Díaz de León, "El Colegio Nacional de San Gregorio," 68.
8. Ibid., 159.
9. Escobar Ohmstede, "El discurso de la 'inteligencia' india en los primeros años posindependientes," 264.
10. Heath, *Telling Tongues*, 58.
11. Duncan, "Political Legitimation and Maximilian's Second Empire in Mexico," 51.
12. Haake, *The State, Removal and Indigenous Peoples in the United States and Mexico*, 91.
13. Cifuentes, *Lenguas para un pasado, huellas de una nación*, 16.
14. Villoro, "En torno al derecho de la autonomía de los pueblos indígenas," 167.
15. Haake, *The State, Removal and Indigenous Peoples in the United States and Mexico*, 91.
16. Weber, *Bárbaros*, 263.
17. Bonfil Batalla, "El concepto de indio en América," 118.
18. González Navarro, "Instituciones indígenas en el México independiente," 209–210; Pellicer, "Oralidad y escritura de la literatura indígena," 41.
19. González Navarro, "Instituciones indígenas en el México independiente," 210.
20. Quoted in Ducey, "Hijos del pueblo y ciudadanos," 127.

21. Escobar Ohmstede, "El discurso de la 'inteligencia' india en los primeros años posindependientes," 265.

22. Ibid., 266–267; Lira, *Comunidades indígenas frente a la ciudad de México*, 83–84.

23. Escobar Ohmstede, "El discurso de la 'inteligencia' india en los primeros años posindependientes," 270. For complete text, see Justicia e Instrucción Pública, vol. 1, exp. 44, folios 285r–286v; "Clamores de la miseria ante el Supremo Goberino"; "Carta de Francisco Mendoza y Moctezuma al gobierno de la República, 1833," vol. 1, exp. 49, f. 298; all Archivo General de la Nación, Mexico City.

24. Escobar Ohmstede, "El discurso de la 'inteligencia' india en los primeros años posindependientes," 268.

25. Juan Rodríguez Puebla was a Nahua intellectual who deserves further research. On his pseudonymous publication "El indio constitucional," see María Eugenia Xilonetl Flores Rodríguez, "Juan de Dios Rodríguez Puebla: En defensa de la instrucción para los indios" (http://www.juridicas.unam.mex). Also see Soberón Mora, "San Gregorio, un colegio transcolonial."

26. Chimalpopoca, quoted in Lira, *Comunidades indígenas frente a la ciudad de México*, 203.

27. The Lancasterian system of education, as developed by British Quaker Joseph Lancaster, had as its basic premise the idea that as each student became proficient in an area of study, he/she would then teach another student (peer learning). This method lent itself to areas where trained teachers were few and far between.

28. Lira, *Comunidades indígenas frente a la ciudad de México*, 203–204.

29. Katz, "The Liberal Republic and the Porfiriato," 49.

30. Kicza, Introduction to *The Indian in Latin American History*, xxi.

31. Lira, *Comunidades indígenas frente a la ciudad de México*, 247; J. Bazant, "From Independence to the Liberal Republic," 9.

32. For one of the more detailed appraisals of the role of the administrador de bienes in nineteenth-century Mexico City, see Lira, *Comunidades indígenas frente a la ciudad de México*, 366–372.

33. Ibid., 258–259. Lira located the complaints and requests that Chimalpopoca received in his capacity as *administrador de bienes* in the following volumes at the Archivo General de la Nación, Mexico City: Gobernación, leg. 1610, Parcialidades, Indiferente General, and Junta Protectora de las Clases Menesterosas.

34. Lira, *Comunidades indígenas frente a la ciudad de México*, 202.

35. Ibid., 243.

36. Duncan, "Political Legitimation and Maximilian's Second Empire in Mexico," 30.

37. J. Bazant, "From Independence to the Liberal Republic," 43.

38. Mexican historiography of the Second Empire is notoriously Manichaean and propagandistic. See Pani, *El Segundo Imperio*, for a "history of the history" of the Second Empire.

39. Quoted in Pani, *El Segundo Imperio*, 49.

40. Ibid.

41. Not all Imperialists were doomed. In her essay "Dreaming of a Mexican Empire," Erika Pani tells us that some were even recycled into the new Republican regime (7).

42. Tafolla Pérez, *La junta de notables de 1863*, 85, 93–95.

43. Pani, *Para mexicanizar el Segundo Imperio*, 239.

44. *La Sociedad, Periódico Político y Literario*, 2, October 4, 1863.

45. Ibid.

46. Zamacois, *Historia de Méjico desde los tiempos más remotos hasta nuestros días*, 295–296.

47. Pani, "¿'Verdaderas figuras de Cooper' o 'Pobres inditos infelices'?" 579–580.

48. Ibid.

49. Krauze, *Mexico*, 183. For full text of the law creating the JPCM, see *Colección de leyes, decretos y reglamentos*, "Decreto imperial que instituyó la Junta Protectora de Clases Menesterosas," vol. 3, t. VI.

50. Meyer, "La Junta Protectora de las Clases Menesterosas," 334–335.

51. Ibid., 337.

52. Pani, "¿'Verdaderas figuras de Cooper' o 'Pobres inditos infelices'?" 584.

53. Ibid., 591.

54. Alfiero Gallegos and González Zamora have compiled a summary of the complaints found in the Junta Protectora file at the Archivo General de la Nación, Mexico City, entitled *Indice del ramo de la Junta Protectora de las Clases Menesterosas* (1977). Other complaints submitted to the JPCM can also be found at the Archivo General de la Nación, Mexico City, in the volumes Gobernación and Segundo Imperio.

55. In his research on the JPCM, Jean Meyer did not encounter a single complaint that went unanswered (336).

56. Jaime del Arenal's essay "La proteccion indígena en el Segundo Imperio mexicano" thoroughly outlines the JPCM's involvement in the development of worker protection rights and three agrarian reform laws (178–188). For a complete listing of "laws from the Empire," see *Colección de leyes, decretos y reglamentos*. Indicative of Mexico's disdain for this episode in their history, these laws do not appear in any of the nation's legislative compilations edited and published since that time. Pani, "Dreaming of a Mexican Empire," 3.

57. Quoted in Meyer, "La Junta Protectora de las Clases Menesterosas," 342. Full text available at Segundo Imperio, box 21, "Diario de extractos del Emperador," Archivo General de la Nación, Mexico City.

58. Dabbs, "The Indian Policy of the Second Empire," 119; J. Bazant, "From Independence to the Liberal Republic," 45.

59. Arenal, "La proteccion indígena en el Segundo Imperio mexicano," 185. Arenal mentions the falsification of land titles in response to lawsuits filed by landowners who insisted that the indigenous communities produce title to the lands in question, reminiscent of Techialoyan codices that appeared in the seventeenth and eighteenth centuries under similar circumstances. During the nineteenth century, lacking the protection afforded them under Spanish rule, Indians resorted to armed resistance and falsification of titles when they could not prove that they had been given the rights to the land by the Spanish Crown or had been in possession of the land as long as could be remembered (186).

60. Krauze, *Mexico*, 183.

61. Ibid.

62. Arenal, "La protección indígena en el Segundo Imperio mexicano," 167.

63. Duncan, "Political Legitimation and Maximilian's Second Empire in Mexico," 65.

64. Quoted in Sepúlveda y Herrera, *Catálogo de la Colección de Documentos Históricos de Faustino Galicia Chimalpopoca*, 15.

65. H. de León-Portilla, *Tepuztlahcuilolli*, 114.
66. Meyer, "La Junta Protectora de las Clases Menesterosas," 353.
67. Cifuentes, "Lenguas amerindias," par. 4.
68. Sepúlveda y Herrera, *Catálogo de la Colección de Documentos Históricos de Faustino Galicia Chimalpopoca*, 12. On the history of the SMGE, see Cifuentes, "Lenguas amerindias" and *Lenguas para un pasado*.
69. Cifuentes, "Lenguas amerindias," par. 6.
70. Ibid., par. 18.
71. Colección Antigua, no. 254, Archivo Histórico of the Biblioteca Nacional de Antropología e Historia, Mexico City. Permission to reproduce the entire document courtesy of the Instituto Nacional de Antropología e Historia (National Institute of Anthropology and History #401–3–11633). The transcription is a faithful reproduction of the original orthography and punctuation.
72. Quoted in Powell, "Mexican Intellectuals and the Indian Question," 21.
73. Sepúlveda y Herrera's *Catálogo de la Colección de Documentos Históricos de Faustino Galicia Chimalpopoca* is the most detailed compilation of the location and description of texts that form part of Chimalpopoca's transcription and translation corpus.
74. The Guadalupan documents transcribed by Chimalpopoca, held at the New York Public Library, include two plays, a song by Joseph Pérez de la Fuente (1719), and two unsigned and undated texts (a sermon and a prayer). Sell, Burkhart, and Poole suggest that the sermon and prayer were possibly written by Chimalpopoca himself: "Since Faustino Chimalpopoca Galicia provides no attribution for the sermon and prayer, it is possible that they are at least in part his own compositions, from the mid-nineteenth century. If this is true, they represent a Nahua scholar's original contribution to the 'Indianization' of Our Lady of Guadalupe. They are the earliest known works in the Nahuatl language to represent her as having an 'Indian' appearance that gives her special relevance to indigenous Mexicans" (*Nahuatl Theater*, 190).
75. Bierhorst, *History and Mythology of the Aztecs*, 12.
76. Garibay, *Historia de la literatura náhuatl*, 27.
77. Ibid., 760.
78. Ibid., 760–761.
79. Garibay, "Estudio previo," xi–xii.
80. Garibay, *Llave del Náhuatl*, 122.
81. Note that Mendoza and Sánchez Solis declined to use the title *Códice Chimalpopoca*. The next translation published in 1945 by Primo Feliciano Vázquez would return Chimalpopoca's name to the title.
82. Ramírez, "Advertencia," 2–3.
83. Ibid., 3.
84. Velázquez, *Códice Chimalpopoca*, xii–xiii.
85. Ibid., xxi.

## Chapter 4

1. Villanueva Hernández, "Tecualnezyolehua," 27.
2. See Segre, "Representing a Model Autochthony," 144.

3. Frances Karttunen has pointed out the paucity of female Nahua writers by drawing our attention to the depiction of a female *tlahucuilo* from the fifteenth century found in the Codex Telleriano-Remensis (30r) and the five-hundred-year gap until the appearance of two Nahua women writers in the early twentieth century. First, we have the academic publications of Isabel Ramírez Castañeda (1881–1943), a native speaker of Nahuatl and the first female Mexican archaeologist, and next doña Luz Jiménez's prose. See Karttunen, "Indigenous Writing as a Vehicle of Postconquest Continuity and Change in Mesoamerica," 435–441. Today, there are still very few female Nahua writers; the reasons behind this phenomenon deserve further study. Yolanda Matías García, a Nahua from the state of Guerrero, publishes her poetry online at http://poesianahuatlyolandamatiasgarcia.blogspot.mx/. According to Adam Coon's recent research ("To *In* or Not to *In*"), Isabel Martínez Nopaltécatl, a Nahua from Zongolica, Veracruz, publishes her poetry on Facebook under the name Yankuik Metztli.

4. This reversal of the gaze—doña Luz looking back at Mexico—is the basic premise of what Karttunen intends to do in a large-scale multimedia project that she has conceived of under the title "Luciana's Worlds."

5. In 1972, Horcasitas published a Nahuatl/English version of *De Porfirio Díaz a Zapata* under the title *Life and Death in Milpa Alta: A Nahuatl Chronicle of Díaz and Zapata*. This version includes doña Luz's original Nahuatl, along with Horcasitas's translation to English of doña Luz's original Spanish version found in *De Porfirio Díaz*. To be clear, the Spanish-language texts in *De Porfirio Díaz* are not direct translations of the Nahuatl. They are instead doña Luz's Spanish-language "versions" of the same story. The translations to English that I provide when discussing *De Porfirio Díaz* are taken from *Life and Death*.

6. Doña Luz's essays published in *Mexhicatl Itonolama* are as follows: September 5, 1950, "Tewewentzin iwan tetepeh"; and October 13, 1950, "Tlohkenawake (sasanilli)."

7. The biographic information on Luz Jiménez is gleaned from her own writing, secondary sources, and conversations with her grandson, Jesús Villanueva Hernández. When there have been discrepancies between the varied sources, I have deferred to the family's versions of Luz's life history.

8. Jiménez, *Life and Death in Milpa Alta*, xvii.

9. Jiménez, *De Porfirio Díaz a Zapata*, 12.

10. Jiménez, *Los cuentos en Náhuatl de doña Luz Jiménez*, 7.

11. Nahuatl-language dictionary entry forms for kinship terms such as *tahtli* (father) or *nantli* (mother) are artificial; these terms would never stand alone in actual discourse. According to Karttunen, even the generic "parent" must use the nonspecific human possessor prefix *te* (*tetah*, *tenan*), "someone's father, someone's mother" (Karttunen, personal communication, November 21, 2012).

12. Jiménez, *De Porfirio Díaz a Zapata*, 24.

13. Karttunen, *Between Worlds*, 195.

14. Jiménez, *Life and Death in Milpa Alta*, xi.

15. As a scholar of testimonio texts, Ana Forcinito has described the genre in Latin America as unfolding in three major phases: 1) politically oriented collection of firsthand stories, in solidarity with the Central American revolutionaries during the 1960s and 1970s; 2) academic privileging of subaltern voices beginning in the 1990s, exemplified by spirited attention to Rigoberta Menchú's text (in collaboration with Elizabeth Burgos), *Me llamo Rigoberta Menchú y así me nació la conciencia*; and, by

extension, 3) anthropologist David Stoll's controversial intervention that challenged the veracity of Menchú's testimony, highlighting issues of collective representation and at times incompatible regimes of truth. See Forcinito, *Memorias y nomadías*, 121n4. Similar to Menchú's experience, the validity of doña Luz's words has also been called into question, particularly since she provided some incorrect dates for wartime skirmishes and held in high esteem two figures who were polar opposites on the political spectrum: Porfirio Díaz and Emilio Zapata. For further reading on the testimonio genre in Latin America, see Beverley, *Against Literature*; Jara and Vidal, *Testimonio y literatura*, 1–21; Gugelberger, *The Real Thing*, 1–19; and Arias, "Authoring Ethnicized Subjects."

16. Jiménez, *Life and Death in Milpa Alta*, 2–3.

17. Beverley, *Against Literature*, 89.

18. León-Portilla, "Lecturas de la palabra de doña Luz Jiménez," 118.

19. Jiménez, *De Porfirio Díaz*, 119, no Nahuatl; *Life and Death in Milpa Alta*, 143.

20. Vaughan, *The State, Education, and Social Class in Mexico*, 13–38.

21. Powell, "Mexican Intellectuals and the Indian Question," 20.

22. For more on dominant-culture theorization of the place of the Indian during the Porfiriato, see Stabb, "Indigenism and Racism in Mexican Thought"; Powell, "Mexican Intellectuals and the Indian Question"; Brading, "Manuel Gamio and Official Indigenism in Mexico"; and M. Bazant, *Debate pedagógico durante el Porfiriato*.

23. Vaughan, *The State, Education, and Social Class in Mexico*, 28.

24. Lund, "The Mestizo State," 1420; Powell, "Mexican Intellectuals and the Indian Question," 22.

25. Powell, "Mexican Intellectuals and the Indian Question," 21.

26. Vaughan, *The State, Education, and Social Class in Mexico*, 14. This reform model has its roots in liberal Mexico: in 1868, Dr. Gabino Barreda wrote a series of laws at the behest of President Benito Juárez, legislating free and obligatory elementary education in the Federal District and its territories. See Vaughan, 19. According to Vaughan, Barreda had identified the nation's problems as the people's "disdain for productive labor and rational entrepreneurial behavior which the Spanish colonial heritage had allegedly produced; clericalism which had inhibited the development of a scientific attitude; and liberal preoccupation with abstract principle rather than social realities and the pragmatism necessary to business expansion." See Vaughan, 19–20.

27. Ibid., 23.

28. Sierra, *México social y político*, 7–11.

29. Ibid., 6–7.

30. Jiménez, *Life and Death in Milpa Alta*, 32.

31. Ibid., 33.

32. Ibid., 100–101.

33. Ibid., 115–117.

34. Ibid., 31–33.

35. Ibid., 33.

36. Jiménez, *De Porfirio Díaz*, 21, no Nahuatl; Jiménez, *Life and Death in Milpa Alta*, 5.

37. Jiménez, *Life and Death in Milpa Alta*, 100–101.

38. Ibid., 27–28.

39. Ibid., 28–29.

40. Ibid., 106.
41. Ibid., 107.
42. Ibid., 99.
43. Ibid., 98.
44. Ibid., 99.
45. Karttunen, *An Analytical Dictionary of Nahuatl*, 143.
46. Jiménez, *Life and Death in Milpa Alta*, 105–106.
47. Knight, "Racism, Revolution, and *Indigenismo*," 73.
48. Karttunen, *Between Worlds*, 194.
49. Ibid., 22–23.
50. Ibid.
51. Jiménez, *De Porfirio Díaz*, 21, no Nahuatl; Jiménez, *Life and Death in Milpa Alta*, 5.
52. Jiménez, *Life and Death in Milpa Alta*, 124–125. "Owlish" in Horcasitas's English translation is a literal interpretation of "tlacatecolotl" or "human-kind-of owl," the early Christian designation for Satan. The force of "owlish" should be read as "devilish" or simply "wickedness" (Karttunen, personal communication, November 21, 2012). See also Burkhart, *The Slippery Earth*, 40–42.
53. Jiménez, *Life and Death in Milpa Alta*, 138–139.
54. Ibid., 134–135.
55. Ibid., 166–167. The English translation of *tatatin* (parents) in *Life and Death* reads "fathers and mothers," but as Karttunen notes, "there were no fathers among the refugees." See Karttunen, *Between Worlds*, 328n48.
56. Jiménez, *Life and Death in Milpa Alta*, 167–171.
57. See Patterson, "An Art in Revolution," regarding the open-air painting schools and their political significance.
58. Charlot, "Jean Charlot and Luz Jiménez," 3.
59. Karttunen, personal communication, November 21, 2012.
60. Karttunen, *Between Worlds*, 192.
61. Karttunen, personal communication, November 21, 2012. Doña Luz wrote about Rivera's monetary gift in a letter to Charlot (undated, more than likely late 1942 or early 1943).
62. See Marta Turok's essay, "Luz Jiménez en el arte popular" in *Luz Jiménez* regarding doña Luz's weaving skills. Villanueva Hernández said that his grandmother "siempre se sintió orgullosa de ser una indígena que desde su infancia había aprendido a usar el telar de cintura. Hay fotos donde se aprecia su rostro alegre al mostrar el uso de este instrumento prehispánico" (was always proud to be an Indian woman who, from her youth, learned to weave with a backstrap loom. There are photos where one can note her obvious joy in demonstrating how to use the loom) (personal communication, December 1, 2008). In the video *Doña Luz: Imagen y palabra de México* (2005), an elderly milpateña woman recalls doña Luz teaching young girls in Milpa Alta how to weave.
63. Karttunen, "The Linguistic Career of doña Luz Jiménez," 268. The maestros rurales program is a classic example of the contradictions between artistic/anthropological *indigenismo* (glorification) and social/political theories and practices (denigration and elimination) of indigenous cultures in the early twentieth century. For example, in 1926, Rafael Ramírez, director of the Departamento de

Enseñanza Rural y Primaria Foránea (Department of Rural and Foreign [Ethnic Outsiders] Instruction) warned the maestros rurales that if they used the Indian language, they ran the risk of turning into Indians, something that apparently was to be avoided at all costs: "Si tú le hablas su idioma perdemos la fe que en ti teníamos, porque corres el peligro de ser tú incorporado. Irás tomando sin darte cuenta las costumbres del grupo social étnico al que ellos pertenecen, luego sus formas de vida, y finalmente tú mismo te volverás indio" (If you speak their language we will lose faith in you, because you run the risk then of being incorporated [by the culture]. You will start, without even noticing, taking on the customs of the socio-ethnic group that they belong to, next their way of life, and then you finally you will turn into an Indian.) See Schmelkes and Núñez, "Alfabetización de jóvenes indígenas en México," 254.

64. Karttunen, "Indigenous Writing," 440.

65. Doña Luz mentions her work with Barlow in a letter to Charlot dated December 11, 1947. I gratefully acknowledge the generosity of the Charlot family and doña Luz's grandson Jesús Villanueva Hernández for copies of forty years of personal letters (such as the abovementioned) between doña Luz and Jean Charlot and their families. The letters are held in the Jean Charlot Collection at the University of Hawaii at Manoa. Karttunen and Villanueva Hernández have worked on the organization and transcription of the handwritten letters over the years, although the transcription of all the letters remains incomplete. For the most part, the letters chronicle work and family life. Horcasitas suggests that there may be unedited texts from the Barlow/Jiménez collaboration in the Archivo Barlow at the Universidad de las Américas, in Cholula, Puebla, as well as the Universidad de las Américas in Mexico City. See Jiménez, *Los cuentos en Náhuatl de doña Luz Jiménez*, 6, and *De Porfirio Díaz* 13.

66. Barlow may have only occasionally cited his "informants" in his own publications, but it should not go unnoticed that the short-lived Nahuatl-language periodical *Mexihcatl Itonalama* (for which doña Luz contributed two essays) was produced in Barlow's home and, furthermore, included all of the names of the indigenous contributors.

67. Barlow, "Un cuento sobre día de los muertos," 77.

68. Fixico, "Call for Native Genius and Indigenous Intellectualism," 45.

69. Charlot provided the illustrations for *The Boy Who Could Do Anything and Other Mexican Folktales*, which more than likely explains why doña Luz sought his assistance in rectifying her lack of acknowledgement and compensation related to the project.

70. Karttunen, *Between Worlds*, 213.

71. Archibald, *Indigenous Storywork*, 1.

72. Million, "Intense Dreaming," 322.

73. Doerfler et al., xxii.

74. On indigenous story as intellectual work, see Archibald, *Indigenous Storywork*; Henry, Pascual Soler, and Martínez-Falquina, *Stories Through Theories/Theories Through Stories*; and Doerfler, Sinclair, and Stark, *Centering Anishinaabeg Studies*.

75. Jiménez, *Life and Death in Milpa Alta*, 10–11.

76. Ibid.

77. Ibid., 53.

78. Ibid., 63.

79. Ibid., 56; 59.

80. Jiménez, *Los cuentos en Náhuatl de doña Luz Jiménez*, 7.

81. *Mictlan* has nine layers, but doña Luz states "chicome," seven.

82. Ibid., 14–15.

83. Ibid., 18–19. This story offers a clear example of the variations between doña Luz's versions of her own stories. In the Nahuatl version she says "caxtilteca nozo cuitlaxcoliztaque." Caxtilteca refers to people from Castille/Europeans, but in the Spanish version she uses the term "la gente capitalina," or city folk instead. See Jiménez, *Los cuentos en Náhuatl de doña Luz Jiménez*, 19. As Karttunen has pointed out, "cuitlaxcoliztaque" is perhaps best translated as lily-livered or cowardly, yet doña Luz's Spanish version renders this term as "gente de panza blanca" or white-bellied people (personal communication, November 21, 2012). Whether doña Luz did not want to come right out and call the Europeans or mestizos of the upper class (such as those that hired her) cowards, or if she assumed that "la gente de panza blanca" conveyed her intended meaning, we cannot know.

84. Ibid., 72.

85. Ibid., 52.

86. In Karttunen's *An Analytical Dictionary of Nahuatl*, 148, "mina" is glossed as "to shoot arrows, to pierce someone with arrows."

87. Scott, *Domination and the Arts of Resistance*, 162.

88. V. Deloria, "Research, Redskins, and Reality," 466.

89. Tuhiwai Smith, *Decolonizing Methodologies*, 173.

90. Ibid., 16.

91. Bruner, *The Anthropology of Experience*, 11.

92. Carey-Webb, "Transformative Voices," 8.

93. León-Portilla, "Lecturas de la palabra de doña Luz Jiménez," 116.

94. Ibid.

95. Jiménez, *Life and Death in Milpa Alta*, 178–179.

96. The Huasteca Region in Mexico encompasses approximately 40,000 square miles of northern Veracruz and southern Tamaulipas, as well as parts of the states of San Luis Potosí, Puebla, and Hidalgo.

97. According to Karttunen and Lockhart, only two extant texts from the colonial period can be said to "exhaustively" utilize the "Jesuit" diacritical system to mark contrastive vowel length and glottal stops: Father Horacio Carochi's grammar and the so-called Bancroft Dialogues. Kartunnen and Lockhart, *The Art of Nahuatl Speech*, 67.

98. On orthographic conventions of Nahuatl, see the introduction in Karttunen, *An Analytical Dictionary of Nahuatl*.

99. Sullivan et al., "Náhuatl tlen naman."

100. These anti-Spanish modified orthographic conventions were adopted by the Aztec Congress in 1940.

101. In his presentation at the 2013 American Society for Ethnohistory annual meeting ("To *In* or Not to *In*"), Adam Coon discussed his current research on the present-day politics of the embrace or rejection of colonial orthographies and lexicon by contemporary Nahuatl-language writers. According to his research with established writers as well as the new generation, publishing houses tend to prefer texts that employ the colonial or "classical" versions of the language.

102. A cursory review of Nahuatl-language grade-school primers produced by the office of the Secretaría de Educación Pública (Secretary of Public Education, SEP)

reveals a general preference for transcriptions using the newer orthographies, although these same texts also reveal a lack of rigorous orthographic standardization within and/or among texts. A thorough investigation of Nahuatl-language texts produced by the SEP has, to my knowledge, yet to be completed. This would be an important study in regards to not only orthographic conventions but also language ideology in general.

103. Sullivan et al., "Náhuatl tlen naman."

104. This point is stressed by the Comunidad de Historia Mapuche, a collective of Mapuche scholars, who point to the presence of indigenous knowledge and indigenous intellectualism in "the lettered sphere," whether or not he or she took up the pen: "La intervención Mapuche en la esfera letrada también involucra a aquellos y aquellas que no escribieron o no escriben pero cuyos conocimientos han sido 'capturados' por las maquinarias escriturales de misioneros, cronistas, historiadores, etnólogos, antropólogos" (16–17) (Mapuche intervention in the lettered sphere also involves those who did not or do not write, but whose knowledges have been 'captured' by the writerly mechanisms of the missionaries, chroniclers, historians, ethnologists, anthropologists.)

105. Lockhart, *Nahuatl as Written*, 32–35, 152–160.

## Chapter 5

1. The Huasteca region extends into several of Mexico's northeastern states, encompassing approximately forty thousand square miles in northern Veracruz and southern Tamaulipas, as well as parts of the states of San Luis Potosí, Puebla, and Hidalgo. While Nahuas are the majority indigenous group in the Huasteca, the region is home to many peoples and cultures, such as the Huastecos and Teneek to the north, and the Otomíes, Totonacas, and Tepehuas to the south. See Valle Esquivel, *Nahuas de la Huasteca*, 6. One of the most impoverished and underdeveloped regions of the Mexican Republic, the majority of the county seats in the Huasteca did not have paved access until the 1980s. Today, there are at least six major highways traversing the area, and one can also fly directly into Tampico or Poza Rica. See Valle Esquivel, 25; Ruvalcaba Mercado and Pérez Zevallos, *La Huasteca en los albores del tercer milenio*, 37.

2. Maya Hernández, "Nauatl grammatical."

3. Acevedo Conde, *Educación interétnica*, 10.

4. Varese, *Proyectos étnicos y proyectos nacionales*, 32–37.

5. Ibid., 37–39.

6. Hernández Díaz, "The Bilingual Teachers," 54.

7. Hamel, "Indigenous Language Policy and Education in Mexico," 302–304.

8. On bilingual/bicultural/intercultural education in Mexico, see Acevedo Conde, *Educación interétnica*; Guzmán Gómez, *Voces indígenas*; Jordá Hernández, *Ser maestro bilingüe en Suljaa'*; and Vargas D., *Educación e ideología*.

9. Hamel, "Indigenous Language Policy and Education in Mexico," 304.

10. Ibid., 309.

11. Calvo and Donnadieu, *El difícil camino de la escolaridad*, 30.

12. Ibid., 30–31.

13. Bhabha, "Of Mimicry and Man," 127.

14. Ibid.

15. Ibid., 129.

16. Wade, *Race and Ethnicity in Latin America*, 107.
17. Hale, *Más que un indio*, 44.
18. Rippberger, "Ideological Shifts in Bilingual Education," 59.
19. Hale, *Más que un indio*, 44.
20. Schryer, "Peasants and the Law," 283.
21. Schryer, *Ethnicity and Class Conflict in Rural Mexico*, 289–291.
22. Ibid., 290.
23. Ibid., 255.
24. In their discussion of the category of the *indio permitido* (a phrase originating with Aymara scholar Silvia Rivera Cusicanqui), Charles Hale and Rosamel Millamán refer to a subjectivity created "when neoliberal regimes actively recognize and open space for collective indigenous presence, even agency" (284).
25. Brazilian Augusto Boal's "theatre of the oppressed" of the 1960s is a method of theater wherein the goal is to transform a formerly passive person or class (proletariat/oppressed) into an active participant on the "social stage." Often the pre-performance activities, and the topics rehearsed and performed, are meant to encourage future action by the participants and/or spectators. See Boal, *Teatro del oprimido*.
26. The Nahuatl and Spanish versions of *Ixtlamatinij* published in *Words of the True Peoples/Palabras de los seres verdaderos* were written by Ildefonso Maya, and the English version (which I cite in this chapter) was adapted/translated by the volume's editors Carlos Montemayor and Donald Frischmann. See Frischmann's excellent introduction ("A Question of Balance") to Mexican indigenous theater and the work of Ildefonso Maya in vol. 3 of *Words of the True Peoples/Palabras de los seres verdaderos*, 19–47.
27. Note the honorific "tsi" attached to the grandfather's name (Juantsi=Juanito). In Nahuatl the "tsi" or "tzin" indicates reverence to the receiver of the "tzin." It can also elevate the entire discourse to a higher degree of respect by discursively bringing the speaker and the receiver closer to each other. This is in contrast to the Spanish "usted," which also connotes respect, but creates and maintains distance. See Hill and Hill, "Honorific Usage in Modern Nahuatl."
28. In Nahua culture it is said that a flicker of a candle or of the cooking fire portends the arrival of a loved one or a messenger. On one of my first visits to a rural Nahua village, an elderly woman told me that she knew to expect me; she had seen the sign in her fire.
29. Maya Hernández, *Ixtlamatinij*, 234.
30. Ibid., 250.
31. Similar to other Mexican indigenous communities, outward migration has resulted in the revitalization and even retrenching of indigenous *costumbre* in Nahua communities since Nahuas working outside the community are able to finance more elaborate celebrations. Many Nahuas are anxious to prove that while they do not regularly reside in the community or carry out the traditional (if not sacred) duties such as tending milpa, they are still members of the community. Financing, and participating actively, in community ceremonial life (even if only once per year) is one such way of strengthening and reinforcing ties to the community.
32. See Sandstrom, *Corn Is Our Blood*, especially chapter 6, "Religion and the Nahua Universe."
33. Bonfil Batalla, *México Profundo*, 13.

34. Quoted in Hamel, "Indigenous Language Policy and Education in Mexico," 303.

35. Memmi, *The Colonizer and the Colonized*, 104–123.

36. Taylor, *Theatre of Crisis*, 37. See Memmi, *The Colonizer and the Colonized*; Fanon, *Black Skin, White Masks*; and Bhabha, *The Location of Culture*, 40–66.

37. Maya Hernández, *Ixtlamatinij*, 232.

38. Ibid., 248. Emphasis added.

39. Ibid., 237.

40. Ibid., 253.

41. Memmi, *The Colonizer and the Colonized*, 103.

42. Maya Hernández, *Ixtlamatinij*, 257.

43. Ibid., 237; 253. Emphasis added.

44. Ibid., 236; 252.

45. Ibid., 236.

46. Ibid., 252.

47. Ibid., 236–237.

48. Ibid., 253.

49. Regarding ceremonial dance in the Hidalgo region of the Huasteca, see Miranda, "'Cuanegros,' Yahualica"; Ramos Castañeda et al., *El Xantolo de Huautla*, 39–57; and the Consejo Estatal para la Cultura y las Artes del Estado de Hidalgo at http://cultura.hidalgo.gob.mx.

50. Maya Hernández, *Ixtlamatinij*, 237.

51. Ibid., 254.

52. Anderson, *Imagined Communities*.

53. Ibid., 6.

54. At present there is little research available related specifically to Nahua women's experiences of migration, education, and work. However, an analysis along these lines focusing on Maya communities in Yucatan has been carried out by anthropologist M. Bianet Castellanos in her book, *A Return to Servitude*.

55. According to Victoriano de la Cruz Cruz (Nahua), the demonstration of a strong command of Spanish is a marker in his own community of being able to take care of oneself (the discourse of "poder defenderse" as reported in Jacqueline Messing's essay, "Fractal Recursivity in Ideologies of Language, Identity, and Modernity in Tlaxcala, Mexico"). Victoriano explained that one needs a decent command of Spanish to be able to sell crops in the market, to avoid being "duped" by outsiders, and to be able to secure work outside of the community if the crop fails or is not enough to provide for the family. While visiting Victoriano's family in Tepoxteco during the summer of 2008, I watched him move fluidly between Nahuatl and Spanish. More often than not his mother, grandmother, and aunts spoke to him in Nahuatl, as expected since they are for the most part monolingual. However, while his father, grandfather, and uncles spoke to him in both Nahuatl and Spanish, Victoriano nearly always responded in Spanish. When I asked him about this, he said he needed to remind his family that he was capable of taking care of himself when he left the community, and he was therefore strategically employing Spanish language.

56. Contemporary Nahuatl orthography in the Veracruz Huasteca region often includes *a*, *c*, *ch*, *cu/uc*, *e*, *hu/uh*, *i*, *l*, *m*, *n*, *o*, *p*, *qu*, *t*, *tl*, *tz*, *x*, *y*, *z*. Spanish-language consonants and vowels such as *b*, *d*, *f*, *g*, *h*, *j*, *r*, s, and *u* are not present in Nahua speech in this region. See Sullivan et al., "Náhuatl tlen naman: Chicontepec, Veracruz."

57. On letter substitution in written Nahuatl, see Karttunen and Lockhart, *Nahuatl in the Middle Years*, 1–14.

58. On hypercorrection in written Nahuatl, see Karttunen and Lockhart, *Nahuatl in the Middle Years*, 14–15.

59. Maya Hernández, *Ixtlamatinij*, 237.

60. Ibid., 237; 253.

61. Ibid., 236; 252.

62. Sandstrom, *Corn Is Our Blood*, 65.

63. Maya Hernández, *Ixtlamatinij*, 235.

64. Ibid., 251.

65. Hernández Castillo, "Indigenous Law and Identity Politics in Mexico," 91.

66. Maya Hernández, *Ixtlamatinij*, 240; 256.

67. Ibid., 239; 256.

68. Ibid., 240; 256.

69. Ibid., 241.

70. Ibid., 257.

71. Ibid., 241–242.

72. Ibid., 258.

73. Ibid., 242.

74. Ibid., 258.

75. Ibid., 242.

76. Ibid., 258.

77. Maya disapproved of the consumption of alcohol and was highly critical of its negative effects in indigenous communities. This particular scene of Epitacio's drunken madness and extreme remorse provides a platform for discussion of alcohol use in the community.

78. Maya Hernández, *Ixtlamatinij*, 245.

79. Ibid., 262.

80. Versényi, "Translation as an Epistemological Paradigm for Theatre in the Americas," 446.

81. Ibid., 445.

82. Escalona, *Tlacuilo*, 26. See n. 30 of the introduction of this book regarding possible female tlahcuilohqueh.

83. León-Portilla, *Aztec Thought and Culture*, 172.

84. Brotherston, *Painted Books from Mexico*, 8.

85. The hot and humid climate of the Huasteca Hidalguense is an inhospitable place for books and papers, and the codices are beginning to disintegrate. Maya wanted to be sure that both indigenous and non-indigenous people alike could benefit from his research, so we cleaned them (with guidance from art historians), photographed each book, and stored them at Maya's home in a manner that ideally will aid in their preservation. To maximize distribution, and ensure that they are freely available, the images can be found at kellysmcdonough.blogspot.com.

86. For a thorough analysis of circulating written versions of the Legend of the Suns in sources ranging from the massive Aztec calendar stone known as the Piedra del Sol to indigenous and European writings (pictographic and alphabetic), see Moreno de los Arcos, "Los cinco soles cosmogónicos."

87. The Great Spirit's fallen eye is symbolized by the mirror in the headdress worn by traditional dancers in the Huasteca today.

88. Hernández Hernández, *El despertar de nuestras lenguas*, 142.

## Conclusion

1. Tierras, vol. 2819, exp. 9, 363f–363v. Archivo General de la Nación, Mexico City. See Paula López Caballero, *Los títulos primordiales del centro de México*, 272–302. Note that the Cuixinco file held at the National Archive has been renumbered since López Caballero's study.

2. For additional commentary on the primordial title of San Matías Cuixinco, see Gruzinski, *The Conquest of Mexico*: 98–145; Wood, "The Cosmic Conquest"; and Wood, "The Social vs. Legal Context of Nahuatl *Títulos*," 212–213. See images from the San Matías Cuixinco documents in Wood, *Transcending Conquest*, 110, 112, 113.

3. Wood, "The Social vs. Legal Context of Nahuatl *Títulos*," 210.

4. Ibid., 208–209.

5. Haskett, *Visions of Paradise*, 23.

6. Wood, "The Social vs. Legal Context of Nahuatl *Títulos*," 203.

7. Lockhart, *Nahuas and Spaniards*, 39–64.

8. Massey, *For Space*, 9.

9. Ibid., 119.

10. Kovach, *Indigenous Methodologies*, 94.

11. Full text of the United Nations Declaration on the Rights of Indigenous Peoples in English, Spanish, and Nahuatl (among other languages) can be found at undesadspd .org/IndigenousPeoples.aspx; full text of the Ley General de Derechos Lingüísticos de los Pueblos Indígenas is available at www.diputados.gob.mx/LeyesBiblio/.

12. See www.inali.gob.mx.

# *Bibliography*


Acevedo Conde, María Luisa, et al. *Educación interétnica*. Mexico City: INAH, 1996.

Adorno, Rolena. "Cultures in Contact: Mesoamerica, the Andes, and the European Written Tradition." In *The Cambridge History of Latin American Literature*, edited by Roberto González Echevarría and Enrique Pupo Walker, 1:33–57. New York: Cambridge University Press, 1996.

Aguirre Beltrán, Gonzalo. *Lenguas vernáculas: Su uso y desuso en la enseñanza. La experiencia de México*. Mexico City: SEP Ediciones de la Casa Chata, 1983.

Alegre, Francisco Javier. *Historia de la provincia de la Compañía de Jesús de Nueva España*. Vol. I, 1566–1596. Edited by Ernest J. Burrus and Felix Zubillaga. Rome: Institutum Historicum S.J., 1956.

Alfiero Gallegos, Alfonso, and Miguel González Zamora. *Indice del ramo de la Junta Protectora de las Clases Menesterosas*. Mexico City: AGN, 1977.

Álvarez Mejía, Juan. "La cuestión del clero indígena en la época colonial." *Revista Javeriana* 45 (March 1956): 57–67.

*Anales de Cuauhtitlán: Noticias históricas de México y sus contornos*. Compiled by D. José Fernando Ramírez. Translated by Faustino Galicia Chimalpopoca, Gumersindo Mendoza, and Felipe Sánchez Solís. Mexico City: Publicaciones de Los Anales del Museo Nacional, 1885.

Anderson, Benedict. *Imagined Communities: Reflections on the Origin and Spread of Nationalism*. London: Verso, 1983.

Andrews, J. Richard. *Introduction to Classical Nahuatl*. Norman: University of Oklahoma Press, 2003.

Archibald, Jo-ann. *Indigenous Storywork: Educating the Heart, Mind, Body, and Spirit*. Vancouver: University of British Columbia Press, 2008.

Arenal, Jaime del. "La protección indígena en el Segundo Imperio mexicano: La Junta Protectora de Clases Menesterosas." *Ars Iuris* 6 (1991): 157–192.

Arias, Arturo. "Authoring Ethnicized Subjects: Rigoberta Menchú and the Performative Production of the Subaltern Self." *PMLA* 116, no. 1 (Jan. 2001): 75–88.

———. "Nahuatlizando la novelística: De infiernos, paraísos y rupturas de estereotipos en las prácticas discursivas decoloniales." *Alter/nativas: Revista de estudios culturales latinoamericanos*, Fall 2013. http://alternativas.osu.edu. Accessed June 27, 2013.

Baber, R. Jovita. "Empire, Indians, and the Negotiation for the Status of City in Tlaxcala, 1521–1550." In *Negotiation Within Domination: New Spain's Indian Pueblos Confront the Spanish State*, edited by Ethelia Ruiz Medrano and Susan Kellogg, 19–44. Boulder: University Press of Colorado, 2010.

Barlow, Robert. "Un cuento sobre día de los muertos." *Estudios de cultura náhuatl* 2 (1960): 77–82.

Basso, Keith H. *Wisdom Sits in Places: Landscape and Language Among the Western Apache*. Albuquerque: University of New Mexico Press, 1996.

Baudot, Georges. *Utopia and History in Mexico: The First Chroniclers of Mexican Civilization (1520–1569)*. Translated by Bernard R. and Thelma Ortiz de Montellano. Niwot: University Press of Colorado, 1995.

Bauer, Arnold. J. *The Search for the Codex Cardona: On the Trail of a Sixteenth-Century Mexican Treasure*. Durham, NC: Duke University Press, 2009.

Bazant, Jan. "From Independence to the Liberal Republic, 1821–1867." In *Mexico: Since Independence*, edited by Leslie Bethell, 1–48. New York: Cambridge University Press, 1991.

Bazant, Milada. *Debate pedagógico durante el Porfiriato*. Mexico City: Consejo Nacional de Fomento Educativo, 1985.

Beverley, John. *Against Literature*. Minneapolis: University of Minnesota Press, 1993.

———. *Subalternity and Representation: Arguments in Cultural Theory*. Durham, NC: Duke University Press, 1999.

———. "Writing in Reverse: On the Project of the Latin American Subaltern Studies Group." *Dispositio* 19, no. 46, Subaltern Studies in the Americas (1994): 271–288.

Bhabha, Homi K. *The Location of Culture*. New York: Routledge, 1994.

———. "Of Mimicry and Man: The Ambivalence of Colonial Discourse." *October, Discipleship: A Special Volume on Psychoanalysis* 28 (Spring 1984): 125–133.

Bierhorst, John. *History and Mythology of the Aztecs: The Codex Chimalpopoca*. Tucson: University of Arizona Press, 1992.

Binotti, Lucia. "La 'lengua compañera del imperio'": Discursos peninsulares sobre la hispanización de América." In *Actas del III Congreso Internacional de Historia de la Lengua Española*, edited by A. Alonso González et al., 621–632. Madrid: Arco/Libros, 1996.

Boal, Augusto. *Teatro del oprimido*. Translated by Graciela Schmilchuk. Mexico City: Editorial Nueva Imagen, 1980.

Bonfil Batalla, Guillermo. "El concepto de indio en América: Una categoría de la situación colonial." *Anales de antropología* 9 (1972): 105–124.

———. *México Profundo: Reclaiming a Civilization*. Translated by Philip A. Dennis. Austin: University of Texas Press, 1996.

———. *Utopía y revolución: El pensamiento político contemporáneo de los indios de América Latina*. Mexico City: Editorial Nueva Imagen, 1981.

Boone, Elizabeth Hill. "*In Tlamatinime*: The Wise Men and Women of Aztec Mexico." In *Painted Books and Indigenous Knowledge in Mesoamerica: Manuscript Studies in Honor of Mary Elizabeth Smith*, edited by Elizabeth Hill Boone, 9–25. New Orleans: Middle American Research Institute, Tulane University, 2005.

———. *Stories in Red and Black: Pictorial Histories of the Aztecs and the Mixtecs*. Austin: University of Texas Press, 2000.

———. "Introduction: Writing and Recording Knowledge." In *Writing Without Words: Alternative Literacies in Mesoamerica and the Andes*, edited by Elizabeth Hill Boone and Walter D. Mignolo, 3–26. Durham, NC: Duke University Press, 1994.

Borah, Woodrow. "Race and Class in Mexico." *Pacific Historical Review* 23, no. 4 (1954): 331–342.

Brading, David A. "Manuel Gamio and Official Indigenism in Mexico." *Bulletin of Latin American Research* 7, no. 1 (1988): 75–89.

Brenner, Anita. *The Boy Who Could Do Anything and Other Mexican Folktales*. Illustrations by Jean Charlot. New York: W. R. Scott, 1942.

———. *Idols Behind Altars*. New York: Payson and Clark, 1929.

Brooks, Lisa. *The Common Pot: The Recovery of Native Space in the Northeast*. Minneapolis: University of Minnesota Press, 2008.

Brotherston, Gordon. *Painted Books from Mexico: Codices in UK Collections and the World They Represent*. London: Published for the Trustees of the British Museum by British Museum Press, 1995.

Bruner, Edward M. Introduction to *The Anthropology of Experience*. Edited by Victor W. Turner and Edward M. Bruner, 3–30. Urbana: University of Illinois Press, 1986.

Burkhart, Louise M. *Holy Wednesday: A Nahua Drama from Early Colonial Mexico*. Philadelphia: University of Pennsylvania Press, 1996.

———. *The Slippery Earth: Nahua-Christian Moral Dialogue in Sixteenth-Century Mexico*. Tucson: University of Arizona Press, 1989.

Calvo, Beatriz, and Laura Donnadieu. *El difícil camino de la escolaridad: El maestro indígena y su proceso de formación*. Mexico City: CIESAS, Cuadernos de la Casa Chata 55, 1982.

Camp, Roderic A. *Intellectuals and the State in Twentieth-Century Mexico*. Austin: University of Texas Press, 1985.

Carey-Webb, Allen. "Transformative Voices." In *Teaching and Testimony: Rigoberta Menchú and the North American Classroom*, edited by Allen Carey-Webb and Stephen Benz, 3–18. Albany: State University of New York Press, 1996.

Carochi, Horacio. *Arte de la lengua Mexicana con la declaración de los adverbios della (1645)*. Translated and edited with commentary by James Lockhart. Stanford: Stanford University Press, 2001.

Carrera, Magali M. *Imagining Identity in New Spain: Race, Lineage, and the Colonial Body in Portraiture and Casta Paintings*. Austin: University of Texas Press, 2003.

*Cartas pastorales y edictos del Ill[ustrissi]mo D. Francisco Antonio Lorenzana y Buitron Arzobispo de México*. Mexico City: En la imprenta del Superior Gobierno, del Br. D. Joseph Antonio de Hogal, 1770.

*Cartas y relaciones de Hernán Cortés al emperador Carlos V*. Edited by Pascual de Gayangos. Paris: Imprenta Central de los Ferro-Carriles A. Chaix, 1866.

Castellanos, M. Bianet. *A Return to Servitude: Maya Migration and the Tourist Trade in Cancún*. Minneapolis: University of Minnesota Press, 2010.

Chacón, Gloria E. "Contemporary Maya Writers: Kabawil and the Making of a Millenarian Literary Tradition." PhD diss., University of California, Santa Cruz, 2006.

Charles, John. *Allies at Odds: The Andean Church and Its Indigenous Agents, 1583–1671*. Albuquerque: University of New Mexico Press, 2010.

Charlot, John. "Jean Charlot and Luz Jiménez." 2007. http://www.jeancharlot.org. Accessed September 2013.

Chimalpopoca, Faustino Galicia. "Devocionario para oír misa en lengua mexicana: Dedicado a los indios," 1848.

———. "Disertación hispano-nahua-latina sobre el origen y modo de contar de los indios nahuacenses," 1858.

———. *El centavo de Nuestra Señora de Guadalupe*. Mexico City: Imp. de I. Cumplido, 1869.

———. *Epítome o modo fácil de aprender el idioma náhuatl o lengua mexicana*. Mexico City: Tipografía de la V. de Murguía è hijos, 1869.

———. *Silbario Mexicano. 1839–1849*. Mexico City: Tipografía de Manuel Castro, 1859.

———. *Vocabulario correcto conforme a los mejores gramáticos en el mexicano o diálogos familiares que enseñan la lengua sin necesidad de maestro*. 1869. *Anales del Museo Nacional de Arqueología, Historia y Etnografía*, 4a época. Mexico City, 1927.

Cifuentes, Bárbara. "Lenguas amerindias de la Sociedad Mexicana de Geografía y Estadística (1833–1874)." *Dimensión Antropólogica* 24 (Feb.–May 2002). http://www.dimensionantropologica.inah.gob.mx/?p=678. Accessed April 6, 2009.

———. *Lenguas para un pasado, huellas de una nación: Los estudios sobre lenguas indígenas de México en el siglo XIX*. Mexico City: INAH, 2002.

Clayton, Mary L., and R. Joe Campbell. "Alonso de Molina as Lexicographer." In *Making Dictionaries: Preserving Indigenous Languages of the Americas*, edited by William Frawley, Kenneth C. Hill, and Pamela Munro, 336–390. Berkeley: University of California Press, 2002.

Clifford, James. "On Ethnographic Authority." *Representations* 2 (Spring 1983): 118–146.

*Codex Chimalpahin*. Vol. 1. Translated and edited by Arthur J. O. Anderson and Susan Schroeder. Norman: University of Oklahoma Press, 1997.

*Códice Chimalpopoca: Anales de Cuauhtitlan y Leyenda de los soles*. 15xx. Translated by Primo Feliciano Velázquez. Mexico City: UNAM IIH, 1975.

*Códice Matritenses de la la Real Academia de la Historia*. 15xx. Facsimile by Francisco del Paso y Troncoso. Madrid: Hauser y Menet, 1907.

*Códice Ramírez: Relación del origen de los indios que habitan esta Nueva España, según su historia*. 15xx. Edited by Manuel Orozco y Berra. Mexico City: Editorial Innovación, 1979.

*Códice Telleriano-Remensis*. *FAMSI*. http://www.famsi.org. Accessed July 1, 2012.

*Colección de leyes, decretos y reglamentos que interinamente forman el sistema político administrativo y judicial del imperio*. Mexico City: Imprenta de Andrade y Escalante, 1865.

Comunidad de Historia Mapuche, eds. *Ta Iñ Fijke Xipa Rakizuameluwün. Historia, colonialismo y resistencia desde el país Mapuche*. Temuco, Chile: Ediciones Comunidad de Historia Mapuche, 2012.

Coon, Adam. "Iahqui Estados Onidos: The Articulation of Nahua Identities in Migration in Contemporary Nahua Literature, 1985–2012." PhD diss., University of Texas, in progress.

———. "To *In* or Not to *In*: The Politics Behind the Usage or Disavowal of Classical Nahuatl Within Contemporary Nahua Literature." Paper presented at the

American Society for Ethnohistory Annual Meeting, New Orleans, September 11–14, 2013.

Cope, R. Douglas. *The Limits of Racial Domination: Plebeian Society in Colonial Mexico: 1660–1720*. Madison: University of Wisconsin Press, 1994.

Cornejo Polar, Antonio. *Escribir en el aire: Ensayo sobre la heterogeneidad socio-cultural en las literaturas andinas*. Lima: Editorial Horizonte, 1994.

Coronil, Fernando. "Beyond Occidentalism: Toward Nonimperial Geohistorical Categories." *Cultural Anthropology* 11, no. 1 (Feb. 1996): 51–87.

Cox, James H. *The Red Land to the South: American Indian Writers and Indigenous Mexico*. Minneapolis: University of Minnesota Press, 2012.

Cruz de la Cruz, Sabina. "Discriminación desde la ley." Tesis de licenciatura, Universidad Autónoma de Zacatecas, 2007.

*Cuéntame*, INEGI para niños. "Hablantes de lengua indígena en México." http://www.cuentame.inegi.gob.mx/. Accessed June 15, 2013.

Cummins, Tom. "We Are the Other: Peruvian Portraits of Colonial Kurakakuna." In *Transatlantic Encounters: Europeans and Andeans in the Sixteenth Century*, edited by Kenneth J. Andrien and Rolena Adorno, 203–231. Berkeley: University of California Press, 1991.

Curcio-Nagy, Linda. *The Great Festivals of Colonial Mexico City: Performing Power and Identity*. Albuquerque: University of New Mexico Press, 2004.

Dabbs, Jack A. "The Indian Policy of the Second Empire." In *Essays in Mexican History*, edited by Thomas E. Cotner and Carlos E. Castañeda, 112–126. Austin: University of Texas, The Institute of Latin American Studies, 1958.

Dean, Carolyn. *Inka Bodies and the Body of Christ: Corpus Christi in Colonial Cuzco, Peru*. Durham, NC: Duke University Press, 1999.

de Certeau, Michel. *The Practice of Everyday Life*. Translated by Steven F. Rendall. Berkeley: University of California Press, 1984.

Decorme, Gerard. *La obra de los jesuitas mexicanos durante la época colonial 1572–1767*. Vol. I. Mexico City: Antigua Librería Robredo de Jose Porrúa e Hijos, 1941.

de la Cruz, Victor. "*Reflexiones sobre la escritura y el futuro de la literatura indígena*." In *Escritura zapoteca: 2,500 años de historia*, edited by María de los Ángeles Romero Frizzi, 487–501. Mexico City: CONACULTA-INAH, 2003.

Deloria, Philip J. *Indians in Unexpected Places*. Lawrence: University Press of Kansas, 2004.

Deloria, Vine Jr. *Custer Died for Your Sins: An Indian Manifesto*. New York: Avon, 1970.

———. "Research, Redskins, and Reality." *American Indian Quarterly* 15, no. 4 (Autumn 1991): 457–468.

Díaz Balsera, Viviana. *The Pyramid Under the Cross: Franciscan Discourses of Evangelization and the Nahua Christian Subject in Sixteenth-Century Mexico*. Tucson: University of Arizona Press, 2005.

Díaz del Castillo, Bernal. *Historia verdadera de la conquista de la Nueva España*. Madrid: Espasa-Calpe, 1968.

Doerfler, Jill, Niigaanwewidam James Sinclair, and Heidi Kiiwetinepinesiik Stark, eds. *Centering Anishinaabeg Studies: Understanding the World Through Stories*. East Lansing: Michigan State University Press, 2013.

*Doña Luz Jiménez: Imagen y palabra de México*. Directed by Juan Carlos Loza Jurado. 2005. Video.

Ducey, Michael T. "Hijos del pueblo y ciudadanos: Identidades políticas entre los rebeldes indios del siglo XIX." In *Construcción de la legitimidad política en México en el siglo XIX*, edited by Brian C. Connaughton, Carlos Illades, and Sonia Pérez Toledo, 127–151. Zamora, Mich.: El Colegio de Michoacán; Universidad Autónoma Metropolitana-Iztapalapa; Universidad Autónoma de México, Instituto de Investigacions Históricas; El Colegio de México, 1999.

Duncan, Robert H. "Political Legitimation and Maximilian's Second Empire in Mexico, 1864–1867." *Mexican Studies/Estudios Mexicanos* 12, no. 1 (Winter 1996): 27–66.

Duverger, Christian. *La conversión de los indios de Nueva España. Con el texto de los coloquios de los doce de Bernardino de Sahagún (1564)*. Mexico City: Fondo de Cultura Económica, 1996.

Errington, Joseph. *Linguistics in a Colonial World: A Story of Language, Meaning, and Power*. Malden, MA: Blackwell Publishing, 2008.

Escalona, Enrique. *Tlacuilo*. Mexico City: Universidad Nacional Autónoma de México, 1989.

Escobar Ohmstede, Antonio. "El discurso de la 'inteligencia' india en los primeros años posindependientes." In *Construcción de la legitimidad política en México en el siglo XIX*, edited by Brian C. Connaughton, Carlos Illades, and Sonia Pérez Toledo, 263–274. Zamora, Mich.: El Colegio de Michoacán; Universidad Autónoma Metropolitana-Iztapalapa; Universidad Autónoma de México, Instituto de Investigaciones Históricas; El Colegio de México, 1999.

Esparza Torres, Miguel Ángel. "Nebrija y los modelos de los misioneros lingüistas del náhuatl." In *Missionary Linguistics III/ Lingüística misionera III: Morphology and Syntax: Selected Papers from the Third and Fourth Conferences on Missionary Linguistics, Hong Kong/Macau*, edited by Otto Zwartjes, Gregory James, and Emilio Ridruejo, 401–412. Amsterdam: John Benjamins, 2005.

Fanon, Frantz. *Black Skin, White Masks*. Translated by Charles Lam Markmann. New York: Grove Press, 1968.

Fernández Rodríguez, Pedro. *Los dominicos en el contexto de la primera evangelización de México, 1526–1550*. Salamanca, Spain: Editorial San Esteban, 1994.

Field, Les. "Blood and Traits: Preliminary Observations on the Analysis of Mestizo and Indigenous Identities in Latin America vs. the U.S." *Journal of Latin American Anthropology* 7, no. 1 (2002): 2–33.

Finnegan, Ruth H. *Literacy and Orality: Studies in the Technology of Communication*. Oxford: Blackwell, 1988.

Fixico, Donald L. "Call for Native Genius and Indigenous Intellectualism." *Indigenous Nations Studies Journal* 1, no. 1 (2000): 43–59.

Flores Farfán, José Antonio, Refugio Nava Nava, Josep Cru Talaveron, Wilf Plum, and Cleofas Ramírez. *Adivinanzas mexicanas: See tosaasaaniltsiin, see tosaasaaniltsiin*. Mexico City: Artes de México, 2007.

Flores Rodríguez, María Eugenia Xilonetl. "Juan de Dios Rodríguez Puebla: En defensa de la instrucción para los indios." In *El estado laico y los derechos humanos en México: 1810–2010*. Vol. 1, edited by Margarita Moreno Bonett and Rosa María Álavarez de Lara, 409–420. http://biblio.juridicas.unam.mx/libros/libro.htm?l=3100. Accessed December 26, 2013.

Florescano, Enrique. *Memoria mexicana*. Mexico City: Fondo de Cultura Económica, 1994.

Florescano, Enrique, and Elsa Malvido. *Ensayos sobre la historia de las epidemias en México*. Mexico City: IMSS, 1982.

Forcinito, Ana. *Memorias y nomadías: Géneros y cuerpos en los márgenes del posfeminismo*. Santiago: Editorial Cuarto Propio, 2004.

Foucault, Michel. "Two Lectures. Lecture One: 7 January 1976." In *Power/Knowledge: Selected Interviews and Other Writings, 1972–1977*, edited by Colin Gordon, 78–108. New York: Pantheon Books, 1980.

Fountain, Catherine. "Colonial Linguistics in New Spain: The Nahuatl Tradition." PhD diss., University of California, Los Angeles, 2006.

Freire, Paulo. "Creating Alternative Research Methods: Learning to Do It by Doing It." In *Creating Knowledge: A Monopoly?* edited by B. Hall, A. Gillette, and R. Tandon, 29–37. Khanpur, New Delhi: Society of Participatory Research in Asia, 1973.

Frischmann, Donald. "The Indigenous Word in Mesoamerica: Orality, Writing, and Contemporary Prose." In *Words of the True Peoples/Palabras de los seres verdaderos: Anthology of Contemporary Mexican Indigenous-Language Writers*. Vol. 1, *Prose/Prosa*, edited by Carlos Montemayor and Donald Frischmann, 16–45. Austin: University of Texas Press, 2004.

———. "A Question of Balance: Indigenous Theater at the Conjunction of Millenia." In *Words of the True Peoples/Palabras de los seres verdaderos: Anthology of Contemporary Mexican Indigenous-Language Writers*. Vol. 3, *Theater/Teatro*, edited by Carlos Montemayor and Donald Frischmann, 19–47. Austin: University of Texas Press, 2007.

Fuchs, Barbara. *Mimesis and Empire: The New World, Islam, and European Identities*. Cambridge: Cambridge University Press, 2001.

García, Genaro, ed. *Documentos inéditos ó muy raros para la historia de México*. Vol. 15. Mexico City: Librería de la Vda. de Ch. Bouret, 1907.

Garcilaso de la Vega, El Inca. *Royal Commentaries of the Incas and General History of Peru*. 1609. Reprint, introduction, and translation by Harold V. Livermore. Austin: University of Texas Press, 1966.

Garibay K., Ángel María. "Estudio previo." In *Historia antigua y de la conquista de México*. 1880 by Manuel Orozco y Berra, vii–xxvii. Reprint, Mexico City: Editorial Porrúa, 1960.

———. *Historia de la literatura náhuatl, 1953–54*. Mexico City: Editorial Porrúa, 1992.

———. *Llave del Náhuatl*. Mexico City: Editorial Porrúa, 1940.

Geertz, Clifford. *Local Knowledge: Further Essays in Interpretive Anthropology*. New York: Basic Books, 1983.

Gibson, Charles. "Aztec Aristocracy in Colonial Mexico." *Comparative Studies in Society and History* 2, no. 2 (January 1960): 169–196.

———. *The Aztecs Under Spanish Rule: A History of the Indians of the Valley of Mexico, 1519–1810*. Stanford: Stanford University Press, 1964.

———. *Tlaxcala in the Sixteenth Century*. Stanford: Stanford University Press, 1952.

Gonzalbo Aizpuru, Pilar. *Educación y colonización en la Nueva España, 1521–1821*. Mexico City: UPN, 2000.

González Navarro, Moisés. "Instituciones indígenas en el México independiente." In *La política indigenista en México: Métodos y resultados*, edited by Alfonso Caso et al., 1: 209–313. Mexico City: INI, SEP, 1954.

Gramsci, Antonio. *Selections from the Prison Notebooks of Antonio Gramsci*. Edited by Quintin Hoare and Geoffrey Nowell-Smith. New York: International Publishers, 1971.

Graña-Behrens, Daniel. "*Itz'aat* and *Tlamatini*: The 'Wise Man' as Keeper of Maya and Nahua Collective Memory." In *Mesoamerican Memory: Enduring Systems of Remembrance*, edited by Amos Megged and Stephanie Wood, 15–32. Norman: University of Oklahoma Press, 2012.

Greenblatt, Stephen. *Marvelous Possessions: The Wonder of the New World*. Chicago: University of Chicago Press, 1991.

Greenleaf, Richard. *Zumárraga y la Inquisición mexicana, 1536–1543*. Translated by Víctor Villela. Mexico City: FCE, 1988.

Gruzinski, Serge. *The Conquest of Mexico: The Incorporation of Indian Societies into the Western World, 16th–18th Centuries*. Translated by Eileen Corrigan. Cambridge: Polity Press, 1993.

———. *La colonización de lo imaginario: Sociedades indígenas y occidentalización en el México español: Siglos XVI–XVIII*. Translated by Jorge Ferreiro. Mexico City: FCE, 1991.

Gugelberger, Georg, ed. *The Real Thing: Testimonial Literature and Latin America*. Durham, NC: Duke University Press, 1996.

Guha, Ranajit. *Subaltern Studies Reader (1986–1995)*. Minneapolis: University of Minnesota Press, 1997.

Gutiérrez, Natividad. *Nationalist Myths and Ethnic Identities: Indigenous Intellectuals and the Mexican State*. Lincoln: University of Nebraska Press, 1999.

Guzmán Betancourt, Ignacio. "Antonio del Rincón (1556–1601: Primer gramático mexicano)." *Estudios de cultura náhuatl* 33 (2002): 253–265.

———. "La política lingüística de la Compañía de Jesús en Nueva España." *Revista Latina de Pensamiento y Lenguaje* 2.2B, *Monográfico: Estudios de filología y lingüística náhuatl* (1995–1996): 381–390.

Guzmán Gómez, Alba. *Voces indígenas*. Mexico City: CONACULTA/INI, 1991.

Haake, Claudia B. *The State, Removal and Indigenous Peoples in the United States and Mexico, 1620–2000*. New York: Routledge, 2007.

Halbwachs, Maurice. *On Collective Memory*. Edited by Lewis A. Coser. Chicago: University of Chicago Press, 1992.

Hale, Charles R., ed. *Engaging Contradictions: Theory, Politics, and Methods of Activist Scholarship*. Los Angeles: University of California Press, 2008.

———. *Más que un indio: Racial Ambivalence and Neoliberal Multiculturalism in Guatemala*. Santa Fe, NM: School of American Research Press, 2006.

Hale, Charles, and Rosamel Millamán. "Cultural Agency and Political Struggle in the Era of the 'Indio Permitido.'" In *Cultural Agency in the Americas*, edited by Doris Sommer, 281–304. Durham, NC: Duke University Press, 2006.

Hamel, Rainer Enrique. "Indigenous Language Policy and Education in Mexico." In *Encyclopedia of Language and Education: Language Policy and Political Issues in Education*, edited by S. May and N. H. Nornberger, 1:301–313. New York: Springer Science + Business Media, 2008.

Haskett, Robert. *Visions of Paradise: Primordial Titles and Mesoamerican History in Cuernavaca*. Norman: University of Oklahoma Press, 2005.

H. de León-Portilla, Asención. *Tepuztlahcuilolli, impresos en Náhuatl: Historia y bibliografía*. Vols. I and II. Mexico City: UNAM, 1988.

Heath, Shirley Brice. *Telling Tongues: Language Policy in Mexico, Colony to Nation*. New York: Teachers College Press, 1972.

Henry, Gordon D., Jr., Nieves Pascual Soler, and Silvia Martínez-Falquina, eds. *Stories Through Theories/Theories Through Stories: North American Indian Writing, Storytelling, and Critique*. East Lansing: Michigan State University Press, 2009.

Hernández Avila, Inés. "The Power of Native Languages and the Performance of Indigenous Autonomy: The Case of Mexico." In *Native Voices: American Indian Identity and Resistance*, edited by Richard A. Grounds, George E. Tinker, and David E. Wilkins, 35–74. Lawrence: University Press of Kansas, 2003.

Hernández Avila, Inés, and Stefano Varese. "Indigenous Intellectual Sovereignties: A Hemispheric Convocation." *Wicazo Sa Review* 14, no. 2 (Autumn 1999): 77–91.

Hernández Castillo, Aída R. "Indigenous Law and Identity Politics in Mexico: Indigenous Men's and Women's Struggles for a Multicultural Nation." *Political and Legal Anthropology Review* 25 (2002): 90–109.

Hernández Díaz, Jorge. "The Bilingual Teachers: A New Indigenous Intelligentsia." In *The Politics of Ethnicity in Southern Mexico*, edited by Howard Campbell, 41–58. Nashville: Vanderbilt University Press, 1996.

Hernández Hernández, Natalio. *El despertar de nuestras lenguas: Queman tlachixque totlahtolhuan*. Mexico City: Editorial Diana, 2002.

———. *In tlahtolli, in ohtli, la palabra, el camino: Memoria y destino de los pueblos indígenas*. Mexico City: Plaza y Valdés Editores, 1998.

Hill, Jane H., and Kenneth C. Hill. "Honorific Usage in Modern Nahuatl: The Expression of Social Distance and Respect in the Nahuatl of the Malinche Volcano Area." *Language* 54, no. 1 (Mar. 1978): 123–155.

INEGI/Instituto Nacional de Estadística Geografía e Informática. "Población hablante de lengua indígena de 5 y más años por principales lenguas, 1970 a 2005." 2007. Sistemas Nacionales Estadístico y de Información Geográfica, México. http://www.inegi.org.mx. Accessed July 1, 2012.

Ireland, Craig. "The Appeal to Experience and Its Consequences: Variations on a Persistent Thompsonian Theme." *Cultural Critique* 52 (Fall 2002): 86–107.

Jara, René, and Hernán Vidal. *Testimonio y literatura*. Minneapolis: Institute for the Study of Ideologies and Literatures, 1986.

Jiménez, Luz. *De Porfirio Díaz a Zapata: Memoria Náhuatl de Milpa Alta*. Translated and edited by Fernando Horcasitas. Mexico City: UNAM, 1968.

———. *Life and Death in Milpa Alta: A Nahuatl Chronicle of Díaz and Zapata*. Translated and edited by Fernando Horcasitas. Norman: University of Oklahoma Press, 1972.

———. *Los cuentos en Náhuatl de doña Luz Jiménez*. Edited by Fernando Horcasitas and Sarah O. de Ford. Mexico City: UNAM, 1979.

Jordá Hernández, Jani. *Ser maestro bilingüe en Suljaa': Lengua e identidad*. Mexico City: Universidad Pedagógica Nacional, 2003.

Justice, Daniel Heath. *Our Fire Survives the Storm: A Cherokee Literary History*. Minneapolis: University of Minnesota Press, 2005.

———. "Seeing (and Reading) Red: Indian Outlaws in the Ivory Tower." In *Indigenizing the Academy: Transforming Scholarship and Empowering Communities*, edited by Devon A. Mihesuah and Angela Cavender Wilson, 100–123. Lincoln: University of Nebraska Press, 2004.

Karttunen, Frances. *An Analytical Dictionary of Nahuatl*. Norman: University of Oklahoma Press, 1992.

———. *Between Worlds: Interpreters, Guides, and Survivors*. New Brunswick: Rutgers University Press, 1994.

———. "Indigenous Writing as a Vehicle of Postconquest Continuity and Change in Mesoamerica." In *Native Traditions in the Postconquest World: A Symposium at Dumbarton Oaks, October 2–4, 1992*, edited by Elizabeth Hill Boone and Tom Cummins, 421–447. Washington, DC: Dumbarton Oaks, 1998.

———. "La contribución del trabajo de Antonio del Rincón a la lexicografía náhuatl del siglo XX." *Revista Latina de Pensamiento y Lenguaje* 2.2B, *Monográfico: Estudios de filología y lingüística náhuatl* (1995–1996): 391–405.

———. "The Linguistic Career of doña Luz Jiménez." *Estudios de cultura náhuatl* 30 (1999): 267–274.

Karttunen, Frances, and James Lockhart. *Nahuatl in the Middle Years: Language Contact Phenomena in Texts of the Colonial Period*. Berkeley: University of California Press, 1976.

———, eds. *The Art of Nahuatl Speech: The Bancroft Dialogues*. Los Angeles: UCLA Latin American Center Publications, 1987.

Katz, Friedrich. "The Liberal Republic and the Porfiriato, 1867–1910." In *Mexico: Since Independence*, edited by Leslie Bethell, 49–124. New York: Cambridge University Press, 1991.

Kicza, John. Introduction to *The Indian in Latin American History: Resistance, Resilience, and Acculturation*. Edited by John Kicza. Wilmington, DE: Scholarly Resources, 1993.

Knight, Alan. "Racism, Revolution, and *Indigenismo*: Mexico 1910–1940." In *The Idea of Race in Latin America: 1870–1940*, edited by Richard Graham, 71–113. Austin: University of Texas Press, 1990.

Kobayashi, José María. *La educación como conquista: Empresa franciscana en México*. Mexico City: El Colegio de México, 1974.

Konkle, Maureen. *Writing Indian Nations: Native Intellectuals and the Politics of Historiography*. Durham, NC: University of North Carolina Press, 2004.

Kovach, Margaret. *Indigenous Methodologies: Characteristics, Conversations, and Contexts*. Toronto: University of Toronto Press, 2009.

Kranz, Travis Barton. "Visual Persuasion: Sixteenth Century Tlaxcalan Pictorials in Response to the Conquest of Mexico." In *The Conquest All Over Again: Nahuas and Zapotecs Thinking, Writing, and Painting Spanish Colonialism*, edited by Susan Schroeder, 41–73. Portland: Sussex Academic Press, 2010.

Krauze, Enrique. *Mexico: Biography of Power: A History of Modern Mexico, 1810–1996*. Translated by Hank Heifetz. New York: Harper Collins, 1997.

Krug, Frances, and Camilla Townsend. "The Tlaxcala-Puebla Family of Annals." 2007, 2010. http://whp.uoregon.edu/Lockhart/. Accessed September 1, 2011.

Las Casas, Bartolomé de. *Bartolomé de las Casas: A Selection of His Writings*. Translated and edited by George Sanderlin. New York: Knopf, 1971.

———. *Obras escogidas de Fray Bartolomé de las Casas*. Vol. 4. Edited by Juan Pérez de Tudela y Bueso. Madrid: Biblioteca de Autores Españoles, 1957–1958.

Latin American Subaltern Studies Group. "Founding Statement." *Dispositio* 19, no. 46 *Subaltern Studies in the Americas* (1994): 1–11.

León-Portilla, Miguel. *Aztec Thought and Culture: A Study of the Ancient Nahuatl Mind*. Translated by Jack Emory Davis. Norman: University of Oklahoma Press, 1990.

———. *La filosofia náhuatl, estudiada en sus fuentes*. Mexico City: Ediciones Especiales del Instituto Indigenista Interamericano, 1956.

———. "Lecturas de la palabra de doña Luz Jiménez." In *Luz Jiménez, símbolo de un pueblo milenario, 1897–1965*, presentación Rafael Tovar, 99–121. Mexico City: Instituto Nacional de Bellas Artes, 2000.

*Lienzo de Tlaxcala* (ex-Stendahl). 15xx. Nettie Lee Benson Latin American Collection, University of Texas Libraries, The University of Texas at Austin.

Lira, Andrés. *Comunidades indígenas frente a la ciudad de México: Tenochtitlan y Tlatelolco, sus pueblos y barrios, 1812–1919*. Mexico City: El Colegio de México, 1983.

Llaguno, S. J. *La personalidad jurídica del indio y el III Concilio Provincial Mexicano, 1585*. Mexico City: Porrúa, 1963.

Lockhart, James. "Introduction: Background and Course of the New Philology." 2007, 2010. http://whp.uoregon.edu/Lockhart/. Accessed July 1, 2012.

———. *The Nahuas After the Conquest: A Social and Cultural History of the Indians of Central Mexico, Sixteenth Through Eighteenth Centuries*. Stanford: Stanford University Press, 1992.

———. *Nahuas and Spaniards: Postconquest Central Mexican History and Philology*. Stanford: Stanford University Press, 1991.

———. *Nahuatl as Written: Lessons in Older Written Nahuatl, with Copious Texts and Examples*. Stanford: Stanford University Press, 2001.

———. *Of Things of the Indies: Essays Old and New in Early Latin American History*. Stanford: Stanford University Press, 1999.

Lockhart, James, Frances Berdan, and Arthur J. O. Anderson, eds. *The Tlaxcalan Actas: A Compendium of the Records of the Cabildo of Tlaxcala (1545–1627)*. Salt Lake City: University of Utah Press, 1986.

Lockhart, James, and Stuart B. Schwartz. *Early Latin America: A History of Colonial Spanish America and Brazil*. Cambridge: Cambridge University Press, 1983.

Lockhart, James, Lisa Sousa, and Stephanie Wood, eds. *Sources and Methods for the Study of Mesoamerican Ethnohistory*. 2007, 2010. http://whp.uoregon.edu/Lockhart/. Accessed July 1, 2012.

Lodares, Juan R. "Language, Catholicism, and Power." In *Spanish and Empire*, edited by Nelsy Echávez-Solano and Kenya C. Dworkin y Méndez, 3–31. Hispanic Issues, vol. 34. Nashville: Vanderbilt University Press, 2007.

Lomawaima, K. Tsianina, and Teresa McCarty. *To Remain an Indian: Lessons in Democracy from a Century of Native American Education*. New York: Teachers College Press, 2006.

Lopenzina, Drew. *Red Ink: Native Americans Picking Up the Pen in the Colonial Period*. Albany: SUNY Press, 2012.

Lopes Don, Patricia. "The 1539 Inquisition and Trial of Don Carlos of Texcoco in Early Mexico." *Hispanic American Historical Review* 88, no. 4 (2008): 573–606.

López Austin, Alfredo. "Aztec." In *The Oxford Encyclopedia of Mesoamerican Cultures: The Civilizations of Mexico and Central America*, edited by Davíd Carrasco, 1:68–72. New York: Oxford University Press, 2001.

López Caballero, Paula. *Los títulos primordiales del centro de México*. Mexico City: CONACULTA, 2003.

Lund, Joshua. "The Mestizo State: Colonization and Indianization in Liberal Mexico." *PMLA* 123, no. 5 (Oct. 2008): 1418–1433.

Maffie, James. *Aztec Philosophy: Understanding a World in Motion*. Boulder: University Press of Colorado, 2014.

Mallon, Florencia E. "Introduction: Decolonizing Knowledge, Language, and Narrative." In *Decolonizing Native Histories: Collaboration, Knowledge, and Language in the Americas*, edited by Forencia E. Mallon, 1–19. Durham, NC: Duke University Press, 2012.

*María Candelaria (Xochimilco)*. Directed by Emilio Fernández. 1944. Film.

Martínez Baracs, Andrea. "Historiadores de la segunda mitad del siglo XVII en Tlaxcala: La historia cronológica de Zapata y Mendoza en perspectiva historiográfica." In *Five Centuries of Mexican History/Cinco siglos de historia de México: Papers of the VIII Conference of Mexican and North American Historians San Diego, California, October 18–20, 1990*, edited by Virginia Guedea and Jamie E. Rodríguez, 1:108–116. Mexico City: Instituto Mora, 1992.

———. *Un gobierno de indios: Tlaxcala, 1519–1750*. Mexico City: FCE, CIESAS, FCHT, 2008.

Massey, Doreen. *For Space*. London: Sage Publications, 2005.

Maya Hernández, Ildefonso. *Ama Tlalnamaquiliztli (Pages/Books of Knowledge): Quen Tiyolque (Origins of Man)*. n.d.

———. *Ama Tlalnamaquiliztli (Pages/Books of Knowledge): Quen Timonempolohque (How We Ruined Ourselves)*. n.d.

———. *Ama Tlalnamaquiliztli (Pages/Books of Knowledge): Quen Tipolihque (How We Perished)*. n.d.

———. *Ama Tlalnamaquiliztli (Pages/Books of Knowledge): Quen Techcoltzahpilocuepque (How the Ancient Birds Returned to Us)*. n.d.

———. *Ixtlamatinij/The Learned Ones*. 1987. In *Words of the True Peoples/Palabras de los seres verdaderos: Anthology of Contemporary Mexican Indigenous-Language Writers*, Vol. 3, *Theater/Teatro*, edited by Carlos Montemayor and Donald Frischmann, 230–281. Austin: University of Texas Press, 2007.

———. "Nauatl gramatical." 1953.

Melton Villanueva, Miriam. "The Nahuas at Independence: Indigenous Communities of the Metepec Area (Toluca Valley) in the First Decades of the Nineteenth Century." PhD diss., University of California, Los Angeles, 2012.

Melton Villanueva, Miriam, and Caterina Pizzigoni. "Late Nahuatl Testaments from the Toluca Valley: Indigenous-Language Ethnohistory in the Independence Period." *Ethnohistory* 55, no. 3 (Summer 2008): 361–391.

Memmi, Albert. *The Colonizer and the Colonized*. 1957. Reprint, Boston: Beacon Press, 1965.

Menchú, Rigoberta. *Me llamo Rigoberta Menchú y así me nació la conciencia*. Mexico City: Siglo Veintinuno Editories, 1985.

Mendieta, Eduardo. "Remapping Latin American Studies: Postcolonialism, Subaltern Studies, Post-Occidentalism, and Globalization Theory." In *Coloniality at Large: Latin America and the Postcolonial Debate*, edited by Mabel Moraña, Enrique Dussel, and Carlos A. Jáuregui, 286–306. Durham, NC: Duke University Press, 2008.

Menegus, Margarita, and Rodolfo Aguirre. *Los indios, el sacerdocio y la Universidad en Nueva España, siglos XVI–XVIII*. Mexico City: Editorial Plaza y Valdés, 2006.

Messing, Jacqueline. "Fractal Recursivity in Ideologies of Language, Identity, and Modernity in Tlaxcala, Mexico." *Proceedings of the Tenth Annual Symposium about Language and Society*, Austin, April 12–14, 2002. *Texas Linguistic Forum* 45 (2002): 95–105.

Meyer, Jean. "La Junta Protectora de las Clases Menesterosas: Indigenismo y agrarismo en el Segundo Imperio." In *Indio, nación y comunidad en el México del siglo XIX*, edited by Antonio Escobar Ohmstede, 329–364. Mexico City: CIESAS, 1993.

Mignolo, Walter. *The Darker Side of the Renaissance: Literacy, Territoriality, and Colonization*. 1995. Reprint, Ann Arbor: University of Michigan Press, 2007.

———. *The Idea of Latin America*. Malden, MA: Blackwell Publishing, 2005.

———. "Philosophy and the Colonial Difference." In *Latin American Philosophy: Currents, Debates, Issues*, edited by Eduardo Mendieta, 80–86. Bloomington: University of Indiana Press, 2003.

Mihesuah, Devon A. Introduction to *Natives and Academics: Researching and Writing About American Indians*. Edited by Devon A. Mihesuah. Lincoln: University of Nebraska Press, 1998.

Mihesuah, Devon A., and Angela Cavendar Wilson, eds. *Indigenizing the Academy: Transforming Scholarship and Empowering Communities*. Lincoln: University of Nebraska Press, 2004.

Million, Dian. "Intense Dreaming: Theories, Narratives, and Our Search for Home." *American Indian Quarterly* 35, no. 3 (Summer 2011): 313–333.

Miranda, Refugio. "'Cuanegros,' Yahualica." In *De Carnaval a Xantolo: Contacto con el inframundo*, edited by Amparo Sevilla Villalobos, 176–184. Cd. Victoria, Mexico: PDCH, 2002.

Molina, Alonso de. "Arte de la lengua mexicana y castellana." 1571. Vol. 1, *Colección de gramáticas de la lengua mexicana: 1547–1673*, edited by D. Francisco del Paso y Troncoso and D. Luis González Obregón. Reprint, Mexico City: Imprenta de Ignacio Escalante, 1904.

———. *Vocabulario en lengua castellana y mexicana y mexicana y castellana*. 1555–1571. Reprint, Mexico City: Porrúa, 1970.

Montejo, Victor. *Maya Intellectual Renaissance: Identity, Representation, and Leadership*. Austin: University of Texas Press, 2005.

Montemayor, Carlos, and Donald Frischmann, eds. *Words of the True Peoples/Palabras de los seres verdaderos: Anthology of Contemporary Mexican Indigenous-Language Writers*, 3 vols. Austin: University of Texas Press, 2005.

Montiel Bonilla, Alejandro. "La fundación de los colegios jesuitas en Puebla." In *Presencia de la Compañía de Jesús en la Puebla de los Ángeles*, edited by María Aurelia Hernández Yahuitl and Xavier Cacho Vásquez, 28–34. Puebla: Universidad Iberoamericana, 1997.

Moraña, Mabel, Enrique Dussel, and Carlos A. Jáuregui. "Colonialism and Its Replicants." In *Coloniality at Large: Latin America and the Postcolonial Debate*, edited by Mabel Moraña, Enrique Dussel, and Carlos A. Jáuregui, 1–22. Durham, NC: Duke University Press, 2008.

Moreno de los Arcos, Roberto. "Los cinco soles cosmogónicos." *Estudios de cultura náhuatl* 7 (1967): 183–201.

Mörner, Magnus, ed. *Race and Class in Latin America*. New York: Columbia University Press, 1970.

Nagel Bielicke, Federico B. "Un acercamiento a la vida de Antonio del Rincón." *Revista Latina de Pensamiento y Lenguaje* 2.2B, *Monográfico: Estudios de filología y lingüística náhuatl* (1995–1996): 445–453.

Nava Nava, Refugio. *Āmo polihuiz in totlahtol: No se perderá nuestra lengua/Ideologías, prácticas y retención del náhuatl en San Isidro Buensuceso, Tlaxcala*. Mexico City: CIESAS, 2009.

———. *Malintzin itlahtol*. Totlahtol Series/Toconehuan. Warsaw: Ministro de Ciencia y Educación Superior, 2013.

———. *Uitsilin*. Tlaxcala: Universidad Autónoma de Tlaxcala, 2012.

Navarrette, Federico. "Chimalpain y Alva Ixtlilxóchitl, dos estrategias de traducción cultural." In *Indios, mestizos y españoles: Interculturalidad e historiografía en la Nueva España*, edited by Danna Levin Rojo and Federico Navarrette, 97–112. Mexico City: UAMUA, 2007.

Nebrija, Elio Antonio de. *Gramática de la lengua castellana*. 1492. Reprint, London: Oxford University Press, 1926.

———. *Introductiones latinae*. 1481. Reprint, Salamãticae: Editorial M. Palaéz del Rosal, 1981.

Nicholson, H. B. "A 'Royal Headband' of the Tlaxcalteca." *Revista mexicana de estudios antropológicos* 21 (1967): 71–106.

Nutini, Hugo, and Barry Isaac. *Social Stratification in Central Mexico, 1500–2000*. Austin: University of Texas Press, 2009.

O'Brien, Jean M. *Firsting and Lasting: Writing Indians out of Existence in New England*. Minneapolis: University of Minnesota Press, 2010.

Olko, Justyna. *Turquoise Diadems and Staffs of Office: Elite Costume and Insignia of Power in Aztec and Early Colonial Mexico*. Warsaw: PTSL, 2005.

Olmos, Andrés de. "Arte para aprender la lengua mexicana." 1547. Vol. 1, *Colección de gramáticas de la lengua mexicana: 1547–1673*, edited by D. Francisco del Paso y Troncoso and D. Luis González Obregón. Reprint, Mexico City: Imprenta de Ignacio Escalante, 1904.

Ong, Walter. *Orality and Literacy: The Technologizing of the Word*. New York: Methuen, 1982.

Ortiz, Fernando. *Contrapunteo cubano del tabaco y el azúcar*. Prólogo y cronología Branislow Malinowski. Barcelona: Editorial Ariel, 1973.

Ortiz, Simon J. "Towards a National Indian Literature: Cultural Authenticity in Nationalism." *Melus* 8, no. 2 (1981): 7–12.

Osorio Romero, Ignacio. *Colegios y profesores jesuitas que enseñaron latín en Nueva España (1527–1767)*. Mexico City: UNAM, 1979.

———. *La enseñanza del latín a los indios*. Mexico City: UNAM, 1990.

Osowski, Edward. "Indigenous Centurions and Triumphal Arches: Negotiation in Eighteenth-Century Mexico." In *Negotiation Within Domination: New Spain's Indian Pueblos Confront the Spanish State*, edited by Ethelia Ruiz Medrano and Susan Kellogg, 79–105. Boulder: University Press of Colorado, 2010.

———. *Indigenous Miracles: Nahua Authority in Colonial Mexico*. Tucson: University of Arizona Press, 2010.

Palomera, Esteban. *La obra educativa de los Jesuitas en Puebla, 1578–1945*. Mexico City: Universidad Iberoamericana, 1999.

Pani, Erika. "Dreaming of a Mexican Empire: The Political Projects of the 'Imperialistas.'" *Hispanic American Historical Review* 82, no. 1 (Feb. 2002): 1–33.

———. *El Segundo Imperio: Pasados de usos múltiples*. Mexico City: CIDE/CFE, 2004.

———. *Para mexicanizar el Segundo Imperio: El imaginario político de los imperialistas*. Mexico City: El Colegio de México, 2001.

———. "¿'Verdaderas figuras de Cooper' o 'Pobres inditos infelices'? La política indigenista de Maximiliano." *Historia Mexicana* 47, no. 3 (1998): 571–604.

Patterson, Robert H. "An Art in Revolution: Antecedents of Mexican Mural Painting, 1900–1920." *Journal of Inter-American Studies* 6, no. 3 (July 1964): 377–387.

Pellicer, Dora. "Oralidad y escritura de la literatura indígena: Una aproximación histórica." In *Situación actual y perspectivas de la literatura en lenguas indígenas*, edited by Carlos Montemayor, 15–53. Mexico City: Consejo Nacional Para la Cultura y las Artes, 1993.

Pérez de Ribas, Andrés. *Corónica y historia religiosa de la Compañía de Jesús de México en Nueva España*. Vol. I. Mexico City: Imprenta del Sagrado Corazón de Jesús, 1896.

Pérez Rocha, Emma, and Rafael Tena. *La nobleza indígena del centro de México después de la conquista*. Mexico City: INAH, 2000.

Pizzigoni, Caterina. "Conclusion: A Language Across Space, Time, and Ethnicity." *Ethnohistory* 59, no. 4 (Fall 2012): 785–790.

Poole, Stafford. "Church Law on the Ordination of Indians and *Castas* in New Spain." *The Hispanic American Historical Review* 61, no. 4 (1981): 637–650.

Powell, T. G. "Mexican Intellectuals and the Indian Question: 1876–1911." *Hispanic American Historical Review* 48 (1968): 19–36.

Pratt, Mary Louise. *Imperial Eyes: Travel Writing and Transculturation*. New York: Routledge, 1992.

*Proceso inquisitorial del cacique de Tetzcoco (1539)*. Preface by Luis González Obregón. Mexico City: AGN, 1980.

Quijano, Aníbal. "Coloniality of Power, Eurocentrism, and Latin America." *Nepantla: Views from the South* 1, no. 3 (2000): 533–580.

Rabasa, José. *Franciscans and Dominicans Under the Gaze of a "Tlacuilo": Plural-World Dwelling in an Indian Pictorial Codex*. Berkeley: UC Berkeley Library, 1998.

———. *Tell Me the Story of How I Conquered You: Elsewheres and Ethnosuicide in the Colonial Mesoamerican World*. Austin: University of Texas Press, 2011.

———. *Without History: Subaltern Studies, the Zapatista Insurgency, and the Specter of History*. Pittsburgh: University of Pittsburgh Press, 2010.

Rabasa, José, and Javier Sanjinés. "Introduction: The Politics of Subaltern Studies." *Dispositio* 19, no. 46 *Subaltern Studies in the Americas* (1994): v–xi.

Rama, Ángel. *The Lettered City*. Translated and edited by John Charles Chasteen. Durham, NC: Duke University Press, 1996.

Ramírez, José Fernando. "Advertencia." In *Anales de Cuauhtitlán: Noticias históricas de México y sus contornos*. Translated by Faustino Galicia Chimalpopoca, Gumesindo Mendoza, and Felipe Sánchez Solís. Edited by José Ramírez, 2–3. Mexico City: Los Anales del Museo Nacional, 1885.

Ramos, Frances. "Succession and Death: Royal Ceremonies in Colonial Puebla." *The Americas* 60, no. 2 (2003): 182–215.

Ramos Castañeda, Nydia, Darío Luis Pantaleón, and Ernesto Ramos Rodríguez. *El Xantolo de Huautla: Rituales de vida y muerte en la Huasteca hidalguense*. Pachuca: IHC, 1992.

Rappaport, Joanne. *Intercultural Utopias: Public Intellectuals, Cultural Experimentation, and Ethnic Pluralism in Colombia*. Durham, NC: Duke University Press, 2005.

Rappaport, Joanne, and Tom Cummins. *Beyond the Lettered City: Indigenous Literacies in the Andes*. Durham, NC: Duke University Press, 2012.

*Recopilación de leyes de los reynos de las indias: Mandadas imprimir y publicar por la Magestad católica del Rey Don Carlos II. Nuestro Señor*. Madrid: Por la viuda de D. Joaquin Ibarra, 1791.

Restall, Matthew, Lisa Sousa, and Kevin Terraciano, eds. *Mesoamerican Voices: Native Language Writings from Colonial Mexico, Oaxaca, Yucatan, and Guatemala*. New York: Cambridge University Press, 2005.

Reyes García, Luis, ed. *Anales de Juan Bautista: Cómo te confundes? Acaso no somos conquistados?* Mexico City: CIESAS, 2001.

Ricard, Robert. *The Spiritual Conquest of Mexico: An Essay on the Apostolate and the Evangelizing Methods of the Mendicant Orders in New Spain: 1523–1572*. Translated by Lesley Byrd Simpson. Berkeley: University of California Press, 1960.

Rincón, Antonio del. *Arte mexicana compuesta por el padre Antonio del Rincón*. 1595 by Casa de Pedro Balli.

———. *Gramática y vocabulario mexicanos por el Padre Antonio del Rincón*. Edited by Antonio Peñafiel. Reprint, Mexico City: Oficina de la Secretaría de Fomento, 1885.

Rippberger, Susan J. "Ideological Shifts in Bilingual Education: Mexico and the United States." *Comparative Education Review* 37, no. 1 (February 1993): 50–61.

Romero Galván, José Rubén. *Historiografía novohispana de tradición indígena*. Mexico City: UNAM, 2003.

Roseberry, William. "Hegemony and the Language of Contention." In *Everyday Forms of State Formation: Revolution and the Negotiation of Rule in Modern Mexico*, edited by Gilbert M. Joseph and Daniel Nugent, 355–366. Durham, NC: Duke University Press, 1994.

Round, Phillip H. *Removable Type: Histories of the Book in Indian Country, 1663–1880*. Chapel Hill: University of North Carolina Press, 2010.

Ruiz Medrano, Ethelia. *Mexico's Indigenous Communities: Their Lands and Histories, 1500–2010*. Boulder: University Press of Colorado, 2010.

Ruiz Medrano, Ethelia, and Susan Kellogg, eds. *Negotiation Within Domination: New Spain's Indian Pueblos Confront the Spanish State*. Boulder: University Press of Colorado, 2010.

Ruvalcaba Mercado, Jesús, and Juan Manuel Pérez Zevallos. *La Huasteca en los albores del tercer milenio: Textos, temas y problemas*. Mexico City: CIESAS, 1996.

Sahagún, Bernardino de. *Coloquios y doctrina cristiana: Con que los doce frailes de San Francisco, enviados por el papa Adriano VI y por el emperador Carlos V, convirtieron a los indios de la Nueva España. En lengua mexicano y española. Los diálogos de 1524/dispuestos por fray Bernardino de Sahagún y sus colaboradores Antonio Valeriano de Azcapotzalco, Alonso Vegerano de Cuauhtitlán, Martín Jacobita y Andrés Leonardo de Tlatelolco, y otros cuatro ancianos muy entendidos en todas sus antigüedades*. Introduction and translation by Miguel León-Portilla. Mexico City: UNAM/FIS, 1986.

———. *Florentine Codex: General History of the Things of New Spain*. Translated and edited by Charles E. Dibble and Arthur J. O. Anderson. 13 vols. Santa Fe, NM: School of American Research; Salt Lake City: University of Utah Press, 1959–1982.

Said, Edward. *Orientalism*. New York: Pantheon Books, 1978.

Salomon, Frank, and Mercedes Niño-Murcia. *The Lettered Mountain: A Peruvian Village's Way with Writing*. Durham, NC: Duke University Press, 2011.

Sánchez Vásquez, Rafael. "Síntesis sobre la Real y Pontificia Universidad de México." 2002. http://www.juridicas.unam.mx/publica/librev/.../cnt10.pdf. Accessed July 2, 2012.

Sandstrom, Alan. *Corn Is Our Blood: Culture and Ethnic Identity in a Contemporary Aztec Village*. Norman: University of Oklahoma Press, 1991.

Schmelkes Guadalupe Aguila, Sylvia, and Ma. de los Ángeles Núñez. "Alfabetización de jóvenes indígenas en México." In *Alfabetización y multiculturalidad: Miradas desde América Latina*, edited by Luis Enrique López and Ulrike Hanemann, 237–289. Guatemala City: UIL-UNESCO and PACE GTZ, 2009.

Schmidt-Díaz de León, Ileana. "El Colegio Nacional de San Gregorio: Una institución formadora de profesionistas en la primera mitad del siglo XIX." In *Historia en la educación superior en México: Historiografía y fuentes*, edited by Oscar García Carmona and Sonia Ibarra-Ibarra, 157–171. Zapopan: El Colegio de Jalisco, 2003.

Schroeder, Susan. "Writing Two Cultures: The Meaning of 'Amoxtli' (Book) in Nahua New Spain." In *New World, First Nations: Native Peoples of Mesoamerica and the Andes Under Colonial Rule*, edited by David Cahill and Blanca Tovías, 13–35. Brighton: Sussex Academic Press, 2006.

Schryer, Frans J. *Ethnicity and Class Conflict in Rural Mexico*. Princeton, NJ: Princeton University Press, 1990.

———. "Peasants and the Law: A History of Land Tenure and Conflict in the Huasteca." *Journal of Latin American Studies* 18, no. 2 (Nov. 1986): 283–311.

Schwaller, John F. "A Catalogue of Pre-1840 Nahuatl Works Held by The Lilly Library." *The Indiana University Bookman* 11 (November, 1973): 69–88. http://www.indiana.edu/~liblilly/etexts/nahuatl/. Accessed July 2, 2012.

———. "The Expansion of Nahuatl as a Lingua Franca Among Priests in Sixteenth-Century Mexico." *Ethnohistory* 59, no. 4 (Fall 2012): 675–690.

Scott, James C. *Domination and the Arts of Resistance: Hidden Transcripts*. New Haven: Yale University Press, 1990.

Scott, Joan W. "The Evidence of Experience." *Critical Inquiry* 17, no. 4 (Summer 1991): 773–797.

Segre, Erica. "Representing a Model Autochthony: The Indian Artist's Model Luz Jiménez and the Mexican Avant-Garde." In *Making Waves Anniversary Volume: Women in Spanish, Portuguese and Latin American Studies*, edited by Ann Davies, Parvathi Kumaraswami, and Claire Williams, 141–167. Newcastle upon Tyne: Cambridge Scholars Publishing, 2009.

Sell, Barry, Louise Burkhart, and Stafford Poole, eds. *Nahuatl Theater*. Vol. 2, *Our Lady of Guadalupe*. Norman: University of Oklahoma Press, 2006.

Sepúlveda y Herrera, María Teresa. *Catálogo de la Colección de Documentos Históricos de Faustino Galicia Chimalpopoca*. Mexico City: Instituto Nacional de Antropología e Historia, 1992.

Sierra, Justo. *México social y político: Apuntes para un libro*. 1885. Reprint, Mexico City: Secretaria de Hacienda y Crédito Público, 1960.

Silverblatt, Irene. *Modern Inquisitions: Peru and the Colonial Origins of the Civilized World*. Durham, NC: Duke University Press, 2004.

Siméon, Rémi. *Diccionario de la lengua nahuatl o mexicana*. 1885. Reprint, Mexico City: Siglo Veintiuno, 1988.

Smith Stark, Thomas. "La grafía del náhuatl de Antonio del Rincón." *Revista latina de pensamiento y lenguaje* 2.2B, *Monográfico: Estudios de filología y lingüística náhuatl* (1995–1996): 407–433.

Soberón Mora, Arturo. "San Gregorio, un colegio transcolonial: De la catequesis jesuita para infantes caciques, a la pedagogía liberal de Juan Rodríguez Puebla." PhD diss., Escuela Nacional de Antropología e Historia. Mexico City: INAH, SEP, 2008.

Spivak, Gayatri Chakravorty. "Can the Subaltern Speak?" In *Colonial Discourse and Post-Colonial Theory*, edited by Patrick Williams and Laura Chrisman, 66–111. New York: Columbia University Press, 1994.

———. "Roundtable on the Future of the Humanities in a Fragmented World." *PMLA* 120, no. 3 (May 2005): 718–720.

Stabb, Martin S. "Indigenism and Racism in Mexican Thought: 1857–1911." *Journal of Inter-American Studies* 1, no. 4 (Oct. 1959): 405–423.

Sullivan, John. "The IDIEZ Project: A Model for Indigenous Language Revitalization in Higher Education." *Collaborative Anthropologies* 4 (2011): 139–153.

Sullivan, John, et al. "Náhuatl tlen naman: Chicontepec, Veracruz." 2006.

Tafolla Pérez, Rafael. *La junta de notables de 1863*. Mexico City: Editorial Jus, 1977.

Taylor, Diana. *The Archive and the Repertoire: Performing Cultural Memory in the Americas*. Durham, NC: Duke University Press, 2003.

———. "Performance and/as History." *The Drama Review* 50, no. 1 (Spring 2006): 67–86.

———. *Theatre of Crisis: Drama and Politics in Latin America*. Lexington: University Press of Kentucky, 1991.

Thiong'o, Ngũgĩ wa. *Decolonizing the Mind: The Politics of Language in African Literature*. Oxford: James Currey, 1986.

Townsend, Camilla. "Don Juan Buenaventura Zapata and the Notion of a Nahua Identity." In *The Conquest All Over Again: Nahuas and Zapotecs Thinking, Writing, and Painting Spanish Colonialism*, edited by Susan Schroeder, 144–180. Portland: Sussex Academic Press, 2010.

———. "Glimpsing Native American Historiography: The Cellular Principle in Sixteenth-Century Nahuatl Annals." *Ethnohistory* 56, no. 4 (Fall 2009): 625–650.

———. "Reading Symbolic and Historical Representations in Early Mesoamerica." *Latin American Research Review* 47, no. 1 (2012): 177–86.

———, ed. *Here in This Year: Seventeenth-Century Nahuatl Annals of the Tlaxcala-Puebla Valley*. Stanford: Stanford University Press, 2010.

Trouillot, Michel Rolph. *Silencing the Past: Power and the Production of History*. Boston: Beacon Press, 1995.

Tuhiwai Smith, Linda. *Decolonizing Methodologies: Research and Indigenous Peoples*. London: Zed Books, 1999.

Turok, Marta. "Luz Jiménez en el arte popular." In *Luz Jiménez, símbolo de un pueblo milenario 1897–1965*, presentación Rafael Tovar, 133–144. Mexico City: Instituto Nacional de Bellas Artes, 2000.

Valle Esquivel, Julieta. *Nahuas de la Huasteca*. Mexico City: Comisión Nacional para el Desarrollo de Pueblos Indígenas, 2003.

Varese, Stefano. *Proyectos étnicos y proyectos nacionales*. Mexico City: FCE, 1983.

Vargas D., María Eugenia. *Educación e ideología: Constitución de una categoría de intermediarios en la comunicación interétnica: El caso de los maestros bilingües tarascos (1964–1982)*. Mexico City: CIESAS, 1994.

Vaughan, Mary Kay. *The State, Education, and Social Class in Mexico: 1880–1928*. DeKalb: Northern Illinois University Press, 1982.

Velázquez, Primo Feliciano. *Códice Chimalpopoca: Anales de Cuauhtitlán y Leyenda de los Soles*. Mexico City: UNAM, Instituto de Historia, 1945.

Versényi, Adam. "Translation as an Epistemological Paradigm for Theatre in the Americas." *Theatre Journal* 59 (2007): 431–447.

Villanueva Hernández, Jesús. "Tecualnezyolehua: La que sublime cosas bellas a la gente." In *Luz Jiménez, símbolo de un pueblo milenario: 1897–1965*, presentación Rafael Tovar, 145–148. Mexico City: Instituto Nacional de Bellas Artes, 2000.

Villoro, Luis. "En torno al derecho de la autonomía de los pueblos indígenas." In *Cultura y derechos de los pueblos indígenas de México*, edited by Patricia Galeana, 161–184. Mexico City: AGN/FCE, 1996.

Wade, Peter. *Race and Ethnicity in Latin America*. Chicago: Pluto Press, 1997.

Warren, Kay, and Jean E. Jackson. *Indigenous Movements, Self-Representation, and the State in Latin America*. Austin: University of Texas Press, 2002.

Warrior, Robert. *The People and the Word: Reading Native Non-fiction*. Minneapolis: University of Minnesota Press, 2005.

———. *Tribal Secrets: Recovering American Indian Intellectual Traditions*. Minneapolis: University of Minnesota, 1995.

Weaver, Jace. *That the People Might Live: Native American Literatures and Native American Community*. New York: Oxford University Press, 1997.

Weber, David J. *Bárbaros: Spaniards and Their Savages in the Age of Enlightenment*. New Haven: Yale University Press, 2005.

Whorf, Benjamin Lee. "The Milpa Alta Dialect of Aztec (with notes on the Classical and the Tepoztlan dialects)." *Linguistic Structures of Native America, Viking Fund Publications in Anthropology* 6 (1946): 367–397.

Womack, Craig S. *Red on Red: Native American Literary Separatism*. Minneapolis: University of Minnesota Press, 1999.

Wood, Stephanie. "The Cosmic Conquest: Late-Colonial Views of the Sword and Cross in Central Mexican Títulos." *Ethnohistory* 38, no. 2 (Spring 1991): 176–195.

———. "Introduction: Collective Memory and Mesoamerican Systems of Remembrance." In *Mesoamerican Memory: Enduring Systems of Remembrance*, edited by Amos Megged and Stephanie Wood, 3–14. Norman: University of Oklahoma Press, 2012.

———. "The Search for Answers About the Cardona." *A Contracorriente* 7, no. 3 (Spring 2010): 389–401. http://www.ncsu.edu/acontracorriente/spring_10/reviews/SWood_rev.pdf. Accessed September 10, 2013.

———. "The Social vs. Legal Context of Nahuatl *Títulos*." In *Native Traditions in the Postconquest World*, edited by Elizabeth Hill Boone and Tom Cummins, 201–231. Washington, DC: Dumbarton Oaks Research Library and Collection, 1998.

———. *Transcending Conquest: Nahua Views of Spanish Colonial Mexico*. Norman: University of Oklahoma Press, 2003.

Wright, David. *Lectura de náhuatl: Fundamentos para la traducción de los textos en náhuatl del periodo novohispano temprano*. Mexico City: Instituto Nacional de Lenguas Indígenas, 2007.

Yannakakis, Yanna. *The Art of Being In-Between: Native Intermediaries, Indian Identity, and Local Rule in Colonial Oaxaca*. Durham, NC: Duke University Press, 2008.

Ybarra, Patricia A. *Performing Conquest: Five Centuries of Theater, History, and Identity in Tlaxcala, Mexico*. Ann Arbor: University of Michigan Press, 2009.

Zamacois, Niceto de. *Historia de Méjico desde los tiempos más remotos hasta nuestros días*. Vol. 17. Mexico City: J. F. Parres y Comp., Editores, 1881.

Zambrano, P. Francisco. *Diccionario bio-bibliográfico de la Compañía de Jesús en México*. Vols. 2, 3, 7. Mexico City: Editorial Tradición, 1961–1973.

Zapata Silva, Claudia, ed. *Intelectuales indígenas piensan América Latina*. Serie Tinkuy 2. Quito: UASB/CECLA-UCH, 2007.

Zapata y Mendoza, Don Juan Buenaventura. *Historia cronológica de la noble ciudad de Tlaxcala*. Edited by Luis Reyes García and Andrea Martínez Baracs. Tlaxcala: Universidad Autónoma de Tlaxcala, 1995.

Zubillaga, Félix. "La provincia jesuítica de Nueva España. Su fundamento económico: Siglo XVI." *Archivum Historicum Societatis Iesu* 37–38 (1968–1969): 3–169.

# Index

*Page numbers in italics refer to figures.*

# *About the Author*

**Kelly McDonough** is an assistant professor of colonial literatures and cultures at the University of Texas at Austin. Her research focuses primarily on Mexican and indigenous studies, with emphasis on postconquest Nahua intellectualism, indigenous cultural and linguistic revitalization projects, and decolonizing methodologies.